England Managers

Other titles by Brian Glanville include:

Arsenal Stadium History
The History of the World Cup
Football Memories: 50 Years of the Beautiful Game
The Comic
Dictators
The Olympian

England Managers
The Toughest Job in Football

Brian Glanville

headline

First published in 2007 by
HEADLINE PUBLISHING GROUP

1

Cataloguing in Publication Data is available from the British Library

ISBN 978 0 7553 1651 9

Typeset in Granjon by Palimpsest Book Production Limited,
Grangemouth, Stirlingshire

England Team Results compiled by Jack Rollin

Printed and bound in Great Britain by
Mackays of Chatham plc, Chatham, Kent

Headline's policy is to use papers that are natural, renewable and recyclable products and
made from wood grown in sustainable forests. The logging and manufacturing processes
are expected to conform to the environmental regulations of the country of origin.

HEADLINE PUBLISHING GROUP
A division of Hachette Livre UK Ltd
338 Euston Road
London NW1 3BH

www.headline.co.uk
www.hodderheadline.com

For Joshie and Samuel

Footballers and football fans

CONTENTS

INTRODUCTION

ROME, 13 MAY 1933. A WARM AND SUNNY AFTERNOON, ON THE occasion of the first match between Italy and England. At half time Vittorio Pozzo, all-powerful and autocratic *commissario tecnico*, or supreme manager, of Italy, emerged from giving his tactical advice to the *azzurri*, to be surprised when his friend Herbert Chapman came out of the England dressing room in shirt-sleeves. When Pozzo asked the celebrated Arsenal manager what he was about, Chapman replied, 'I'm doing for my team what you are doing for yours.'

The substantial difference being that Chapman was acting quite unofficially. While Pozzo had, on and off, been in charge of the Italian team since the 1912 Stockholm Olympics, and would clock up twenty consecutive years, from 1928, during which Italy twice won the World Cup, England would have no manager at all till 1946. And even then Chapman would not remotely have the powers enjoyed by Pozzo. Bizarrely and illogically, his teams would be picked by a so-called selection committee, formed by directors of Football League clubs, until the advent of Alf Ramsey in 1962.

England's team that day in Rome contained two of Chapman's leading young stars – Eddie Hapgood, making his debut at left back, and Cliff Bastin, at outside-left, scorer of England's goal in a 1–1 draw witnessed from the Tribune of Honour under a yachting cap by

Il Duce, Benito Mussolini, himself. At one point, Hapgood inadvertently kicked a football into his lap.

It is impossible to think of Italy achieving as much as they did in those inter-war years without Pozzo, the great irony of his stewardship being that his tactics were based on what he had studied as an impoverished student in the Midlands and North of England before the Great War, conversing with such titans of the English game as the prolific Steve Bloomer of Derby County, and Manchester United's versatile centre half, Charlie Roberts.

By 1933, Arsenal under Chapman were eight years into the Third Back Game, conceived, as he always insisted, by their illustrious veteran inside right, Charlie Buchan, who had returned that year from Sunderland under an unorthodox £100-a-goal transfer to the club he had abandoned as an amateur in 1909.

These tactics, with a stopper or third-back centre half, full backs moved out of the centre to the flanks, wing halves moved into the middle, were a response to the 1925 change in the offside law, whereby it needed only two, rather than three, players to put an attacker onside.

Pozzo would have none of it. He continued with the methods he had seen and approved in England, with a fluid centre half and an emphasis on attack rather than counterattack. Like Chapman, he was essentially a paternalist. 'Kind, but with a strong hand,' he once explained his philosophy to me. 'If I let them make mistakes, I lose my authority.' A French journalist once called him the Poor Captain of a Company of Millionaires.

Both he and Chapman were formidable practical psychologists in an era when the present practice of employing a professional psychologist would have seemed chimerical. Chapman, a Yorkshireman who'd been thrown briefly out of football soon after the war over illicit payments made when managing Leeds City, had returned to win consecutive championships with Huddersfield Town. 'He told you how to dress, he told you how to do your hair!' Hapgood once happily said to me. Far ahead of his time in so many novel ways, Chapman possessed what has been described as an hypnotic power of convincing his players.

Tom Whittaker, who, as is largely forgotten, actually became the first ever England manager for the 1946 end-of-season friendly internationals against Continental opposition, owed his remarkable career as a trainer to Chapman who told him in the summer of 1925, when he returned to Highbury from an Australian Football Association tour with a crippling knee injury, that he would make Tom the finest trainer in the world.

Pozzo himself had all sorts of stratagems to deal with his players, so much more volatile than their English equivalents. If during a training game a player disagreed with him, he would simply await his chance then sidle up to him and say, 'You know, I've been thinking about what you've just said; you are right.' Except that what the player had supposedly said was what Pozzo had told him. And if two players had fallen out in a League game, he would simply set them to share the same bedroom, coming in next morning to ask, drolly, 'Well, cannibals, have you eaten each other yet?' To which the answer would be embarrassed grunts, each man coming to him in turn to say, 'He's not really such a bad fellow. The crowd set me against him.'

Unlike Chapman, who had been a player of modest achievements with such as Tottenham Hotspur in their Southern League days, Pozzo had never been a professional footballer. Did it make a difference? None that was remotely evident. Long afterwards, in the 1990s, Italy appointed as manager Arrigo Sacchi who had never even played decent amateur football, but whose dictum was, 'You don't have to have been a horse to be a jockey.' Ironically, as we shall see, the first permanent English manager, Walter Winterbottom, would be widely disparaged, not least by the seasoned professionals in his initial teams, for never having been a pro himself, when in fact he had played successfully for Manchester United.

Pozzo differed from Chapman in his far superior educational background. He was a polyglot, fluent in English and French, but the essential thing was that he could communicate so easily and effectively with his players. The same might broadly be said of the man who made up a trio of outstanding leaders, Hugo Meisl of Austria, a friend of them both. Another highly educated polyglot, from a wealthy Viennese Jewish family, Meisl, as supremo of what came to be known as the Austrian *Wunderteam*, was another who brooked no opposition from his players. The difference from the other two was that he employed the outstanding English coach, a little Lancastrian called Jimmy Hogan, whom he had schooled and inspired when Hogan first coached with difficulty in Vienna.

Yet it is pertinent to ask, how much difference does a manager make? Not least because even without one, *pace* Chapman's brief episode in Rome, the England team between the wars had a decent enough record, and never lost a game at home. Did this mean that a manager was superfluous in an era when the leading professionals were arguably far more resilient and self-contained than those of later years, coddled by their clubs, if they were stars, and subject to the tactical diktats of managers and coaches? Perhaps, too, the selection committees, by and large, did at least an adequate job.

The fact is that England did not even lose a game abroad until 1929 when Spain beat them 4–3 in Madrid on a ferociously hot day. Two years later at Highbury a crowd eager for revenge battered down the gates to get in, to see Spain annihilated 7–1. It was perhaps the only time that the Spanish goalkeeper, Ricardo Zamora, was hopelessly inept. The prolific Everton centre forward Dixie Dean, who was among the England scorers, told me long afterwards that at the post-match reception the interpreter told him of Zamora, 'He says he is nothing in Madrid, tonight.' To which Dean somewhat callously replied, 'Tell him he's not much here, either.' Yet 1931 was the year in which England crashed on the Continent for the first time and which came to be seen as something of a watershed.

It happened, in fact, just a few months before Spain came, saw and were conquered at Highbury. England's 5–2 beating in Paris, by a French team which had never before escaped defeat and had lost to England in Paris just a couple of years earlier, fell, wrote the principal German soccer magazine *Der Kicker*, 'like a bombshell over the Continent'.

Certainly the English selectors had chosen what seemed a resourceful team, described as 'a good, business-like side, strong in defence and with penetrative power in attack'. The full back combination of Tom Cooper and Ernie Blenkinsop was a famous one, and Aston Villa's Pongo Waring was a formidable centre forward, wont to tease Herbert

Chapman when Villa played Arsenal, 'You'd like to buy me, wouldn't you, Herbert?' Even Gabriel Hanot, the Grand Panjandrum of French football journalism, wrote, 'Our team has no chance of winning,' and went on, somewhat quaintly in retrospect, to hope that the English players would remind the French that the charge was still part of football.

They hardly had the chance to do so. Where the English selectors failed badly was to allow the England players ten days off training; and to ignore the advice of Peter Farmer, who was then managing Racing Club de Paris: 'I could plainly see that what beat our team was their tactics,' he declared. 'Surely after this disaster our countrymen at home will waken up to the fact that the Continentals are providing opposition of a formidable nature.'

On a hard, baked pitch the French forwards, regarded as the weakness of their team, simply outplayed England's defence. And attempts at mitigation by the selector in charge, a Mr Arthur G. Kingscott, asserting that the French 'had been in training and were consequently in the pink' proved a futile excuse. Gaston Barreau, the French selector, devastatingly rejoined that the French team had been brought together only on the eve of the match. He also brushed aside Mr Kingscott's excuse that seven England players had been injured, though Kingscott did have the grace to admit, 'They were yards faster than our men, their passing was better and their goal-keeping was infinitely superior.'

As for M. Barreau, he was generous enough to emphasise, 'French officials, pressmen and players do not regard their footballers as the equal of English professionals; they are satisfied with the victory and nothing more.'

It should be recorded that foreign teams came to play in England often in a state of fear and trembling, such was the colossal prestige of the 'fathers of football'. Given the contemptuous crushing of Spain, the defeat in France could be dismissed and forgotten as a fluke, a freak, a passing aberration. And heavy reverses such as the 5–1 victory of Scotland's Wembley Wizards in 1928 could be absorbed as coming, so to speak, within the family.

True, there were warning voices to be heard, notably those of James Catton, the tiny, bowler-hatted figure whose influential career spanned the nineteenth and twentieth centuries, and Ivan Sharpe, the former amateur Derby County and United Kingdom outside left, who followed him as the editor of the germinal *Athletic News*. In 1923, Catton had written: 'If England is to retain her prestige in the face of the advance of other nations, all players, whether they be forwards or backs, must use more intelligence, and by constant practice obtain control of and power over the ball with the inside and outside of each foot. Unless players get out of the rut into which they have fallen, the game will lose its popularity and Great Britain her fame. Call me pessimist, shake with Homeric laughter and write me down senile and silly, but the truth will prevail and this is the truth.' For his part an equally minatory Sharpe would succinctly write, 'They coach, we don't.'

Indeed, training at almost all English clubs was and for decades would remain bewilderingly primitive, largely consisting of endless lapping of the pitch; training grounds for clubs lay far in the remote future. The bizarre theory was that if a player didn't see the ball in the week, he would be all the more eager to see it on the Saturday, though what he was supposed to do with it then went unexplained. Until around the time of the Second World War, Scottish players constituted an accomplished exception to prove the rule, brought up as they were in the tradition of the tanner ba', with a high premium placed on skill. The word was that they tended to be slow and thus needed time to adjust to the higher pace of English football, but in that inter-war period, two of the Wembley Wizards such as Arsenal's playmaking inside left Alex James and the tough, doomed little peripatetic centre forward, Hughie Gallacher, were among the most coruscating players in the Football League.

Jimmy Hogan also sounded warnings about the state, and problematic future, of the English game. When his and Hugo Meisl's *Wunderteam* came to Stamford Bridge in 1932, it was to give England a tremendous run for their money, with their superb technique in passing, in a gloriously oscillating game. In the end England prevailed 4–3 – and in fact had the ball in the net again just as the final whistle blew – but the victory had surely flattered them.

Austria and Italy, Meisl and Pozzo, were intense rivals. For all his cultivated background, Pozzo could be a ruthless competitor, and there is no doubt that though he was never a Fascist himself, he derived advantage from the overblown chauvinism of the times. When, before kick-off in Italy's opening 1938 World Cup match against Norway in Marseille in 1938, his team gave the usual Fascist salute and were jeered by the expatriate dissidents in the crowd, he told his players to hold the salute until the jeering died.

He did not hesitate to strengthen his sides with *oriundi* – South American stars of Italian origin – among whom was the ruthless Luisito Monti, a thuggish centre half who, as fate would have it, precipitated in November 1934 the 'Battle of Highbury' when he limped off after ninety seconds with a toe broken in a clash with the burly Arsenal centre forward, Ted Drake. Italian double standards would persist right into the 1980s under Enzo Bearzot, another well-educated manager with contempt for chicanery, yet all too reliant on such bruising players as Claudio Gentile and Romeo Benetti.

It should be said that with a few notable exceptions such as Herbert Chapman himself, who once spent an hour or so criticising the single goal given away by an Arsenal team which had subsequently won with ease, English club managers were hardly tacticians. The so-called tracksuit manager lay in the post-war future. By and large, the manager stayed in his office. Leslie Knighton, who had begun as the office boy with the little Yorkshire club Castleford, would subsequently manage Arsenal, Chelsea, Birmingham, Manchester City and Bournemouth. Always very shrewd in acquiring players, perhaps the most 'tactical' thing he ever did was to give, in 1925, Arsenal's men mysterious silver-coated pills given to him by a Harley Street fan, which led to raging thirst and super-abundant energy.

During those inter-war years, when the rest of the football world was catching up so fast, the English game lived in a state of splendid isolation. Having in 1928 left FIFA, the international body, with which relations had been brittle ever since its foundation in 1904, England and the other British countries could not enter the World Cup. And while they regularly met the various European teams in 'friendly' matches – what was friendly about the Battle of Highbury? – they never came up against such powerful South American teams as

Argentina and Uruguay, who won two Olympic titles and the first, admittedly underpopulated, World Cup of 1930, played at home, in Montevideo. Not till May 1951 did a South American team, in the shape of Argentina, come to England, narrowly and unluckily losing 2–1 to England at Wembley. England themselves did not play in South America till 1953.

Meanwhile, though England narrowly lost a number of summer friendlies on the Continent, they also had their refulgent successes, not least when, after being obliged to give the Nazi salute before the match against Germany in Berlin's Olympic Stadium in May 1938, they thrashed the opposition 6–3. The Germans, on the eve of the World Cup finals in France, promptly appointed a new manager in Sepp Herberger who would remain in office for the next twenty-four years, winning the World Cup against Hungary and all the odds in 1954. Such longevity overshadowed even Walter Winterbottom's sixteen bureaucratic years in charge of England.

Herberger's Greater German team, including several Austrians after the Anschluss, was quickly eliminated in France, but he himself would emerge as a highly competitive, relentless force, maintaining tight tactical discipline. This, in contrast with the man who became his second-in-command, Helmut Schoen who, succeeding Herberger after the 1962 World Cup, would institute a more open and expensive policy, ultimately embracing Total Football. Herberger liked to lampoon his own supposed authoritarianism. One remembers, during the 1958 World Cup, in Gothenburg, when a Swedish newspaper had alleged that he knew his players only by numbers, he finished a press conference by smiling and saying that he was now going back to see numbers one, two and three.

Generalising about international team managers is a futile occupation. They come, you might say, in all shapes and sizes. Say that their careers are all essentially finite – rather on the lines of the adage that all political careers end in failure – and you can point to the sad, declining years of Alf Ramsey, after his World Cup triumphs. Yet Pozzo and Herberger lasted a couple of decades each, Pozzo ultimately succumbing because, in the 1940s, he could never come to terms with the Third Back Game.

Curiously enough, in a country which for so many years past has been obsessed with tactics, it wasn't until 1939, after England had drawn with Italy in Milan, that they woke up to the existence of the Third Back Game. A further oddity was that it was 'discovered' in the *Corriere Dello Sport* of Rome, by none other than Fulvio Bernardini, previously an elegant attacking centre half, ruthlessly discarded from the Italian team by Pozzo in favour of the harder, harsher and more functional Monti. It was Bernardini who christened the Third Back Game *sistema*, as opposed to the more traditional *metodo*.

Then there is the ever-pervasive question of luck. When Napoleon thought of promoting a general to the rank of marshal, the salient question he asked was, 'Is he lucky?' The problem being that, in football, luck can run suddenly out. This it did to Bobby Robson in the 1986 World Cup finals in Mexico. England made an abysmal start in Monterrey against Portugal, not least because Robson insisted on deploying his namesake Bryan, the skipper, though Bryan's shoulder dislocated at the drop of a hat. But when it happened again against Morocco, when Ray Wilkins, sadly off form, was sent off, Bobby was obliged to revolutionise his team, which then suddenly came to life, only to be eliminated in the quarter-finals when Diego Maradona punched his notorious Hand of God goal. Four years later, in Italy, Bobby and his team were hardly lucky to be knocked out by West Germany on penalties in the semi-final.

In the 2006 finals in Germany, you might well say that the French manager, Raymond Domenech, was lucky, up to a point. A slightly comic figure as he pirouetted on the touchline, he infuriated Zinedine Zidane, a supreme player but certainly out of sorts against South Korea, by substituting him. Zidane stalked off the field incensed, without a glance at his manager. He was suspended from the next game and Domenech brought in David Trezeguet to play profitably up front beside Thierry Henry. That, one assumed, was the end of Zidane; the man who had spectacularly headed those two goals from corners in the 1998 final against Brazil.

But probably overcoming his displeasure with Zidane, and against all expectations, all indications of form, Domenech brought Zizou back for the ensuing match against Spain. Zidane gave an inspired performance as he did again in the match with Brazil. But when it came to the final against Italy, which Zizou began by netting the coolest of penalties, he allowed himself to be provoked late in the game by Italy's Marco Materazzi, butted him in the chest and had himself sent off, thereby effectively sabotaging his team's chances. Luck . . . and bad luck.

And into what kind of category would you fit the ebullient little Yorkshire coach George Raynor, winner with Sweden of a sparkling Olympic football tournament in London in 1948, beaten World Cup finalist in Stockholm against Brazil ten years later, third placed, heavily depleted, team in the Brazilian World Cup of 1950?

Nils Liedholm, a star of Raynor's teams in 1948 and 1958, later a notable club manager himself in Italy, once called George 'a good manager for a happy team'. Yet he was rather more than that. I came to know him well during the tumultuous 1954–5 season in Rome when, having failed to make progress at Juventus, he was parachuted in to save Lazio from a disastrous campaign: which he ultimately did; he even achieved a sensational victory in the Roman derby against the seemingly superior Roma, managed by another Englishman in the Liverpudlian Jesse Carver.

Raynor, by his own admission, was 'a second-class player', first with Sheffield United, then with Aldershot. But – luck, again? – he found himself during Army service in the war managing the Iraqi national team and thus coming to the notice of the all-powerful Football Association Secretary, Stanley Rous. It was Rous who plucked him out of the chorus, sending him to manage Sweden where at first the press greeted him with disdain. A splendid success in his first game put an end to that and, coach as well as tactician, he travelled the country coaching the men he wanted for his team.

He could scarcely have been more of a contrast with the reigning England manager, tall, pedagogic Walter Winterbottom, yet when it came to playing the resplendent Hungarians in 1953, he had much the better of it. Raynor, as we shall see, took his team to Budapest, promised his men that if they won he'd 'paint Stalin's moustache red', and got a 2–2 draw with his astute tactics. Two weeks later at Wembley, Winterbottom got everything wrong, and England, never before beaten at home by a foreign team (I don't count Eire in 1949) were thrashed, 6–3.

Mention of Rous and subsequently of Winterbottom leads us to the salient part Rous played in English and international football. Born in Suffolk, he became at once a games master at a Watford grammar school, and an international referee, who in England achieved the crowning kudos of refereeing the 1934 FA Cup final. He then became Secretary of the Football Association, in succession to the antediluvian Sir Frederic Wall, and at once embarked on a sustained campaign to modernise the English game. He did not succeed in getting England back into FIFA till after the Second World War. Nor did England accept what was, in fact, a quite gratuitous invitation – not being members of FIFA – to take part in the 1938 World Cup in France. A pity, really, since England at that time had a successful team which had just beaten France in Paris; the vacancy had been created by Austria's disappearance into the Anschluss, and the outbreak of a bitter civil war in Spain. Rous, however, magisterially redrafted the Laws of the Game, and showed his commitment to coaching by appointing, with surprising lack of success, Jimmy Hogan to run courses, shortly before the Second World War.

That Rous was a snob and an authoritarian could hardly be gainsaid. There were times when he seemed almost embarrassed by the fact that his increasing social status, his access to kings and queens, all depended on young men in shorts running about muddy fields. When Denis Follows, whom Rous despised and who reciprocated his hostility, unexpectedly was voted FA Secretary as Rous's successor in 1962, I remember sitting in a BBC radio studio anteroom before interviewing Follows, who remarked, 'The Secretary is meant to be the servant of the Football Association, but we all know what happened. The servant became the master.' Which, overall, was just as well.

But Rous was not popular with England's players and had frequent stand-offs with the press. All in all, he was little concerned with the troops on the ground, as evidenced by the fact that throughout his long regime, England's team never travelled abroad, even to World Cups, with their own doctor.

I remember a significant episode during the 1962 World Cup in

Chile. Garrincha, the dynamic Brazilian right winger, had been sent off in Santiago in the semi-final against the host nation – as had the Chilean centre forward, Landa. Garrincha, in the absence of the injured Pele, had been the outstanding figure of the competition, and the Brazilians lodged an appeal, which seemed doomed to failure. Such was the frenetic anxiety in Brazil itself that it was said that the President himself was listening to developments through headphones, during Mass. The world of football waited with him. I was staying in the Emperador Hotel on the busy Avenida O'Higgiñs, together with the BBC television commentator, Kenneth Wostenholme. Eager to know what decision had been taken on Garrincha, Kenneth said, 'I'll ring Stanley.' This he did, the response to his question being, 'Oh, the disciplinary committee met this morning.'

'But what did they decide?' Kenneth asked.

'I've got my papers here,' said Rous, and shuffled through them. 'Seven and nine,' he said, at last, 'seven and nine. Seven was cautioned and nine was suspended.' Which was how we learned that seven, alias Garrincha, could play, however controversially, in the final.

Yet Rous's support for Winterbottom as England manager was not wholly consistent. In May 1955, when I was living and working in Rome, Jesse Carver, the Liverpudlian who was then managing Roma, one of his many Italian clubs, told me that he had an appointment with Rous at the Hotel Quirinale in Via Nazionale and that I might care to come along; it could do me some good.

Rous awaited us, silver haired, formidably tall. 'Did you have a good journey, Sir Stanley?' I dutifully asked him.

'Yes, yes, yes,' he said, impatiently. 'Who are you?'

Little interested when I told him, he then proceeded, in my obscure presence, to offer Winterbottom's managerial job to Carver. 'It's about time we brought Walter back into the office,' he said. It didn't happen. Nor, deciding this was a private conversation, did I report it for twenty-five years or so. Carver, always full of new ideas, once manager of Holland – one of the many jobs on which he abruptly walked out – would probably have made a very good England manager, though goodness knows how long he would have stayed. So Winterbottom remained in office for another seven years.

Had Rous had his way, Winterbottom would have been the sole selector, as was largely the fashion elsewhere. But the stubborn, selfish mediocrities from the League clubs, jealous of their privileges and peregrinations, refused to bend. Indeed, it was even hard for Rous to get them to accept a team manager at all. When Alf Ramsey ultimately succeeded Winterbottom in 1962, his insistence that he should manage alone was non-negotiable. Yet the greedy old men still insisted on a Senior International Committee, whose motto, I once suggested, should be, 'They also serve who only eat and drink.' And as we'll see, in due course these vindictive parasites would have a spiteful revenge on Ramsey. I published a rhyme about them once:

'You are old, Councillor William,' the young man roared,
'and are obviously quite out of touch.
And yet you incessantly travel abroad.
Don't you think at your age it's too much?'

'In my youth,' Councillor William replied with disdain,
'I spent all my time making money.
But now I can travel the world without paying,
I really don't see what's so funny.'

'You are old,' said the youth, 'as I've mentioned before,
and are gravely reluctant to think.
And yet for an ancient reactionary bore,
it's amazing how much you can drink.'

'When Sir Alf,' said the Councillor, 'took over the team,
he robbed me of any real function.
Now drinking for England's my pride and my joy,
nor have I the smallest compunction.'

'You are old,' said the youth, 'and you stand in the way
of anyone younger than you.
And yet you're perpetually having your say
on what English football should do.'

'I *am* old,' said the sage, 'you are perfectly right,
but I'd rather be old than be clever.
Do you think you can change the whole game overnight?
Be off, or I'll stay here for ever!'

1 WALTER AND THE STANLEYS

Walter Winterbottom 1946–62
Key Game: England v Hungary, November 1953

SO WALTER WINTERBOTTOM, IN 1946, TOOK CHARGE OF THE England team with one hand tied behind his back. Or, to vary the metaphor, with the dead weight of the selection committee holding him back. It could perhaps, were one cynical, be said to act as a kind of protection. If he couldn't pick the teams, how could he be held responsible? By the time it came to the 1958 World Cup finals in Sweden, the feeling among the travelling press was that though the selection committee remained, Walter was largely getting his own way. Little groups of selectors would assure journalists that they would certainly make changes in an unimpressive team, but when they emerged from their meetings with Winterbottom, it was simply to say, 'No change.'

The ambiguity of the situation was such that, even now, it is difficult to sort fact from speculation. Thus, during the World Cup in Sweden, the young Bobby Charlton didn't get a game. Billy Wright, the England captain, subsequently wrote that it was because Winterbottom had been overruled by the selectors. But when Wright and Winterbottom contributed to a book edited by the leading football writer Bob Ferrier soon after that tournament, it was to disparage Charlton for his supposed inadequacies.

The truth was that he was still profoundly shaken by his appalling experiences in the Munich air crash suffered by Manchester United the previous February, when Charlton had been hurled still strapped in his seat clean out of the aircraft and into a field. The guilt of the survivor you might surmise, since so many others had died or were so badly hurt that they would never play again. There remains no doubt in my mind that Walter in Sweden was calling the shots.

Watching the England players training in the old Ullevi stadium, situated next door to the cantilevered new World Cup one, an unfamiliar figure was to be seen, red faced, red jerseyed, a sergeant major figure, trapping and passing with the members of the squad. Middle aged, he could hardly be a reinforcement to a squad which, though two short of its permitted complement of twenty-two, had left at home both Nat Lofthouse, Bolton's formidable centre forward, and the ageing but irrepressible Stanley Matthews. The name of this mystery figure was Chalwyn, and it transpired that he was a friend of Stanley Rous whose hospitality Rous had enjoyed in Australia.

Four years later in Coya, up in the hills beyond Santiago at England's Chilean World Cup training camp, astounding to see, there was Chalwyn participating in a training game! 'We're playing the Chalwyn Plan!' joked Bernard Joy, the *Evening Standard* correspondent and once Arsenal's amateur centre half. But still no team doctor, which was arguably why when Peter Swan, the reserve centre half, fell gravely ill, there was no one to treat him but the doctor of the Braden Copper Company at Rancagua where the team played its eliminators. He could have died.

Luck? You might think that Winterbottom's and England's ran out with the appalling Munich air crash, depriving the team at one cruel stroke of three of its crucial players: Duncan Edwards, the powerful, driving young left half, Roger Byrne, the captain and left back, and the free-scoring centre forward, with foot or head, Tommy Taylor. Vittorio Pozzo, attending the tournament as a journalist, was scathing about Derek Kevan, Taylor's successor, strangely preferred to Nat Lofthouse. 'To choose a player like Kevan,' Pozzo censoriously told me, 'is paving the way to brute force. He scored a goal [against the USSR] with the *outside* of his head.'

When England were obliged to meet the USSR a second time in a play-off, once more in Gothenburg, Bobby Charlton still couldn't get a game. Surprisingly England chose two young players who had never yet been capped, the Chelsea right winger Peter Brabrook and the Wolves inside right, Peter Broadbent. Brabrook hit the post early in the game but England – without the injured Tom Finney after the initial match with Russia, more bad luck – lost 1–0.

Bad luck? England and Winterbottom surely had it four years earlier when Neil Franklin, the elegant Stoke City player, fulcrum of the defence, that rare phenomenon of the time, a footballing centre half, lied to the FA. He wished to miss the World Cup because his wife was pregnant, only, suddenly and surreptitiously, to fly to Bogotá in Colombia, where he had been lured by the Santa Fe club, offering him a £50 a week wage which was far in advance of what he was earning with Stoke. Santa Fe could do this, because Colombia at that time were no longer members of FIFA.

Not that this could be seen as an excuse for the most humiliating defeat in the history of the England team: its 1–0 loss to a rag-tag and bobtail USA team, in Belo Horizonte. It was one of the three worst results in Winterbottom's sixteen-year reign, the other being the two humiliating defeats, 6–3 at Wembley, 7–1 in Budapest, by the brilliant Hungarian team.

Those last two disasters could be laid at Winterbottom's door, but the 1950 American fiasco should surely not be. After what looked a formidably talented team, including such as Bert Williams in goal, Billy Wright at right half, Alf Ramsey at right back, Tom Finney, Stanley Mortensen, Roy Bentley and Wilf Mannion in attack, they should have annihilated such obscure opposition. The Americans were captained from right half by Eddie McIlvenny, a Scotsman who'd just been given a free transfer by Wrexham of the Third Division North. Though they had in John Souza from Fall River – long a remote American football oasis in a country where soccer was an un-American activity – an inside left of exceptional quality, and gave both Spain and Chile a run for their money.

The only goal went past England's gifted goalkeeper off the head of Joe Gaetjens, a Haitian centre forward, fated, years later, to be murdered in that tormented island by the Tons Tons Macoutes. A fluke? Gaetjens' team mates insisted that he often scored that kind of goal. England, though they dominated play on a tight and bumpy pitch, having changed in their hotel rather than in the primitive dressing rooms, could score none at all.

Wise after the event, it has been suggested, even to this day, that all would have been well had Stanley Matthews, a last-minute call-up from an FA tour of North America, played. His absence was blamed by some on the sole selector, a Grimsby fish merchant called Arthur Drewry, who allegedly refused Winterbottom's request to pick Matthews. But, given the apparent strength of the England team, how should it have seemed remotely necessary?

'Of course we had chances, dozens of them,' said Winterbottom, after the game. But posts, bar and a defiant American goalkeeper in Frank Borghi kept the English out. America's coach, a Scotsman called Bill Jeffries, said exultantly, 'That's all we need to make the game go in America.' It wasn't. The great American sporting public simply turned over and went to sleep. The result made tiny, bottom-of-the-page paragraphs in the newspapers. The ball which had beaten Williams lurked, deflated, a symbol, for years in a cabinet in the American Soccer Association's minuscule office in the Empire State Building in New York.

That Winterbottom found it so hard to speak the language of the led is beyond doubt. Nevertheless, much of the criticism initially made of him by famous and experienced England players was inaccurate and unfair. 'That PT teacher,' Tommy Lawton, a majestic centre forward, scathingly called him, while Raich Carter, a celebrated inside forward, scornfully derided Walter's training exercises, which, he said, involved skills which he had learned as a schoolboy. Stanley Matthews found Winterbottom irrelevant. Bobby Charlton, later on, inveighed, 'He'd never been properly in the professional game. He didn't know how to handle players, how to talk to them.'

The second part of his accusation was probably true, the first was simply and demonstrably unfair, for Winterbottom had indeed been a professional and I once had the *Topical Times* magazine photo card to prove it. In it, Walter stood in a Manchester United shirt, heavy shin pads bulging out his socks. A good enough centre half to hold a first-team place till the outbreak of war, he had used his wages as a footballer to pay his way through Carnegie physical education college. In the war itself he achieved the rank of Wing Commander in the Royal Air Force, worked in the Air Ministry, played as a full back guest for Chelsea, and was once picked as an England reserve. That he was a rather academic figure, well spoken, fluent, rational, something of a Corinthian figure you might say, set him apart from the young, working-class professionals he had to manage.

Moreover, he did not even consider the job of England manager his principal one. I well remember his telling me, in a 1952 interview in the FA headquarters in Lancaster Gate, that he believed his more important role was that of Director of Coaching. The coaching scheme unquestionably began well. Walter that day described coaching to me as 'a means of showing how to practise', and it initially produced such talented disciples as Ron Greenwood, who would revolutionise West Ham United and ultimately — though too late in his day, alas — manage England himself.

The problem was that the longer the coaching scheme lasted, the more it became ossified in jargon and orthodoxy. Arthur Rowe, a fine coach and the author of Tottenham Hotspur's splendid one-touch push-and-run teams of the early 1950s, when told of the term 'peripheral vision', said, 'You know what that means? It means seeing out of your arse!' John Arlott, the famous cricket commentator and a long-time lover of football, once spoke to Walter of the ability of some players almost to photograph the field, before the ball even came to them. 'Yes,' said Walter, 'we know about that. We call it Environmental Awareness.'

It is instructive, meanwhile, to look back at that 1950 World Cup and examine just what part tactics played. By then, the European teams were all playing the Third Back Game. Brazil's defensive system was termed the Diagonal, its weakness, finally and disastrously exposed in the deciding World Cup game in Rio — there was no final as such — by Uruguay, allowed opponents too much potential space on its left flank. Yet in the final pool matches, Brazil simply overwhelmed Spain 6–1 and Sweden 7–1, their dazzling inside forward trio of Zizinho, Ademir and Jair playing so well that the *Corriere dello Sport* published a headline, '*Come Resistere?*' How to resist? In the event, the

Uruguayans, with a superbly powerful, versatile and adventurous centre half in Obdulio Varela, did indeed resist and win, with no concession to Third Back football.

Aside from basic, elementary tactical errors, such as Winterbottom made against Hungary, it is arguable that tactics per se are secondary to individual talent. In Europe in the 1950s, the chief novelty was that of the deep-lying centre forward, as practised so devastatingly at Wembley against England by Hungary's Nandor Hidegkuti. In that famed Hungarian team, the inside forwards, Sandor 'Golden Head' Kocsis, and Ferenc Puskas, of the phenomenal left foot, stayed well up the field. But the defence had a third back in the burly Gyula Lorant.

Uruguay beat Brazil in that dramatic game not through any tactical advantage, but because of a number of superb individual performances: Varela both in defence and later, when he surged into attack, Rodrigues Andrade, the resilient black defender, Roque Maspoli, indomitable in goal, and the two scorers – the lean, pale, inventive and elusive inside left Juan Schiaffino, and the little, flying right winger, Chico Ghiggia. Varela was a genuine captain, as, for better and ultimately for worse, was Puskas for Hungary. In neither case was a strong, inspirational manager behind the team's success.

Walter's problem was that he could neither inspire nor tactically innovate, though Billy Wright, his faithful captain, tells of an early game against Belgium when Winterbottom made decisive tactical changes. The indicative tale is told of Len Shackleton, a glittering maverick of an inside forward, lying on the grass at the Bank of England grounds at Roehampton where England were training before a game; one of the scandalously few occasions on which the so-called Clown Prince of Soccer was chosen for an international. Mistrusted, like so many other maverick talents from Charlie Buchan, through to Stanley Matthews, Glenn Hoddle and Paul Gascoigne, by an English football establishment ever wary of the unorthodox star.

Winterbottom announced that he wanted all five forwards to run down the field interpassing till they reached the penalty area, when they should put the ball into the empty goal. 'Shack' looked up wearily. 'Which side of the goal, Mr Winterbottom?' he asked.

Where Winterbottom was fortunate was in inheriting, when he took office, an England team full of outstanding players. It was sadly ironic that it had probably reached its peak in the war, when only Scotland and Wales could be encountered. The all-Army half back line of Cliff Britton, Stanley Cullis and Joe Mercer, and the attack formed by Matthews, Raich Carter, Tommy Lawton, Jimmy Hagan and Denis Compton, were formidable. In an international in Manchester against Scotland in 1943, England won 8-0.

Denis was a gloriously exciting batsman, a ball-playing left winger with a fierce left foot. Yet owing to the paradoxes of the war years, he never won a full England cap, while his far less gifted brother Leslie did. Wartime internationals were not 'official', and the closest Denis came to full recognition was when, on his return from Army service in India, he played for the England team, beaten 1–0 in a Victory International in Glasgow.

It was a sore point with Winterbottom that he was obliged to include in two of his teams, in a four-day spell, the then 38-year-old Leslie Compton, by then a dominating Arsenal centre half, who had spent seven pre-war years as a reserve full back at Highbury, though he made several England appearances during the war. But there was no appeal from the choice of the selectors. Walter once remarked that three or four of his players picked themselves, 'So I can concentrate my arguments on the most important of the others, knowing that I am pretty sure to be outvoted on one or two positions.'

His overall record in 139 matches was: won 78, drew 33, lost 28. He never failed to qualify his team for the World Cup finals, though this was made relatively easy on the first two occasions, when the British Championship was generously made a qualifying group by FIFA. And if England fell at the first, group-stage, hurdle in 1950 and 1958, they reached the quarter-finals in 1954 and 1962.

His original team could call not only on the likes of big, resourceful Frank Swift in goal, Wilf Mannion, a small, blond, hugely talented inside forward, one of the few British stars who served in the Army abroad rather than in the Physical Training Corps at home, and Tommy Lawton, but on such gifted newcomers as Tom Finney, a remarkable winger who had also served abroad, Neil Franklin, Billy

Wright and the lively little Manchester United left half, Henry Cockburn.

Almost at once, the selectors, and Walter himself, were faced with the Matthews–Finney dualism. Both were outside rights, both exceptional players, but which should be picked? Matthews, nicknamed the Wizard of Dribble, was, in his day, irresistible. His amazing swerve – 'Don't ask me how I do it, it just comes out of me under pressure' – had put an infinity of left backs on the wrong foot, as he swept the ball past them with a flick of the outside of his right foot, and disappeared at speed up the touchline.

Finney, naturally left footed, originally an inside left, nicknamed the Preston Plumber for his other occupation, was a more orthodox but still supremely elusive winger. His balance was exceptional, he had pace, he was equally adroit with either foot, he would always score more goals than Matthews who, though he had scored a famous and crucial hat trick for England against the Czechs at Tottenham in 1937, when an injury to right half Jack Crayston caused him to be switched inside, was always more the maker rather than the taker of goals – ideally with his ability, which Finney shared, to get to the by-line and pull the ball back dangerously into the middle.

That Finney should initially be preferred to an excluded Matthews could have come as no great surprise even to Matthews himself. In 1946, falling out with an intransigent manager, Bob McGrory, he had even left his home town club Stoke City for Blackpool, where he had played as a wartime guest and owned a boarding house. Beloved by the fans – it was reckoned that whenever he played in London he'd put an extra ten thousand people on the gate – Matthews remained an eternal enigma. Billy Wright was known to criticise him strongly for his alleged self-indulgence, only, with another volte-face, to eulogise him in his valedictory book.

Matthews' second game for England as a nineteen-year-old had happened to be at the notorious Battle of Highbury in November 1934, when Italian boots and elbows flew, after the fearsome Luisito Monti left the field injured in ninety seconds. Seldom in the story of sporting journalism can words have come so devastatingly home to roost than those of the *Daily Mail* sports columnist, Geoffrey Simpson, who wrote, 'I saw Matthews play just as moderately in the recent inter-League match, exhibiting the same slowness and hesitation. Perhaps he lacks the big match temperament.' *Matthews?*

In the first four internationals of the 1946–47 post-war season, Tom Finney was preferred to Matthews. England could hardly have got off to a better start under Winterbottom, thrashing Northern Ireland 7–2 in Belfast with a hat trick by Wilf Mannion, in his first official international. Two days later, however, England could only scrape a 1–0 victory over the Republic of Ireland, in Dublin, Finney's scrappy goal after 82 minutes being flatteringly decisive. Billy Wright would later observe that the whole team had eaten all too well, escaping from the post-war English austerity.

In the fourth international Holland were annihilated 8–2 in Huddersfield, with four for Tommy Lawton. But when, in April, it came to the then classic encounter with Scotland at Wembley, it was Matthews who was preferred to Finney, a game in which the Scots unexpectedly and deservedly forced a 1–1 draw.

By the same token, when it came in May to the match between Britain and the Rest of Europe in Glasgow, won by the British by a resounding 6–1, it was Matthews who appeared on the British right wing. Not till 25 May 1947, in Lisbon, did the penny finally drop, Matthews being selected on the right wing, Finney on the left, for an overwhelming 10–0 victory. Lawton scored another four goals. Stanley Mortensen, his inside right, whose first international appearance had been at Wembley as, bizarrely, a wartime substitute for Wales, celebrated his first full cap with four more.

A year later, in Turin, with Matthews and Finney again on the wings, Finney scored twice in a 4–0 win which somewhat flattered England. Italy had been on top early in the game, till Mortensen got away to score a goal that was to be remembered in Italy for decades to come – a shot from an 'impossible' angle, almost on the right-hand goal line, which somehow found its way into the near, top corner of the net. Matthews, irresistible, tormented poor Alberto Eliani, Italy's deputy left back. Winterbottom later told of how he went into the England dressing room at half time to find his players wilting in the heat; he encouraged them by telling them that in the dressing room next door, the Italians were being sprayed with soda siphons!

That Matthews should initially not be chosen for the 1950 World Cup squad was further evidence of the ambivalence with which he and his unorthodoxy were regarded by the English football establishment. When he did eventually play against Spain, in Rio, it was for an England team which, probably playing its best football of the competition, had claims to have scored a valid goal when Jackie Milburn, the Newcastle centre forward, was given offside, but eventually went down to a single goal.

If George Raynor, three years later, showed a tactical flair with his Swedish team in Budapest which wholly eluded Winterbottom a fortnight later at Wembley, I suppose Sweden's 7–1 annihilation by Brazil in the 1950 World Cup final pool might in some way be seen as a parallel to England's twin debacles against the Hungarians. Raynor, after all, had watched powerless as his defence was swept utterly aside. Yet the devastating Zizinho–Ademir–Jair inside forward trio had played only once before, in the third Group A match, against Yugoslavia in the Maracana, goals by Ademir – used for the first time at centre forward – with Zizinho making his World Cup debut at inside right, bringing a far from easy victory. In fact, if Yugoslavia's clever inside right, Rajko Mitic, hadn't cut his head on an exposed steel girder as he left the dressing room, things might have been somewhat different. As it was, Ademir gave Brazil the lead in three minutes, before Mitic could get on the field.

Raynor knew that his gifted, young inside forwards, Kalle Palmer and Nacka Skoglund, were physically frail. 'With two stronger inside forwards,' he told me in Rome, five years later, 'Sweden would have done much better. Give Palmer the ball and he can split any defence. But both he and Skoglund were physically very weak.' His plan was to seek an early goal: 'We had two chances before they even moved.' But on nineteen minutes Ademir scored and the floodgates opened. Note, though, that Brazil, managed by Flavio Costa, showed no great tactical innovation. That was to come, of course, in 1958. All depended on supreme individual skill and sublime execution.

In October 1953, England, at Wembley, met a FIFA selection to celebrate the ninetieth anniversary of the Football Association. There were no South Americans and no Hungarians, Gustav Sebes, the Hungarian Deputy Minister of Sport, being quoted as saying he had no desire to accommodate a bunch of English idiots. The FIFA team was polyglot, all European, but by no means the easy prey the Rest of Europe had been at Hampden in 1947. Instead the cosmopolitan group of players quickly found a common language. The English defence was especially troubled by the fact that the big Swedish centre forward, Gunnar 'The Fireman' Nordahl, who had left Sweden after the 1948 Olympics to score abundantly for Milan, chose to drop behind the firing line. Derek Ufton of Charlton, making his one and only appearance for England, was bewildered by this, and stood back, allowing Nordahl to dictate much of the play. With the blond Italian *jeune premier* Giampiero Boniperti and the thick-thighed, much-travelled Hungarian, Ladislao Kubala, scoring twice each, England were lucky to survive with a very late and somewhat doubtful penalty, converted by Alf Ramsey, to draw 4–4. So the unbeaten home record was narrowly preserved.

Raynor's Sweden had largely nullified the threat of Hungary's own deep-lying centre forward, Nandor Hidegkuti, by close-marking him with a different forward in each half. What would England do? Winterbottom asked his centre half, Harry Johnston, whether he preferred to man-mark Hidegkuti or stand off him. Johnston replied that he preferred to stand off him, the logical corollary of which would clearly be to assign another player to shadow Hidegkuti. Amazingly, it wasn't done. So it was that the Hungarians – given a team talk by their captain, Puskas, who told them to ignore a long oration by Sebes (so much for supposed managers) – took the lead in ninety seconds; and it was Hidegkuti who scored. With a clever feint, he put Johnston on the wrong foot in the wall of English defenders, and drove the ball fiercely through the gap.

Finney, alas, was missing; in another of those strangely irrational choices by the selection committee, his place went to the Tottenham outside left George Robb, given his first and only cap, not long after he had given up his amateur status. England resisted as best they could against a team hugely superior in touch and movement. Jackie Sewell actually equalised, but by half time, with Hidegkuti in command and on his way to a hat trick, the Hungarians were 4–2 up and on their own way to a 6–3 victory. The last goal, England's third, arrived on the hour from another of Ramsey's penalties, this one indisputable, after Gyula Grosics, the Hungarian keeper – famed for his ability to act as a virtual sweeper if his defence was breached – brought down Robb. If there was a major tactical change from the Hungarians' previous game against the Swedes, it lay in the fact that their quick, clever wingers, Laszlo Budai and Zoltan Czibor, looked for the ball rather than waiting for it to come to them. It had not been one of Matthews' better Wembley days; six months after, in what became known as 'the Matthews final', he had at last won his first ever FA Cup gold medal, playing havoc in the closing minutes with a Bolton team reduced to nine fit men.

He did not play in the ill-fated return match in Budapest the following May. Instead, in another case of obscure selection, the outside right position went to Portsmouth's Peter Harris, whose only previous appearance had been almost five years earlier, at Everton, where England had lost 2–0 to the Republic of Ireland. Another strange choice, and presumably not Winterbottom's, was that of the Fulham centre forward Bedford Jezzard; to make his international debut in an England team which was overwhelmed 7–1, was hardly ideal. That the Hungarians would show themselves greatly superior to any team England might at that time have deployed was unquestionable. But knowing what Winterbottom did about their strengths and methods, surely it would have been possible at least to devise a plan to limit the damage.

So it was that England went on to the World Cup in Switzerland just as they were to do four years later in Sweden, in the shadow of a thumping defeat. There would, however, be one major, effective difference from the debacle of Budapest. For the first time, Billy Wright would play at centre half. Ever Winterbottom's protégé, just as Winterbottom was that of Rous, Wright in fact had first been picked for England in early 1946 in a transitional international against Belgium at Wembley at inside left. But when the chosen right half, Frank Soo, dropped out, Wright was switched with great success to right half. There he would stay till the 1954 World Cup, though in

November 1951, in a most unusual display of tactical innovation, the selectors chose Wright to play not at wing half but at inside left. This was clearly an attempt to counter the fulcrum of a gifted Austrian team, the majestic, roving centre half, Ernst Ocwirk. In the event, however, Billy Nicholson of Spurs, selected at right half, was injured, and Wright was withdrawn to his customary position of right half.

Nicholson, who never won another cap, having scored on his debut the previous May against Portugal, would eventually of course become an outstanding coach and manager. It was he, in Gothenburg in the 1958 World Cup, acting as assistant to Winterbottom, who cleverly devised a strategy to contain the Brazilian attack. Neither Pele nor Garrincha was yet playing, but the Brazilians were still a forbidding opponent. Nicholson's tactics put Don Howe, then the West Bromwich Albion right back, in a central defensive position, using the wing half Bill Slater to play tight on Didi, the playmaker of the Brazilian side, while freeing Eddie Clamp, his Wolves colleague, usually a right half, to attack up the touchline as a wing back. The plan overall worked well, and England might even have won through a penalty when the Brazilian captain and centre half Hilderado Luis Bellini seemed clearly to have fouled Derek Kevan in the box.

As for the 1954 tournament, England emerged from it with some credit; certainly with a great deal more than Scotland, who were thrashed and humiliated 7–0 by Uruguay. Matthews in this tournament was picked and prominent from the first. In the opening group game against Belgium, he was restored to the team after the fatuous experiment with Harris. Making light of his thirty-nine years, elusive and ubiquitous, he was never subdued by a Belgian team which however exploited the failings of an English defence in which Wright was yet to play at centre half, drawing 4–4 a game which seemed beyond them.

Matthews, injured, missed the 2–0 victory against the hosts, Switzerland, when Wright made his debut at centre half. But he returned in ebullient form in an oscillating quarter-final against the holders, Uruguay, who eventually won 4–2, despite injury to three players. Among them the imposing Varela who, like Matthews, belied his thirty-nine years. Matthews himself played a clever ball behind

Varela to engineer the first English goal. Frequently – as against Belgium – moved into the middle, Matthews hit a post and had a shot saved by the keeper Maspoli, but inept goalkeeping by England's Gil Merrick, who had long been living on borrowed time, doomed England to elimination.

Yet even the mighty Hungarians were fated to failure. Given the revelations, so many years after the event, that suspicions the Germans had been using stimulants were all too well justified, perhaps it is irrelevant to talk about tactics. When, after their sensational triumph over the Hungarians in the final in Berne it was found that so many of the team had gone down with jaundice, it was widely believed that drugs had been used. But in those innocent days, drug tests were unknown. And it has to be asked – given the ultimate revelation that syringes were found in the drains of the German dressing room – how often they had been used before in the tournament. Thus it made redundant any kind of assessment of the tactics imposed by Sepp Herberger on a team which had risen from the ashes of its initial 8–3 defeat by Hungary, thrashing Austria 6–1 in the semi-final.

Ferenc Puskas himself, who had forcefully talked his way back into Hungary's final line-up despite not having yet recovered fully from injury, insisted at the time that he had been in the German dressing room after the match and seen their players vomiting. It is perhaps arguable that, all talk of tactics aside, the kick which won West Germany the World Cup was the one inflicted by the German centre half, Werner Liebrich, on Puskas in the course of the 8–3 game. Puskas was obliged to drop out, but the Hungarians still flourished, moving Czibor off the left wing to inside left, only for Puskas, always the dominant figure (whatever the role of Gyula Mandi, the team manager, and Gustav Sebes, the politician), not only to impose himself on the team for the final but to insist on the exclusion of the capable outside right, Budai. In the event, there was some reason to think that Puskas was denied a valid equaliser at 3–3 in the final, when controversially given offside by a Welsh linesman, Mervyn Griffiths, and the English referee, Bill Ling.

In retrospect, this was probably England's best World Cup performance under Walter Winterbottom. If the 5–0 defeat in Belgrade's heat had been potentially traumatic, the well-deserved draw in Moscow against the USSR – due to be met again in Sweden – was a significant recovery. But both in that 1958 tournament and in Chile, four years later, the England attack was largely firing blanks.

As for Brazil, still all but in mourning for the last-gasp defeat by Uruguay in the 1950 decider, hoping perhaps to banish memories of it by even changing the colour of their shirts from white faced with blue to the now familiar yellow, they had fallen out of the 1954 World Cup after the notorious Battle of Berne, when their players had run amok against the Hungarians in the quarter-final. A Third Back was now being used, but there were still defensive problems.

These became evident when Brazil, on tour, came to Wembley in May 1956 when their supposed Third Back defence was a thing of gaps and disasters. It quickly became clear that the Brazilian defenders had little idea of the pivotal covering essential to Third Back defence, and England raced happily through the resultant chasms, scoring four goals and even missing a couple of penalties. The game was remarkable for the dominance of the now forty-one-year-old Stanley Matthews over Nilton Santos, reputedly one of the best left backs in the game. Matthews turned him inside out, and after the game, in the England dressing room, spoke bitterly of those critics who declared he was too old to play: 'There's times I want to tear the paper across.'

By the time it came to the 1958 World Cup, however, Brazil had not only found a new defensive system; they had found one which would go out to conquer the world of football, sweeping aside the previously dominant Third Back game. Resisted only in Italy where catenaccio – sweeper defence – originated by Karl Rappan when the Austrian was coaching Switzerland, it would be in dour vogue for many years.

Four–two–four, as it began, played by the Brazilians, was supposedly invented by a Paraguayan coach, Fleitas Solitch, working in Rio. Instead of having three men at the back, two full backs pivoting around a centre half, Brazil now deployed four defenders in a line: two full backs and a centre half, supported by what might be described as a defensive wing half. In front of them played two men in the midfield, one being Didi, a classical inside forward, a supreme passer of the ball, adept with so-called 'falling leaf' free kicks, which faded insidiously away from bewildered goalkeepers; the other a wing half, initially in the shape of the attacking Dino Sani, then in that of the more restrained Zito. Up front played two wingers, a centre forward, and an inside forward playing just off him. Yet from the first, the tireless energy, the phenomenal stamina, of the outside left, Mario Lobo Zagallo, enabled him to drop deep to defend whenever necessary, as well as playing a major role in attack. So the formation could at a moment's notice become 4–3–3, which by the time it came to the 1962 World Cup in Chile, it was.

Winterbottom's luck, or the lack if it, in 1958, went beyond the crucial loss of Edwards, Byrne and Taylor, to embrace the poor form of several of his team. It was unfortunate for him and for England that the last weeks of the season had seen an intensely contested Second Division promotion battle between three clubs: Fulham, Blackburn Rovers and Charlton Athletic. The consequence was that Johnny Haynes and Bobby Robson, the Fulham inside forwards whose team had finished fourth, were weary; Haynes, in addition, being troubled by blistered feet. Tired too were the Blackburn pair Bryan Douglas, the talented and adroit little right winger, and the right half Ronnie Clayton, who didn't, in fact, play until the ill-omened play-off against the USSR.

Haynes, who had been a national figure ever since, as a fifteen-year-old inside left, he played at Wembley in a televised schoolboy international for England against Scotland, was expected to be the creative force in the English midfield in Sweden but, in fact, he was largely ineffectual in a malfunctioning attack. Four years later in Chile, alas, he was again unable to bear the burden placed on him, though on this occasion, when he proved a somewhat sullen captain, it seemed evident that the opposition had read his long-passing game all too well.

To qualify for the 1962 finals, as they had been obliged to do outside the comforting shelter of the British International Championship since the previous World Cup, England did well to eliminate the strong Portuguese side, drawing with them in Lisbon, beating them in London. En route to Chile, playing Peru in Lima, they found a new star: 21-year-old Bobby Moore of West Ham.

Tall, blond, strongly built, precociously and impeccably calm, Moore had begun at West Ham as a centre half, somewhat compromised by a lack of pace and indifferent command in the air. Yet from his earliest days at Upton Park, his coolness under any kind of pressure had been impressive. Moving to wing half, and in time to the role of second stopper, it was clear that any physical lack of speed was largely compensated by his lightning quick anticipation. The only way to disconcert him was to play a fast, elusive forward close up on him – though there were times when his almost casual approach to the game could lead to expensive error, notably many years later in Katowice, in a World Cup eliminator against Poland.

Moore had done so well against Peru that he was a logical choice to keep his place in the World Cup tournament itself. The problem was that Moore as a defensive half back in a 4–2–4 formation too closely resembled the other blond wing half, Ron Flowers of Wolves. This meant that an especially heavy burden rested on Johnny Haynes in midfield. Unlike Didi, who had Zito to complement him, Haynes was largely operating on his own. 'Why is everything with England number 10?' asked the Yugoslavian manager, Milovan Ciric. 'Number 10 takes the corners! Number 10 takes the throw-ins! So what do we do? We put a man on number 10! Goodbye England!'

And goodbye it was when England opened their programme in the rickety Braden Copper Company stadium in the little town of Rancagua. Hungary put Gyuza Rakosi on Haynes, who in consequence was largely ineffectual. The Hungarians, with only Gyula Grosics in goal surviving from the famous team of the 1950s, were far more creative, Florian Albert an elegant and versatile centre forward, well supported by the tall, blond, skilful right half, Erno Solymosi. The hard-shooting Lajos Tichy put Hungary ahead from long range, exposing the dangerous vulnerability of England's keeper Ron Springett, so brave in the box, to shots of this kind. Ron Flowers equalised from a penalty given for handball, but a glorious solo goal by Albert deservedly won the game for the Hungarians. 'You *want* us to lose,' Haynes admonished the English press.

Winterbottom's coach this time was the right half and captain of Burnley, Jimmy Adamson, who has just been voted Footballer of the Year though, bizarrely, he would never win an international cap.

A lean, dark Geordie who would eventually manage his club, and specialise in developing young players from his own North-east, Adamson would quite soon be offered Winterbottom's job, but turn it down. Only then did the FA approach Alf Ramsey. Winterbottom, meanwhile, had to come to terms with the knowledge that he had failed to succeed his mentor, Stanley Rous, as Secretary of the Football Association. Rous, on his retirement, was elected to the presidency of FIFA, the international organisation.

For Winterbottom, who had spent sixteen years in office as a kind of civil servant, impervious to change, unafflicted by results, it was a fearful blow. He seemed, after all, ideal for such a job, far more so than for the role of international manager. A decent, well-educated, intelligent, honest man, with no delusions of grandeur (by contrast, it might be thought, to the man he should have succeeded), an accomplished footballer in his own time, his intellectual superiority to the men he was expected to lead need not have counted against him, as it never did against the highly educated Pozzo. But Pozzo was the quintessential father figure, with a force of personality which gave him the ascendancy over his players. Winterbottom's inability to relate to them — the exception to the rule being Billy Wright — meant that there must always be a barrier between them.

This was exacerbated by the fact that under the aegis of Rous, the FA was essentially a hierarchy even if, at the last, Rous was unable to get his way. He was undermined and outflanked by the machiavellian Professor Sir Harold Thompson, eager to revenge himself for the years in which Rous time and again swatted him like a fly. Thompson, a Yorkshireman, was a highly gifted scientist, specialising in infra-red spectroscopy, with a chair at Oxford University. There he not only presided over the University soccer team — not averse to purloining many of their share of FA Cup final tickets — but was the chief inspiration of the Pegasus football club, formed by former Oxford and Cambridge blues, founded in 1948, and twice resplendent winners of the FA Amateur Cup at Wembley.

Alas Thompson — notorious for lubricious attention to women — was ever a contentious and disruptive presence, arguably as much responsible for the eventual disintegration of the club as for its foundation. Thompson's strategy for frustrating Winterbottom was simple but deviously effective. On the morning of the vote by the sere and yellow ranks of FA councillors, he approached them one by one with a copy of that morning's *Observer* newspaper, in which Clement Freud, the future Liberal MP and grandson of Sigmund, had eulogised Winterbottom as the next FA Secretary. Were they, Thompson asked them, prepared to be corralled into voting for Winterbottom by a mere newspaper article?

Absurdly, his campaign succeeded. The old gentlemen seemingly bridled, and decided against all logic and good sense to do Winterbottom down, voting instead for the FA Treasurer, Denis Follows, whose chief appointment had been with the British Airline Pilots Association.

He and Rous had no warm feelings for each other. Rous regarded him as a mediocrity. He had no real background in football, scant authority and no innovative dynamism. Thompson, in fact, would make his life a misery, for he had none of Rous's contemptuous ability to brush Thompson aside, and ultimately he was driven into a heart attack. Yet it seems arguable that the vote against Winterbottom was essentially a vote against the autocracy of Rous.

That Winterbottom should have remained in office for so long, despite results which overall were so unexceptional, and, in the case of those two Hungarian games, disastrous, made little sense, and could be seen as a prolonged exercise in nepotism by Rous himself. Unlike the cases of Pozzo and Herberger, longevity had no correlation with success. There could scarcely be a greater contrast between Winterbottom, who would duly become head of the Central Council of Physical Recreation, and the man who succeeded him. A man who, as England's right back, had been able to view Winterbottom's academic approach from close quarters.

Yet in Chile, England did have one impressive game, defeating Argentina 3–1 in Rancagua, thanks in large measure to an iridescent display by Bobby Charlton, now functioning as an outside left. His pace, his ball control, his ability to use his left foot as easily and effectively as his stronger right, made him the ideal winger. Though it was with his right foot that he gave England a 2–0 lead, it was with his left that he set up the first English goal. His cross was neatly headed on by the tall, straight-backed young Middlesbrough centre forward, Alan Peacock, making his first appearance. Ruben Navarro, the centre back who gave Peacock a hard and painful battering from behind, handled the ball, and Flowers scored his second penalty of the tournament.

England ran out winners 3–1, with Bryan Douglas, who had appalled Jimmy Adamson on arriving with the team at its mountain retreat in Coya by sitting on his suitcase and saying, 'I feel homesick already,' showing form far livelier on the right wing than he had against Hungary, or in Sweden four years before.

I remember going, after the game, into the Argentine dressing room where one official after another came up consolingly to Juan Carlos Lorenzo, later to become the nemesis of English football, kissing him on the cheek and saying, *'Muy bien, Juan Carlos, muy bien!'*

It was rather too good for England to be true. Their next match, again in Rancagua, was an excruciatingly dull goalless draw against Bulgaria. But it was enough to qualify for the quarter-finals. 'Don't tell me you're going to give us to beat Brazil!' said Haynes to the reporters, after the game.

It would have been a wild surmise, even though Pele had dropped out of the Brazilian team. In the picturesque little stadium at Viña del Mar, where pelicans sat on the rocks and the sea wrack drifted over the ground, Garrincha, now the essence of versatility, was simply too much for England to resist. He actually, all five foot seven of him, outjumped the towering England centre half Maurice Norman, to give Brazil the lead, to an exultant beating of samba drums on the terraces. In the second half, though England had equalised through their centre forward Gerry Hitchens after Jimmy Greaves hit the bar, two devastating, swerving shots from long range by Garrincha gave Brazil the game. The first bounced off Ron Springett's chest to be put in by Vavá, the second flew in on its own.

Greaves, like Haynes, proved another disappointment when so much had been expected from him, a precocious and prolific young goalscorer with an electric turn of pace, a deadly left foot, and an uncanny ability to find space in a crowded penalty area. 'There are some good teams here and they're playing some bloody rubbish,' he once told me, 'because they're frightened of being killed.'

Whatever the reason, his form was a colossal disappointment and again, as in the case of Haynes, one could hardly blame Winterbottom. Luck, again. Had both men played to their full capacity, England might not have beaten Brazil, the eventual winners, but their performances would have been enormously better.

But it was for Greaves himself that bitter disappointment would be waiting, four years later.

2 'YOU DID IT, ALF!'

Alf Ramsey 1963–74
Key Game: England v West Germany, July 1966

'YOU DID IT, ALF! WE'D BE NOTHING WITHOUT YOU!' CRIED A tearful Nobby Stiles, as he stood on the Wembley turf after England's victory in the 1966 World Cup final. He was surely right. Ramsey indeed did it, in the sense that he coaxed and inspired the success of a team of which the whole, thanks to his influence and strategies, was so much greater than the parts.

The day before that final, writing in the *New Statesman*, the Austrian-born musicologist and admirer of the pre-war Austria *Wunderteam*, Hans Keller, wrote, 'Next week I shall describe how England won the World Cup, and what we can do about it.' His words reflected the unease with which many had regarded Ramsey's tactics, however finally successful. The emphasis on sheer work rate, the implementation of the so-called Wingless Wonders, seemed all too likely to produce a legacy of functional football, at the expense of flair and freedom. Arguably, so it did, even if Ramsey's 1970 team – which, despite mythology, he never thought superior to the 1966 side – were so unlucky to go out in the quarter-finals in Mexico, beaten by West Germany, the team England had overcome in the World Cup final of 1966.

Ramsey's is an extraordinary story, beginning in virtual penury, ending in undeserved, virtual poverty. England have never had a manager like him, and will probably never win the World Cup again.

Dedicated to the point of obsession, ineluctably xenophobic, socially inept, his remarkable career doomed to end in sad anticlimax, Ramsey's command of his players was all but absolute. Even if, in the earlier stages, he had had to quash rebellion.

Alf was brought up in what was then rural Dagenham, in a family of five children, their house a primitive wooden affair with no inside lavatory, no running water, no electricity; his father, Herbert, had a smallholding, kept pigs, drove a horse-drawn dustcart. Asked, in his England managerial days in an interview where his parents were, Ramsey famously replied, 'In Dagenham I believe.' It has variously been said that the family was of gypsy origin – which once elicited from Bobby Moore, Ramsey's captain, a wounding jibe as the team bus passed gypsy caravans on a Balkans tour – and that Alf took elocution lessons. Neither assumption seems justified. Ramsey's was an Essex family with roots well in the past, while if his public speech was strangulated, so often the object of parody and ridicule, it seems to have been the product of embarrassment and the BBC. Alf supposedly listened carefully to the patrician accents then prevalent on the radio.

That his accent was, in the vernacular of the time, Sarn't Major Posh, might even have something to do with the fact that he served as a sergeant in the Army. In these demotic days, it tends to be forgotten how class conscious was the era in which Ramsey grew up. There is a significant contrast between Ramsey's accent and the confident Cockney of his Dagenham-born successor as an England manager, Terry Venables, who grew up in a later, urbanised Dagenham, with no such complexes.

In those remote days, moreover, a talented young footballer could blush unseen for many years. The current Children's Crusade, which sees ten-year-old boys snapped up by predatory clubs, was unknown. Ramsey, from boyhood days, was plainly a talented footballer, picked eventually for district teams, but totally ignored by professional clubs and condemned, after he had left school, for two years to playing no football at all, obliged as he was to work on Saturdays for the Co-op shop, first as a delivery boy, then behind the counter.

In 1936, however, by now aged sixteen, he was able to play for a newly formed local team, at centre half. Portsmouth noticed him, sent him amateur forms to sign, and when he duly returned them, had neither the wit nor the decency to contact him again. So it was, after he had joined the Army which he insisted was the making of him, that he eventually joined Southampton.

There, he would settle down as a resourceful right back. Heavily built, never quick, no overlapper – tactics that lay in the future, and which he'd encourage in his own England team – what he possessed was a cool head, fine positional sense, exact distribution, and supreme authority. When he joined Tottenham Hotspur in the summer of 1949, already an England international, he'd soon gain the nickname of The General. He wasn't the captain – that role was filled by the exuberant Welsh international left half, Ronnie Burgess – but he was undoubtedly the major influence on a team which tended to look bereft when he wasn't playing.

He was, however, fortunate in the supportive presence of Billy Nicholson, the right half, a firm tackler and a shield for him in defence, and the outside right, Sonny Walters, happy to drop back and, as some said, 'do his running for him'. This was the Spurs team of the exuberant push-and-run, one-touch era, encouraged by a progressive new manager in their pre-war centre half Arthur Rowe, who himself had learned much when coaching in Hungary on the eve of the Second World War.

It might somewhat uncharitably be said that Ramsey was in difficulty when a quick, strong winger, careless of reputations, called his bluff, took him on, and sped past him thanks to pace, close control and initiative. There were those who believed that Ramsey's antipathy to Scottish football, well known in his England managerial days, was caused by the various Scottish left wingers who flew past him, such as Liverpool's powerful Billy Liddell, Newcastle's elusive Bobby Mitchell, and little Jimmy Kelly, of Barnsley.

It was with Ipswich Town that Ramsey would establish himself as an outstandingly innovative manager. When he joined them, they were no more than a Third Division South club, the indulgence, you might say, of the powerful Cobbold family. The club, which had just been relegated after a brief sojourn in Division Two, played on a splendid pitch in a rickety stadium, where the occasional cow was known to pay a visit on market day.

Ramsey would revitalise the club, as clever in his tactics as he was shrewd in the transfer market. Perhaps his most productive stroke was to sign the veteran Scottish inside forward Jimmy Leadbetter, a reserve team player when he arrived, and convert him into a deep lying outside left – a role in which he confused and exploited innumerable rival defences. Reanimated, too, was the rangy inside left Ted Phillips, a country boy, adept with a catapult, whom Ramsey encouraged to turn into a prolific striker, playing off the centre forward, Ray Crawford, who had seen Army service in the Malayan jungle. He came from Portsmouth in 1958 for a mere £5,000. Though originally none too keen to move, he would form a hugely effective partnership with Phillips.

Jimmy Adamson having refused the England managership, Ramsey's appointment, for once in a largely unhappy history, would prove inspired. Before he accepted, he made it a condition that the selection committee should be abandoned, leaving him in sole charge not only of coaching but of selecting the team. His demand was non-negotiable, and had to be accepted, but plainly with deep reluctance and resentment. Over the years, Ramsey showed manifest contempt for the so-called Senior International Committee, which took the place of the former selectors; the essence of sinecure. On a South American tour, he actually told a group of such committee men that he would far rather have four extra players, but that at least the officials saved him from attending functions. For years to come, the humiliated conspirators would be lurking in the shadows, eager to pounce when things went wrong, as, in the end, they did.

Early in 1963, Ramsey took charge of England for the first time, in a European Nations Cup qualifying match in Paris which he scarcely took seriously, evidently content to assess what kind of a team had been left to him. It was thrashed 5–2, Ron Henry, the Spurs left back, remarking pungently afterwards that every time he looked up, 'All I saw was a line of arseholes disappearing over the horizon.'

The Nations Cup had been innovated as a two-year competition in 1958, and England had refused to take part in it. At that time, even

Vittorio Pozzo, the arch competitor, expressed his distress that football now had to be dragooned into competitions. Over the years, his fear would be all too well justified. The Nations Cup, which became the European Championship, was at least, initially, a tournament confined in the last stages to just four surviving teams, which contested the semi-finals, third-place match and final in one of those countries.

Alas, it would grow exponentially, more and more teams being added to the final stages, and the qualifying rounds themselves bloated after the collapse of the Soviet empire by a plethora of smaller nations. Thus, the friendly international, a staple for decades of the game, would become marginalised, even farcified when, by the twenty-first century, teams would ludicrously throw in as many as ten substitutes. So such classic friendlies as Italy against Austria, and England against a variety of foreign teams, became no more than a mere relic. And as both the World Cup and the European Championship relentlessly expanded, so greater and greater pressure was placed on elite footballers, now often fated to play as many as sixty games a season.

It was on England's summer tour of 1963 that Ramsey first put his stamp on the team. So far as the press were concerned, this was emphatically the honeymoon period. Relations – which, to give Walter Winterbottom his due, had usually been cordial enough under the previous aegis – were friendly to a degree. Indeed, even in later years, when Ramsey's disdain for what he deemed the relevance of the press, was all too plain, he never adopted the policy of sheep and goats embraced by his successors. Access to the players was easy. On prolonged flights across Latin America, there was no exclusion zone; players and journalists sat with one another without let or hindrance – a custom unthinkable in later times.

Yet Ramsey's quasi-religious dedication to the game – which for him was hardly a game – excluded all non-initiates, be they journalists, administrators or fans. Just as the choleric novelist Evelyn Waugh would dismiss any critic on the grounds that he was American, so Ramsey set no store by the options of anyone outside the magic circle of his chosen players. It was the journalist Hugh McIlvanney who pertinently observed that in embracing such a philosophy, Ramsey risked alienating the public at large.

On this 1963 tour, however, all was geniality, the more so as the results were so good. In Bratislava, where the first match, against Czechoslovakia, was to be played, Ramsey at his pre-game press conference cheerfully outlined his strategy, which would change so radically when it came to the 1966 World Cup. He was keen, he told us, to use two orthodox wingers who could, in the classic style, beat the back, get to the by-line and pull the ball back into the box, as Stanley Matthews and Tom Finney of course had done so well. The wingless wonders then were not even a mirage, and when Ramsey did employ such tactics, he insisted that it was not out of principle, but because the wingers he initially used simply hadn't filled the bill.

The wingers on this occasion would be Terry Paine, the quick little Southampton player, and Bobby Charlton, still a left winger at the time, though due eventually to become England's deep centre forward. Charlton told me how impressed he was by training sessions, in which Ramsey got his players to stand where they thought they should be, then told them where he wanted them to be.

After Croatia had humiliated England in a World Cup qualifying match in October 2006, the combative Croatian manager, Slaven Bilic, who had declared before the game that England, as they did, would play a 3–5–2 formation at their peril, declared, 'Systems are dead.' Rather as Henry Ford had opined long before, 'History is bunk.' One saw what Slaven, who once played for Everton and West Ham, broadly meant, though in the event, it was perfectly clear that the English players in Zagreb found 3–5–2 unfamiliar and alien to them. What might more exactly be said is that systems in themselves will never be enough. Ramsey, who started with 4–4–2 and wingers, obtaining a convincing 4–2 victory with Jimmy Greaves scoring two goals, would over the years chop and change frequently.

Though the World Cup was won, it could be argued that, especially in his latter years as England manager, he made a number of costly mistakes. Partly this was thanks to his obvious aversion to the introduction of substitutes, which did not happen till the World Cup of 1970. When England so dramatically and disappointingly lost in the quarter-final in Leon 3–2 after going 2–0 ahead, the blame was largely put on the hapless goalkeeper, Peter Bonetti, deployed at the last moment after Gordon Banks, the outstanding goalkeeper, had succumbed to food poisoning. Yet it was surely equally relevant to reflect that in the intense heat and at the high, breathless altitude, the England full backs, Keith Newton and Terry Cooper, had run themselves to exhaustion, Cooper in particular being easy prey when the shrewder German manager, Helmut Schoen, brought on a fresh substitute in the outside right, Jurgen Grabowski. In addition, after Franz Beckenbauer had reduced England's lead to 2–1, Ramsey bewilderingly pulled off Bobby Charlton, whom Beckenbauer had been marking, giving Beckenbauer freedom to break forward at will. The accepted view was that Ramsey, convinced the game had been won, preferred to rest Charlton, in anticipation of the semi-final.

West Germany would again prove the nemesis in the spring of 1972 when, in the first leg of the Nations Cup quarter-final at Wembley, Ramsey put out a midfield without a ball winner, thus largely giving the flamboyant Gunter Netzer the freedom of the park, which he proceeded to enjoy. Yet when it came to the return leg in Berlin, Ramsey, all confidence seemingly drained, picked a side full of hard men, which would never be capable of the substantial victory he needed, leading to a useless 0–0 draw, with a disenchanted Netzer coming off at the end, remarking, 'The whole England team has autographed my leg.'

And when, against Poland in Katowice in the early summer of 1973, pace was plainly of the essence if England were to win this vital World Cup eliminator, Ramsey kept his fastest player, Mike Channon of Southampton, on the bench throughout. But all those travails were far in the future.

One of the most positive decisions of the England tour of 1963 was that, at long last, a doctor was officially designated to accompany the team. And Alan Bass proved an important choice. Not only was he a specialist in physical medicine, a consultant both at Paddington and St Charles' hospitals, destined eventually to become a professor of medicine in Canada, but his bluff, cheerful, humorous personality made him a great favourite with the players, and a solid support to the manager.

It was a happy party which set off for the next game in Leipzig. There had been jollifications in the Bratislava hotel bar, enlivened by the presence of the girl skaters of a travelling ice show. Walking down the aisle of the plane, Alan Bass confided to journalists, naming a leading star, 'Gastroenteritis. Hangover, actually!' Later, Jimmy Greaves was heard to cry, 'What chance have *we* got? Look at the old doc!' At which point Bass was relaxing across three seats. There is no doubt that apart from ensuring first-class medical treatment to the players on tour, for the first time ever, he also proved a valuable bridge between Ramsey and the press, enjoying the confidence of both sides.

Going through the sombre streets of Communist Leipzig, where loudspeakers constantly hectored the populace, Gordon Banks, the England keeper, remarked, 'They walk and they whisper.' Banks, destined to be a World Cup-winning goalkeeper and the author in Guadalajara in 1970 of one of the finest saves in the history of the World Cup, had been rebuked by Ramsey after only his second game, a friendly at Wembley against Brazil which preceded the European tour. 'They all need help,' Alf once said, 'they all need encouragement. They all need to be punished by the tongue, sometimes.'

Which Banks indeed was after letting through a left-footed free kick, low, from long distance, by Pepe, the Brazilian outside left, about which Ramsey had specifically warned him. Brave, alert by and large, gymnastically agile, Banks at his best was a superb goalkeeper, but there were such moments when his attention strayed. Another came in Belgrade on the 1965 European tour when, playing against Yugoslavia, Banks distractedly stood behind his own defensive 'wall' of players when the Yugoslavs took a free kick. 'I have just been up to his room,' said Alf afterwards in his all too imitable accent. 'I told him, "One of these days I shall lift up a dagger and fuckin' well kill you!"' Even before the 1966 World Cup final, one recalls Banks saying, 'Alf's convinced me, my mind's not got to wander.' And indeed it didn't.

Tact with Alf was never of the essence. Not long after he had taken on the England job, in the 1962–63 season, I remember driving to watch Ipswich play Milan with Gerry Hitchens, the exuberant former

Shropshire miner, who, with limited success, had played centre forward for England in the Chilean World Cup, and was now playing in Italy for Torino. 'Must wish good luck to Alf!' cried Gerry. 'Must say hallo to the lads!'

Arriving at the San Siro stadium, we walked along the dressing room corridors in the bowels of the building until Alf came in view. 'Hallo, Alf!' called Gerry.

'Oh, yes,' said Ramsey, coolly. 'You're playin' in these parts.'

Throughout the match, when Gerry was sitting beside me in a largely empty press box, he inveighed about it. 'Prat! Prat! "You're playin' in these parts!" Prat!' He never got another game for England.

England duly won 2–1 in Leipzig then with a largely reserve team, annihilated Switzerland 8–1 in Basel. Bobby Charlton scored three of the goals, and Ramsey gave a first cap to the combative, red-haired Sheffield Wednesday wing half, Tony Kay. Ramsey had spoken in Bratislava of his admiration for Kay: 'It would be like putting a tiger in midfield.' But not for long; Kay was doomed to be implicated with two other Wednesday players, one of them Peter Swan, of fixing a match against Ipswich Town and was suspended *sine die*.

Press relations with Ramsey would never be as good again but you wonder, in retrospect, how much this mattered. Italy, for example, under the managership of Enzo Bearzot, went to great lengths during the 1978 World Cup in Argentina to accommodate the volatile Italian journalists. Gigi Peronace, the effusive little Calabrian player-agent, made General Manager for the squad, went even further, to the extent of every day holding a press conference complete with players at their headquarters in the Hindu Club, outside Buenos Aires.

One morning, the players were a little late in coming down, and one of the younger journalists threw himself into an impassioned if synthetic frenzy, shouting that this was an insult to the press. 'I can't grab them by the neck,' said Bearzot, glumly. Eventually, the players arrived.

The following morning, the scene resembled one from a film by Antonioni. True, the players were to be seen, but only through a glass partition, from behind which they occasionally smiled and waved. The *azzurri* did well enough in the tournament, beating the hosts,

Argentina, eventually losing to Holland in Buenos Aires, and to Brazil in the third-place match.

Four years later, in Spain, there was no such co-operation with the press, whom Peronace had agonisingly described as *giornalisti d'assalto*, journalists of attack. One newspaper had run a scurrilous article accusing two of the *azzurri* of having a homosexual affair. The outraged footballers promptly and inexorably imposed press silence. All press conferences were addressed only by the grave veteran captain and goalkeeper, Dino Zoff. They won the World Cup. By the same token, in 1990, and with rather less justification, the England players in Italy would refuse to talk to the English journalists. This, because the two outraged Robsons, Bobby and Bryan, the manager and captain respectively, believed they had been badly traduced in the tabloid press. In Bobby's case, old stories of his allegedly erotic adventures when manager of Ipswich Town were exhumed. For his part, Bryan was accused of following a girl with amorous intentions into the women's toilet at an Aylesbury hotel, after England had played an exhibition game.

Following the lead of the incensed Robsons, the England squad collectively turned its backs on the football press. This was both irrational and unfair, since the scandalous articles had been written not by football journalists but by general news reporters. The Robsons and the players did not differentiate. So far as they were concerned, all journalists were tarred with the same brush. The football journalists insisted that the guilty parties were 'The Rotters', alias the news reporters, who hovered like jackals around the England scene. Once again, however, there was no evidence that this exclusion of the press had any negative effect on the performance of the team, which eventually reached the semi-final, losing only on penalties to Germany.

Ramsey had given substantial hostages to fortune on his appointment, declaring that England would win the 1966 World Cup. Fast forward to the eve of the World Cup final, the last training session and press conference at the expansive Bank of England sports fields at Roehampton. Asked by a journalist whether he still thought England would win the World Cup, there was a protracted hiatus until Ramsey finally, and almost reluctantly, said, 'Yes!'

The new international season began with a flurry of goals. In what was then the habitual autumn fixtures in the British International Championship, doomed to wither away under the huge proliferation of 'official' tournament matches, England put four goals past Wales in Cardiff and then thrashed Northern Ireland 8–3 at Wembley. Four of those goals went to Jimmy Greaves, three to Terry Paine, deployed again at outside right in a team with two wingers. Neither, as we know, would last the course in the 1966 World Cup finals.

Greaves, so ineffective as we have seen four years previously in Chile, for all his unquestioned talents, the formidable opportunism he had demonstrated from the moment he made a precocious teenaged debut for Chelsea at Tottenham, would never be Ramsey's kind of player. Ramsey, indeed, was bang in the English football tradition of mistrusting the maverick. 'Greaves?' he was heard to say, in the hotel, after that same game in Belgrade in 1965 when Banks had been at fault. 'Wants fuckin' stranglin'!'

With England the 1966 World Cup hosts, there would be no qualifying matches – always something of a mixed blessing. True, the diet of 'friendly' internationals posed no real pressure, but by the same token, nor did they provide the challenge which would keep a squad sharp. Sandwiched between the two home internationals was an entertaining affair at Wembley against a Rest of the World team, to celebrate the hundredth anniversary of the Football Association. It was chiefly notable for a glorious performance by the giant, black-jerseyed Russian keeper, Lev Yashin, England's opponent in Gothenburg in the World Cup of 1958, and the virtuosity of Alfredo Di Stefano, the veteran Argentine inspiration of Real Madrid's triumphant European Cup teams.

Reality would set in the following April, when England played the traditional last and most significant game of the International Championship against Scotland, at Hampden Park, and lost 1–0. Lost, deservedly to a superior Scottish team, forever Ramsey's *bête noire*, whether as player or manager. Alan Gilzean, the tall, effective striker, got the only goal. It was a match with portents for the future. In the first place, Ramsey was surely induced to think again about his policy of wingers. Neither Terry Paine nor Bobby Charlton proved able to beat his full back on the outside, the classical winger's move, which ideally would take him to the by-line where he could of course pull the ball menacingly back into the goalmouth.

In addition, it was Roger Hunt of Liverpool rather than Jimmy Greaves who occupied the role of second striker. Penetration by the England attack, devoid of Greaves, was minimal. I wrote of Hunt as being 'too stolid'. He was a strong, unselfish, functional player, and as such, more to Ramsey's taste than the mercurial Greaves. At least he could be pretty sure of what Hunt, whom he would praise – occasionally to some critical derision – for 'making space', would contribute. And it was Hunt rather than Greaves who, to Greaves' despair and dismay, would figure in the 1966 World Cup final, missing one excellent chance, which arguably turned the whole game.

Ramsey, however, had no doubts about him. Before the first leg of the Intercontinental Cup final of 1967 at Hampden Park, between Celtic and Racing Club of Buenos Aires, I found myself having tea, amiably, with Ramsey, in the North British Hotel. We went outside, hoping to catch a taxi to take us to the game. No such luck. Eventually, a somewhat battered blue jalopy full of young Scottish fans drove past and drew up beside us.

'Och, it's Sir Alf, get in, get in,' which we did. The badinage soon began. 'That England team that won the World Cup! So many poor players!'

'Well,' said Sir Alf, as by then he was. 'For example, who?'

'That Roger Hunt; he's a poor player.'

'Roger Hunt,' said Ramsey, 'scores twenty-five goals a season, every season. Yes, Roger Hunt's a poor player!'

He would remain a deeply reluctant visitor to Hampden; at least when his England team were involved. Once, arriving with his squad at Glasgow airport, for an international game, he was accosted by a voluble local journalist: 'Welcome to Scotland, Sir Alf!'

'You must be fuckin' jokin',' said Ramsey.

The summer of 1964 saw Ramsey put acutely to the test by a mutinous bunch of his players. It was a confrontation which was essential for him to win, were he to maintain his authority. As it transpired, he did, but it was an unpleasant episode. Drink was at the root of it.

England were due to play Portugal in Lisbon, Ireland in Dublin, then to fly to New York to take on the United States, a team which was hardly expected to be as formidable as the one which had astonished England fourteen years earlier in Belo Horizonte. After that, in a thoroughly ill-planned tour, the party was due to take the long flight to Rio, where there would be just a couple of days to acclimatise before meeting Brazil – and Pele.

The players assembled in a modest hotel near to Lancaster Gate, the headquarters of the Football Association. That evening seven of the squad, led by the captain Bobby Moore and his inseparable pal, and fellow Eastender, Jimmy Greaves, set off on foot towards the West End. Greaves, doomed alas to alcoholism after his disappointment in the 1966 World Cup final, once said that Moore was matched by few 'in a drinking contest'. The difference was that however much Moore drank, he somehow managed to absorb it; even to the point of training with West Ham the following morning. On or off the field, his cool self-discipline was paramount.

Eventually the hardly magnificent seven found their way to a bar called the Beachcomber, known for serving a strong, rum-based drink called 'the Zombie'. Not till one o'clock in the morning did the seven find their way back to the England hotel, and on his bed each found his passport and his packed case.

Ramsey said nothing to them till after the first training session in Lisbon, after which he remarked, 'I think there are seven gentlemen who would like to stay behind and see me.' He then told them forcefully that if he'd had enough players with him, all of them would have been dropped. 'Just learn a lesson,' he concluded, 'that I will not tolerate the sort of thing that happened in London before we left.'

Dissidence, however, was not wholly ended. In New York, preparing for the American game, Bobby Moore protested against the rigour of the training schedule, in great heat. He won no support from Dr Bass, still less from Ramsey, and the training continued. Ramsey however did not easily forgive and forget. When it came to the opening international of the following season, versus Wales in Cardiff, he delayed choosing Moore as the captain till the last possible moment. Despite his vast, inspirational importance to the team, well recognised by Ramsey, Moore probably had the least comfortable relationship with Ramsey, who even replaced him for a brief while before the 1966 World Cup with Leeds United's Norman Hunter. 'Pushed Bobby Moore!' Alf once told me with a smile.

It is interesting to note that in the latter months of the 1963–64 season he gave free rein to ball-playing attackers, to the exclusion of the big, traditionally physical English centre forward in the shape of Tottenham's Bobby Smith. Instead, there was abundant room for the elegant, creative George Eastham, whose father had been a pre-war England inside forward, and for the elusive, incisive West Ham United centre forward, Johnny Byrne. Byrne had been controversially excluded from the 1962 World Cup party in Chile, supposedly because he'd had a confrontation in the tunnel after a game with the former England right back Don Howe.

England won narrowly 4–3 in Portugal, with a hat trick by Byrne. They would play the Portuguese again in Sao Paulo in the second match of the mini-tournament though this time it would be a 1–1 draw.

The opening match against Brazil, however, was a disaster and is worth studying for the light it casts on Ramsey's tactical failings, in this early stage of his stewardship. Pele was bound to be the major threat, accepted as the greatest player in the world, a glorious amalgam of skill, power and surprise. There was also Julinho, the strong, fast outside right who had preceded Garrincha ten years earlier in Brazil's World Cup side and had scored a spectacular goal against Hungary in the Battle of Berne.

Five years after that, having just returned to Brazil after distinguished service in Italy with Fiorentina, he played for his country in Rio against the hapless Jimmy Armfield, inexplicably deployed at left back on his international debut, on his wrong foot. Brazil won 2–0 on that occasion, but this time, England would be totally outplayed.

With strategic aberration, Ramsey had somehow decided that the way to play Brazil – or so the story went – was not to man-mark Pele, but to close-mark the other Brazilian attackers. With Tony Waiters in goal rather than the more experienced Banks, England could do nothing with a superb Brazilian attack and lost 5–1, two of the goals going to the left winger, Rinaldo, one each to Pele and Julinho and Roberto Dias.

In Brazil's ensuing match against their old foes Argentina, Pele was indeed man-marked by the ruthless Jose Agustin Mesiano. After sustained ill treatment, Pele, never inclined to be a passive victim, retaliated by breaking Mesiano's nose. But he was then so distressed that he played little further part in the game and Roberto Telch, who came on to substitute Mesiano, proceeded to score twice in a 3–0 Argentine victory.

England, in Rio again, lost their third match 1–0 to an Argentina team which included only a couple of the players who would face them in the notorious Wembley World Cup quarter-final of 1966; one of them was the towering midfield pivot Antonio Rattin, whose expulsion at Wembley would provoke such contention. Watching Brazil in their final game, Ramsey somewhat enigmatically informed his players that the Brazilian defence was there to be taken; Brazil would not win the World Cup. He'd be proved right, though at that time he could hardly have known that Brazil would send to England a team full of spent veterans, and a physically vulnerable Pele.

Ramsey announced that he wished to use the following season, 1964–5, to judge players he didn't know much about. Yet the impression he gave, certainly until the spring, was that he was losing his way. True, results were unimpressive rather than catastrophic, no games were lost, but successes were meagre, and selection inconsistent. Press relations deteriorated. Ramsey's natural distrust and suspicion of journalists began to assert itself. Bobby Charlton and Greaves both played against Holland in a 1–1 draw in Amsterdam, but Ramsey's response to criticism was a curt 'No comment!' How could journalists understand?

Suddenly, when it came to the annual game against Scotland, this time in April at Wembley, Ramsey would strike gold, bringing in two players who in their different ways would be essential to his quest for the World Cup. If this was intended to be a season to test new talent, you could say that he was finally and amply vindicated.

The contrast between Jack Charlton and Nobby Stiles was physically extreme. Charlton, the centre half, was tall and raw boned.

Stiles, a right half, was small and, seen off the field, the very antithesis of a professional footballer, let alone one who could succeed at the highest level. He wore spectacles, and would take out his upper false teeth before a game.

Jackie Charlton, Bobby's older brother, and in several ways as great a contrast to him – both in character and physique – as he was to Nobby Stiles, may have owed his international career to Ramsey, but the manager who had transformed a career in the doldrums was unquestionably Leeds United's Don Revie. When Revie, himself an inside forward and deep-lying centre forward of exceptional talent, was made manager of Leeds United, Charlton's career, in the vernacular, seemed to be going nowhere.

Fishing and shooting seemed to absorb his attentions as much if not more than football, to which his attitude was almost casual. But Revie saw the potential in him, and steadily inculcated in Charlton a far more dedicated and professional approach. As Jack himself readily admitted, there was no comparison between himself and 'our kid', the enormously gifted Bobby. Even their relations with their mother, the dominant Cissie Charlton, who came from a family of footballers, was in contrast. There were those who thought that Jackie rather than Bobby was the preferred son, and the brothers would fall out bitterly when Cissie was dying. Jackie felt his brother, whose wife had never been fully accepted by Cissie, failed to attend to his mother as he should.

Jackie was the one member of Ramsey's eventual World Cup team – save the occasional contretemps with Bobby Moore – who would sometimes dispute Ramsey's tactics, even to the point of swearing at him. It availed him little. After one such outburst on the training field, Ramsey's response was, 'Do it my way or else.'

'Or else what?' asked Jackie. 'Or else,' was the reply, 'you are out.'

Where Bobby patiently suffered maltreatment without retaliation, Jackie's approach was altogether more confrontational. He was once quoted as saying that he had a little black book in which he entered the names of opponents who had displeased him. Nobby Stiles, in his way, was equally combustible. When the two of them had a furious row on the training field, Ramsey – ever the practical psychologist –

simply stood by and let them get on with it. The two eventually became good friends.

It so happened that I had first seen, and admired, Nobby Stiles at Wembley itself, where he was destined to play so influentially, if controversially, in the 1966 World Cup. That was in a schoolboy international when he was at right half for England against Wales and much the most impressive player on the pitch, constantly driving up the right flank in attack, in sharp contrast with the kind of game he would play for Ramsey's England.

Fine words, with Alf, buttered no parsnips. When Charlton was once rash enough to ask why he had chosen him, Ramsey replied, 'Well, Jack, I have a pattern of play in mind and I pick the best players to fit that pattern. I don't necessarily pick the best players.'

The best players? Nobby Stiles scarcely seemed to fit into either category when first brought into the team in 1965. With the World Cup finals looming the following summer, Ramsey seemed seriously to have lost his way. Stiles was no longer the adventurous young player one had seen in that schoolboy international. After a flaccid display at Wembley in October 1965 against a modest Austrian team which won 3–2, I wrote in the *Sunday Times*:

> It was John Wilkes who said that the peace of Paris was like the Peace of God; it passed all understanding. He might just as well have been talking about Mr Alf Ramsey's England teams.
>
> Next Wednesday, against [Northern] Ireland, he fields the great bulk of the side which drew laboriously at Cardiff, and lost so shabbily at home to Austria. When one has made due allowances for consistency, generosity and the abysmal lack of talent in the League, his choice is still remarkable. Above all, in continuing to choose Stiles of Manchester United as the linking right half, he is pursuing a course which is as obstinate as it is inexplicable, a course which leads one seriously to doubt if the team is being picked on any rational basis.
>
> This is not to criticise Stiles, a hard, courageous, defensive footballer who fills that role well for his club, and does not pretend to be anything more. Even if he did, the fact that Manchester

United employ him, week after week, in a destructive function, would make it almost impossible for him to develop. Against Wales, he had a poor match. Against Austria, he had a disastrous one, culminating in the clumsy piece of football which allowed him to be shaken off the ball by Austria's outside right, who went straight on to score the winning goal.

It is worth recalling the exact circumstances of Stiles' debut for England; an ironic occasion in which, by playing well in the role for which he was not intended, he confirmed his place for the European tour. It will be remembered that England, playing Scotland last April, were reduced to ten men and then nine fit men, by injuries to Wilson and Byrne. Stiles, who had surprisingly been picked as a linking half-back, thus found himself committed to the job he does best and most bravely; that of back-to-the-wall defence. No one can deny that he did it wonderfully well; so well, indeed, that it would have been a cruel recompense to drop him. This, nevertheless, was the logical move, unless Ramsey intended to drop the 'official' defensive wing-half, Bobby Moore – which was then unthinkable. So Stiles remained, played twice on the Continental tour, and played well.

Again, however, the circumstances were rather special ones. These were difficult away matches, in which breakaway goals were all that we were likely to score, and in which a compact defence was essential. Stiles, with his energy and his communicable spirit, did much to guarantee that; though in use of the ball he fell notably below even Flowers, who took his place against West Germany. And Flowers, after all, has scarcely been renowned, across the years, as the most creative of half-backs.

In choosing Stiles again against Ireland, I feel that Ramsey – fundamentally a shrewd and thoughtful man – has made an emotional rather than a programmatic choice. What he is expressing, in effect, is loyalty to Stiles, loyalty in the teeth of bad form and a hostile press. But there are two ways of being influenced by the newspapers, and Ramsey, whether he appreciates it or not, has clearly been very strongly influenced indeed.

I went on to question severely the choice at centre forward of Alan Peacock, who had long fallen out of favour since his promising performances in and soon after the World Cup finals of 1962, in Chile. In Cardiff, against Wales, only his heading had passed muster. 'Yet I myself,' I resumed,

have lost faith neither in Ramsey, despite these strange perversities, nor in the potential of the England team. During the long home season, Ramsey appears to become now obstinate, now confused. Get him away to the relative tranquillity of the Continent, give him the players to himself, and his talents and qualities are better revealed. I think it is arguable that we should not have abolished, in effect, the selection committee. Perhaps a compromise might have been achieved, on the Portuguese pattern, whereby there is a sole selector and a team manager, who pick the team together. This, at least, provided a corrective.

But by July [1966], I conclude, there is ever hope that Ramsey will have made his errors, found a more rationally conceived team and injected his players with his own determination.

So it would happily transpire.

In the event, England gave another tenuous performance against Northern Ireland at Wembley, scraping through 2–1. The team was still deeply in the melting pot, even if any suggestion at any time to Ramsey that he should share responsibility with a selector would plainly have been fiercely rejected. Fred Pickering of Blackburn, Frank Wignall of Everton, Barry Bridges of Chelsea – once a youth team colleague of Jimmy Greaves – Mick Jones of Sheffield United, who did well in the last two matches of the 1965 summer tour of Europe, Alan Peacock of Leeds: all were tried at centre forward and discarded. Not till the April international of 1966, won vertiginously 4–3 against Scotland at Hampden, was Bobby Charlton at last used there, but in the less orthodox role of operating behind a spearhead of Roger Hunt, till then in and out of the team, and a powerful newcomer in West Ham United's Geoff Hurst, formidable in the air, an explosive shot, who moved unselfishly off the ball to open spaces for his fellow attackers.

That was a game in which Alan Ball of Blackpool was used for the first time on the right wing. Small and red haired, with the fiery temperament associated with his kind, Alan was twice turned down in boyhood by Wolves and Bolton. Bolton's manager, Bill Riddick, patronisingly and expensively said, 'You'd make a good little jockey.' Alan would, in fact, make a dynamically active inside forward with Blackpool, making a successful debut on the 1965 England tour in Belgrade against Yugoslavia, on his twentieth birthday. Yet it was on the right flank in the 1966 World Cup finals that he would leave indelible memories.

There was a curious disagreement between Ramsey and the English press in Gothenburg, where England played Sweden and beat them 2–1 in the last game of a successful tour. Ramsey's equivocal responses led journalists to believe that Jimmy Greaves, who had missed the 1–0 win in Nuremberg against West Germany, had been dropped. An angry Ramsey insisted that Greaves in fact had been injured, but eventually and honestly admitted that he might unwittingly have been misleading. Alas, there was an unfortunate, if indicative, postscript to Alan Ball's successful England tour. He was suspended for fourteen days in England, having been booked half-a-dozen times. In Vienna, playing for England Under-23 against Austria, he was sent off for throwing the ball at the Hungarian referee, who had told him to move the ball back for a free kick. Doubts about his temperament were inevitably resuscitated. Yet on tour with England in Belgrade, he made light of heavy treatment by his Yugoslav marker and when push almost literally came to shove, Ball kept calm.

1966: Ramsey's Wembley Lions

As the World Cup finals approached, optimism oscillated; as did Alf Ramsey's selection. He still seemed to have no clear idea of what kind of team, what kind of tactic, he wanted, though there were sporadic shafts of light. Especially in Madrid where, without Jimmy Greaves in early December 1965, England beat Spain 2–0. One of the goals was scored by little Joe Baker, a tough and mobile centre forward, Scottish to a degree, who happened to be born in Liverpool.

'England,' said Spain's manager, Jose Villalonga, 'were just phenomenal tonight. They were far superior in their performance. They could have beaten any team.'

Barely a month later, it was back again to sustained mediocrity, a rare match played away from Wembley in Liverpool and drawn 1–1 against Poland. At least George Cohen, the ebullient Fulham right back who had replaced Jimmy Armfield, kept his place, despite having tackled Ramsey, once after all a right back himself, so fiercely in Spain that Alf landed on his head and lay there, groaning. Cohen watched apprehensively till Ramsey at last looked up and said, 'George, if I had another fuckin' full back, you wouldn't be playin' tomorrow.' As it was both Cohen and his fellow full back Ray Wilson played well, and their crosses were to be instrumental in England's successful World Cup campaign.

Could Peter Osgood be the saviour? Eighteen years old, a precociously effective centre forward, tall and strong, clever on the ground, powerful in the air, eulogised by his Chelsea manager Tommy Docherty, the risk surely seemed worth taking. But the word went round that Ramsey, though he would put Osgood on his list of forty possibles, thought he should be saved until the next World Cup. As it transpired, he would indeed go to Mexico, with only a couple of appearances as substitute. Ramsey's deep, utterly English caution, his mistrust of the maverick, was all too evident again. But the matter became sadly academic the next season when Osgood broke his leg in a clash with Emlyn Hughes, then with Blackpool, and a future England captain.

So it was, when England came to play a weakened West German team at Wembley in a friendly, that Ramsey, at centre forward, preferred to pick . . . Nobby Stiles. Not, plainly, expecting him to play an orthodox striker's game, yet the choice seemed the essence of perversity; even if Stiles scored the only goal of a tediously lukewarm game. No newspapers would tell Alf what to do!

Yet in retrospect, it is tantalising to dwell on what might have been; and what actually was. What, you wonder, if Ramsey had given Osgood his chance, conquering his aversion to the unorthodox, and Osgood had flourished? That, presumably, would have barred the way to Geoff Hurst, who became the unexpected hero of the last World Cup stages, the scorer of a hat trick in the final. Indeed, I still remember, somewhat tactlessly, perhaps, that it was to Hurst that I lamented Osgood's disappointing absence during the pre-World Cup European tour in which the West Ham man scarcely excelled. 'Instead of me, I suppose,' said Hurst, bitterly. Unlike Osgood, he had never been a Boy Wonder. Initially a wing half and son of a former professional player, Hurst had almost been sold to Southend United, only at the last moment for West Ham boss Ron Greenwood to change his mind, and in due course to convert him with such success into an attacker.

There was another setback for Ramsey, and England, in March when, at Newcastle, a Football League team which included several first-choice England players, including the Charlton brothers, Alan Ball on the right flank and Jimmy Greaves, was utterly outplayed – something, alas, unthinkable nowadays – by the Scottish League team, which won 3–1. Particularly embarrassing for Ramsey, given an aversion to wingers which had already been noted and criticised in the New Year, was the fact that the little, red-haired Celtic outside right, Jimmy Johnstone, had tormented Keith Newton, the Football League left back.

It is interesting to note that Ramsey, this early, was already answering criticism of his 'non-wingers' policy by insisting that the wingers just were not there. In the Football League game, Bobby Charlton was deployed on the left wing. The indications were that Ramsey's tactics were still in a somewhat amorphous state. Using Bobby Charlton behind the front line was a strategy innovated only the following April against Scotland, when Jimmy Johnstone would again play havoc with an England defence which not only gave away three goals against an unbalanced Scottish side, but were also lucky not to concede a penalty.

Over the years, the received wisdom has been that Ramsey as strategist was a shrewd operator in both his World Cups – apart from the misconceived substitutions against West Germany in the 1970 quarter-final – and began making costly mistakes only in 1972. Yet hindsight – that impeccable aid to being right – suggests that he found his way to England's ultimately successful 1966 World Cup formation only as the product of trial and frequent error. Dr Alan Bass, however, had no doubt of Ramsey's qualities. He praised Alf's 'man management, the handling of your men at all times. These are very high-spirited men, in many cases just matured or on the brink of maturity. It's wonderful to see how Alf does this.' Indeed, there was no doubting Ramsey's ascendancy over players who admired him and respected him, in sharp contrast to his beleaguered predecessor. But respect could hardly be the ultimate criterion. Many mistakes had been made.

There was a seven-week hiatus before the squad set off on its 1966 European tour, giving Ramsey the opportunity to train his players hard and long at the Lilleshall training centre. It was beyond doubt a battle hardened team, both physically and psychologically, which set out for Europe. Jimmy Greaves, now recovered from an attack of jaundice, his stomach, in the words of one columnist 'as flat as a spade', was especially optimistic. 'I think every player senses this in the England team,' he reflected, 'that we could all be on the edge of virtual immortality, as far as the football's concerned.' Greaves' fate, alas, was to remain on the edge.

To be pushed to the margins could hardly have been anticipated, after he ran riot in the second match against Norway in Oslo. England were strangely slow to get into gear, but once they did, Greaves scored four, sweeping the Norwegians aside in a 6–1 win.

The third game of the tour was in Denmark, against a team whose Copenhagen pitch was in abysmal condition. England, however, won 2–0, with Geoff Hurst by his own admission giving 'the worst performance of my international career'. He would not come into the World Cup until the quarter-final, when his splendid near-post header would give England their laborious win against a ten-man Argentina.

The immaculate cross from the left – a typical West Ham ploy – was curled in by his club mate, Martin Peters, capped for the first time in early May at Wembley against a Yugoslavia team beaten 2–0. Peters that evening played at right half, his customary role, rather than Nobby Stiles, but it was one of Alf Ramsey's most inspired notions to make him, so to speak, a 'false', right-footed, outside left. Peters, Ramsey would subsequently enthuse, was 'ten years ahead of his time'.

No true winger, certainly, but a creative source in a team which badly needed it.

Using Bobby Charlton 'in retreat' behind the two strikers was certainly effective in its way, but not because Charlton was any real kind of a play-maker. His massive crossfield passes, usually from right to left, would bring loud roars of appreciation from the crowd, yet as often as not did not gain his team a yard's advantage. What he could unquestionably do with his ball skills was to take on the opposition from his deeper role and, by beating a man, or men, give the England attack a numerical superiority. Plus, plainly, his tremendously powerful shot, with either foot.

As it transpired, Peters would make his first appearance on the left flank in England's qualifying group only in the second game, against Mexico. One remembers the bewilderment of the Uruguay coach Ondino Vieira, before the opening game against England, when he heard that the choice for the left flank position would be between Peters and John Connelly. In what was almost an interior monologue, when he sat outside in the sunshine at the Harlow motel where Uruguay were based, he mused that he couldn't understand how Peters might be preferred: 'How is it possible they can put out a great player like Connelly and put in a half back? Because I've seen Connelly play, he's a great winger, a great *puntero*. They must have a defensive idea if they do, not an attacking one, tremendously defensive.'

Memorably, he declared, 'Other countries have their history, Uruguay has its football,' but lamented the fact that four of his best players – Pavoni, Matosas, Silveira and Cubilla – had been denied him by their Argentine clubs. In that time, inexplicably, FIFA regulations enabled them to do so. Uruguay would capably nullify the England attack in a dull opening game, but would disgrace themselves in the quarter-final against West Germany when frustration turned into violence.

Taking advantage of a break in the England tour, Ramsey, accompanied by a gaggle of us journalists, flew to Gothenburg to see Brazil, the World Cup holders, play a friendly against Sweden. Dr Milton Gosling, long an essential figure in the Brazilian hierarchy, told us he thought the present team better than the world champions of 1962.

Did he really believe that? Against the Swedes Brazil were palpably at half pace, vulnerable through the middle, inconsistent in midfield, where Gerson, of the fabulous left foot and the infinity of cigarettes, had yet to reach full maturity. Garrincha, the true hero of 1962, came on after half time, beat his man once, and wholly disappeared. Pele, given the freedom of the park, had moments of sublime originality, magical control. There was a throbbing, latent power about him, as there seemed, misleadingly as it transpired, about the team at large. After the game, Gosling said, 'The problem with Garrincha is he has recovered [from a serious motor accident] but not completely. He can't play as often as he used to play; his recovery is quite slow, now.'

Vicente Feola, that rumbling Buddha figure, was in charge again, as he had been in 1958. There were worries about his health; and his weight. Gosling said, 'We try to take with us an old and a young player,' to cover each position. As it transpired, a kind of gerontophilia afflicted Brazil's World Cup selection. Elderly defenders were deployed – Bellini, Orlando and Djalma Santos. Pele, enjoying none of the freedom of Gothenburg, was severely kicked by the Bulgarians and Portuguese, under the tolerant eye of two English referees. Hungarians and Portuguese would rout Brazil.

England completed their successful tour in Poland, arriving in Katowice after what seemed an endless journey by coach from Copenhagen. Ramsey waxed sardonic. Greaves, on reaching Silesia, stepped off the coach and said, 'All right, Alf, you've proved your point. Now let's go home!' A well-struck goal by Roger Hunt decided the match.

Little notice was taken of the warnings of Stanley Rous, and the former French left winger, Jean Vincent, of the menace of the unknown North Koreans, who had twice thrashed Australia in play-offs in Phnom Penh. Overall, whether or not out of courtesy, it was agreed among the various coaches that England, on their own territory, must be among the favourites.

I stayed behind in Copenhagen after England's game there to talk to the Italians, who had flown in for a friendly. Their recent results had been formidable, though all had been obtained at home. Under their tiny manager, Edmondo ('Topolino' – The Mouse) Fabbri, they wanted, he said, 'to demonstrate above all that we're a rational team, anxious to acquit itself on the human plane and on the sporting and technical plane'. England, he believed, would win the World Cup, 'above all because they are strong'.

But before hostilities began, something never, I think, disclosed till now occurred. Dr Alan Bass, by then in charge of medical control at the competition, received for examination from Gigi Peronace, the voluble and volatile little Calabrian player-agent, a urine sample. It arrived unlabelled. When Bass tested it, he said, the results were alarming. He replied to Gigi that whatever was in the sample, there was no way it could be used in the tournament. A tournament in which, of course, the Italians would be humbled by North Korea, who were taken to the hearts of the Middlesbrough crowd.

So England opened the competition; anticlimactically. It had been clear that against a Uruguay team likely to pack their defence, England couldn't employ the counter-attacking style successful in Poland. England, indeed, attacked as best they could, but with scant hopes of breaking through a Uruguay team which showed so little ambition to attack on their own behalf. Once, in the 65th minute, a flick by John Connelly bounced for a corner off the chin of the able Uruguayan keeper, Mazurkiewicz, but that was about as close as England came. The portents were not good.

It could be argued, indeed, that England played only two good games in this World Cup; in the semi-final and the final. True, they proceeded now to account in turn for Mexico and France by the same 2–0 score, but in neither game were they fully convincing. Indeed, it was after the French match that Ramsey, back at the Hendon Hall Hotel, subjected his team to angry criticism.

The Mexicans were even less ambitious than the Uruguayans and substantially less able. Yet not till the 37th minute, by which time the crowd were plaintively singing, 'All we are saying is give us a goal!' did England score, thanks to a piledriver by Bobby Charlton. Moving out to the right, from near halfway, he finally pivoted to strike, from long range, a tremendous right-footed shot, which tore past the keeper, Ignacio Calderon, and into the far top corner of the net.

After that, no deluge. Not till the 76th minute did England breach a far from solid Mexican defence again. That was when Bobby Charlton, now maker rather than scorer of goals, sent a well-judged pass through to Jimmy Greaves, who ran on to shoot with his celebrated left foot. Calderon could only push the ball out and Hunt, who had done little else, tapped it home.

Even against a French team handicapped by injury to two players, Robert Herbin early in the game, and clever Jacky Simon, badly fouled by Nobby Stiles, in the second half, England made heavy weather of success again, though Peters was vigorous and progressive on the wing. Ian Callaghan figured on the other flank, replacing Terry Paine who had been concussed in the match against Uruguay.

Hunt got both the English goals, the first another tap-in, after Jackie Charlton had headed Greaves' corner against a post, the second with a strong header from Callaghan's cross. Jimmy Greaves, kicked so hard on the shin by Joseph Bonnel that the wound necessitated four stitches, was obviously and seriously handicapped. He would miss the rest of the tournament.

Stiles' dreadful challenge bizarrely was not even booked, let alone was he sent off by the Japanese-Peruvian referee, Arturo Yagasaki. FIFA made minatory noises. Ramsey was called before the International Committee who demanded that Stiles be condignly punished; suspended at least for the coming game. Ramsey, whose contempt for the committee had been evident almost since his first foreign tour, regardless of future consequences, would have none of it. He valued Stiles, he said, had no intention of omitting him, and if Stiles went, then so would he. Before such an ultimatum, the committee capitulated. But this, too, would plainly be remembered.

England's quarter-final opponents would be Argentina, their victims in Chile in 1962, managed again by Juan Carlos Lorenzo, who now had a team with a far more abrasive attitude. They had comfortably held West Germany, including the elegant 21-year-old attacking right half, Franz Beckenbauer who had played against England in that flaccid friendly at Wembley. The South Americans played for much of the game with ten men, their central defender Albrecht having been sent off for kicking in the stomach Wolfgang Weber, who was destined to score West Germany's last-gasp equaliser against England in the final.

Argentina's formation was highly flexible, and there was such skill in the team that in retrospect it seems absurd that they should sacrifice finesse to thuggery. Had they played to their undoubted strengths – and kept all men on the field – you wonder whether England could have held them. Their initial tactics, before the bitterly contested dismissal of their towering captain, Antonio Rattin, were to have four men across the back and the left back, blond Silvio Marzolini, as ready to break forward as he had been in Rancagua in 1962. The skilful Ermindo Onega, who had scored an elegantly taken solo goal against Switzerland in their previous game, operated slightly ahead of Rattin with the other midfielder, Alberto Gonzalez, sometimes moving to the right flank. Luis 'The Handsome' Artime was a technically adept and elusive centre forward.

For their part, England now brought in Geoff Hurst in place of Greaves. A more orthodox attacker, without the sporadic brilliance of Greaves at his best – which he had hardly been in this tournament – Hurst was bigger, stronger and immeasurably more effective in the air.

From the start, alas, it was clear that Argentina were less keen on playing themselves, for all their high potential, than in stopping England from doing so. I wrote of 'the total cynicism of their disregard for the laws of the game'. Foul followed petty foul almost whenever England attacked, and when Alan Ball was tripped just inside the box, it was hard to see why little bald Herr Rudolf Kreitlein, largely so pedantic, gave no penalty. Somewhat incongruously, given the huge disparity of their heights, Herr Kreitlein was endlessly hectored and loomed over by the towering Rattin. Strutting about the field, bald head gleaming in the sunshine, he put name after Argentinian name into his notebook, almost like some schoolboy collecting engine numbers. At last, perhaps because he had no pages left, he'd had enough of Rattin and, nine minutes from half time, expelled him. 'For the look on his face,' he subsequently said.

But Rattin wouldn't go. An irony of the affair was that his previous booking had been for a somewhat trivial foul on Bobby Charlton. Now he was inveighing against the booking of a team mate. Lorenzo and several of his players ran outraged to the touchline, remonstrating first with Kreitlein then with Ken Aston, the head of the referees' committee. Aston pacified the enraged Argentines as best he could, while Rattin made his way very slowly round the ground, accompanied by a trainer who exchanged insults with the crowd, himself stopping once, perhaps symbolically, to wipe his hands on the miniature Union Jack in service as a corner flag.

After a protracted hiatus, the game at last resumed, and the poverty of England's methods, the lack of constructive flair, would be all too clearly shown. Just as in their match against West Germany, the ten Argentinians showed themselves coolly capable of keeping the opposition at bay. Yet it was only an astonishing save by their goalkeeper, Antonio Roma, four minutes after half time, which prevented England exploiting one of the few created chances.

Bobby Moore, a supremely authoritative and dominating captain throughout the tournament, rightly nominated its finest player, found Ray Wilson free on the left. The full back made ground, then dropped his centre neatly over the defence to Hurst. For one alarming moment, Hurst seemed to have lost the ball helplessly between his feet. Then he recovered it to let fly a stinging, point-blank shot, flying just inside the near post. Somehow, with a jack-knife bound, Roma reached the ball, to turn it for a corner. Up in the press box, Alfredo Di Stefano, the greatest Argentine never to play for them in the World Cup, was hollering his imprecations.

Even though outnumbered, Argentina still mounted the occasional dangerous attack, with Artime and the abrasive little left winger Oscar Mas so quick on the turn, well supplied by Onega, not to mention the occasional overlapping by the full backs. Yet on seventy-seven minutes, with victory becoming more and more of a mirage, England at last produced a splendid move and a glorious winning goal. Wilson to Peters on the left, and in came, as it so often had for West Ham, the insidious curling cross which Hurst, so well used to it, perfectly anticipated with a huge leap above Roma at the near post, to head the ball home. Yet almost from the kick-off the unquenchable Mas – who had even cuffed a ball boy in his impatience – broke through, forcing Banks to come out of his area to scramble the ball away.

There was a torrid aftermath. As George Cohen began to exchange shirts with Alberto Gonzales, a furious Ramsey grabbed the jersey, inveighing, 'You're not changing shirts with that animal!' Afterwards, an edited version had Ramsey acting to prevent players stripping in front of the Royal Box, but that was essentially for public consumption. Argentine players rushed menacingly towards Kreitlein, who had to be escorted off the field by police. Down in the bowels of the stadium, unperceived by press or public, Argentinians urinated against the walls of their dressing room and banged on the door of England's, trying to break in.

It was with all this freshly on his mind that Ramsey came upstairs for an immediate press conference, delivering words which would make him the *bête noire* of Latin America for years to come. He hoped, he said, that England's opponents in the forthcoming semi-final would want to play football, 'and not act as animals'. Xenophobic he unquestionably was, but given the circumstances, his outburst was surely understandable. It had been anything but a famous victory, whatever the excesses of the opposition, but a victory nonetheless. I remembered the response of Jimmy Armfield, England's 1962 right back and reserve in 1966, when asked at Roehampton before the match what hope England had of ultimate success. 'Slight,' he answered.

Should the upcoming semi-final have been played at Wembley, rather than at Everton? Even Stanley Rous seemed confused. Foreign critics cried conspiracy, but a close reading of the World Cup rule book made it clear that Wembley was the legitimate venue. Portugal would be the difficult and dangerous opposition. True, they had cynically and brutally disabled Pele when the teams met, but much of their football had been coruscating and in the lithe, graceful Eusebio, with his dynamic right foot, they had arguably the most dangerous attacker of the competition; in which indeed he would finish as top scorer. It was his four goals, two from the penalty spot, which had dramatically turned the tide in the quarter-final against the sensational North Koreans, who had sped into a 3–0 lead in twenty minutes only to pay the price of their ultimate naivety, and Eusebio's supreme virtuosity.

What team would Ramsey field? Greaves was now fit, but Hurst stayed in. Clearly England's chief problem would be how to contain

Eusebio and it was here that Nobby Stiles, villain of the piece against France, unable to contribute anything constructive in midfield, would at last come into his own. In Stiles' own words, the England players had celebrated victory over Argentina by getting 'well and truly drunk'. Ramsey, shrewd enough to know when to let his men off the leash, simply sat in a corner as a passive spectator. Yet at other moments, he had brooked no opposition to his careful plans. When the players, tiring of the long coach journey from Hendon Hall to Roehampton, asked whether the training venue might be changed, the answer was brusquely no; similarly, when Bobby Charlton asked whether sartorial regulations could be eased, the manager refused to bend.

Stiles, now, would be assigned to mark Eusebio. Told by Ramsey he must take Eusebio out of the game, Stiles responded, poker faced, 'For one game or a whole career?' His sortie was greeted by laughter. As it transpired, he contained Eusebio not only with great efficiency but with great tactical skill, seldom neglecting him, but carefully standing off him, refusing to be lured into the tackle. When Eusebio went left, as he often and dangerously had in previous games, Stiles simply went with him.

But it would emphatically be Bobby Charlton's evening, his display one of supreme versatility and skill, operating à la Nandor Hidegkuti, behind Hurst and Hunt, back heeling, reverse passing, springing, shooting – and scoring both England's goals. After half an hour, an inspired pass by Wilson sent Hunt away. Costa Pereira, the Portuguese keeper, raced out of goal to block the eventual shot. The ball, however, ran to Charlton, who stroked it into the empty goal. But several other chances went begging. One wondered whether England, with an orthodox left winger such as John Connelly, might have been able to exploit the failings of the Portuguese right back, Alberto Festa.

As it was, the resilient Portuguese called the tune in the first ten minutes of the second half. Keeping them at bay, England at last regained ascendancy and, on seventy-nine minutes, scored their second. Hurst, on one of his muscular runs, this time down the right, brushed off the Portuguese defender, Jose Carlos, got to the goal line, and pulled back the most dangerous pass in the game, usually the speciality of genuine wingers. Charlton comfortably put it away.

Yet England in these final minutes seemed curiously to lose confidence; or maybe they were simply tired. Driven on by their talented left-sided midfielder, Mario Coluna, a goalscoring hero of the Benfica European Cup-winning teams, Portugal grasped the initiative, and the threatened goal arrived after eighty-two minutes, from the penalty spot. Nor could there be any argument about the penalty. Simoes, the fast, elusive little outside left, crossed high. For once Banks didn't get there and the ball was heading inexorably for the head of Jose Torres, the giant centre forward. In desperation, Jackie Charlton punched it away. Eusebio took the kick. Banks had studied the two penalties Eusebio had scored against the North Koreans and duly went that way, but in vain. England, however, held out to win 2–1 largely on merit.

The final, then, would be between West Germany and England. The Germans had never yet beaten an England team and they had been trying one way or another since 1901, when their rudimentary national team was beaten 12–0 by an all-England amateur side at Tottenham and 10–0 by the professionals in Manchester. Under Helmut Schoen, it was a more fluent, technical side than those which had played under Sepp Herberger. Schoen, who had been his assistant manager, was at last able to express his own ideas through the team, though to those who somewhat caustically implied that he was still under Herberger's spell, he would politely reply that, of course, they were sometimes in contact.

Schoen, however, was prepared to go so far; and no further. That is to say, he resisted the ambitions of the young Franz Beckenbauer, a precocious strategist, who was already playing as an attacking *libero*, or sweeper, for his club Bayern Munich, thus initiating the polymath style which would come to be known as Total Football. Beckenbauer had conceived the idea, he said, when watching the big Italian international left back Giacinto Fachetti – who like most of his Italy team had such a disappointing World Cup – surging into attack from deep positions. If a full back could do it, reasoned Beckenbauer, then why not a *liberor*?

Ironically enough, Fabbri had omitted from his Italian squad the doyen of Italian sweepers, Armando Picchi, who interpreted the role purely in terms of defence, but practised it resiliently. So Picchi attended the World Cup only as a spectator which was how, to my astonishment, that I found myself one Sunday morning playing side by side with him – wearing his underpants! – in a pick-up game in Battersea Park. One in which, quite typically, he played with a commitment suggesting we were indeed involved in the World Cup itself.

As for England, the main question was whether Jimmy Greaves would play. Certainly he was quite fit again. And if he were to play, presumably he could scarcely hope to displace Geoff Hurst, whose contribution had been invaluable in the previous two games. Greaves or Hunt, then, one assumed; but for Ramsey, if not for the critics and supporters at large, Hunt was important.

Truth to tell, Hunt in the World Cup final was guilty of two howling mistakes, which could well have cost England the game. Three minutes from half time, with the score at 1–1, Ray Wilson, with a typically fast and incisive overlap, finished with a searching cross. Hurst leaped above the German defence, flicking the ball accurately to Hunt, on his left. But the best, or worst, that Hunt could do was to strike an inadequate shot with his weaker left foot, saved by the German keeper Hans Tilkowski, perhaps more by luck than judgement, when he threw up his arms in seeming hope.

On eighty-six minutes, with England 2–1 ahead and the Germans desperately in search of parity, Hunt blundered again. This time, he was favoured by a glorious defence-shredding pass by an inspired Alan Ball. He had both Hurst and Bobby Charlton to his right, with only the big German defender Willi Schulz in his way. All he had to do was to draw Schulz and give the ball right, to one or other of his team mates. Instead, his pass to Charlton was too soon and too square. Charlton sliced wildly at the ball in his evident surprise, and the vital chance had gone. The Germans thus went on to equalise.

Hard indeed to forget the Friday morning press conference at Roehampton before that final and Alf's strangulated confirmation that England would win. Jimmy Greaves had the weight of the world, let alone the World Cup, on his shoulders, wondering whether he'd be picked. Yet he was still able to say to me with a smile, 'We must have another game next season, Brian!' Meaning of all things a game in Essex between his Tennis All Stars of Abridge against my little Sunday side, Chelsea Casuals, games in which Jimmy played combatively in goal. But that weekend there would be no game for Jimmy, though the sad descent into alcoholism was apparently precipitated not by this massive disappointment, but by his dejection when, transferred from Spurs to West Ham, he found there a Ron Greenwood disillusioned with football and no longer the same, innovative figure. This grew all too clear when Greenwood was elevated to the England role.

It might well be said that Helmut Schoen gave the game away when he detailed Franz Beckenbauer to man-mark Bobby Charlton. In so doing, he may well have largely subdued Charlton, but only at the enormous cost of restricting Beckenbauer to such a negative role, when up till that point he had been the fluent, adventurous inspiration of the German midfield. It was widely believed that the two players cancelled each other out, but if they did, it was at West Germany's expense, rather than England's.

It was a tribute to England's morale that they should fight back after such a potentially traumatising opening goal. After thirteen minutes the usually so reliable Ray Wilson headed Siggi Held's left-wing cross aberrantly straight to the feet of Helmut Haller, and into the net it went.

Another of those West Ham combinations got England back into the game; a quickly taken, perfectly judged free kick by Bobby Moore from the left; a perfectly judged run and header by Geoff Hurst. Tilkowski and his team mates berated one another.

Ramsey's instructions to Ball had been to draw the German left back Karl-Heinz Schnellinger constantly into the middle, which for some time he did, with success; only in the latter stages of the game to overwhelm 'Schnelli', out on the right flank, with all the pace and elusiveness of the true winger.

Playing their own version of *catenaccio* which had availed the Italians so little, with Willi Schulz as the uncompromising sweeper, and Wolfgang Weber, due to score that breathless equaliser, at centre back, the Germans were by no means committed merely to defence. They were flexible and menacing, with Haller supporting the drive of Held on the left, and the irrepressible Uwe Seeler drifting to the right. Gordon Banks had to make a double save from Wolfgang Overath, the chief playmaker, and the big left winger, Lothar Emmerich.

The second half was largely indifferent, though the gap on England's left flank, save when Wilson advanced to fill it, was notable. After seventy-eight minutes, however, England went ahead with a somewhat fortuitous goal, Peters, notionally committed to that wing, popped up in the box to score after Weber had blocked Hurst's shot. That seemed to be that; but controversially it wasn't.

With barely a minute left came West Germany's disputable equaliser. Disputable, because the free kick which produced it was probably a foul by Held, backing in on Jackie Charlton, rather than against him. Emmerich, hesitant till then, now had the chance to strike the crucial free kick from the left of the box, into the goalmouth. There, it hit Schnellinger in the back, was driven across goal again by Held, and struck home on the far post by Weber.

As his weary, dejected players sprawled on the turf, awaiting extra time, Ramsey strode magisterially on to the field to tell them they had won the World Cup once; now they must win it again. With a derisive gesture at the equally recumbent Germans, he declared, 'Look at them! They're finished.'

It would be the apotheosis now of Alan Ball. Well might Ramsey tell him afterwards that he would never play a better game for England. Within ninety seconds, Ball was racing down the wing, giving the lie to any notion of wingless wonders, ending with a shot which Tilkowski, seemingly troubled throughout by the shoulder he had hurt playing in the semi-final versus the Soviet Union, turned over the bar. Shoulder or no shoulder, Tilkowski proceeded next to turn a searing drive by Bobby Charlton for a corner.

A hundred minutes had been played when a searching pass to the right by Stiles reached Ball. 'Oh, no!' Ball told himself. 'I can't get that one! I'm finished.' He had, he later declared, 'already died twice'. Yet somehow he found the strength, pace and energy to get the ball indeed, and leave Schnellinger panting in the rear. Geoff Hurst met his cross on the near post with a searing right-footed shot. After which – eternal controversy.

That the shot beat Tilkowski all ends up was palpable. That it struck the underside of the bar was indisputable. Whether or not it then crossed the goal line has been disputed to this day. Roger Hunt, turning away in triumph without bothering to make sure of the goal, seemed quite convinced. Herr Gottfreid Dienst, the Swiss referee, wasn't sure. He turned to his Azerbaijan linesman Tofik Bakhramov, to his right, a man with the flowing grey hair of a concert violinist; Bakhramov pointed his flag emphatically towards the centre. England 3 West Germany 2.

With the Germans desperately in quest of an equaliser, leaving gaps galore, a West Ham partnership turned the trick again. Moore's long ball out of defence, capping his immaculate display, and there was Hurst, blowing out his cheeks, to crash the ball left footed past Tilkowski. Was he trying to score, or simply blasting the ball away, willy nilly, as the seconds ebbed? No matter. It was a spectacular goal, England's fourth, and the first hat trick ever recorded in a World Cup final.

So Ramsey had won the World Cup, as he said he would, England's best coming last, or in the last two games. Had he and they been lucky? Lucky to play every game at Wembley? Perhaps, but there was nothing illicit about it. And unlucky surely to concede that late equaliser, in such dubious and potentially disheartening circumstances. That the team was able to pick itself up, dust itself off and start all over again was surely a tribute to his influence and inspiration.

As to the future, he could hardly be blamed entirely for the arguably negative effect of his wingless and work-rate tactics on the English game at large, any more than Arsenal after 1925 could be blamed when almost every other leading English club adopted the Third Back Game with its breakaway implications.

It would not be a victory much eulogised abroad. For conspiracy theorists Hurst's second was the Goal That Never Was; and if England had played their semi-final at Wembley rather than at Goodison Park, that was the work of Stanley Rous. Even though he had mistakenly opposed it. For Latin America, Rattin had been a guiltless victim, and the reference to 'animals' was an unforgivable insult.

Even in England itself, there were mixed feelings about the way the World Cup had been won by a team seen as essentially functional rather than exhilarating. Yet what had the once exhilarating Brazilians contributed to a tournament in which they had been woundingly swept aside both by the Hungarians and the Portuguese?

Given the players at his disposal, and not only the twenty-two whom he eventually picked, could Ramsey have done better? Might there, you wondered, have at least been an opportunity for George Eastham, the only genuine, playmaking inside forward in the squad, with his clever close control and his subtle use of the ball? Eastham never got on the field, but had he done so, the pattern which had Bobby Charlton as withdrawn centre forward and notionally the chief purveyor would have had to be varied radically. Ramsey's answer would be that, in the last analysis, his way worked.

Four years later, in Mexico, England would give a rejuvenated Brazil a thrilling run for their money and play enough good football against West Germany to deserve better than they got. As for luck, it deserted Ramsey in the cruellest way; even if he contributed to his and England's own downfall.

1970: Mayhem in Mexico
Scarcely had the 1966 World Cup been won than the qualifying rounds for the European Nations Cup began. UEFA, as generous as FIFA had been when the British Championship was originally made an eliminating group, emulated the international body. It was almost as though England had been given a bye through to the eventual quarter-finals. Predictably, in England's opening game against Northern Ireland in Belfast, doubly valid, Ramsey chose to field his complete World Cup-winning team. It won 2–0 with confidence rather than brilliance, through goals by Roger Hunt and Martin Peters, though the inimitable George Best was the star of the show, never subdued.

A pedestrian Czech team came to Wembley for a dull draw in a friendly, a game in which Nobby Stiles, cast as a putatively advanced rather than a strictly defensive midfielder, did little of note. His admiration for Ramsey remained undimmed. Talking to him in Manchester, he told me: 'Knowing Alf, best to leave him alone. He doesn't like praise. I admire him for it. He's made me a better player in meself. He's so straightforward, you know he says things to people which they think might be upsetting them, but it's a good thing. I think he's done an awful lot for me.'

Commenting after the 5–1 demolition of a shambolic Wales in the British Championship, Ramsey, with a certain, smiling diffidence, at last gave hostages to fortune when he told us, 'This is a great team.' The following April, at Wembley, the 'great team' lost, though in pardonable circumstances, to the Auld Enemy, to the ecstatic acclaim of the Scottish fans. But on the Scottish side at least, tensions remained. Denis Law, that splendidly acrobatic forward, scorer of one of the goals that helped his team beat England 3–2, had refused to watch the World Cup final on television, preferring to go out to play golf.

The 1970 World Cup, with its substitutes, had yet to come; and England would end the match with eight fit players. After only thirteen minutes, Jackie Charlton limped off the field following a clash with Scotland's Bobby Lennox. He stayed off for another thirteen minutes. On his return, he was obliged to hobble about at centre forward, though even then he contrived to head a goal and forced an accomplished save by the veteran Scottish goalkeeper, Ronnie Simpson.

My somewhat disenchanted match report was met with a fusillade of scornful resentment from north of the border, but in truth it had hardly been a famous victory. Yet, even when at full strength, England had scarcely had a distinguished season. Jimmy Greaves was recalled for the Scotland game, but, as one of the injured English players, he was hardly able to reassert himself.

To Ramsey's justified displeasure, his team were condemned to a half-baked so-called Exposition tournament in Montreal, with dismal accommodation. Ramsey did not hide his disdain when, on arrival with his squad at Montreal airport, he was accosted by a garrulous Canadian television journalist: 'Sir Alf, I've got great news for you! I'm going to take you straight to our studio and put you on television. Fifteen minutes of prime-time Canadian television!'

'Oh, no, you fuckin' ain't!' said Alf.

England began the 1967–68 season, in Cardiff, with nine of their World Cup final team, the only absentees being Ray Wilson, replaced by Keith Newton at left back, and Nobby Stiles by Alan Mullery. Mullery, a strong, forceful and sometimes adventurous wing half, vigorous rather than elegant, should in fact have been on England's foreign tour of 1964, only to rick his back while shaving in a freakish accident. A Londoner, he, like George Cohen had grown up at Fulham, though by now he had moved across London to Spurs.

England's 3–0 victory, wingless again, demanding as it did endless running by their flank men, was absurdly flattering. Though Bobby Charlton was at his most fluent and inventive, and England were a goal up through Peters at half time, a resurgent Welsh team dominated most of the second half, needing a defiantly agile Gordon Banks to keep them out, and only in the last three minutes did England score twice, to put a misleading gloss on the game.

England's win at Wembley against a Northern Ireland team without George Best, and Scotland's previous, surprising 1–0 defeat by the Irish in Belfast meant that the world champions were virtually guaranteed a place in the European quarter-finals.

There followed a somewhat laborious 2–2 draw at Wembley against the Soviet Union with Cyril Knowles, Tottenham's left back, playing at right back and David Sadler, an elegant and versatile performer, at centre back alongside Bobby Moore. But the match was chiefly interesting for what you might call the redemption of Igor Chislenko. The Russian outside right, that evening reminding Ramsey of what a real winger could do, scored both his team's goals, thus to some extent effacing the bleak memory of the 1966 World Cup semi-final against West Germany at Goodison Park. Then, fiercely and painfully tackled by Schnellinger, Chislenko lost the ball. Adding insult to injury, 'Schnelli' had gone on to set up a German goal. An infuriated, hobbling Chislenko had then decided to take revenge on the opponent closest to him, kicking the wholly innocent Siggi Held, and being instantly sent off.

Unusually, the annual fixture with Scotland was played in February rather than April. England needed a single point to qualify for Europe and they got it in a 1–1 draw on a treacherous pitch, muddy on top but hard below. After a fine right-footed drive by Martin Peters scored England's goal, an equally fine, twisting header by Celtic's John 'Yogi Bear' Hughes brought Scotland's equaliser.

In a sudden, untypical moment of euphoria, Ramsey disclosed his hope and belief that one day, his England team might surpass the Hungarians who had won 6–3 in November 1963. It seemed most unlikely, even if, in one sense, Ramsey's England had already surpassed the team of Puskas, Kocsis and Hidegkuti, having won a World Cup, the ultimate prize that had so cruelly eluded Hungary.

Ramsey's belief in the immense potential of his team was again hard to share when it squeezed through the first leg of the quarter-final against Spain 1–0 at Wembley, with a goal by Bobby Charlton. The English defence never managed to subdue the powerful, clever, fast Amancio on the Spanish right wing while England's own lack of genuine wingers was all too plain again versus a team which, at Wembley, demanded to be attacked rather than counter-attacked. Nor was the absence of Geoff Hurst a help.

In the second leg in Madrid, however, a counter-punching approach was legitimate and profitable. No Hurst, again, and Ramsey abandoned even the pretence of having any kind of real wing player on the left flank, preferring to choose the notoriously abrasive Norman 'Bite Your Legs' Hunter there, essentially a defensive left half though, in the ironic event, he would score England's second goal in a 2–1 success.

In those less overloaded days, the custom was to limit the last stage of the European tournament to four clubs, the semi-finalists, playing on the soil of one of them: in this case, Italy. England's opponents would be a talented but bruising young Yugoslav team, to be met in Florence, where England, on their only other visit, had drawn 1–1 in May 1952. This time they lost, to a goal taken with supreme skill by Dragan Dzajic – the gifted Yugoslav outside left – never one for rough methods. But Dobrivoje Trivic, the Yugoslav midfielder, kicked Alan Ball so violently that he was frightened to take off his boot, so badly did his ankle swell. A crude foul by Norman Hunter lamed the chief Yugoslav playmaker, the tall Ivica Osim, who, admittedly, had been carrying a previous injury: yet he scarcely deserved to be called a clown by an unsympathetic Alf Ramsey.

So England were consigned to the third-place match, in Rome's Olympic Stadium. A curtain raiser to the final between Italy and

Yugoslavia, which was distorted when a deeply compromised Herr Dienst, the World Cup final referee of 1966, refused an obvious penalty to the Yugoslavs. So the game was drawn, Italy going on to win the replay.

England, for their part, played brightly and briskly to beat the Soviets 2–0 with goals by Bobby Charlton and a returning Geoff Hurst. The match marred by the sustained, vituperative whistling and jeering of Nobby Stiles by the vindictive Roman crowd. This behaviour induced Indro Montanelli, the doyen of Italian political writers, incensed by the praise the crowd had had at large, to write a bitterly critical piece under the heading 'Magnificent Public', deploring such insensate behaviour.

Qualified as holders for the 1970 World Cup finals, England's ensuing season was something of a time out of war; until it came to the summer 1969 tour of Latin America and its preparations for defence of their trophy. This was Ramsey's second summer visit to Mexico, for he had attended the 1968 Olympic football tournament which, despite the huge putative advantages accruing to the hosts in terms of the breathless altitudes and the searing heat, was ultimately dominated by European teams.

Well dressed and imperturbable in Mexico City, even when a tiny Mexican stabbed a golden pin into his lapel with a cry of 'So you will always remember Mexico!' – he would have greater cause than that – Alf Ramsey surmised that were England to be based in Guadalajara, substantially lower than Mexico City at 7,200 feet above sea level, they would find that 'The lower you go, the hotter it gets.' Indeed, FIFA's decision to stage the World Cup in Mexico in May, in the heat of summer, seemed even more crass than that of the international Olympic Committee to stage their tournament there in October 1968.

Ramsey reflected, 'What I would say is that we should come out here and spend as much time in acclimatisation as we can. I would think that if we are to be based in Guadalajara, we would stay there. We would acclimatise in Mexico City and then go down to Guadalajara. Normally we don't do badly under heat. Whether it would affect us over a time, I don't know. I'm thinking of Canada last year, where we were playing, and in Italy this year. Canada especially, where it was over 90 [degrees], and in Guadalajara it will be over 100. It was over 100 when I was there.'

As it transpired, the England players would make use of a chemical called slow sodium which certainly seemed to help them in Guadalajara, but was of limited effect when they met West Germany in the quarter-finals on the heights and in the equally ferocious heat of Leon.

England's form during the 1968–69 season was hardly encouraging. After three successive draws against East European opposition, somebody, Ramsey promised, was going to get a terrible hiding, and in March, it turned out to be France; thrashed 5–0 at Wembley. Wonder of wonders, England played with two wingers, the effervescent Francis Lee on the right, and Mike O'Grady, capped just once in 1962 against Northern Ireland, and swiftly if ruthlessly to be jettisoned. There might even have been a recall for Jimmy Greaves, about whose absence Ramsey was almost apologetic; though it emerged that Greaves had stipulated that he would join the squad only if he were guaranteed a game, which he must have known would never be countenanced by Ramsey. Another surprising feature of the victory was that it was achieved without either Bobby Charlton or Alan Ball, though a revitalised Geoff Hurst was in his most majestic form, grabbing a treble including two penalties.

For the first time, the British International Championship was stuck on the end of the season, thereby plainly presaging its ultimate doom. Ramsey's reaction was pertinent. Were the British Championship to be an end-of-season affair before the World Cup finals in 1970, there would be two alternatives: 'One, that you don't compete in the British Championship. This is purely a personal thought. This would mean we would get the minimum period of acclimatisation. The second is, of course, that you select your strongest party, take them to Mexico, and you compete in the British Championship with the rest.'

In the event, prior to the 1969 expedition, England won all three of their British Championship matches, with the final satisfaction of an easy 4–1 victory against Scotland at Wembley, 'There was no doubt of Scotland's courage,' I wrote, 'still less of England's superiority.' Two goals each for Martin Peters and Geoff Hurst, one a penalty, both revitalised after dull displays in Belfast against Northern Ireland. Six of the 1966 World Cup winners played, the newcomers being the full backs Keith Newton and Leeds United's Terry Cooper, originally an outside left with a winger's penchant for overlapping, together with Alan Mullery at right half, Brian Labone, the solid Everton centre half, and Francis Lee, on the right wing.

Arriving in Mexico City for the first match of the tour, Alf Ramsey gathered the journalists and gave us a little homily on how important it would be to win friends and influence people. Alas, the cloven hoof of his own xenophobia would quickly show through.

The match against Mexico, played in the yet to be rebuilt Azteca Stadium, was a 0–0 draw in which the England players, with minimal time to acclimatise, were plainly struggling for breath in the closing stages. Afterwards, Ramsey gave a press conference. When asked by the Mexican journalists if he would say something to them, he responded: 'Yes! There was a band playin' outside our hotel at five o'clock this mornin'. We were promised a motor cycle escort to the ground. It never arrived. When our players went out to inspect the pitch, they were abused and jeered by the spectators. I would have thought the Mexican public would have been delighted to welcome England. Then, when the game began, they could applaud their own team as much as they liked. But: we are delighted to be in Mexico, and the Mexican people are a wonderful people!'

In Guadalajara, where England would subsequently be based, an England B team won easily against a Mexican XI. When a group of Mexican journalists penetrated the subterranean tunnel to the dressing rooms, Ramsey angrily drove them out again, telling them they had no right to be there. The following day, the local paper reflected bitterly, 'What would you expect from someone who calls the Argentines animals?'

The promising young striker Allan Clarke scored two of the goals in Guadalajara, but was made all too conscious of Ramsey's emphatic discipline when, laughing loudly at the back of the aircraft, he found Alf looming over him. 'You enjoyin' yourself, Allan?' Alf asked. Clarke said he was.

'Well,' was the retort, 'you don't fuckin' enjoy yourself with me, remember that!'

From Guadalajara come the long flight south to Montevideo, winning there 2–1 for the first time, despite the phantom free kick from which Uruguay's elusive little right winger, Luis Cubilla, headed an equaliser. Francis Lee, in insidiously good form, wriggled through a baffled defence to score, and made the winner for Hurst. Gordon Banks distinguished himself with a fine save from Cubilla.

Next, the daunting prospect of Rio, and Brazil, who had thrashed England there in 1964. Here, beaten despite looking the better team for some eighty minutes, England would surely have done better were it not for the first evidence of Ramsey's uneasy grasp of substitutes, two of whom would be permissible in the coming World Cup for the first time.

Leaving Geoff Hurst to toil alone up-field throughout the game in the exhausting heat and humidity was always going to be a dangerous policy, not least because Bobby Charlton, notionally his fellow striker, had long been used to playing a deeper role. Allan Clarke and the West Bromwich centre forward Jeff Astle, who had scored the other two goals in Guadalajara, would surely have been potential partners up front for Hurst, who ran himself to exhaustion.

Colin Bell, the metronomic Manchester City inside right now a fully fledged member of the squad, gave England the lead, when a shot by Hurst was deflected to him. Even with Pele in the Brazil team, England looked superior, and when Brazil were given a penalty and their right back Carlos Albertol took it, Banks saved.

In the closing minutes, however, a weary England gave away goals to Tostao, Brazil's centre forward, and their right winger, Jairzinho, to lose 2–1. On Copacabana beach the following day, opposite the team's hotel, a cheerful and relaxed Alf Ramsey, by no means at odds with the press, joined a group of sunbathing journalists and conceded he might have done things differently. Yet overall, the omens for 1970 were good.

The following season, with the British Championship – which was to be an anticlimax, as widely predicted – not due till April, the England team were put on a meagre diet of friendlies with foreign opposition. There was a promising win in Amsterdam against Holland where Francis Lee was ebullient again but none could compare with the virtuosity of Holland's Johan Cruyff. Altogether less promising, come December, was a dismally mediocre performance at Wembley against a weakened Portugal. Ironically, in view of what would so disastrously happen in Leon, the hero of the evening was Peter Bonetti of Chelsea, standing in for Gordon Banks, who made three spectacular saves. He had looked highly impressive, too, in Amsterdam. But Hurst was badly missed and a packed midfield did little of consequence till Martin Peters came on as a late substitute. The only goal of the game was resourcefully — and significantly — scored by Jackie Charlton.

When Ramsey, somewhat prematurely, announced a list of thirty possible players, many of us were distressed to see no Peter Osgood on it. Despite his precocious form as Chelsea's teenaged centre forward, he was ignored in the run-up to the previous World Cup. In the interim, he had broken his leg, but come back to play just as effectively as an attacking midfielder. The New Year gave scant cause for hope with a display at Wembley in the return game against Holland when the fans were chorusing, 'What a load of rubbish!' Ramsey, one felt, was the only man at Wembley who thought they were booing the Dutch. Preferring Norman Hunter to the majestic Bobby Moore seemed an aberration. Ian Storey-Moore was, at least, a true winger, but contributed little. Bobby Charlton was off song. Cooper scarcely overlapped. Jackie Charlton looked decidedly vulnerable, far from the dominant if ungainly figure of 1966.

Yet in February, against Belgium, Osgood, however grudgingly, at last got his chance. The manner of his choice was the pure quintessence of Ramseyism. The Saturday before he announced his squad, Ramsey went to QPR to watch an FA Cup tie against Chelsea, with three goals from a resplendent Osgood. Subsequently Ramsey stood in a corner of the team room, darkly justifying his policies: 'Tell them [England fans] that we need experienced men, will you? Tell them that Belgium have deliberately switched to a smaller ground, because they want to win.'

Interviewed later that evening on television, Ramsey, with sublime perversity, eulogised the eighteen-year-old Chelsea inside right, Alan Hudson, but limited his appraisal of Osgood to conceding that he'd taken his goals well. Would Osgood have played in Belgium at all, had Bobby Charlton not been needed by Manchester United for an FA Cup tie while his replacement, Colin Bell, dropped out, injured? Thus did Ramsey show that, while he refused to be bullied, he was not inflexible, that he would concede to public pressure only when it suited him. Optimism would surge again after an impressive 3–1 win with Hurst, Peters and Labone back to their best, Bobby Moore and Alan Ball returning with impact, Emlyn Hughes, of Liverpool, far more at home in midfield than as a right-footed left back. In Mexico, all Osgood would get, to his chagrin – in later years he would insist that England could have done better had he played – was a couple of spells as substitute.

World Cup 1970

So to Latin America for a month's acclimatisation, initially on the 7,200 feet, pollution-shrouded heights of Mexico City, after which the squad flew higher still, to the breathless peaks of Bogotá in Colombia, Quito in Ecuador.

Two matches were played in each city, one by the B team, one by the full international side. All four were won, but these results were dwarfed by the cataclysm of Bobby Moore's arrest in Bogotá, en route from Quito back to Mexico. In the meantime, Ramsey had cut his squad in Quito by half a dozen players, including that unlucky Liverpool winger Peter Thompson, who thus missed the cut for the second successive World Cup; a player of undoubted talent, strong, fast and elusive, yet fatally inconsistent.

Moore's arrest, for the alleged theft of a bracelet, caused global astonishment. Nowhere was his guilt believed. 'Pardon the vehemence that I've put into this article,' wrote the recently supplanted Brazilian team manager, Joao Saldanha. 'I know Bobby Moore well enough as a player to say that he's the pride of English football and I should be glad to have him in my team, in the certainty of winning the World Cup. And as a person, I consider him a clean man.'

The accusation against Moore, by a female shop assistant in the

Fuego Verde jewellery shop at the Tequendama Hotel where England had stayed in Bogotá, was that after he and Bobby Charlton had left the shop, it was found that a bracelet had disappeared. Ominously, it was not the first time that such an accusation had been made against a visiting celebrity. The proprietor of the shop endorsed it and there was even a mysterious 'witness'– of dubious background – who would subsequently vanish.

For all that, Moore was arrested, and consigned to house arrest, under the aegis of the President of the Colombian Millonarios football club. Strange echoes of the Neil Franklin affair, shortly before England were due to compete in the 1950 World Cup, and their Stoke City centre half defected to play for the Santa Fe club of Bogotá.

After diplomatic intervention, Moore was let out on 'bail' to join the squad in Guadalajara, to the immense relief of his manager and team mates. For a few months, the pantomime of spurious charges continued, then faded gradually away. Moore emerged as cool, calm and unperturbed as though nothing had happened, with the sang-froid which had always characterised his presence on the field. He would go on to play with as much, if not more, authority and influence as he had when voted best player of the previous World Cup.

'Drunks and Pirates Arrive!' was the beneficent headline in a local paper when the England team returned to Mexico City airport. Jeff Astle, it is true, was in dire plight, his clothes rumpled, palpably the worse for alcohol. He was terrified of flying, and it was rumoured that a mischievous England colleague had been plying him with drink.

Brazil were ominously included in England's Guadalajara qualifying group. Now under the managership of 'Lucky' Mario Lobo Zagallo, after Saldanha had gone in a blaze of controversy, they had already charmed and placated the locals. With an array of flags, smiles and banners, they had seduced Guadalajara, only then to retire behind the impregnable stockade of their training camp, outside the city, where entry was denied to all but initiates.

Zagallo had deployed his team with extreme tactical skill. Where Saldanha, in a burst of suicidal aberration, had actually planned to drop Pele, Zagallo welcomed a player who initially had promised he would never play in another World Cup, after seeing on the official World Cup film how brutally he'd been kicked by the Portuguese in the previous competition. Faced with an embarrassment of riches in the shape of his two formidable left-footed playmakers, Gerson and Rivelino, Zagallo resolved it by using them both, Gerson as a virtual inside left, Rivelino as the deep-lying left winger; where once Zagallo himself had so tirelessly played.

With Tostao, the clever, linking, centre forward and Jairzinho on the right wing powerfully continuing the tradition established by Julinho and Garrincha, it seemed of secondary importance that Brazil were by no means as impressive in defence where Felix, the goal-keeper, would seem alarmingly erratic, not least when it came to flapping at high crosses.

In their opening game against the Czechs the Brazilian defence did indeed look porous, and Ladislav Petras actually put the Czech team ahead. But Brazil then swept them aside with superb attacking football to win 4–1. Pele scored a fine goal, but almost scored a still more memorable one when his lob from almost halfway bounced just past a post. Alan Ball derided the Czechs: 'They played basketball football. As soon as the Brazilians got the ball, they all ran back, seven of them. The midfield was wide open.'

Before England's opening match against Romania, as Ball later admitted, 'We were terrified . . . of having a bad result against Romania. I've never been as frightened in my life as when we went out. I always write home to my wife and my parents on the afternoon of a game for England, it's a superstition. I wrote to my dad: "I'm really looking forward to it, but I'm frightened to death!" Normally I'm not that kind of lad, but I was really keyed up the other day. But when we got it over, relief came over the camp in general. We'd got the hardest ever, and now we think we can beat these [the Brazilians].'

The unusual optimism caused by the 1–0 victory over Romania, achieved through Hurst's forcefully taken left-footed goal, was well enough deserved. Feeble refereeing by the Belgian Vital Loraux enabled Mihai Mocanu, the Romanian left back, to stay on the field despite three vicious fouls against England players. But the night before the game against Brazil, opposition came from unexpected quarters:

a virtual siege of the Hilton Hotel where England, centrally and some-what unwisely, were staying.

As one who was staying there myself, I had a close-up view of the organised cacophony outside which went on well into the small hours, with motor bikes roaring across the front steps of the hotel. Ramsey had to move his men from one side of the hotel to the other to enable them to sleep as best they could. And the match would, outrageously, kick off in the fierce heat of noon. Alas, FIFA and the World Cup committee, not exempting Sir Stanley Rous, then FIFA's President, had as little concern for footballers as the generals of the First World War. Television ruled, and European broadcasters needed matches to be played at high noon.

It proved to be a fascinating game. Brazil lacked the injured Gerson, the fulcrum of so many of their attacks, but were otherwise at full strength. Terry Cooper, who had overlapped so exuberantly down both flanks against Romania, would find himself wholly occupied with trying to contain the dynamic Jairzinho. And when, in the first half, Jairzinho streaked past him to deliver a probing cross, Pele's bouncing header seemed irresistible. He himself was actually shouting, 'Goal!' when Gordon Banks launched himself to deflect the ball, one handed, up and over the bar. Met afterwards in the hotel lift, he remarked of Pele, 'He got up like a salmon out of bright water!'

In the second half Jairzinho scored the only goal, when Pele delicately turned the ball on to him, though later study of television suggested that Bobby Moore, again in imperious form, had been obstructed by Tostao as he moved to clear. Jeff Astle, brought on as a second half substitute, had an ideal opportunity to equalise when a desperate defender headed the ball straight to his feet, but could only shoot over the bar. Sitting disconsolate next morning by the Hilton's swimming pool, one heard Alan Ball's high voice lamenting, 'How could Jeff miss that chance?'

Confident of qualifying, Ramsey – like the Brazilians, in their third game against Romania – put out a much-diluted team against the Czechs, and nearly paid for it. It was a dismal display. Jackie Charlton in defence looked clumsy and superannuated. Astle and Clarke were ineffective in attack though Clarke, from the most doubtful of penalties, scored the only goal of an abysmal game. Rene Machin, a French referee given to controversial calls, awarded a penalty when Ladislav Kuna appeared to fall and handle the ball as he challenged Colin Bell, but asserted that the spot kick had been given for a trip. Both sides hit the bar.

The quarter-final now pitted England against their victims in the 1966 final, West Germany, in Leon, where heat, oppressive in Guadalajara, was compounded by altitude. England were quartered in a motel where, the evening before the game, I sat at a non-functioning bar with Bobby Moore and others. How typical it seemed of Moore, the epitome of nonchalance, that his one preoccupation had nothing to do with the game, but with whether two of his London friends, Morrie and Phil, would be able to find a hotel room.

The following morning I emerged from sleeping on a colleague's chalet floor to be greeted by an alarming sight: Gordon Banks, pale and plainly distressed, staggering across the hotel's lawn on the arm of the England doctor, Neil Phillips. Food poisoning had affected him and, disastrously for England, put him out of the game. How had it happened; and only to him? Many years later, when I spoke to him about it, Banks insisted that he had eaten and drunk the evening before exactly the same as any other player.

Though it may be merely a wild surmise, it could be worth recording that when the *Daily Telegraph* reporter Bob Oxby subsequently broke his journey home in Washington to visit his cousin, the well-known Senator Stewart Symington, the senator laughingly told him, 'That was the CIA! You don't think we were going to let England beat Brazil, do you?' – Brazil at that time being in a state of political turmoil. The mystery may never be solved, but, beyond all doubt, Banks's illness was fatal for England.

His place would go to Chelsea's Peter Bonetti, alias 'The Cat', author as we know of two coruscating performances for England earlier in the year. Yet it was an ill-omened moment for Bonetti. In the first place he had not played a game in anger for many weeks. In the second, it is known that he was worried about his wife, Frances, from whom he would later be divorced, and who was among several players' wives who had been brought out as a publicity stunt by a commercial organisation; they seemed to be enjoying themselves greatly in a Guadalajara hotel.

Bonetti in the event would have a wretched game, but whatever his deficiencies on the day, they were not the only factor in England's surprising defeat. Bonetti's mistakes were compounded by the tactical misjudgements of Alf Ramsey. A game which should have been well won was thrown away. Persistent themes assert themselves. Luck, or the lack of it. Strategy.

In West Germany's favour was the fact that at long last, after generations of trying, they had managed to beat a below-strength England, in Hanover in 1968, albeit in a poor game in which the only goal was scored when Franz Beckenbauer's shot was deflected in off Brian Labone.

On form, the Germans had now to be favoured. They had been playing far more convincing, productive football than England with Gerd 'Der Bomber' Muller blending well with his popular predecessor, Uwe Seeler, up front; a particular success for Helmut Schoen, though he had yet to give Beckenbauer free rein to operate as he wished, as an attacking *libero*. England's tactics had moved from 4–3–3 to 4–4–2, with Francis Lee moving from the right wing to centre forward. There were those such as the old England, Everton and Arsenal wing half, and prominent manager, Joe Mercer, who felt the front men carried too much of a burden. The one-man strike force which has become so common lay in the future.

But in the earlier stages of this game, England played by far their best football of the tournament. On the half hour, an inspired Alan Mullery, playing unquestionably his finest game for England, swapped passes with Lee, sent Keith Newton tearing down the right flank, and himself raced diagonally across field to pop up on the near post to convert Newton's cross. On fifty minutes, the inexhaustible Geoff Hurst sent Newton flying down the right wing again, and this time it would be Martin Peters, resuscitated, who would exploit his cross.

Shortly after this, Helmut Schoen made an all too significant substitution, taking off the right winger Reinhard Libuda and sending on

Jurgen Grabowski. Terry Cooper, who like Newton had been over-lapping with speed and success, by now was plainly paying for his exertions in the heat of noon and at the breathless altitude. He was in no condition to counter the fresh Grabowski. And when Beckenbauer advanced for an unexceptional shot, the hapless Bonetti allowed it to slip under his body, for 2–1. Note that it was only after this goal that Ramsey so controversially took off Bobby Charlton. The subsequent belief in some quarters that he had done so *before* Beckenbauer scored, thereby allowing the West German captain to break forward at will, was quite wrong. Though with Charlton gone, Beckenbauer certainly enjoyed more leeway.

Charlton it's true had begun to show signs of fatigue, but the general feeling was that Ramsey, convinced that the battle was won, substituted him so he'd be fresher for the semi-final. Colin Bell took his place. Ramsey's second substitution seemed almost aberrational: Norman Hunter for Peters. As if this were not odd enough, Hunter, who one assumed had been brought on to bolster the defence, was soon to be seen taking a corner!

So it was that West Germany equalised with what might be considered a virtuoso or a freakish goal. When Brian Labone's weak clearance was lobbed back again by Schnellinger, Seeler leaped with his back to the goal and somehow managed to head the ball over an out-of-contention Bonetti. The keeper would be blamed, but the header was an extraordinary one.

Extra time would be played, with England now plainly under pressure. Yet surely, one felt, they scored a valid goal when Lee dodged past Schnellinger on the right-hand goal line and pulled the ball back in the true winger's way; as England so far had never yet done. Hurst shot home but the goal was disallowed, for no evident reason: Hurst could not have been offside. Surprisingly little was made of this in the English media and even by Ramsey himself.

The *coup de grâce* came when Grabowski once again beat Cooper and crossed the ball for Johannes Loehr, the other winger, to head the ball back from the left. Muller scored with a ferocious volley. Afterwards, the England players sprawled exhausted on the motel lawn. David Miller of the *Daily Telegraph* and I took Geoff Hurst in our taxi back to Guadalajara. The poor fellow was utterly spent and appallingly thirsty. We stopped the car in front of a tiny village store where I bought him a soft drink and found in my jacket a solitary salt pill. It seemed to give him some small comfort.

Had Banks played, England would surely have won. Had Ramsey been as alert as Helmut Schoen, they might still have done.

Decline and Fall

The following season was something of a ceasefire, reality kept at bay until hostilities resumed. Ramsey was still paid a tight-fisted £6,000 a year and the FA had paid England's players a meagre £1,000 each for winning the World Cup. As George Cohen bitterly emphasised years afterwards, this thorough financial ineptitude had condemned the Association to pay a quarter of a million unnecessary pounds in tax.

Ramsey now showed himself quite ready to rebuild his team, even to the controversial extent of dropping Bobby Moore and Bobby Charlton. An easy 3–1 win at Wembley against a poor East German side, deploying a 4–3–3 formation rather than the 4–4–2 used in Mexico, made one regret that it hadn't been used in the World Cup.

The Great White Hope was the new centre forward, Martin Chivers, first capped in a frustrating European Championship qualifying game in Malta where, on an appalling pitch, England prevailed only on Martin Peters' goal. Chivers had the qualities which should have made him one of the outstanding players of his British, even of his European, generation. He was tall, he was strong, with the powerful physique of the traditional English centre forward. What he had, as such players seldom had, was great skill and technique into the bargain. But what he lacked, at times when it was badly needed, was the confidence and commitment to exploit his gifts. Once – I believe it was when England lost crucially in the Championship at Wembley to West Germany in 1972 – he turned to Alan Ball, the quintessence of commitment, and pleaded, 'Say something to gee us up, Alan!'

Ramsey deplored the difficulty of persuading clubs involved in European competition to release their players. I wrote at the time that, 'It is easier for a camel to pass through the eye of a needle than for an unorthodox player to get into the England team. While far from eschewing the destructive player, Sir Alf seems to have a positive need to have one in his side.' The latest, abrasive, example was Peter Storey of Arsenal, the *reductio ad absurdum* to come, the following year, in Berlin.

My reservations over Ramsey's teams and tactics seemed all too bleakly justified in the 1971–72 season when, in the European Championship qualifiers, modest Switzerland were met in Basel. England's 3–2 victory against a Swiss team which tired in the latter stages and could never subdue Chivers, was laboriously won, largely thanks to fearful errors by Marcel Kunz, the Swiss goalkeeper. No Bobby Charlton, even though Bell and Ball were injured. Ramsey seemed to have confined his former favourite to the dustbin of history.

Soon afterwards, at Coverciano, the Italian coaching centre outside Florence, I heard the team manager of the *azzurri*, Ferruccio Valcareggi, say:

> I would rather not play England. They're cool, they know how to hold their own, even if they haven't any technical qualities. They don't lose their lucidity. They don't worry about things going wrong. Banks is a player you can always be sure of. Bobby Moore remains for me one of the greatest players in the world. Mullery is really combative, a player who may not be spectacular, but really makes a contribution. Then there is Chivers, who is a great revelation. A really positive player, in every way. He has power, skill, a good turn of speed, even if he doesn't get off the mark that quickly, and he is impossible to counter in the air, because when he goes up, he hangs there like a basketball player. Lee, for me, is the key player, because if he beats his man, which he is always trying to do, he finds the head of Chivers or Hurst. He is always creating danger.

When Ramsey had watched the Swiss beat Turkey, he had left well before the end. 'He thought he had seen everything,' said Valcareggi, 'but he hadn't.'

Louis Maurer, Switzerland's manager, observed, 'We had studied

the play of the English in films of their World Cup matches and we
understood that to neutralise them, we had to keep the ball on the
ground. We succeeded in this in terms of play, we dominated them.
Our final deterioration was caused not by lesser concentration but by
lesser athletic preparation.'

There was to be no such deterioration when the Swiss came to
Wembley in November 1971 and, against an England team with a
few somewhat strange choices, forced a 1–1 draw. Ramsey, however,
was hardly helped by the characteristic insularity of the Football
League, who insisted on playing League Cup games a mere couple
of days before the international. Chivers, one of those who had been
thus involved, came on only well into the second half, when the Swiss
defences were well dug in. Ramsey deplored the fact that so many
England passes had gone astray, but failed to draw the plain corollary that the answer was to pick players who could pass the ball.
Storey, presumably chosen for his man-marking abilities, signally
failed to subdue the blond, elegant Karl Odermatt, who struck a spectacular equalising goal.

Yet in the next game, the European qualifier in Athens against
Greece, Ramsey surprisingly, and perhaps significantly, swung to the
other extreme, eschewing Storey, who might well have contained the
clever playmaker Dimitri Domazos, opting instead for a midfield of
the three creative players, Ball, Bell and Peters. It worked against
Greece, eventually, with Hurst's fierce left footer giving England the
lead, Chivers notching the second. Surely such tactics would be fatal
in the ensuing quarter-final against West Germany?

I remember arriving that April evening at Wembley and being
surprised and alarmed that Ramsey had chosen no ball winner against
the Germans. Moreover, he'd bewilderingly picked Bobby Moore at
centre half, a position he hadn't filled since his days in West Ham's
youth team. Only when Ron Greenwood, his manager at the time,
had switched him to defensive left half did his career take off. He
was never fast, never a great header of the ball. Alas, he had a dreadful
evening. He conceded the first of West Germany's three goals by
trying to dribble in his own penalty box, and conceded a penalty for
the third, by tripping Siggi Held.

But above all, England had no one to contain the rampant German inside left, the blond Gunter Netzer, of the size 11 boots. Throughout the game, he ran wild and free, carrying the ball in raid after raid. Ramsey had got things horribly wrong in a match which might be seen as the turning point, the watershed, of his international career. It meant that going to Berlin for the return, England had to overturn a 3–1 deficit. Ramsey didn't even try. Never before had he approached a game with such defeatism, with such a deeply untypical lack of belief. Malcolm Allison, that maverick manager and coach, told me that before the game, he spoke with an agonised Alf Ramsey, discussing possible tactics, deep into the night. The team he eventually picked was one clearly incapable of turning the tables, capable at most of saving a modicum of face.

Not to put too fine a point on it, he chose a team full of renowned hard men: Peter Storey, Norman Hunter, Mike Summerbee, a team which was never going to be much of a threat to the German defence, however defensively capable itself. And so it proved, in a sterile 0–0 draw. Ramsey, of all people, had simply lost his nerve.

Questions, not for the first time but now with special cogency, were being asked. Not least over Ramsey's failure to use Alan Mullery, a tackling midfielder par excellence, in either game against West Germany, even though Mullery had fully recovered from a pelvic injury. He was so distressed he announced that he never wanted to play for England again. And if, after defeat at Wembley, Alf had criticised his back four for being slow to push upfield, then Malcolm Allison had made that exact criticism of England's tactics in the Leon World Cup quarter-final, when, in his view, excessive use of the long ball had led directly to the second German goal. Booted carelessly out of the English defence, the ball was promptly returned, finding Uwe Seeler in an onside position, and able to head his extraordinary goal.

With the new season came the task of qualifying for the 1974 World Cup finals, hardly insurmountable, with the opposition coming from Poland and Wales, even if the Poles were much improved of late. True, another patchwork England team drew 1–1 with Yugoslavia in a Wembley friendly, thanks in no small measure to the saves of the burly young Peter Shilton, now first choice in goal. The major consolation was the ebullient form of the debutant Mike Channon of Southampton, a right-sided attacker with the pace which, he himself would observe, was essential for success at this level. His arm-whirling celebrations after he scored became well known.

England's first two World Cup qualifiers, both against Wales, were anything but reassuring. In Cardiff, a dreadful game was decided by a goal from Colin Bell. 'What are they trying to do?' demanded one disenchanted young English club manager. 'Kill off football?' But to give Ramsey his due, he was at least trying new talent and it was hardly his fault if the results were negligible. Rodney Marsh, tall, strong, a superb ball player, was one of the great maverick figures of his football generation, but on the basis of his show in Cardiff, time might have passed him by. Kevin Keegan, a self-made star but none the worse for that, failed at the first fence; but he at least would jump higher in the future. Ramsey complained that his team made chances, but failed to take them.

In January came the return match at Wembley, a still gloomier disappointment. Even Ball, so bright in Cardiff, and Bell, were incoherent in a 1–1 draw, in which Norman Hunter got another of his rare goals for England. Disappointed, the players sullenly refused to shake hands with their opponents after the game. 'Very boring, very stereotyped,' Mike England, the Welsh centre half, termed them, while Terry Yorath, a future manager of Wales, was equally scathing: 'Once they got to our box or about twenty-five yards out, they had no idea. They just knocked balls into the box.' Yet Ramsey, in another of those oddly self-destructive decisions due disastrously to be repeated in Poland, had dropped the fleet Mike Channon. If there was any kind of extenuation, perhaps it lay in the words of a First Division coach who rhetorically demanded, 'How can you play football when you've got players on the field who'd kick their own grandmother?' Wales, would be seen when they played Poland, certainly had one or two of those.

Yet how, in such circumstances, to explain the St Valentine's Day Massacre of Scotland at Hampden, even if the Scots defence was so weak, giving England's attack, with Channon and Clarke restored, such leeway? It was a strange celebration of the centenary of the Scottish Football Association, and when the teams met 'officially' in May at Hampden in the British Championship, England won only by a single goal.

Ramsey and England had every reason to be grateful to Wales for beating the Poles 2–0 in Cardiff in March 1973. The manner of their victory was quite ruthless, above all in the fearsome presence of the bearded left half, Trevor Hockey – a piratical figure in his headband, tearing into challenges which sometimes made the blood run cold. It would run hot and often when the Poles took their physical revenge in Katowice the following September. Yet Hockey could play, as well as destroy. This he showed when, winning the ball in another of his fierce tackles, he ran on to beat the big goalkeeper, England's eventual Wembley nemesis, Jan Tomaszewski. 'I don't approve of that fellow,' remarked Alf Ramsey, afterwards, 'but I'm glad he was playing.'

England's victory in the now devalued British Championship was all a mere prelude to a European tour in which the game against the Poles in Katowice loomed so large. Would Ramsey, you wondered, never learn? Yet again, against the Czechs in Prague, he risked a Ball–Bell–Peters non-tackling midfield. Enzo Bearzot, the shrewd Italian coach, came, saw and was unimpressed. 'Not one of your three midfield players is a true midfield man,' he observed. 'You badly miss Bobby Charlton. He was quality in the midst of quantity. Few players hit a long ball like he did.' (Even, one couldn't but reflect, if it simply went laterally from one side of the field to the other.) 'England's strength is that they play and run for ninety minutes. Very well, they equalised in Prague in the last minute, but a football match goes on for ninety minutes and after that, Chivers could have won the game.'

It ended 1–1, the significant irony being that despite England having three supposed playmakers in midfield, it was the Czech Kuna, who dominated that area.

So to Katowice and the moment, or the ninety minutes, of truth. Truth without Channon. Not only did Ramsey leave him out – and indeed he had been unimpressive in Prague – but he failed to bring him on when the match was slipping away from England and Channon's sheer speed might have made such a difference.

Yet you could not put all the blame on Ramsey. Once again, the matter of luck comes into the reckoning. It was debatable whether, after only eight minutes, the Poles should have been awarded a free kick out on the left. Roy McFarland, by then the England centre half, argued furiously that it was unmerited. Curiously enough, when it was taken, an inswinger, there had, as the England defenders later admitted, been too many of them in the wall, thereby causing confusion. Jan Banas, for Poland, made contact with the ball, which touched Bobby Moore and eluded Peter Shilton on its way into the goal.

Early in the second half, Martin Chivers was plainly tripped in the Polish box, though no penalty was given. So it was that the Poles doubled their lead, thanks to one of those rare but calamitously gratuitous mistakes which littered Bobby Moore's otherwise distinguished career. When McFarland played the ball back to him, instead of clearing it, he tried in a moment of hubris to beat the oncoming Polish attacker, Wlodzimierz Lubanski, their outstanding player of the moment, in a tackle. He came off worse. Lubanski won the ball, and ran on alone to beat Shilton. Yet it was to be a still more disastrous day for Lubanski; in another challenge with Moore, he was so seriously injured as to put an end to his career – one which had already had a long hiatus, caused by recklessly taking too many of the pills prescribed him.

'The second goal was a killer, wasn't it?' asked Allan Clarke, after the 2–0 defeat. 'I think it sickened all the lads.' Nor were England helped when Alan Ball foolishly got himself sent off. As for Ramsey, his response seemed manifestly to beg the question. 'I was so satisfied with the first-half display that I didn't contemplate experiments.'

Would using Channon have constituted an experiment? However, he did use him when the team flew on to Moscow, where Channon played havoc with the Soviet defence. Yet once again, Ramsey seemed all at sea with substitutions. With England 2–0 up and dominating, he took off three players, Channon among them, and a grateful Soviet team, suddenly handed the initiative, scored and all but equalised.

Next, in Turin, Italy would beat England for the first time in forty years, and their victory was comprehensive. Not once did England get a shot on goal, while Italy scored twice through Pietro Anastasi, that rarity, a Sicilian centre forward, and Fabio Capello, a future manager of renown, quite unimpressed by England. 'Your play is too predictable,' he said, then reiterating the views of Enzo Bearzot. 'In my view, you lack a player like Bobby Charlton to switch the ball about. In the crosses, you take too much time to get there and make them. You miss Cooper a lot. He was a real winger . . .' – or what, in Ramsey's tactics, passed for one.

Channon, for his part, got scant change out of the towering Italy left back, Giacinto Facchetti, himself best known for his overlapping. 'The Italians,' Channon complained, 'are the best in the world for nudging and obstructing. The big number three was always up my back. I thought he was going to come for a drink with me. The times I got to him and he nudged me! They come in and play through you, push you, obstruct you. Referees are hypnotised by them.'

Getting on to the plane for the flight home, I remarked, in all sincerity, to Ramsey that there was no one really to be blamed for the defeat. 'Blame me!' he smiled. Not this time.

Ahead loomed the decisive match at Wembley against the Poles which had to be won. They had outplayed Wales in a sanguinary encounter in Katowice, taking brutal revenge for the excesses of Hockey in Cardiff. That same night at Wembley England had a largely meaningless 7–0 win over a supine Austria, Clarke and Channon looking sharp, Chivers distracted. In the meantime, the Welsh players were being kicked and butted, though only Hockey was sent off. And though Lubanski had gone, a fast and penetrative right winger in Grzegorz Lato was clearly a new threat.

At Wembley three weeks later, England had enough of the play to have beaten Poland, but given the nature of the Polish goal, and the appalling foul by McFarland which arguably cost them another, you could scarcely say the Poles were lucky. Not least in the way England carelessly conceded a vital opening goal. Tony Currie, a blond inside forward of unquestioned talent, functioning out on the right but once again – the old, familiar story – anything but a true winger, gave the ball away to the Polish left back, Adam Musial. The cause was not yet lost, but two more errors followed. First, Norman Hunter was beaten down the flank by Lato, who had switched there. When

Lato crossed, Jan Domarski, the centre forward, was able to squeeze the ball between Shilton and his near, left-hand post; a goal surely avoidable.

Though England attacked furiously, thwarted time and again by the desperate interventions of a sometimes reckless keeper, Tomaszewski – gratuitously called 'a clown' on television by that most garrulous and confrontational of managers, Brian Clough – somehow the ball stayed out; if Tomaszewski was ever beaten, there was someone to clear on the line.

Moreover, England could well have conceded a second goal when Lato, breaking clean through, was stopped only by McFarland, shamefully, seizing and hauling him back. When a 'last defender' rule was later properly enacted, McFarland's foul would have meant an automatic expulsion. As it was, he stayed on the field and Poland had been cheated.

For all their frenzied pressure, and the fact that overall, this was arguably England's best performance in their qualifying group, their only goal came from a debatable penalty converted by Allan Clarke. Only ninety seconds were left when Ramsey, demonstrating yet again his confusion with substitutes, at last sent on the Derby County striker, Kevin Hector, who promptly hit the bar. Ramsey admitted afterwards that he had lost track of time. England drew, England were out, failing for the first time ever to reach the World Cup finals.

For Ramsey, the writing was all too luridly on the wall. Now Italy came to Wembley and beat England on their own soil for the first time, 1–0. Fabio Capello scored again, though the architect of the goal was the big Lazio centre forward Giorgio Chinaglia who once, as an impecunious Swansea Town reserve, used to steal milk bottles off doorsteps for his breakfast. He rounded Bobby Moore on the right-hand goal line like a classical winger, shot against Shilton and Capello did the rest.

'The usual English play,' said Enzo Bearzot, the *azzurri* manager. 'Sustained rhythm and big, high crosses. We have defenders who deal very effectively with these.' Franco 'The Baron' Causio, the clever outside right from picturesque Lecce in the South, agreed: 'We always know how the English play. We closed the spaces and didn't allow them the initiative. We blocked them on the wings, so they were reduced to putting over high crosses. We have the defenders to counter that. For me, they lack a man to put order into midfield. They no longer have Bobby Charlton.'

Seldom can a player have achieved such stature by his very absence. Ramsey's response was not to resign, even though his days seemed numbered. Instead he asked the Football Association to double his absurdly meagre £6,000 a year salary. There was no chance of that. The knives were out, none sharper than that wielded by the serpentine Professor Sir Harold Thompson, who had lurked in ambush for so long – ever since, it was rumoured, Ramsey had brusquely asked him not to smoke his pungent cigar in the neighbourhood of England's young players.

There was still time for Ramsey, all unaware of the gathering storm, to take a much altered team to Lisbon for a 0–0 draw with Portugal. In the absence of several regular players, he enterprisingly picked six debutants – such young talents as Trevor Brooking, the gifted and constructive West Ham inside forward, the latest product of Upton Park's so-called 'academy of football arts and sciences'; the resilient Derby County defender Colin Todd, and the accomplished Burnley right half Martin Dobson, not to mention one of the salient mavericks of his time, the supremely left-footed inside forward and inveterate gambler, Stan Bowles of Queens Park Rangers. They all showed promise, but it was too late.

Early in May, the International Committee, which he had so long despised, announced that he must go. The announcement was timed with exquisite insensitivity, when Ramsey had already announced his squad for the next seven matches, the British Championship and a European tour. If revenge was sweet, it was also deplorable.

Ramsey did not, initially at least, go out of the game. He became manager of Birmingham City, but there had been a radical sea change. Suddenly, he seemed to have lost that essential rapport with his players, the mutual trust and respect, which had been the bedrock of his success. It seemed at once significant, almost symbolic, that he should fall out even with the young, precociously gifted, initially shy attacker, Trevor Francis, but they grew bitterly at odds. When Ramsey imposed sanctions on Francis, it seemed essentially a corollary of his lost authority.

Those were sad days of anticlimax at St Andrews and they did not last long. He retired to a modest home in Ipswich on the miserable pension given him by the niggardly and vengeful FA. He had a devoted wife and a stepdaughter, but no children of his own. Once, in a moment of pure pathos, when Nigel Clarke, who 'ghosted' his articles for the *Daily Mirror*, lamented the fact that he had never really been close to his father, Ramsey suddenly exclaimed, '*I'll* be your father.' If Clarke needed a father figure, then Alf plainly wanted a son.

He had no real hinterland; football had been the warp and weft on his life, given an almost religious importance. The depths of his bitterness may be gauged from the fact that though Bobby Robson, like Alf, was a successful manager of Ipswich Town who also had his home there, Alf never sought his company and even criticised him in his column.

Perhaps it was not wholly surprising that Ramsey, in the end, should succumb to Alzheimer's. Isolated, grotesquely unrewarded, his occupation, like Othello's, gone; what had he left?

And what was his legacy? Above all, surely, the winning of the World Cup, even though it was played in England, even though there were those who felt his tactics would subvert the English game. It is hard to think that any other manager, given the men at his disposal, could have done as much. And four years later, in the utterly contrasting and infinitely less favourable conditions of Mexico, England, in slightly different circumstances, could well have gone through to the final even if there, they would probably have met their nemesis in Brazil.

And if all managerial careers in football are essentially finite, above all at international level – Vittorio Pozzo and Sepp Herberger with their twenty years each being the exceptions who proved the rule – then the ten largely productive years of Ramsey's reign seem laudable enough.

Nobby Stiles was right. They'd never have done it without Alf.

3 FIRST JOE: THEN REVIE

Don Revie 1974–77
Key Game: Italy v England, November 1976

THERE FOLLOWED WHAT WAS SOMETHING OF A HOLIDAY interlude – with the grisly exception of what happened to Kevin Keegan at Belgrade airport – an interlude in which the veteran Joe Mercer took over the England team for seven largely successful matches. A brief period in which tactical winter seemed to have turned to spring, in which the ball players and even the mavericks were allowed to flourish. It is I think legitimate to wonder what would have happened had Mercer remained in command, with his laissez-faire approach, to the exclusion of the tormented, obsessional Don Revie. If England needed a holiday from Alf Ramsey's over-functional tactics, they got it. Dressed in a lightweight suit, while the new FA Secretary, Ted Croker, once a Charlton pro, put on an England tracksuit and trained with the team, 'Uncle Joe' was geniality person-ified.

In his playing day Mercer had been an adventurous, attacking wing half with pre-war Everton ('You'd have liked me then, Brian,' he once told me), a member of the vibrant Britton–Cullis–Mercer all-Army England half-back line of wartime; from 1946, he had been a shrewd, if less ebullient, captain of Arsenal, who had helped him recover from a serious injury, whereas Everton had neglected him.

'For all the crocodile tears,' I wrote, 'the ten-pound-a-plate dinners, the truth is that Sir Alf Ramsey's going has opened the door to talent.

The very fact that Joe Mercer is a man without rigid theory gives the Channons, Brookings and Worthingtons a chance not only to be chosen but to play their own game.'

Frank Worthington might be said to have personified the new, relaxed atmosphere; a maverick's maverick, unorthodox in his ways both on and off the field, tall, elegantly left footed, strong in the air, he was the antithesis of Ramsey's ideal player, and in fact he would not last long under Don Revie's regime. First capped in May 1974 as a substitute in a meagre 1–0 win against Northern Ireland at Wembley, retained at Hampden in the 2–0 defeat by Scotland, he and the team would really come into their own when Mercer deployed the three-man attack of Channon, Worthington and Keegan against Argentina at Wembley, with Channon and Worthington scoring. It was a 2–2 draw, both Argentine goals, one a penalty, going to another, still more distinguished, left footer in the young Mario Kempes, destined four years later to become the hero of the World Cup final in Buenos Aires.

On the ensuing European tour in Leipzig, England hit the woodwork four times and had to be content with a 1–1 draw. 'An old-fashioned manager and old-fashioned posts,' said Mercer. 'You've got no bleeding chance.' Channon paid tribute to Worthington's importance. 'With a target man, it's obviously much easier. It's good if you've got somebody binding the whole team together. I wouldn't pretend to be able to do that, any more than play goal. I've always had a free role, wherever I play.'

Bulgaria were beaten 1–0 in Sofia, far more comprehensively than the score suggested, Worthington again getting the goal. Next to Belgrade, and the grim fiasco at the airport. A confused travel agent had to share the blame. Failing to take account of the fact that there was a one-hour time difference between Sofia and Belgrade, he obliged the England party to arrive one hour earlier than they were expected, which meant that there was no one from the Yugoslav Federation or the British Embassy to meet them. This was compounded by the fact that the English players had been allowed to dispense with their usual official uniforms, and dress casually. Clearly so far as the Yugoslav security personnel were concerned, a bunch of exuberant young tourists had arrived, an illusion doubtless exacerbated by the fact that one of the England players started to fool about on the luggage carousel.

Kevin Keegan meanwhile, somewhat the worse for wear after the flight, was sitting quietly apart, holding a large paper bag of purchases. A small man in a shabby brown suit suddenly accosted him and tried to wrench the bag out of his grasp. Keegan vigorously and volubly resisted, at which a huge, grey-uniformed, jackbooted policeman strode on to the scene, picked up poor Keegan at one end while the brown suited man took the other and carried him bodily out of the entrance hall. When eventually he returned, he was in tears. He had been beaten up.

Officials arrived, explanations and excuses were made and the party eventually departed for the Yugoslavia Hotel, on the banks of the Danube. On a subsequent visit to Belgrade, I was told by the British ambassador that the outrage was the product of Yugoslavia's ambiguity. In a Western democracy there would have been no area out of bounds, such as the one in which Keegan was innocently sitting. In an Iron Curtain country, no access to such an area would have been possible. As it transpired, a resilient Keegan may be said to have had the last word, scoring for England in a 2–2 draw. The Mercer 'holiday', with a record of three wins, three draws and one defeat, was over.

So, exit Mercer, enter Revie. Ultimately, to the deep disappointment of those of us who had at first welcomed his arrival. In his playing day, Revie had been an outstanding playmaker, initially as a young inside right with Leicester City, whom he had joined from junior football in his native Middlesbrough. His apogee had come in the semi-final of the 1949 FA Cup at Highbury, when his masterly display had enabled Second Division Leicester to astonish then powerful Portsmouth, on their way to the First Division title. Alas, Revie couldn't play in the final; he was fighting for his life after a dreadful blow to the nose had caused torrential bleeding.

He would rise again with Manchester City, transformed into a deeplying centre forward, splendidly pulling the strings of a gifted attack, gaining consolation for the woes of 1949 by inspiring the victory of his team in the so-called Revie Final of 1956, against Birmingham City.

Leeds United had been his last club. There he became player-manager then manager, but by now there had been a radical change in his approach to the game. He was, in fact, not the first creative player who, turning to management, had embraced a policy of blood and iron. Eventually though, under his control, Leeds would become a paragon of glittering football.

It could be argued that Revie was never cut out for the relative loneliness of international management, which has none of the intense day-to-day contacts of running a club. Even Ramsey admitted there were times he wished he was managing a team again. Revie's demons seemed to catch up with him. He was an anxious, superstitious man, given to wearing a 'lucky suit' indefinitely when Leeds United played; he gave the impression that his apparent greed – for which he would be castigated by a High Court judge – derived from a fear of one day waking up poor. Moreover, there were alarming questions about his earlier days in charge of Leeds, when he was trying to bring them out of the Second Division; questions of attempted bribery. Bob Stokoe, who won the FA Cup when manager of Sunderland and a former centre half for neighbouring Newcastle United, once publicly declared that Revie had tried to bribe him to fix a game.

Revie, moreover, was exceptionally vulnerable to criticism, thin skinned, hyper-sensitive, to a degree. As England manager, he used a ghosted newspaper column to respond to his detractors. I was astonished when he agreed, certainly not at my behest, to debate with me on the BBC's Saturday evening radio programme, *Sports Report*. I told him of my surprise. 'You,' I told him, 'are *the* manager of *the* England team. I am *a* journalist working for *a* newspaper.' Subsequently, he asked Barry Davies, the BBC television football commentator, what he had thought of the exchange, to which Barry replied, 'I assume the return will be at Elland Road.'

At Leeds, Revie's players were devoted to him. When the abrasive Brian Clough, a bitter critic of the team and its methods, surprisingly, even suicidally, took over the club when Revie left, he met extreme hostility from the players and lasted a turbulent forty-four days. Yet as England boss Revie never remotely matched the splendid football Leeds played at their best, with Billy Bremner and Johnny Giles the creative hub of their midfield, Jackie Charlton commanding the defence, and the gifted Scottish wingers, Peter Lorimer and Eddie Gray.

Revie was hardly given an easy initiation. The very first game would be a European Championship qualifier at Wembley, against what seemed a promising young Czech team. Despite the impressive form shown by Joe Mercer's England on their Continental tour, Revie had cautiously announced that it would take three years to build the team he wanted. In the match programme, he exhorted the crowd to sing 'Land of Hope and Glory', only to hear them singing, with deep feeling, as the match went on, 'All we are saying is, give us a goal!'

In the end, they were given three, when the young Czech team manifestly tired in the closing minutes, but I wrote: 'It might prove something of a Pyrrhic victory if we place too much emphasis on the goals, and not enough on the wasteland of football that went before.' So much of the approach play seemed as archaic as 'Land of Hope and Glory'. There was some consolation in the bright debut of Queens Park Rangers' Dave Thomas as substitute, that rare species, a true winger, who showed great pace, skill and enterprise. As against that, there was no Frank Worthington, no true centre forward as a valid point of reference. With Total Football, as practised by the Dutch and West Germans, very much the new reality, Mercer's England had come closer to it than Revie's, whose full backs, Emlyn Hughes and Paul Madeley, simply trundled down the flanks and booted in high crosses. Keegan, warmly praised by Revie and a success on the tour despite his Belgrade vicissitudes, ran and ran but accomplished little.

By the end of the season, it was hard to make a valid judgement on Revie's stewardship. True, Wembley had seen two five-goal performances, but the first, all five being scored by Malcolm Macdonald, left-footed idol of Newcastle, had been against lowly Cyprus, the second against a Scottish team whose star-crossed keeper, Stewart Kennedy, had given away three embarrassing goals. Shades perhaps of poor, disastrous Frank Haffey who had let in nine at Wembley in 1961. Scottish keepers were figures of fun.

Moreover, for much of the European Championship qualifier

against Cyprus, they alarmingly showed up the limitations of an un-inventive, unimaginative England team, which laboured to get its five goals. Moreover, one divined a very worrying change in the behaviour of the crowd. Jeering the visitors' national anthem, it is true, had by then become almost a ritual. But there was a time when underdogs were treated with a modicum of sympathy. Not now. When a Cypriot player went down injured, not least when a brave keeper in Makis Alkiviadis was painfully fouled by Kevin Beattie, uneasy in the unfamiliar role of left back, supporters whistled and jeered. And from the banking behind each goal came endless choruses of, 'Shit, shit!'

Much exaggerated praise greeted a 2–0 victory in March in a friendly at Wembley against a West German team which seemed indifferently committed. In particular, Chelsea's skilful young inside right Alan Hudson was eulogised, yet Helmut Schoen, the German manager, in his courteous way, brought matters into perspective. When an eager English journalist gushingly asked him if he thought that the 1974 World Cup finals would have turned out differently, had this England team been involved, he replied that while he didn't want to drop water in the wine, this was not the best international ever played at Wembley.

In Limassol, on an appalling pitch, England had some excuse for beating Cyprus only 1–0, with a goal by Kevin Keegan, but the display was mediocre, the match a protracted bore. Trevor Brooking, however disappointing he may have been in that drawn game against the Portuguese, surely had claims to be reconsidered, and the Czechs' 5–0 win against that Portuguese team which, in England's second European qualifier, had held them grimly and goallessly at Wembley, was an ominous portent.

One of the rare consolations was the dominant form of the centre backs, Dave Watson of Sunderland and Colin Todd of Derby County, a proper successor in the role of Bobby Moore. But the team had been endlessly chopped and changed. 'The best one can say of this commonplace England side,' I wrote, after a dreary goalless draw in Belfast – England's first visit there for four troubled years – is that they have still, under the leadership of Don Revie, not given away a goal. A negative recommendation for what is, let it be reluctantly admitted, a thoroughly negative team.'

Four days later at Wembley, the Welsh scored twice, and only a dynamic appearance as substitute of Aston Villa's Brian Little, never to be capped again, spared England's blushes. There was, though, the consolation of seeing David Johnson, a far more fluent centre forward than Macdonald, scoring twice on his debut, with another to come against the Scots. Two more were scored that day by Gerry Francis, a strong and intelligent inside right with an unusual tactical grasp of the game, destined to become the England captain.

The following October, in Bratislava, bleak reality intervened. The Czechs, well beaten there on Ramsey's first tour in 1963, were met twice. The first game was fogged off, the second was disastrous, a defeat which starkly exposed Revie's deficiencies at international level. It was the watershed, arguably the point of no return.

It was preceded by a dire friendly against Switzerland in Basel, won 2–1, the goal given away by a shocking error from Ray Clemence, strangely erratic in goal. One of those three men all 'creative', non-tackling mid-fields didn't work. It was weird to hear both Revie and Gerry Francis, now made captain on only his fifth appearance, insist on how hard it was to mark two attackers with a four-man defence. The prolix theory seeming to be that with the full backs out on the flanks marking wingers, the two in the middle became vulnerable. Well, if none of the midfielders was a ball winner, perhaps that was so. 'Ray lost it in the lights,' said Revie, attempting to exonerate Clemence, who was honest enough to insist that there was 'no excuse'.

Fluent Daniel Dupeux, the talented Swiss attacker, was indulgent about England's display. 'They no longer play like the English did,' he said, 'with long centres; they play more on the ground. It is diffi-cult to judge them on this game, because after five minutes the game was won. We haven't seen the real England team. When you were winning 2–0, you eased up. The Swiss played better as the game went on, because we are beginning to find ourselves now. But there are fewer personalities in the England team than there were four years ago like Bobby Moore. It lacks a *patron*.'

Under Revie, England now travelled with a bloated entourage that was, as I wrote, 'so heavy with acolytes, functionaries and super-numeraries that you fully expected to find Mother Courage in her cart bringing up the rear'. Plainly this would be the moment of truth for Revie, who had been in power for a year without remotely producing a good team. Could his supposed 'luck' carry him and England through? There was certainly the luck that the Czechs had abruptly run into a dip in form, held at home by the Swiss and the Hungarians. Alas, he was destined to emerge from the fixture almost as a figure of fun, the last thing you would have expected when he was appointed on the basis of his formidable years at Leeds. This because, cloistered in a hotel far from Bratislava itself, far from any hint of intrusion, he burdened his players with dossiers on the opposition, heavily detailed, and encouraged them to play . . . carpet bowls. Later, *qui s'excuse s'accuse*, he would publicly defend himself from ridicule – most players were known to have used the dossier pages to record their card game scores – and insisted in a newspaper interview that the dossiers enabled the players 'to do more work on the training field'.

Singling me out for counter-criticism, he defended his policy of a 4–3–3 formation in which Kevin Keegan, essentially an attacker, was used in central midfield, by recalling that I had criticised Alf Ramsey for his defensive tactics. Which simply begged the central question: that deploying Keegan in that role led to a fragile midfield. 'I thought he did it very well,' he said, 'because we did not give them space to play.' In fact, supposedly marked by Keegan, the Czech midfielder Jaraslav Pollak had the freedom of the park. It transpired, bizarrely, that Revie's whole tactical policy had been based on the fact that Anton Ondrus, the giant Czech centre back, was wont to drop back to receive the ball short from his keeper at goal kicks.

The choice of the Queens Park Rangers left back, Ian Gillard, who had failed on his previous game for England, seemed the more perverse in that David Nish of Derby County had recently mastered the clever Czech right winger, Marian Masny, in a European club game. Sure enough, it was Pollak's fine crossfield ball to Masny which set up the winning goal. England had gone ahead with a dazzling goal of their own by Mike Channon, but that was about the sum of their effective efforts. By contrast, the first Czech goal was the product of a fiasco in defence, at a corner.

So to keep the Czechs at bay England urgently needed to win their return match in Portugal, and it was no great surprise when they failed to do so, drawing 1–1. A miss by Macdonald which I described as a cameo of clumsiness cost his team dear and once more illustrated that notwithstanding his five goals against Cyprus and the many he scored at club level, he would never be an international centre forward. I argued at the time that it would have been far more sensible to take a brilliant maverick such as Arsenal's Charlie George to Lisbon. But as we shall see, when George, powerfully built, an exceptional ball player and passer, strong in the air, was at last picked, it would come to a bitter and premature end. An end, indeed, of an international career which had barely begun. Revie's 'luck', which he had publicly pleaded was a fiction, hardly ran here: Keegan had what looked a good goal annulled for offside, a resilient Colin Todd was blatantly fouled before an inept Austrian referee gave the free kick from which Rui Rodrigues scored a spectacular goal. That Trevor Brooking, who had made his England debut here eighteen months before, should, belatedly recalled, play with such finesse and authority left a bittersweet taste, given his long and illogical exclusion.

'Patience' was now the word Revie used like a mantra, but if patience might at last exclude the long-ball tactics traditionally the curse of the English game, it could hardly be an end in itself. It was hard to resist the conclusion that a year had been largely wasted. Futile for Revie to complain that the Football League was full of speed rather than skill when he stubbornly continued to pick players who had failed, thus spurning the chance to try those who might play better. His complaints that the team simply hadn't had enough time together might have been more germane had he succeeded, over the previous fifteen months, in getting and keeping together a better conceived and more impressive squad. Alone in his Lancaster Gate office, he had far too much time to make mistakes.

Revie did pick Charlie George in his squad for the Welsh centenary match in Wrexham in March, only for George to cry off, injured. Thereafter, he would have to wait until the following season for his one ill-starred chance, though in fairness to Revie it must be said that

George's abundant talents were too often overshadowed by an explosive temperament.

At the end of the season England then went off on a short tour of the USA, losing 1–0 to Brazil in Los Angeles, with a display light years ahead of the previous mediocrity. With Trevor Brooking returning from injury to shine, and his fellow Londoner Gerry Francis complementing him vigorously in midfield, defeat by Roberto's very late goal was hardly fair to a team which had suddenly blossomed.

Encouraging too was the 3–2 victory over the Italians, due now to play England in the imminent World Cup qualifying tournament. At Yankee Stadium, New York, where the sandy midfield constituted a notable hazard, an England team full of untried talent rebounded from a half time 2–0 deficit to win 3–2. England's second-half performance simply swept the previously superior Italians aside and seemed to furnish a glittering portent for the World Cup games to come. Mike Channon, scorer of two fine goals, was aflame, young Ray Wilkins of Chelsea as inventive in midfield as Trevor Brooking. Had Revie got it right at last?

An easy 3–1 win against so-called Team America in Philadelphia, even though it included Pele and Chinaglia (no caps awarded), wound up the tournament and the tour on a sudden and unexpected note of high optimism. This mood was sustained when, in June, England travelled to Helsinki for their first World Cup qualifier and brushed the Finns aside 4–1, with a couple of goals from Keegan.

Gerry Francis, England's young captain, who played in the first and last matches, was exuberant: 'I'm never frightened of playing against Brazil if you ignore the myth that people have given them over the years, and I think we went a long way to stuffing that myth, and to showing that British football is one of the best in the world. The Brazilians play in this sunny climate all the year round, and it must help their ball control, and obviously they must have a lot more touches than we have, but we've got as many skilful players, and I think tactically we're a lot better than the Brazilians in every way. The only way you're going to beat the South Americans in South America is to play them at their own game. I don't think you can go out there with your typical long-ball game.'

Hopes then were high for the World Cup qualifiers, after the American expedition and the Finnish success; had Italy, after all, not been beaten by an England team made up largely of reserves? But Italy when the chips were down, Italy when it mattered, Italy no longer under the forty-year Indian sign, would prove a different and more dangerous proposition. Their preparation for the incipient first meeting in Rome was meticulous to a degree. Time and time again their dedicated, able, engaging manager, Enzo Bearzot – destined in time to win the World Cup himself – would come to England to run the rule over leading players, accompanied always, like Sancho Panza to his Don Quixote, by the little Calabrian ex-football agent, Gigi Peronace.

Gigi, whom I had known for so many years, had at last found himself a role worthy of his ambitions. He was not merely interpreter to Bearzot, who never spoke a word of English, not merely his ever-present amanuensis – clinging to Enzo like grim death to a knobstick – he would ultimately be designated as General Manager to the Italian team. Rising from obscurity in the deep South of Italy, initially, thanks to his knowledge of English organising fixtures with the occupying British troops in the war, he'd gone to Turin to study engineering, becoming interpreter to two British managers of Juventus, first Willie Chalmers, then Jesse Carver: the man to whom Stanley Rous, in my presence, had offered the England job.

As an agent, his great coup had been to bring John Charles – celebrated in Turin as King John, the Gentle Giant – to Juventus. Settling in England, he had persuaded a naive bank manager to lend him fortunes, building a marble staircase in his Twickenham home, only in 1980 to die virtually bankrupt in Bearzot's arms from a huge heart attack in a Roman hotel just before the *azzurri* set out to play in Uruguay.

It was Benjamin Disraeli who opined that 'the defects of great men are the consolation of dunces', and even Bearzot could get things wrong. As assistant coach to the *azzurri* in the West German World Cup of 1974 he'd been sent to scout the Argentina team before they met Italy. He came back declaring that little Rene Houseman, the clever Argentine left winger, was a midfielder. So Italy marked him with their own genuine midfielder, Fabio Capello who, being no kind of defender, was run ragged till the Italians realised their mistake and relieved Capello from his torment as an unwilling right back.

Where Bearzot excelled was in what he called 'disintoxicating' his players, purging them of the pains and pressures of the ever-oppressive and demanding Italian *campionato*. Yet like Pozzo before him, he could be curiously ambivalent about ruthless players. Pozzo had Luisito Monti, Bearzot had Claudio Gentile and Romeo Benetti. An honest and well-educated man, like Pozzo, a classical student, originally with plans to become a doctor, Bearzot, so far as his hard men were concerned, would become curiously unaware. Even in New York, in a match of no ultimate consequence, the Italians had lost their heads near the end. Notably and surprisingly Giacinto Facchetti, the towering, overlapping, left back, when denied a goal threw punches at the England full backs, Dave Clement and Mick Mills, who admirably kept their composure.

Alas, it was back to bleak reality when in September England were embarrassingly shown up by a far more inventive Republic of Ireland team. True, four first choices were absent, Channon and his pace particularly missed, but that hardly explained another of Trevor Brooking's strangely opaque, if rare, exhibitions. As for Charlie George the truth is that, whatever his subsequent spleen, on the night he was tried and found wanting. George, I wrote, 'was neither fish nor fowl, neither striker nor creator, presumably he expected to be the first, but lacked the pace and the appetite required for it at the highest level'.

George himself saw things very differently. He was essentially the victim, set up for a fall. At the team's hotel, he was surprised and sceptical when 'we played bingo that night . . . The whole thing was rather weird, like forced entertainment for adults . . . It was better than carpet bowls to be fair, but can you imagine Michael Owen and the other punters in the England team being ecstatic playing bingo?' Much worse was to come, when Revie told him he wanted him to play behind the front line, rather than as a striker, where he had been operating for Derby County. And at half time, to his outrage, he was ordered by Revie to play on the left flank. 'What?' exclaimed George.

'I'm not a left winger.' He made his disagreement clear, and when he saw Gordon Hill, who was indeed an authentic left winger, warming up on the touchline, he knew his hour had struck. As he left the field, duly substituted by Hill, and Revie tried to shake hands with him, George shouted at him, 'Go fuck yourself!' For all that, as George remembered, 'he had me in the squad again once, or was it twice?' But that first cap was the last. As for that match, it was a 1–1 draw in which Ireland looked far better than England.

England's tactics that evening were to use a sweeper behind man-to-man markers, a system then foreign to the English game. Yet eventually, versus Finland, the tactics modulated into 4–2–4, with the four at the front – surely by then a long outdated strategy – restricting space and surprise, rather than creating it. This was exacerbated by the choice of two full-backs unused to the position, who kept galloping wildly into the maelstrom. The injured Gerry Francis was severely missed, as he was destined to be in Rome; another loss was the sturdy Stuart Pearson at centre forward. Too great a midfield burden was placed on the inexperienced Ray Wilkins. Rome, looming on the horizon, did not seem quite a lost cause. Beating Luxembourg 4–1 in their group game, Italy hardly seemed invincible. Yet but for an appalling foul by Clemence on an encroaching Finnish forward, for which he certainly deserved to be expelled, things could well have been worse than the tight 2–1 victory.

And so to Rome, with the experiment of using that slender 'fantasist' Stan Bowles, tried without success in 1974, as the central striker in a trio which would be man-marked out of the game. Bowles, unimpressed by the Italian team, had minimal chances of fitting into an England side whose pack had yet again been reshuffled by Revie; though he couldn't be blamed for a number of significant absences, not least that of Gerry Francis. Trevor Brooking, the one incontestable success in the England team, could hardly prevail on his own.

Bearzot, who, ironically, was hoping to wean away his Italian team from the sweeper defence and man-to-man marking, observed that it was precisely this close marking which rendered the English trio ineffective; that a ball player can show what he can do with the ball only when he is given time to get it under control; that had Keegan been playing for Italy, he would have shone. As indeed, he would the following year in the same Olympic Stadium, making light of the close marking of Berti Vogts, inspiring Liverpool's victory in the European Cup final against Borussia Moenchengladbach.

The effervescent Franco 'The Baron' Causio was behind both Italian goals. The first, by Giancarlo Antognoni in the opening half, was helped by a large deflection. The second was expertly taken by the elegant Roberto Bettega, exploiting momentary hesitation and confusion in the England defence. Dave Clement, the right back, said afterwards that he had moved out to cover Romeo Benetti and assumed he would be covered in his turn. In a radio interview just after the game, in which he, Francesco Graziani, the centre forward, and I took part, Bettega remarked, 'There is a tendency among British defenders to say, "That's your man, not mine."'

That afternoon, Italy's man-markers, Marco Tardelli, Antonello Cuccureddu and Claudio Gentile looked impregnable. Yet against England's reserve players in New York, Italy's defence had looked anything but; nor would it again, when the following month the *azzurri* were beaten in Portugal. Nor, for that matter, when they came to Wembley twelve months later, for the return.

In England, and in Italy too, a great debate about man-marking ensued. George Best, most elusive of forwards, told me that 'man-to-man marking could be beaten when your men have got more ability than the men who are marking them, and as far as the England team are concerned, they haven't got more ability. Can you imagine a manager sending his team out to mark the great Real Madrid side man-to-man?' In a similar vein, Rodney Marsh, a notable maverick and one who never quite made the leap from club to international football, praised the Dutch method of retreating into midfield, luring the man-markers to pursue them, and thus creating space behind them to be exploited.

Nils Liedholm, then Roma's manager, previously a famed Swedish international, observed – as a coach bringing zonal defence into the Italian game – that whatever its advantages up to the penalty box, therein the marking had to be absolutely rigorous. 'In the past,' he pursued, 'there were great dribblers like Matthews and Finney who put the Italian defenders in difficulty. But there seems to be a lack of quality among the players.'

In February 1977, Holland came to Wembley and took England apart. A 2–0 defeat was made all the more embarrassing by the fact that modest Northern Ireland, the previous November, had played the Dutch in Rotterdam and forced a 2–2 draw. 'Don Revie,' I wrote, 'has now had charge of the England team for two-and-a-half years, and look at it! It has no pattern, no apparent tactical purpose, no consistency in personnel.' Enzo Bearzot, in London to watch the game, ever diligent, ever shadowed by Peronace, asked sadly why was it that an English team no longer came out and played like an English team, throwing away instead the old weapons of aggression, in the best sense, and commitment? Yet in no way was he taking Italy's qualification for granted. Any team that plays England, he observed, whatever its technical superiority, was liable to be overwhelmed if it, too, were not superbly fit.

Brooking, so strangely inconsistent at this point in his notable career, was badly off the boil again. By comparison with the graceful Dutch, the England players looked ponderous, reminiscent of Liedholm's view that they needed more callisthenics in their training. Revie himself had averred that the revolution necessary to improve the English game could take fifteen years. It seemed that his own harsh and parsimonious Leeds teams, whatever the quality of their key players, had hardly pointed the way to better things, though at least they were effective. Walter Winterbottom had, for better or for worse, spent sixteen years in office, and never missed a World Cup. Were Revie to stay for another fifteen, I doubt he would have made much difference.

Yet was British football really bankrupt? On the very spring evening that England's 5–0 World Cup qualifying win against little Luxembourg was wondrously achieved at Wembley, a depleted Wales thrashed the Czechs, the European champions, while Eire beat France; both winning teams composed of Football League players. 'Revie's endless frenetic fiddling with the mechanism of his ever-changing England team,' I complained, 'evokes nothing so much as the apocryphal words of President Eisenhower to his egregious Secretary of State, John Foster Dulles: "Don't just say something, stand there!"'

The South American tour of June 1977 which followed an abject defeat at Wembley to the Scots, would, in retrospect, be remembered less for the three somewhat illusory results against famous rivals but for the deceitful machinations of Don Revie. Declaring that he had another match to watch, he missed the initial fixture in Rio against Brazil, leaving his assistant, the former Leeds United trainer, Les Cocker, in charge. Instead, he flew to Dubai, surreptitiously to agree a £350,000-a-year contract with the team of the United Arab Emirates.

England drew all three games in Brazil, Argentina and Uruguay. It was the first time an England team had avoided defeat in Rio, and was gained in spite of the dreadful pitch at the huge Maracana Stadium, and sapping humidity. As the twenty-year-old Ray Wilkins, then at the bright dawn of a career which would taper off in sterility, complained, 'In the first half, the grass took it out of your legs. In the second half, the sweat was pouring into your eyes.' Kevin Keegan, mysteriously deployed in midfield, despite his recent triumph against Borussia Moenchengladbach in the European Cup final, shone in the first half, but admitted that he was so exhausted in the last half hour, he might just as well have left the field. A goalless draw was a decent enough achievement. England might, indeed, have won had they exploited several good chances in the first half. Cocker, to his credit, created a relaxed and positive atmosphere.

Revie returned, and the team flew on to Buenos Aires and drew 1–1 with Argentina, Stuart Pearson, so off song at Wembley, now back in predatory form, snapping up the English goal. Disgracefully, Trevor Cherry, most convincing at left back, was expelled together with the Argentine scorer, Daniel Bertoni, who'd punched him in the mouth.

Long haired, chain smoking Cesar Luis ('El Flaco', The Thin One) Menotti, Argentina's manager, who insisted he was trying to wean his teams away from violence, was disappointed by England. In his office, he told me, 'They surprised me. I thought they would exploit the attacking potential of the team. But when I saw them play in Rio, I just saw them looking for a result. The level of English football in general is so much higher than that of the England team that I was surprised. I saw Keegan, on television, play against Borussia, and he was another player. He was everywhere. Over here, he was a half back. It was a sad team. It was a team with no joy in playing.'

It was Revie's team. A dull, goalless draw in Montevideo against Uruguay completed the tour. Bearzot was there, of course, as he had been in Buenos Aires. 'England seemed shocked by their two home defeats [against Holland and Scotland],' he said. 'They played like they did in Rome, a containing game. Yet in games which didn't count.' He added diplomatically, 'Italy haven't got their ticket for Argentina yet, though. Football is full of surprises, even if we now have the better chance.' But by the time it came to Wembley and the return game, it would all be academic.

Having defected, Revie genially remarked that were he to have had another chance in charge, he would have built 'a real bastard of a team', which was what many people thought he had done at Leeds. An outraged Professor Sir Harold Thompson, by then FA Chairman, impulsively acted as both judge and jury by implementing a ten-year ban on him for bringing the game into disrepute.

Thus it was that in early December 1979, Revie sued the FA in the High Court for the rest of his money. Dracula, I wrote at the time, meets the Wolfman. 'A plague on both their houses, one has felt, sitting in court, regarding now the tight-mouthed, haggard uneasiness of Don Revie, now the endless compulsive swapping of spectacles by Sir Harold Thompson, as he waffled in the witness box.' The judge was Mr Justice Cantley, fresh from his controversial handling of the trial of Jeremy Thorpe. In the present case, Cantley was more rational. He damned Revie as greedy and dishonest, but ruled in his favour, as Thompson had abused his powers. The belated end of a horrid affair.

4 UNDER THE GREENWOOD TREE

Ron Greenwood 1977–82
Key Game: Spain v England, July 1982

WITH REVIE GONE, HAROLD THOMPSON SEARCHED FOR AN antidote, and the chosen antidote would be Ron Greenwood. Thompson, the *faute de mieux* kingmaker, picked him with idealism rather than objectivity. After the subterfuge and greed of Revie's going, Thompson wanted a manager who would be a symbol of probity. It seemed plain enough that he chose Greenwood less because he had for many years been the inspiration of West Ham United's admired 'academy of football arts and sciences' than because he had known him previously as the coach to the Oxford University football team over which he himself autocratically presided. The problem was, as would soon become clear, that Greenwood by then was no longer the coach he had been, but a man deeply disillusioned by what he perceived had happened to the game, and to himself; ultimately kicked upstairs by West Ham, and driven into an unhappy retirement.

It was, indeed, arguable that Greenwood did far more to help England's cause, to bring about their victory in the 1966 World Cup before he was manager, by the fact that at Upton Park he nurtured and encouraged three crucial members of that England team – Bobby Moore, Geoff Hurst and Martin Peters. Moore and Hurst, as we know, were converted by Greenwood from their original roles into roles far better suited to them, Moore emerging as the most dominant of 'second' centre backs, Hurst, once a mediocre wing half, into a resilient striker.

It was all too significant and symbolic that when Greenwood chose his first team to play Switzerland at Wembley in September 1977, he astonishingly omitted a player who at West Ham had been his cherished protégé, Trevor Brooking. Instead, in a team replete with seven Liverpool players, he preferred Ian Callaghan, once a right winger discarded in the 1966 World Cup by Alf Ramsey, now an industrious but uninspired central midfielder, with none of Brooking's constructive flair.

Predictably, it was a team that floundered, a team without illumination, giving some justification to Greenwood's initial appointment being on only a temporary basis. Wembley, it might be said, had bulked large in his football life from a very early age. Growing up poor in Burnley, he and his family had come down before the war to London, where on leaving school he found himself working on the scoreboard at the Empire Stadium. A talented footballer, he would soon be signed by Chelsea, a club to which he was destined to return many years later, actually winning a Championship medal in 1955, making 21 of the 42 appearances at centre half.

Initially a precocious eight-year-old inside left, he served during the war in the Royal Air Force, and afterwards was transferred for a substantial fee to Bradford Park Avenue; doomed, alas, to virtual extinction as a professional club. From Bradford, he moved first to Brentford then, after over 300 games, successfully to Chelsea, helping them to win their first, and for many years to come, their only Championship, seeing out his career with nearby Fulham. Successfully coaching the amateur Eastbourne club, he became an innovative coach at Arsenal, his novel methods very popular with the players, till he moved to Upton Park. 'The crowds at West Ham,' he once remarked, 'haven't been rewarded by results, but they keep turning up because of the good football they see. Other clubs will suffer from the old bugbear that results count more than anything. This has been the ruination of English soccer.'

It would have been impossible then – and it was the very year in which he was appointed to the England job – to conceive not only that he would exclude Trevor Brooking but that later, when Glenn Hoddle made a superb debut for England against Bulgaria at

Wembley, capping it with a spectacular goal, Greenwood would drop him from the next match with the bizarre words, 'Disappointment is part of football.' Here was a man who, alas, appeared to have lost the courage of his convictions.

The selection of a Liverpool bloc, I suggested before the game, was unlikely to work, not least as it was without the services of Steve Heighway, an Irish international and an essential complement to Kevin Keegan. And work it didn't, turning out, I reflected, 'still more depressing and disastrous than it had seemed in prospect'. Callaghan in the event won the praise of the ever-present Enzo Bearzot who thought the now 35-year-old was 'a great success, he kept the midfield nice and solid, he got everyone into the game'. But he was surprised that Greenwood hadn't gone the whole hog – or much of it – by omitting Jimmy Case, a major factor in the Liverpool midfield.

Switzerland, the opposition, forced that depressingly familiar goalless draw, and while they were fresh were vastly superior in technique and imagination, not least in the person of the much maltreated René Botteron, a thorn in England's side in the past. England, by comparison with the Swiss, simply looked clumsy, their three-man midfield – where the addition of Case might have helped – lacking pace and flair. Ray Wilkins, who had shown such promise on the South American tour, did not appear until the last ten minutes. As to the defence, Greenwood himself was obliged to confess that on a couple of occasions, players were going for the same opponent. *Catenaccio*, invented in Switzerland when the Austrian Karl Rappan ran the national team, not only served them well in defence but gave the full backs more space to attack. There was cold comfort in Bearzot's parting remark that all England now needed was 'a couple of outstanding players'. But who?

The following month, still without Brooking, England gained their predictable win in Luxembourg, but only by 2–0. Three days later the Italians thrashed Finland 6–1 in Turin, with four goals by Roberto Bettega, a result that certainly helped their goal difference in this tight qualifying group. Bettega, not long since a sufferer from tuberculosis, was inspired, headed three of his goals and sent another header against the post. Yet Bearzot, who made his centre forward 'Ciccio' Graziani his key man, was still not fully satisfied. 'We still don't know how to rest while we're playing, like the Dutch,' he complained. 'We run more in the international team than in club football. The Dutch possession football is the way to play when you are tired.'

England, without an injured Keegan and Brooking, scored in Luxembourg through Ray Kennedy, the big Liverpool midfielder, once an Arsenal striker, and Paul Mariner, the Ipswich Town centre forward, a newcomer never destined quite to establish and assert himself in the England team.

So to November and the impossible dream, for victory over Italy would still leave the *azzurri* with a final match in Rome, against Luxembourg. Greenwood at last took his courage in both hands and selected a team more in tune with his own true predilections. There would be Keegan. There would be Bròoking. Above all, there would be two genuine young wingers: little, tireless Steve Coppell of Manchester United, an economics graduate, on the right; blond, sinuous Peter Barnes of Manchester City, on the left.

Trevor Brooking belatedly returned. The bizarre obsession with Liverpool players was at an end, though Phil Neal would keep his place at right back and, following a disastrous afternoon against Leighton James, the Queens Park Rangers and Wales outside left, put in a performance of cool aplomb. Kevin Keegan, lately so disappointing, would be at his devastating best, helped perhaps by another of Bearzot's rare mistakes – having him marked by Renato Zaccarelli, essentially a midfielder rather than a defender. Another of Bearzot's mistakes would be to keep 'Ciccio' Graziani, vital to the efficiency of the attack, after he had cut his head and was clearly groggy, far too long on the field.

Brooking had a splendid match. Marco Tardelli, very much a marker and a ruthless one at that, did better when switched to mark Keegan. Romeo Benetti was lucky not to be expelled. Claudio Gentile scythed Barnes to the ground and snarled at him, 'English pig!' But Barnes, despite his obvious inexperience, did well enough, as did the Zagallo-like Coppell, till he inevitably tired. The one gamble which did not succeed was that of giving the big Birmingham centre forward Bob Latchford his debut. He was out of his depth and eventually gave way to the more effective Stuart Pearson. Dave Watson was a dominant centre half and provoked a glorious save from Dino Zoff.

The man-to-man marking which had suppressed England in Rome was now ineffectual, while another of those three-man midfields without a tackler this time posed no problems, such was the dominance of the England team. Even if the shrewd little former Inter manager and Italy outside right, Annibale Frossi, may have had a point when he averred that England's tactics had been hand-to-mouth. He also questioned the commitment of some of the Italian players.

But England won with two excellent goals, Keegan in the first half, Brooking in the second and the victory was inspiriting, bringing the two nations level on goal difference. As it transpired, Italy would win 3–0 in Rome against little Luxembourg, finishing level on ten points with England, but with a goal total of 18–4 to England's 15–4. The painful truth was that as in 1974, England had fallen on the road to the World Cup finals. Still, at long last there was cause for English optimism. Revie's barren years, Greenwood's dull beginning, could be consigned to the memory hole.

There was a hiatus till the following February, when a friendly against world champions West Germany in Munich, though lost on a contentious free-kick goal by Rainer Bonhof, was cause for renewed optimism. More fool Charlie George to reject, self-defeatingly, an olive branch from Ron Greenwood. 'A beautiful defeat,' said the smiling Enzo Bearzot. 'To say that the English lost unjustly,' pursued Bearzot, 'is the best compliment you can pay to Greenwood.' Ron was once again blessedly following his own instincts.

It was a game which showed us, to paraphrase Mark Twain, that the reports of the death of English football had been greatly exaggerated. It showed that Greenwood's new regime had brought optimism and good humour into an ambience soured by the fear-ridden attitudes of Don Revie. And, while the fact that Wales had drawn in Germany in December put England's performance into some perspective, it was clear that the balance of power in European football was delicate. Above all, perhaps, it showed that it's players and not tactics who make teams.

The idea that West German football had everything right and thus bestrode the world game was gainsaid not only by what happened in Munich and what Wales achieved but by the victory of England's B team in Augsburg on the previous day. However solid the foundations of the West German game, however positive manager Helmut Schoen's policy of encouraging artistry and skill, success was still something to be prayed for. With Franz Beckenbauer turning his back on German football for a contract with the Cosmos in New York, with no post-Gerd Muller centre forward available for the Munich game, West Germany were diminished.

Not that England, though they led at half time by Stuart Pearson's well-taken goal, looked incisive enough to win. Bearzot called Ray Wilkins, in transcendent form, and the flying Peter Barnes 'the true protagonists of the game', with Kevin Keegan also on song, but there was clearly still progress to be made. Coppell again did his Stakhanovite duty on the right flank, but wondered afterwards, cogently, whether he might thus have sacrificed his contribution to the attack. A 2–1 defeat was somewhat cruel.

Results for the rest of that season continued to be satisfactory. Greenwood had blessedly seen no need to build 'a real bastard of a team'.

In April, Brazil under manager Claudio Coutinho, essentially a physical education man, came to Wembley in front of 92,000 and thoroughly disgraced themselves. The feeble Dutch referee, Charles Corver, who would plunge the depths of craven ineptitude at the World Cup semi-final of 1982 when he allowed Germany's vicious keeper, Toni Schumacher, to stay on the field after a brutal assault on France's Patrick Battiston, was pitifully flaccid. He should have sent off both Edinho and Ze Maria for appalling, recidivist fouls. Brazil, wasting the gifted Cerezo so deep in defence, had a handful of dazzling moments, not least when their right winger, Gil, accelerated, pivoted and scored. But overall, they were a rancid team. It was England, supposedly Brazil's inferiors in flair and finesse, who provided the grace notes of the game, especially Kevin Keegan – their scorer – in midfield with Tony Currie of Leeds United: an abundantly gifted playmaker, who never quite fulfilled his international promise.

Results for the rest of that season continued to be satisfactory, with wins in all three home internationals and a 4–1 dismissal of Hungary. Greenwood had blessedly seen no need to build 'a real bastard of a team'.

Yet football is eternally and ineluctably fickle. Come the following September and England's debut in Copenhagen versus Denmark in the European Championship qualifying competition, you wondered if it had all been too good to be true. There, two ludicrous defences surpassed one another in fiasco. The marking of the English defenders was often non-existent. Only Keegan, Brooking and Ray Clemence, so often exposed in the English goal, gave satisfactory shows. Ron Greenwood's vulnerable 4–2–4 formation ultimately lay in tatters, embarrassingly seen for what it was. A 4–3 victory was something to be appreciated, given the points it brought, but in every other way the match was a disaster.

Greenwood came away from the ensuing European game, drawn 1–1 in Dublin, whistling merrily, one felt, to keep his spirits up. Yes, the defence this time had given away one goal rather than three, but never at any time, gambling again with a midfield that had no ball winner, did they remotely subdue the most influential player on the pitch, Arsenal's gifted left-footed playmaker, Liam Brady. Johnny Giles, the Irish manager, in his prime such a tough and influential inside forward himself, observed when quizzed on the subject, 'England were playing a 4–2–4 with the wingers wide. You've got to pay the price somewhere along the line.' England, not for the first time, seemed to believe they were playing 4–4–2, when to the neutral eye they were plainly playing 4–2–4. For all that, Trevor Brooking had a magisterial first twenty minutes, largely compensating for the indifferent form of Wilkins, and came back on song late in the game; but England were dicing with death.

And though England conceded just the one goal, the defence ineptly gave it away, leaving Gerry Daly unmarked from Brady's free kick. Big Bob Latchford, given yet another chance at centre forward, headed the English goal but missed several others and yet again looked short of true international class. How long could Greenwood persist with the same dubious strategy?

The Czechs came to Wembley the following month for a friendly and this time the English defence managed a clean sheet, largely attributable to the splendid goalkeeping of Peter Shilton, recalled to the colours. For much of the game the Czechs dominated proceedings with almost embarrassing ease. Yet again, the lack of a ball winner in midfield was crucial. By contrast, an error on the icy field by the Czech keeper Pavel Michalik led to Coppell's second-half goal and England's unmerited success. Greenwood hadn't yet got it right. But the debut of Nottingham Forest's accomplished right back Viv Anderson at least gave the match an historic significance, for he thus became the first black footballer to play for England.

Still, with Northern Ireland on the same night, in the same group, beating Bulgaria 2–0 in Sofia, it seemed a racing certainty that England would qualify for the next stage. When they did play Northern Ireland at Wembley the following February, before the second consecutive 92,000 crowd, they brushed them aside, 4–0. This time the difference in quality between the teams was such that having no tackler in midfield made little odds. Bob Latchford got a whole game and scored two second-half goals. Ron Greenwood opined that teamwork and understanding – a somewhat roseate view – were at the root of England's positive run, but wisely admitted that some problems remained to be solved. Arguably the choice of a genuine tackling wing half in Liverpool's Terry McDermott for the first two games of the British Championship in May 1979 was an attempted solution.

A debutant in the goalless game against Wales, and one destined to win many more caps, was the muscular little left back Kenny Sansom, who won praise from Greenwood, predictably disappointed with his team's poor finishing. Bulgaria, beaten 3–0 in the one game of the tour which really counted, the European qualifier in Sofia, and Sweden, held 0–0 in Stockholm, couldn't breach England's defence either; but Austria, surprisingly, scored four times in Vienna when England's defence – with no midfield ball winner – crumbled; two of Austria's goals were scored by their big centre back, Bruno Pezzey. England came back from 3–1 down to equalise, but Pezzey and Austria had the last word when he headed the winner. Putting as brave a face on such a defeat and such shaky defending, the Panglossian

Greenwood insisted, 'We certainly proved that we are a team with plenty of character and spirit and there is enough evidence to suggest that we are progressing in the right lines.'

Greenwood resumed his discourse when, in October 1979, England overwhelmed Northern Ireland 5–1 in Belfast. He said that much had been learned in Vienna the previous June, where the Austrian forwards were given too much space. Did it really take the lesson of four goals and defeat to teach what should have been abundantly learned in so many previous internationals? And when Danny Blanchflower, once such a notable captain of the Irish team before becoming its manager, reflected after the Belfast game that England's defence had looked surprisingly uneasy under early second-half pressure, he was not being deliberately perverse; merely objective, not least when he unfavourably compared England's defence with Holland's.

The bright new reality of the England team, however, was the ebullient form up front of Trevor Francis, Britain's first million-pound player, scorer with an untypical header of Nottingham Forest's winner against Malmo in the final of the recent European Cup; after which he went on to play incisively in Bulgaria. That Kevin Keegan should declare that England would need a robust attacker such as Bob Latchford, against stronger defences than Northern Ireland's, smacked of a mild case of green eye. Keegan, twice voted European Footballer of the Year, had worked wonders on his game, with restricted natural talent. Francis, by contrast, was supremely and naturally gifted, the epitome of fluency and elegance.

Another vibrant newcomer to the attack was Francis's Nottingham Forest team mate, Tony Woodcock, quick of foot and mind, scorer like Francis of a double in Belfast. Neither could strictly be called a centre forward, but as a pair they constituted the best England spearhead for many years. Typical of Francis's prowess and his partnership with Woodcock was the goal he set up for Tony in the second half. With an astonishing burst of pace, he whipped the ball away from the Irish left back, Sammy Nelson, then crossed, enabling Woodcock to head home.

Neither of them, in fact, had played in the opening international of the season, a meagre 1–0 win at Wembley in the European return match against Denmark, resolved by a goal from Keegan; a margin which might well have been greater had Francis and Woodcock been present. But with Ireland thrashing Bulgaria 3–0 in Dublin on the day England romped home in Belfast, Greenwood could be sure of a place in the much-expanded European finals in Italy. Elephantiasis, again.

Credit where credit was due. Greenwood, after a timorous and uncertain start in which he seemed reluctant to follow his true promptings, had lifted the miasma of fear, foreboding and negativity which was the relic of the Revie years. People wanted to play for him and they wanted above all to play football. But what kind of football, and who should those people be? International competition was now so intense, so tactically sophisticated, so swift to exploit potential weaknesses, that analysis had to be hard and self-critical. Thus, it had to be asked whether England's 4–4–2 formation, however effective against weak opposition, poor defences, was itself defensively watertight. How was it that even in Belfast, where England exploited a feeble pair of full backs, Ireland should have pressed for the first fifteen minutes of the second half, with only a fine save by Peter Shilton depriving them of a goal? And even in the facile victory against Bulgaria in Sofia, Phil Neal, never the most reliable of full backs, was given a hard time by the opposing left winger, Tchavdar Zvetkov.

Liverpool's Ray Kennedy was brought back in the return against Bulgaria at Wembley, which meant some cover for the moments when the enterprising Dave Watson moved forward from centre half to strike for goal; which indeed he would, with success. The other goal was majestically scored, right footed from long range, by the debutant Glenn Hoddle, a supreme long passer of the ball, technically exceptional, an adept ball player. He once told me he had taught himself every trick he knew bar one in his own back garden by the time he was eleven years old. As we know, Greenwood, looking a gift horse stonily in the mouth and again denying his own basic principles, left him out of the next game at home to the Republic of Ireland. Charlie Buchan, Len Shackleton, Glenn Hoddle, Paul Gascoigne. What was it, you wondered, about the way England's selectors and managers turned their backs on unorthodox talent? The words of George Raynor, arch strategist with Sweden, are so often relevant here: 'Ball players are important, because they create unorthodox situations.'

Bulgaria having been seen off 2–0, Ireland were not expected to present real problems though the Irish had their complement of stars: Liam Brady, Gerry Daly, Frank Stapleton, Steve Heighway. Significant was the choice of the all rounder par excellence in midfield, young Bryan Robson. In fact neither he nor McDermott, whose forte – running into spaces – had really yet to be seen in England colours, was on song. Robson on his debut, even looked slightly bemused, but the best was emphatically yet to come. Keegan, coming from behind, scored twice, but Greenwood should surely have settled long since on tactics and a basic team. Perpetually recalling players who had not made the grade, while leaving out those who had, was a wasteful and self-defeating policy. From that point till the finals in June, Greenwood should surely end such meaningless experiments, pursue a policy of *realpolitik*, discard the weak, persevere with the strong and decide once and for all what tactics he meant to use. There, surely, lay salvation.

As early as the following month, in Barcelona, it seemed it had been found. Perhaps it would have been, were it not for the wretched misfortune of the injury to Trevor Francis, destined to keep him out of the European finals. At the Nou Camp, he and Woodcock, strangely below par against the Irish, were simply irresistible against a woeful Spanish defence. Slow and spiteful, the home defenders were overwhelmed, Francis and Woodcock happily co-existing with Keegan who, as the ubiquitous Enzo Bearzot observed – Italy would be in England's European group – was valuable to his team above all for his ability to beat his man, and thus to commit one more defender. As for Woodcock, Bearzot remarked, 'You can see a player's gifts even when he's playing against nobody,' adding that, with strikers such as Woodcock and Francis, 'England didn't need their usual long, deep crosses.'

Spain's attack was better than their defence, obliging Peter Shilton to make several excellent saves, while Coppell and Wilkins, somewhat below par with Manchester United, rose buoyantly to the occasion. Overall, this looked the most promising and positive team for years, but there were still doubts over whether it could cope with a more talented team than Spain's.

In mid-May, at Wembley, it never began to contain a dazzling Diego Maradona, but Argentina were beaten, 3–1, just the same. Whenever Maradona had the ball, the England defence wobbled like a jelly. Keegan, restored to the firing line in the absence of Francis, flourished, scoring one of England's three goals. The other two went to the Liverpool centre forward, David Johnson, but neither he nor his club mate, Ray Kennedy, looked truly adequate at this level. By contrast, when the debutant Garry Birtles, the centre forward Nottingham Forest discovered at non-League Long Eaton, came an as substitute for Johnson, he seemed happily at home. No one, however, could match the power, pace, skill and devastating solos of Maradona, who procured the only Argentine goal when a desperate Kenny Sansom brought him down in the box, and Daniel Passarella scored from the penalty.

After that, the subsequent British International Championship seemed more than ever a historical relic. A patchwork England team even managed to lose to Wales 4–1 in Wrexham and only to draw 1–1 at Wembley with Northern Ireland; though the traditional climax, against Scotland at Hampden Park, saw England – without Francis, Woodcock or Keegan – beat Scotland 2–0 with goals by Brooking and Coppell. The Glaswegian crowd was as fanatical as ever, but their team's defence was simply not equal to the occasion.

European Championship, Italy 1980
Off, then, to Italy and anticlimax. A draw, a defeat and a meaningless victory. Crowd trouble in Turin, where rioting English fans were subdued with tear gas, and more peaceful fans were terrorised in the city streets.

By the time England had left the tournament, hardly trailing clouds of glory rather than tear gas, one wondered why Laurie Cunningham, now of Real Madrid, had been ignored, why the gifted Glenn Hoddle, capable with his passing and shooting of transforming any game, had been subjected to Catch-22 treatment. Because Greenwood had ignored him for so long – though he'd sent him to Australia recently for a meaningless international played by England's virtual reserves – he lacked the 'experience' to be used until the last match against Spain, when he did so well that one could only mourn his previous exclusion.

By and large England beat in vain at the massed ranks of a Belgian side due to improve and to contest the final vigorously against West Germany. Only Ray Wilkins and Kenny Sansom emerged with credit in the Turin heat. 'It just boiled down to the fact that we didn't start playing,' admitted the honest Tony Woodcock. 'Nine or ten men in defence; you could have had Maradona playing, and he would have found it difficult, but if you're going to win, you've got to break it down. I wasn't happy. I'm not particularly strong in the air. They [England] were throwing balls in, there was a Belgian there twice as big as I am. I might as well have not been there.' It was not until the closing minutes that England achieved any dominance.

Next up: Italy. Enzo Bearzot admitted that his team had been wearily there for the taking in the latter stages of their goalless draw against Spain. If England attacked, he predicted, it would be a very fine game. Surprisingly, he saw the *azzurri* themselves as an attacking team: 'When our team closes up, it's finished. We can't do what the Belgians do. We haven't the physical strength to close up for long periods. Juventus, who have many players in our team, tried to do that against Arsenal [who had recently beaten them in Turin in the European Cup-Winners' Cup] and they lost.'

Which begged the question of whether Juventus should have been allowed to contest the game at all. Italian football was still rocking from the appalling scandal of the *Totonero*, black football pools, in which a couple of small-time Roman crooks, Trinca and Crociani, had bribed leading Italian teams and players at will to throw matches. Paolo Rossi, an outstanding centre forward, had been banned for three years, later conveniently commuted to two, enabling him to play and score six goals in the 1982 World Cup. Juventus, his former club, were bang to rights in almost comically drawing a game at Bologna in which, to the horror of their players, they had taken the lead, only to achieve a draw with a headed own goal. The Italian Federation turned a blind eye, just as they had in the 1970s when Juve were plainly guilty of trying to bribe the Portuguese referee of a European match at Derby County.

After the 1–1 draw with Belgium, England gave away another goal in Turin but seldom looked remotely likely to score themselves. Greenwood gave Garry Birtles another chance, but this time he was innocuous. The lack of a genuine wing half was yet again painfully evident, the use of Keegan in midfield rather than up front no better than confusing. Romania's shrewd manager, Stefan Kovacs, once successfully at Ajax, remarked, 'He has the same fault as Johan Cruyff, he goes back for the ball. Too deep. He's lost his punch.' The comparison was less odious than ludicrous and Keegan in fact had not lost his punch; it would be evident again in the last match against Spain in Naples, when Greenwood conquered what one called his 'Keeganitis', putting him up front again.

Phil Neal at right back, without the protection he always received from the self-sacrificing Jimmy Case, looked sadly and typically vulnerable, neither the much put-upon Ray Wilkins nor the overburdened Steve Coppell being able to look after him. Ciccio Graziani, who had looked a spent force against Spain, strolled round him with humiliating ease to make Tardelli's goal. He, Benetti, Gentile and even the elegant sweeper Gaetano Scirea, doomed, alas, to die a horrible death on a Polish road, put it about, the emblem of Enzo Bearzot's ambivalence towards hard men. But this was a palliative rather than an excuse for an England team so ineffectual in attack, so uneasy in defence.

Against Spain, Greenwood profitably used Keegan as a striker, with plenty of evidence of Hoddle's potential at this level in midfield. Brooking and Woodcock scored, Dani replied from a penalty. It was not as comprehensive a win as when the teams had last met in Barcelona, but then this time there was no Francis to complement Woodcock. If luck or the lack of it is an underlying theme of this book, then Greenwood's luck in this respect at least had been minuscule. Still, it did him no credit to lament England's bad luck when they had laboured miserably against Belgium, could have given four goals away to Italy and were unconvincing winners against Spain. A less than distinguished contribution to the tournament by England and their unruly followers.

* * *

Now with the new season came the World Cup qualifiers, Norway first up at Wembley in early September, albeit without two of their best players. And now, alarmingly, Greenwood was beginning to chop and change like a latter-day Revie. What of the philosophy which had seemed so bright and clear at Upton Park? His sheer ambivalence, the old English mistrust of the maverick, could scarcely have been more starkly illustrated than in his treatment of Laurie Cunningham. His explanation for not taking him to Italy was fatuous: that he had to play in a national cup final for his club– but then so did Woodcock, who of course was picked for England.

Now, when injuries caused withdrawals, Greenwood appealed to the generous Norwegians to let him bring Cunningham over from Madrid after the squad lists had closed. So Cunningham came – and never got off the bench. It was fair to reflect that Cunningham had yet to play well for England, but this was indecision bordering on absurdity.

In the event, England won by what seemed a handsome margin, 4–0, but only because the Norwegians tired in the closing phases. Still no Trevor Francis, further opportunities for players such as Paul Mariner and Terry McDermott who'd yet to show true international class – though McDermott scored twice, once from a penalty, and Mariner scored another. The midfield debutant Eric Gates, Mariner's Ipswich team mate, was another who would for all his activity fail to make the ultimate grade. A good club player, out of his depth though he did near the end produce a couple of searching passes. The Arsenal deep left winger, Graham Rix, looked, by happy contrast, no hewer of wood and drawer of water. He seemed easily to adjust to the international game, a natural left footer, beating men with skill, playing the ball about with imagination, manifestly enjoying himself. Strange, though, to think that Bryan Robson, later to make such an impact on the team and its midfield, should again look diligent but limited. The best was yet to come. It could hardly come soon enough.

Meanwhile, a bleakly mediocre season would stretch until the following June when England, inspired by Trevor Brooking and his goals, at last came to life in Budapest. In the autumn there were two World Cup qualifiers to negotiate: the first against Romania, some-what unluckily lost 2–1 in Bucharest, and then a win at home against

Switzerland. For the Romania game Greenwood again chopped and changed, picking players such as Gates and McDermott who again showed they were not up to scratch, and pulled off Garry Birtles, given another chance, just when his partnership with his former Nottingham Forest team mate Woodcock seemed to be paying off. Greenwood insisted that Birtles' legs, at that point – and it was a moment when the Romanian defence was beginning to falter – had gone. It seemed more likely that Birtles was suffering from a knock on the ankle. This time Laurie Cunningham did at last get a game, or part of one, coming on as substitute, playing wide where another striker was needed and, truth to tell, doing very little.

No Glenn Hoddle, again, to provide the flair which Stefan Kovacs the Romanian guru declared that England lacked, in midfield: 'No good play, no passes, no shots at goal.' A justified criticism perhaps of Rix, ploughing his endless, weary furrow down the left, no longer what he'd been at Wembley. However, at least Bryan Robson was now starting to make his mark.

'There was no leader,' said Kovacs, pertinently. The swift left winger Marcel Raducanu scored the first Romanian goal, though overall, Phil Neal, in improved form, contained him well. His fellow full back Kenny Sansom was a little unlucky to concede the penalty from which Anghel Iordanescu scored his team's second goal. Woodcock replied for England, whose chances of reaching the World Cup finals still seemed alive to me.

A 2–1 victory against Switzerland the following month at Wembley at least maintained those hopes, if only mathematically. Before the game Greenwood, plaintively and significantly, publicly appealed for people to stop denigrating his team and encourage it instead. Which may have been why, despite a plodding performance, the 70,000 spectators restrained the slow handclap till the 90th minute, greeting the final whistle with an all too apposite outburst of booing. Markus Tanner put through his own goal to give England the lead, Mariner got the second, while Hans-Jorg Pfister replied for the Swiss. Gloom.

In March, at the third time of asking, Spain got the better of England at Wembley 2–1, in a game where their playmaker Zamora dominated midfield, while their right winger Juanito did much as he pleased.

Hoddle, who scored, was back, as indeed was Francis, but, ominously, neither they nor Trevor Brooking could turn the tide.

At the end of April 1981, following a home defeat in the friendly against Spain, came the return with Romania, and again England were firing blanks; a barren goalless draw, even with the Francis–Woodcock duo restored. Paul Breitner, the West Germany left back, ever loquacious and contentious, had just dismissed English football as 'stupid', lacking subtlety, relying for goals on mere pressure. In fact, there was nothing stupid about an England team which, even without the injured Hoddle, had skill in abundance and had now in Bryan Robson, marking the scheming and sometimes violent Iordanecu, the tackling midfielder so long needed.

Woodcock, alas, was for once ineffective on the left, McDermott, a late choice, was again pedestrian, Anderson's tackling an embarrassment. Yet England started well, against a nine-man Romanian defence, Francis an elusive centre forward, Brooking and Coppell prominent. But when an early goal wouldn't come, the virtue seemed to drain out of England, who beat in vain against the packed opposing defence.

Might Keegan, had he been available, have made the difference? He was absent, too, at Wembley in May from the below-strength team beaten 1–0 through the clever Zico's goal, by Brazil. West Ham's Alvin Martin at centre half, big ponderous Peter Withe at centre forward, not to mention McDermott were hardly the kind of players to match the abundant skills of Zico, Socrates, Junior and Cerezo. Ron Greenwood was now peddling the bizarre theory that the trouble with English football was that its clubs played so many different styles – something which would surprise any half-competent foreign observer. Whatever the differing tactics, the English essentially had speed, strength and stamina; straightforward, perhaps, to a fault. Then, after the irrelevance of the British tournament, in which England were goalless yet again, a 0–0 draw at Wembley with Wales, a 1–0 defeat by Scotland, with no team willing to travel to troubled Belfast, came the happy surprise of Budapest: and Brooking, who had played in none of these three matches.

It was preceded, making it all the more unexpected, by a humiliating

World Cup defeat by the Swiss in Basel; again without Brooking, though Francis and Keegan played. But Keegan looked a spent force, Ron Greenwood, with his tactics, a busted flush. If Bryan Robson were to play, why was he not put on to the most creative and dangerous Swiss player, Botteron, rather than being allowed eventually to drift aimlessly about in midfield? The current complaint that England had 'no players' surely defied logic. The players were there; they simply had to be chosen and deployed effectively. Hadn't Liverpool, a team hardly replete with stars, just won another European Cup, in Paris? How obscure it was that the Football Association should persevere with a team manager who had long since lost all direction, consistency and coherence. By contrast the Swiss had recently, when things were going awry, sacked one manager in Leon Walker and profitably installed another in Paul Wolfisberg.

England did at least manage to score their first goal – by McDermott, another marginal player – for four games, but Alfred Scheiwiler and the incisive striker, Claudio Sulser, replied for the Swiss. Thus, for England to retain any chance at all of reaching the World Cup finals, victory in Budapest was essential.

And they blessedly achieved it, on a ground where they had not won since 1909, and where indeed they had been thrashed 7–1 in 1954. Brooking, so long out of his old club manager's favour, transformed the attack, lean Phil Thompson, the Liverpool centre half, the defence. Keegan had his best international game for many moons and coolly put away his penalty. McDermott was suddenly inspired, Bryan Robson sharp and versatile.

The Hungarians threatened in the opening minutes, but in the eighteenth, a fine move involving Keegan, Robson, Coppell and Neal was consummated by Brooking, shooting calmly inside the near post. A vociferous crowd was shocked into silence. But Hungary equalised at that delicate moment just before half time through the adventurous centre back Imre Garaba, beginning and ending a fine, fluent move. On the hour, a little unexpectedly, England regained their lead, Brooking receiving from Keegan, his fulminating shot stuck dramatically in the top left-hand corner of the net. Almost a symbol. Keegan's penalty completed the success. One could not but feel happy, whatever one's many reservations, for Greenwood, in his triumph in a city whose football had always meant so much to him. Thus the World Cup finals became rather more than just a faint glimmer on the horizon.

A glimmer, or a false dawn? Come September, disaster loomed in Oslo, where at the end of a game in which Norway, inspired by outside left Hallvar Thoresen and the veteran attacker, Tom Lund, laid waste to a shaky England defence, an ecstatic radio commentator reached crescendo: 'Mrs Thatcher, your boys have taken such a beating!' Outside the plate glass window of the room where Ron Greenwood was giving his press conference, a disgusted young fan was mouthing inaudible insults, finally tearing off his England scarf and stamping on it. England were lucky to lose 2–1.

Lame performances abounded: Russell Osman of Ipswich looked anything but an England centre half; Neal, McDermott, Hoddle, Mariner, even Keegan and Francis were ineffectual, Francis perhaps still feeling the aftermath of an Achilles tendon operation, his pace impaired. Neal missed the covering of the absent Coppell. Only Peter Barnes, when he emerged as a substitute, and Phil Thompson impressed among the wreckage, though at least Bryan Robson took his goal well.

'In the first fifteen minutes,' admitted Age Hareide, Norway's Manchester City centre half, 'it was a nightmare out there, but after they got the goal, the pace went. It was easy to mark a man. They played the same style all the time.'

Tom Lund, who proved so influential when he moved inside from the flank, and suffered a slight concussion, said, on the treatment table, 'I had to move about to get some movement into the team, else it would have been very easy for the defenders. We had to get some more happening into our game, because it was very dead.' He and Thoresen emphatically did, dominating midfield.

'Of course Keegan was moving around a lot,' continued Hareide, 'but he wasn't the same player any more.' Incontestably. So, back again to square one and pending disaster. Avoiding defeat against Hungary at Wembley in November became imperative, and it would be achieved without panache.

Coppell and Brooking returned, Francis was absent. Paul Mariner kept his place and scored the game's solitary goal. Yet a draw would have been enough, thanks to England's rivals in the group beating one another. Meditating nostalgically before the game, Greenwood reflected, 'Football's emotional, it's involved, it stirs everyone's imagination. That's why it's such a beautiful game; there are so many opinions.' The wrong man for the wrong job, surely, but so much nicer than most of those who might succeed him.

Clever Tibor Nyilasi, who had headed against the bar in Budapest, was making aggressive if somewhat illusory noises, talking about laying the ghost of the great Puskas–Kocsis–Hidegkuti team which had annihilated England 6–3 in 1953. There was no doubt that on their day he, Andras Torocsik and the dynamic striker, Laszlo Kiss, could test a porous England defence. The Hungarians, Greenwood forecast, would come with 'a relaxed attitude'. So in fact they had on their most recent visit to Wembley when they'd been battered 4–1, but, of course, there were different ways of relaxing.

As it transpired, only a dreadful goalkeeping error, giving Mariner the decisive goal, enabled yet another dreary England team to win. Four years after Greenwood took over, I sadly recorded, nearly eighteen months after England collapsed in the European Championship in Italy, he was still nowhere near to building a sufficient side. That talent was limited had to be conceded, but Greenwood had neither been deploying nor properly exploiting such as there was. There were reported mutterings from the somnolent, irrelevant Senior (oh, how senior!) International Committee, but needless to say, nothing was done; though flanking Greenwood with an assistant such as Bobby Robson would have made sense.

Such inactivity however may have seemed justified when, in the prelude to the World Cup finals, England proceeded to win all their matches, with a largely reserve team drawing 1–1 in Iceland. How interesting it was when, hard on the heels of the surprising Swiss victory in Bucharest, which opened the door for England, that Jackie Charlton rather than Bobby Robson or Brian Clough should be the first choice of readers in a *Sunday Times* competition to name an alternative manager to Greenwood.

Charlton did, in fact, eventually apply for the post, only to be shamefully snubbed by the FA who did not even reply to his request. Later, of course, he would prove himself a greatly effective manager of the Republic of Ireland, with whom he achieved extraordinary success, though his highly functional methods may not have suited England, from whom much more, however excessively, was demanded. At that time, Jackie Charlton was gradually improving a Sheffield Wednesday side down in Division Two, but 14.1 per cent of the perceptive voters put him top – admittedly hardly a resounding vote.

How interesting, even significant, it was, however, that Brian Clough, so often canvassed in the tabloids as The People's Choice, should, with his essential Man Friday, Peter Taylor, have finished behind Charlton on 10.2 per cent. Bobby Robson, who would eventually inherit the role, scored just 4 per cent. Readers seemed to feel he might crack under pressure. He was even outscored by Southampton's Lawrie McMenemy, on 7.5 per cent. And 5.6 per cent wanted Greenwood to stay.

Stay for the moment he did. The voting took place in a week when McMenemy's Southampton were tactically humiliated by Sporting Lisbon. As for Clough, I had just written,

> The patriot cry for Brian Clough and Peter Taylor goes up every time England lose a match, but what guarantee is there that the methods which have worked so well at club level would be effective in the international field? Peter Taylor's book on Clough made it perfectly clear what many of us had known all along, that they are an authoritarian couple, ruling essentially by fear. Between the wars, in the days of the illustrious and commanding Arsenal manager, Herbert Chapman, the fear was of unemployment. Today, though we have unemployment again, the fear is of losing the huge rewards which clubs like Forest can provide. No such hold could be established over international players. Treat them peremptorily, and they would certainly rebel.

Clough's methods had worked small wonders both at Derby County and at Forest, twice remarkable winners in consecutive years of the

European Cup. But in a brief spell at Brighton they had utterly demoralised a Third Division team which crashed 8–2 at home to Bristol Rovers and were knocked out of the FA Cup at home to amateur opponents. While in his nightmarish forty-four days at Leeds United, Clough endured the hostility and recalcitrance which anyone less insensitively egocentric could have predicted, given that he had derided and scorned the success of the club under Don Revie, both before – at a banquet – and after he got to Elland Road, excoriating what he saw as the intimidatory cynicism of Revie's team.

Ironic and strange to think that we awarded the prize to a reader who suggested Graham Taylor, manager of the long-ball Watford team which for a time shocked and in the view of many of us corrupted English football. Though it was to be emphasised that the award was given not on the basis of the reader's sound judgement, but because his letter made us laugh. He suggested Taylor, whose Watford team was then in the Second Division but threatening to achieve the First, because he felt Taylor could destroy the apathy among players 'which has produced a new concept in world football . . . the all-seater football squad'. As a matter of interest, Kevin Keegan received two votes as a potential player-manager.

In late April, the 1–0 British Championship win in Cardiff against Wales found an England team still in the melting pot. On the positive side, an all-round performance by Bryan Robson which showed the problem of a genuine half back in midfield had at last been solved, fine, eventual, overlapping by Kenny Sansom from left back. Less happily, the vulnerability of the other back, Phil Neal, the increasing caution in midfield of Ray Wilkins, the failure of the Aston Villa pair Peter Withe at centre forward – why did he start rather than his livelier substitute, Cyrille Regis? – and left winger Tony Morley. Claims made for the absent Kevin Keegan, on the grounds that he was England's 'only world-class player', seemed a good two years out of date. And why was McDermott deployed yet again?

Things looked up at Wembley a month later where Holland in a friendly were beaten 2–0, with goals by Woodcock and Mariner. From his old club, West Ham, Greenwood chose Alan Devonshire, a slim, quick flanker who had come straight out of non-League football with London's suburban Southall; but he wouldn't make the cut for Spain.

The experiment of playing Wilkins as a sweeper, tried in the game against Northern Ireland, had wisely not been renewed. Unfortunately, injury prevented recourse to Regis, who had looked so much better a prospect at centre forward than the clumsy Withe or the not quite adequate Mariner; though Mariner like Robson would get another couple of goals in an undemanding 4–1 win over Finland in Helsinki. A match, however, which again demonstrated Greenwood's penchant for Keeganitis. Now with Southampton, Keegan seemed a source of confusion in midfield, negligible in attack where despite England's superiority, the Finns marked him out of the game. And so to Spain.

Greenwood Falls: World Cup, Spain 1982

England were based in the Basque region, in pro-English Bilbao, where they'd already played the local Athletic club in a kind of courtesy game. France, the Czechs and the unfancied Kuwaitis would be the group opposition in a World Cup now bloated to twenty-four teams by the ineffable FIFA President Joao Havelange. Described to me once by a German journalist as one who 'has fifty new ideas every day and fifty-one of them are bad', his eventual successor Sepp Blatter, FIFA Secretary, was waiting in the wings.

By now an improved England, defensively tightened by their recently appointed coach Don Howe, of Arsenal fame, an essential adjunct to the waning Greenwood, looked capable at least of reaching the second round. Tony Woodcock, after two years playing in the Bundesliga for Cologne, had no fears were England subsequently – as indeed they did – to meet West Germany. 'In fact, I'm looking forward to it. They can get goals, but they're suspect in defence.' That he should stress the fact that the German right back Manny Kaltz was better attacking than defending would in retrospect emphasise the bizarre moment in Greenwood's press conference after the eventual draw with the Germans. He was amazed, he told us reporters, that we hadn't asked a certain question. When nobody answered, he explained, 'We didn't let Manny Kaltz get in any crosses.'

In Bilbao, England against France made the most electric of

beginnings. Only twenty-seven seconds had been played when Bryan Robson scored the fastest goal in the history of the competition. Steve Coppell took a long throw in from the right. Terry Butcher, the centre back, flicked it on, Robson drove the ball home. Bravely hurling himself among the flying boots, he headed a second; a clear competitor to Holland's Johan Neeskens as that rarity, the genuine, all-round midfield man.

Neither Trevor Brooking, with pelvic trouble, nor Kevin Keegan, with back problems could play. Nor would they till both came on as substitutes in what proved the ultimate match, against Spain. Brooking was severely missed; Keegan should surely never have had his way and been recalled, palpably off form, missing the vital chance which would have won the match for England and put them into the semi-finals. Afterwards, Ted Croker, the FA Secretary, congratulated himself on the fact that Keegan's trip to Germany during the tournament for treatment to his back had been concealed from the press. His satisfaction seemed thoroughly misplaced. A stronger manager than the wearied Greenwood would surely not have let him have his way.

After their well-deserved victory, in oppressive heat, England would meet a Czech team which had laboured in its opening match against outsiders Kuwait. 'We sat there in cold towels in the dressing room at half time,' said Ray Wilkins, after the initial victory, 'and the heat came off us like steam.' But morale, after a well-deserved 3–1 success, had soared. Bryan Robson, the hero of the hour, doomed alas – Greenwood's luck? – to pull a groin in the next game – remarked, 'I think the way results are going, it's given the lads a bit of heart that we can go all the way. I'm not saying we're going to, but when you see things like Algeria and Germany [Algeria had won 2–1] it just gives you that little bit of heart. The teams aren't as exceptional as we thought when we came here.' He had, he said, been happier when moved from the left of midfield into the centre, where he could certainly exert more influence.

Greenwood's evident problem, till Robson was injured, was something of an embarrassment of riches; how to accommodate Robson, Wilkins and Hoddle, who would substitute Robson against the Czechs, in the same midfield. Robson and Hoddle, of course, were two very different breeds of cat, Robson perpetual motion, Hoddle the classical, perceptive, creative inside forward. His through-passes, when he came on, confused the Czechs and ignited Trevor Francis.

'That's the type of ball these defences don't come up against very often,' reflected Hoddle. 'Because their build-up's a very slow and lethargic build-up. That would be a lovely dream come true, to play Brazil in the final. But let's take one stage at a time.' Francis relished the service, long or short. 'I'm finding in this competition there's a definite reluctance of forward players to go past defenders. So when I get the ball, I try to commit defenders and go past them, and they don't like it. I think you've got to be positive, because there are so many negative players about.'

By turns amiable, expansive, tetchy and vulnerable, Greenwood's contribution to success could, in all fairness, easily be underrated. If Don Howe had been able to work happily and profitably with the admiring England players, it had been under, one might say, the Greenwood tree. Now that Greenwood had dropped, or been encouraged to stop, his fetishism about certain players, it would not seem wholly perverse at that point to see the partnership continuing into the future. But that was before Keegan got his way against the Spaniards.

Of Don Howe, Steve Coppell – that rare bird amongst footballers, a university graduate, with an economics degree – enthused, 'He's a coach who talks a lot of common sense. You find a lot of coaches who are so steeped in football, some of their ideas seem a little bit vague and strange. Don has his feet on the ground. The players can relate to him, because he talks in simple football terms. He relates well to every player, and seems to understand every player's problems and quirks.'

After the deserved 2–0 win against the Czechs, the English team gave a strangely strangulated performance, again in Bilbao, against Kuwait, with a laborious 1–0 win. Still, this gave England a 100 per cent record and comfortable qualification in their group, and put them, in yet another perversely organised World Cup, into Group 2 with West Germany and Spain. These were mini-leagues; there would be no knock-out matches till the semi-final.

Against the Germans, in Madrid, Bryan Robson would play, 95 per cent fit according to Greenwood, but a great deal less so to a more objective eye. With Robson restrained, Hoddle unused, there was scant service for Francis and an ineffectual Mariner, both rigorously policed by the blond German Forster brothers.

Overall, this was an evening of drab sterility, illuminated only by a couple of splendid runs down either flank by Paul Breitner, previously a critic of England's football, now back from international retirement as a playmaker, a nineteenth-minute header by Bryan Robson turned over the bar, a shot against the England bar by Karl-Heinz Rummenigge. When Enzo Bearzot, World Cup winner, heard afterwards of Greenwood's pride in containing Kaltz, he smiled and said his own team simply hadn't worried about the full back.

So came the decisive game at the Bernabeu against a Spanish team humiliated by Northern Ireland — whom they had kicked considerably — with no hope of further progress (they had also lost to West Germany). Coppell withdrew, injured, but there was still no place for Hoddle; Tony Woodcock was included in a three-man attack which again, surprisingly, included Mariner. After sixty-three minutes, Greenwood sent both Brooking and Keegan on to the field. For twenty minutes, largely unmarked, Brooking held sway to such an extent that one wondered how much difference he might have made had he been on from the beginning.

Spain threw away three fine chances. Arconada, largely a suspect goalkeeper, thwarted a splendid effort by Brooking. And Keegan, six minutes after his appearance, headed wide after Bryan Robson had put the ball on his head. England were out, without losing a match. Greenwood retired. The era of Bobby Robson now began.

5 BOBBY AND THE HAND OF GOD

Bobby Robson 1982–90
Key Game: England v West Germany, July 1990

ENTER BOBBY ROBSON, CANVASSED FOR SOME TIME AS THE OBVIOUS candidate to the succession. A former England international both at inside right and right half, a World Cup player, if somewhat muted, in 1958, a successful manager of Ipswich Town, there had been some slight doubt about a volatile temperament. But, like Alf Ramsey before him, it was his achievements at Ipswich Town, not least in European football, that had won him the role.

Like Ramsey, he would guide England in two World Cups, though he won neither of them. Undone in Mexico in 1986 by Diego Maradona's notorious Hand of God; unlucky enough to go out of the 1990 semi-finals on penalties. Was he a lucky manager? Certainly he had none when Maradona punched that goal, but previously, in Monterrey, injuries to two out-of-form players had obliged him to revise – and galvanise – a team which seemed to be heading to extinction. In between these two World Cups, there was the disaster area of the European Championship finals in West Germany, when all three games were humiliatingly lost, and Robson became an Aunt Sally.

Working, often with success, in Spain and Portugal, he became in his later years, managing Newcastle United, a kind of latter-day saint, beloved by the media. In his earlier days with England, however, his relations with the press had often been sour and sullen. I remember him sitting gloomily in the lounge of the England team's hotel before a press conference in 1985, during the pre-World Cup mini-tournament in Mexico. 'Bastard!' he exploded, at a photographer surreptitiously taking a picture of him, which he thought would be unflattering. 'Pressure?' he addressed the journalists. 'There isn't any pressure. You people provide the pressure. If you people didn't exist, my job would be twice as easy and twice as pleasurable.' Five years later, in Italy, after the tabloid invasion of his romantic life, press relations would be barely minimal.

With Ipswich, there had been a radical change of tactics, from long-ball methods to a more measured, sophisticated approach when he acquired two cultured Dutch midfield players in Arnold Muhren and Franz Thijssen. With England, his firm preference was for a 4–4–2 formation. He went on record before the 1990 World Cup finals to insist that British players were uncomfortable with the sweeper forma-tion, but under player pressure in Cagliari, he adopted it – only to declare, after England in Naples had so narrowly survived against Cameroon, changing tactics through injury, 'A flat back four saved us.'

Sheer good fortune saved England again in Copenhagen where Robson made such an ill-starred beginning. True, he had scarcely had time to get his feet under the table at Lancaster Gate when, in late September 1982, the first European Championship qualifying match was due in Denmark. The ludicrous irony of it was – illustrating Walter Winterbottom's dictum that soccer differs from other sports in the sheer difficulty of scoring goals – that the one which little left winger Jesper Olsen so dazzlingly scored was actually the Danish equaliser, when they should long have been several goals ahead. It took some twenty minutes for the Danes to realise just how poor England were, and they then played the kind of scintillating football which put the mediocre opposition to shame if not to waste. If Bobby Robson had done anything at all, it was to put the clock back.

The senselessness of his selection, one lamented, the inadequacy of his perverse tactics, the inflexibility of his posture when things had so manifestly gone wrong, gave no ground for optimism. You couldn't go back to players who have proved so utterly insufficient in the past?

What was Phil Neal doing at right back, run ragged by Olsen, two years after the inelegant Graziani had danced round him to set up Italy's winner in Turin? What was Russell Osman doing at centre back, after he had failed so lamentably against Norway in Oslo and at a time when he was even floundering in the Ipswich Town team? Why was Tony Morley there when he himself admitted he'd been out of form and why, being two footed, was he kept throughout on the right wing? Why was Mariner lurching around at centre forward after his failure in the World Cup? What case could be made for Graham Rix, so uninspired in all but the first two World Cup games, even if he had stopped Manny Kaltz getting in any crosses? Yes, Bobby Robson was unlucky that the injured Glenn Hoddle and Steve Coppell had to be excluded, but when things went wrong, what did he try to do to put them right? The case against him was that rather than take risks, he picked a team of jaded revenants. Trevor Francis, now in Italy with Sampdoria, looked sharp; but who was to give him the ball?

Thanks to luck and the defiant goalkeeping of Peter Shilton, England came away with a 2–2 draw, both their goals being scored by the alert Francis. But the omens were grim. Not till the 84th minute did Robson bring on Luton's playmaking inside right, Ricky Hill, but he started him at Wembley in the next match, a friendly lost 2–1 to West Germany. Karl-Heinz Rummenigge, a player of true international class, elegantly scored both the German goals. Mariner was inexplicably there again, this time beside the far more incisive Regis, centre forwards who cancelled rather than complemented each other; it would be Regis who was substituted, Woodcock only coming on as a sub. And those three substitutes, shades of Alf Ramsey, brought on, absurdly, only ten minutes from the end.

In Bobby Robson's defence, it had to be said that he was without Francis, Hoddle and Bryan Robson, but the choice of Armstrong, a pedestrian midfielder from Middlesbrough, and the unexceptional Luther Blissett, a Watford forward cruelly nicknamed Miss It Blissett, was hardly reassuring.

Hopes rose in November when a better balanced England team, still without Francis, Coppell and Hoddle, comfortably won the second

European qualifier against Greece in Salonika. This time, Bobby Robson had the wit to incorporate the busy little Liverpool midfielder, Sammy Lee, wide on the right, so he could protect his club colleague Phil Neal as Jimmy Case had diligently done before him. Lee's was a name constantly touted at Anfield since he was a teenager, as that of a precocious inside forward. Perhaps he should have been given a much earlier regular place in the side, for when he did at last attain it, he showed a deferential attitude to his seniors which prevented him from expressing his full talents. Nevertheless, he was a hard working, self-sacrificing, efficient player.

Beware of Greeks bearing gift goals. The Greeks had plainly moved the match to Salonika in the hope that their team would be lifted by the passion of the crowd, but a traumatising goal by Tony Woodcock in eighty seconds set the pattern of the game, subduing the Greek players and crowd alike. Thrown back on their own inadequate abilities, the Greeks could do little but kick the English strikers and come briefly to life at the very end. Only the unhappy Tony Morley, given another chance, comprehensively threw it away. Even Paul Mariner had a brave and effective first half. An Ipswich player, Bobby Robson's talisman, the manager insisted he should stay even though he bizarrely admitted Mariner seldom scored goals. Woodcock scored twice, Lee once.

Most encouraging of all was the form in midfield of Tottenham's Bristolian wing half Gary Mabbutt, played out of position in the previous game at right back, where he defended indifferently but overlapped well. He and Bryan Robson at last gave bite as well as drive to the English midfield. A 9–0 December win against feeble Luxembourg in another European game gave Blissett the chance to score three, but it was essentially an essay in rabbit killing. Hoddle and Coppell returned. Even Phil Neal scored a goal.

It was interesting to hear Mabbutt say, 'I see myself as a real wing half in the old fashioned expression. Lots of youngsters wouldn't know what you meant by wing half. I was lucky enough to have my father, who used to play for Bristol Rovers, and so I associate myself with that position. I enjoy getting forward and getting goals, as well as, for want of a better word, scrapping. I don't mean fisticuffs. I mean challenging and winning the ball and getting things going from there, which I can do more from a central role than a wider role.'

So for Bobby Robson and England the year ended far more positively than had earlier seemed likely: but there was trouble ahead. Ominous indeed was the failure to beat or even score at Wembley in the return match against the previously overwhelmed Greeks. Perhaps, one reflected, the most surprising if not encouraging aspect of a dire evening was that the crowd choruses of, 'What the blanking hell is this?' followed by the slow handclap did not erupt till five minutes from the end. Sterility, technical inadequacy, bleak lack of imagination, addiction to the shortest and crudest route to goal by the long ball – all had been seen only too often at the Empire Stadium.

There were sinister implications of this, adumbrated in the match programme where Bobby Robson inexplicably eulogised what Graham Taylor had done as the manager both of Watford and of the current England youth team. For many critics, what Taylor had done, was, along with the FA's Director of Coaching, Charles Hughes, poison the wells of English football. At that time it seemed all too probable that Bobby Robson was becoming complicit in that process.

Taylor and Hughes, given free destructive reign at the FA by the weak leadership of the Chief Executive, Graham Kelly, were to turn the clock back and adopt the dubious 1950s theories of a certain Wing Commander Charles Reep. This non-flying RAF man had devised a system known as Match Analysis, pursued in the columns of the long-defunct daily *News Chronicle* with a plethora of squiggly diagrams, which purported to show the efficacy of long-ball football, cutting out the midfield – a method all too common in the history of English football.

As long ago as 1932, when the Austrian *Wunderteam* came to play England at Chelsea, their famous English coach, Jimmy Hogan, and his players were appalled four days before the international when they watched Chelsea play Everton at Stamford Bridge. Each team had a famous centre forward, Scotland's Hughie Gallacher for Chelsea, Dixie Dean for Everton; and all both teams did was to boot the ball down the middle in search of these two. Now, though the two men denied it, there was no doubt then that Robson was greatly under the influence of Hughes, a dogmatic and arrogant theorist, and that there were plans to extend the long-ball football played – without ultimate success, even with home advantage in the European finals – by the youth team, under Taylor. In a bewildering choice by the palsied International Committee, Taylor would later be given charge of the full England team.

Reep's salary was paid out of Taylor's own pocket, and when he was ultimately dismissed and appealed for compensation to Watford, they were able, rather as Henry V dismissed Falstaff, to say, 'Old man, we know thee not.' With Hughes deploying his brainwashed FA coaches and imposing his obsolescent ideas on the whole coaching system, English football was truly in peril, though eventually and fortunately Bobby Robson drew back from the brink.

The paradox of the Greek game was that Robson ineptly chose two quick, clever strikers in Trevor Francis and Tony Woodcock who essentially needed the ball on the ground, rather than having it lumped towards them in the air. It defied logic that Robson afterwards should deplore the fact that there had been no player to do damage in the air. Only the previous week, in Genoa, Francis had deplored to me the English tendency to hit long balls towards besieged strikers. 'I think my game is based on running,' he said, 'getting away from defenders. It's essential to my game that I've got somebody who can provide me with passes.'

Aston Villa's adroit little playmaker Gordon Cowans, who had done well at Wembley the previous month against Wales, might have done as much, but never even got on the field. Mabbutt, ball winner and infiltrator, could do little in the misbegotten tactical pattern. Clearly the efficacy of the long ball when properly used couldn't be denied, but as Enzo Bearzot had observed, 'Clearly the long pass is the decisive one, but there are fewer and fewer players in the world with the peripheral vision to make that pass.' Glenn Hoddle was emphatically one of them, but he wasn't playing in either game. Besides, he was never a player to Bobby Robson's taste even if, as we shall see, there was a Damascene conversion, just before the 1986 World Cup. What was now all too plain was that Robson, for all his experience, was not his own man.

Four weeks later, however, in his roller-coaster regime, Robson had the relief and satisfaction of seeing England win their next game, a vital European qualifier against Hungary at Wembley. This they won 2–0 after surviving an awkward and tormenting half hour in which the Hungarians dominated the field, and should certainly have gone ahead on thirty minutes when the English defence pitifully broke down, leaving the goal at the mercy of the skilful Tibor Nyilasi and the less experienced Gyula Hajszan, as they pursued a long ball from the centre back Garaba, a previous thorn in England's side. Nyilasi would surely have scored, but Hajszan beat him to the ball, and Peter Shilton raced off his line for a gallant block.

Football being the cruelly perverse game that it can be, England promptly went ahead with an excellent goal, a cleverly curled free kick by Gordon Cowans, with a brave and perfectly timed header by Trevor Francis. At which point the virtue and the morale went out of a dejected Hungary. England dominated the second half, with Peter Withe a centre forward transformed, suddenly confident, intelligent and incisive, taking the weight off an inspired Francis. Hoddle and Bryan Robson were again absent, but Cowans cleverly kept the wheels turning, and England made light of the Hungarians' physical excesses, disregarded by Pietro D'Elia, a hopelessly permissive Italian referee.

Qualification for the next stage no longer looked chimerical; it would merely prove illusory. There were still doubts in defence, where Neal badly needed Lee to look after him, and now centre halves seemed alarmingly at a premium. Meanwhile, the malign influence of Long-ball Charlie Hughes appeared to be on the wane.

Denmark would again be met in September 1983, Denmark would win, and the European Championship was closed to England. Though he did not remotely make the best of a bad job, given the spate of absentees, Bobby Robson was certainly afflicted by the absence of the injured Gordon Cowans, Bryan Robson and Steve Coppell – kicked by a Hungarian and fated never to play again. Yet there was scant excuse for ignoring the inventions of Glenn Hoddle even if, at that moment, he had been so controversially dropped by Spurs. Nothing of creative consequence would come from the likes of Sammy Lee, Ray Wilkins and the straightforward Queens Park Rangers half back,

John Gregory. Nor from Bobby Robson's King Charles' Head, the pedestrian Paul Mariner. No service for gifted Trevor Francis.

The irony of it was that Denmark, recently in stunning form including beating Hungary 3–1, devastating but unlucky a year earlier against England in Copenhagen, didn't even play particularly well at Wembley. England's defence, yet again including at centre back Russell Osman, Bobby Robson's Ipswich player who'd been exposed in Copenhagen, fell apart early in the game, when Michael Laudrup should have scored. He'd atone for this by dancing round Terry Butcher, the other centre back, and company on the goal line, to gain the penalty from which the clever little Allan Simonsen won the game with the only goal.

Bobby Robson, dourly inflexible, kept the potentially dynamic Watford attacker John Barnes marooned throughout on the left wing, when the situation cried out for him to be moved into the middle. That England by and large lacked talent to call on was beyond dispute – though Sepp Piontek, Denmark's manager, didn't think so. The problem was that Bobby Robson did so pathetically little, persisting with players whose inadequacy at this level had so long been evident. Even the Welsh and Northern Irish at that moment were, with still more limited resources, giving a better account of themselves.

That England, with Hoddle and Robson back but without Trevor Francis, should go to Budapest the following month and thrash Hungary 3–0 was scant consolation. There, Hoddle bestrode the field, making it the more regrettable that he'd been excluded against the Danes. His answer, in Budapest, was to come out swaggering with almost contemptuous brilliance. From the start, he was performing small feats of virtuosity, chest traps, sidesteps and the like, which put the traditionally gifted Hungarians to shame on their own ground.

He was also distributing the ball splendidly and imaginatively. He nearly scored in the opening minute, and did score from a spectacular free kick, after which the Hungarians wilted, Lee and Mariner getting the other goals. But so far as the European Championship was concerned, the die was all but cast.

It seemed right to blame Bobby Robson, who had learned good sense too late. He made a fiasco of the opening European game in

Scoring a hat trick, and Hungary's sixth goal, Nandor Hidegkuti was the hero of the game in November 1953. It was the first time England had been beaten at home by a foreign team – partly due to Winterbottom's lack of man-marking tactics.

A preoccupied Walter Winterbottom leaves the field at Wembley at half time, flanked by left back Ray Wilson and centre half Peter Swan. Switzerland were the opponents, weeks away from the 1962 World Cup finals in Chile.

February 1963. Alf Ramsey with members of the now-neutered Senior International Committee, including Joe Richards (on Ramsey's left), and Chelsea's Joe Mears, top right. Geniality would be short lived.

MIRRORPIX

World Cup final against West Germany at Wembley, 1966. England's trainer Harold Shepherdson exults. Ramsey will tell him to sit down. Team doctor Alan Bass and assistant trainer Les Cocker are on Ramsey's right.

EMPICS

In or out? Geoff Hurst's ever-controversial third England goal.

EMPICS

Don Revie advises Trevor Cherry during England's 2–0 defeat by Italy in a World Cup qualifier in Rome, November 1976.

Don Revie arrives at the High Court in December 1979. He got his money from the FA but the judge called him greedy and dishonest.

World Cup, Spain, 1982. Drawing 0–0 with the host nation, England would go out unbeaten. Well might Ron Greenwood look worried.

Greenwood consults Terry Venables and Bobby Robson in training before the previous draw in Spain against West Germany.

World Cup, 1986, Mexico City. Diego Maradona punches his notorious 'hand of God' goal for Argentina, outjumping the 6' 1" Peter Shilton.

World Cup, 1990. The semi-final in Turin. Bobby Robson talks, in vain, to Stuart Pearce before the disastrous penalty shoot-out. Paul Gascoigne intently listens.

COLORSPORT

Gary Lineker, within a goal of the England record, is notoriously pulled off by Graham Taylor against Sweden in Stockholm, in the 1992 European Championship finals.

Does he not like that? Graham Taylor, outraged on England's bench – with assistant manager Lawrie McMenemy and ex-keeper Peter Bonetti beside him – and about to lose to Holland in October 1993.

MIRRORPIX

COLORSPORT

Euro '96 semi-final, Wembley, England v Germany. Terry Venables discusses tactics before extra time with his assistant manager, Bryan Robson.

Still with a 1–1 scoreboard after extra time, the game goes to penalties. Gareth Southgate misses the vital kick.

EMPICS

Rome, October 1997. Glenn Hoddle intently watches England's decisive drawn World Cup qualifier against Italy. England doctor John Crane and coach Glenn Roeder are on his right, physio Gary Lewin on his left.

World Cup, France 1998. Glenn Hoddle consoles Paul Ince, who has just missed in the penalty shoot-out against Argentina.

Charleroi, Euro 2000. Kevin Keegan exults after England beat Germany. Joy will be short lived.

Wembley, three months later. Germany again in a disastrous World Cup qualifier. Keegan despairs. He'll later resign.

Deutschland   Olympiastadion
               München

England

1 : 5

01.SEP.
2001

English ecstasy. The scoreboard in Munich shows the triumphant margin of their World Cup qualifying win against a seemingly impregnable Germany.

A depressed Sven-Goran Eriksson and David Beckham after England's defeat by Portugal in the 2006 World Cup.

Steve McClaren gestures in vain. His fatal 3–5–2 selection is on its way to defeat by Croatia in Zagreb in a European qualifier in October 2006.

Denmark, gave himself another chance with the win in Salonika, but then slid steadily into bewildering basic error. Not that there was any good new reason for believing that Brian Clough, the People's Choice, who had spitefully attacked Bobby Robson on the previous weekend, had the credentials to take over.

Yet if English football was in the doldrums, it was salutary to remember that in 1953, after the Hungarians' annihilation of England at Wembley, a book appeared called *Learn to Play the Hungarian Way*. What Hungarian way, one might now well ask?

In Budapest, Luther Blissett played, and must have felt this a blessed release from his club football. Then with Milan, he had lived in a nightmare, subject to full-page inquests. In his own weird, unorthodox, exciting way, he set up the second England goal, missed a couple in the second half, never showing the class, control or composure of an international striker. Nor, alas, of one who could succeed in the Campionato.

The rest of the season was inevitably an anticlimax, as Denmark duly won the qualifying group; though there would be consolations on the close-season tour of South America. There was the formality of a 4-0 win in Luxembourg in the last European qualifier, Bryan Robson scoring two of the goals, after which Bobby Robson spoke vaguely about one door closing and another one opening. Which? Form, like Bobby Robson himself, continued wildly to oscillate. Things fell apart, the centre did not hold, in Paris, where Graham Roberts and Terry Butcher at centre back looked a couple of cart horses, ridiculed by a dazzling Michel Platini, scorer of both French goals (the first a defensive horror), while the Luton strike pair of Brian Stein and Paul Walsh made a dismal debut. France won 2–0. Woodock and John Barnes got on only as 88th-minute substitutes. Chaos.

After a win, a draw and a defeat in the British Championship, the USSR now came to Wembley and won with abysmal ease, overwhelming England's 4–2–4 system in the midfield, seriously outnumbered. When right back Mike Duxbury fell flat, the Soviets scored. In the last minute, when the celebrated Oleg Blokhin eluded England's plodding defence, Shilton couldn't hold his shot and Oleg Protassov hit home.

After that, the decision to embark on a South American tour, especially with Brazil in prospect, seemed a hostage to fortune. Even if a rebuilt Brazil, under a new manager in Edu, were an unknown quantity. Against all logic and prognostication, England won in the now crumbling vastness of the Maracana with a goal from John Barnes which, in its sheer virtuosity, ranked with any ever seen there. Brazil's gamble of playing veterans in midfield went badly awry. Bobby Robson's gamble – he insisted it wasn't one – on using two wingers in a 4–2–4 came off. Cutting in from the left flank, cruising at speed past man after man, Barnes eventually gave England the lead. Don Howe, the coach, praised him. 'To run with the ball that distance and keep it at his feet was absolutely great. Running with the ball on that surface was not impossible, but it was very difficult. It was like running on straw, sticking all the time. Magnificent run, that.'

It was indeed, and, against Argentina in Mexico City in the 1986 World Cup, Barnes would have two more to match it. Yet in subsequent times, he would be booed by the England fans, convinced that he was not giving his all. The fact was that he was almost constitutionally relaxed, and had come into professional football almost by chance. Son of the Jamaican military attaché in London, he was playing amateur football on a public park at seventeen when a Watford fan spotted him, recommended him, and he effortlessly made the transition to League football.

His perfect centre gave the big young centre forward Mark Hateley, then in the Second Division with Portsmouth but due, like Ray Wilkins, shortly to join Milan, England's second, powerfully headed, goal. Mark had the same aerial power of his father, the much-travelled Tony, though he said it had been hard – with two wingers – to find people to pass to.

Defeat by Uruguay in Montevideo was something of an anticlimax, the two goals conceded on a penalty against Hateley for hands – unjust, he believed – and after an untypical error by the new centre back, Dave Watson, misjudging a high centre. A dull goalless draw played out by a tired team in Santiago followed. The World Cup qualifiers loomed; at last there was cause for hope.

But at the start of the new season, it was soon clear that Bobby

Robson was a worrying, cautious, anxious manager, at least at international level, where a manager perforce must spend so much time alone. In the Wembley friendly against East Germany in September 1984, he decided to drop Hateley, and restore the old warhorse, Paul Mariner, who, to be fair, lumbered about to reasonable purpose. Moreover, Robson assured us, with nearly two years to go, that this would be the team he'd field in Mexico. Dropping Hateley so soon after such a splendid tour seemed an ideal way to demoralise a young player. So much for psychology. Significantly, a mere 23,000 turned up to watch England squeeze another of their 1–0 victories. And why always Wembley, when other leading nations, Italy especially, played in numerous venues?

Still, Northern Ireland, concurrently, had done England a good turn by beating Romania, their chief rivals in the World Cup group in Belfast. First up for England were Finland at Wembley, and this time, Mariner having pulled a muscle, Hateley returned, dynamically. Chasing, challenging, galvanising, scoring twice in a 5–0 win. Yet he would not even be in Istanbul four weeks later, when, imperiously, England annihilated the Turks 8–0. True, the home team were known to be horribly vulnerable, without a win for a year, beaten even by modest Finland, but the margin was still unexpected.

Three of the goals went to an irresistible Bryan Robson, surging through from midfield. Ray Wilkins, revitalised by his months in Milan, inspired the attack, yet on arrival in Istanbul he'd found the players 'really quiet. There should be more joking around. Whether they were a bit apprehensive, I don't know.' It didn't last long. When Bryan Robson scored his first from a corner, the Turks cravenly collapsed. 'Even when we were eight up,' pursued Wilkins, 'I was saying, come on, we've got to get more if we can. You just can't see Turkey helping us out, so we've got to give them a bloody good hiding.'

In Belfast the following February, Hateley would return and score the only goal. Bobby Robson spoke somewhat smugly of 'battle'. To the less subjective, it resembled a battle between dinosaurs, a wilderness of stratospheric punts by both keepers. 'Typical English Championship play,' said Romania's sophisticated young manager and former captain, Mircea Lucescu. 'More play in the air than on the ground.' What happened to Ray Wilkins, in such dazzling form for Milan, but so deep in Belfast that he largely fed his goalkeeper? 'I don't think I was myself,' he admitted. At least Hateley's goal was a fine piece of opportunism. 'When I saw Pat Jennings [the Irish keeper] putting every ball on Kenny Sansom's napper, I knew just what they were going to do.' But did England have to emulate them?

In March, there was a meaningless and incoherent 2–1 win against the Republic of Ireland in a Wembley friendly, with Bobby Robson, who'd excoriated the press for lambasting the fiasco of Belfast, lurching from depression to euphoria, forgiving the dreadful mistake whereby the new keeper, Gary Bailey, had given Liam Brady his goal near the end. The crucial test came on May Day in Bucharest against Romania and it ended goalless, Gary Lineker, destined to score so many goals for England, getting on the field only for the last seven minutes. In those early international days, there was no doubt about his pace, skill and opportunism, only about his finishing. Had Hateley been fit, it might have been an English victory; something which Lucescu had expected.

Hateley would be back to score against Finland in Helsinki in May, the next European game, but consistency was as remote as ever in Bobby Robson's teams in a miserable 1–1 draw. The midfield was a disaster. Three days later to Hampden in a wholly superfluous match, the so-called Stanley Rous Cup – switched from Wembley for fear of the violent and aggressive Scots supporters – England lost there for the first time in nine years. This time it was Glenn Hoddle whom Lineker replaced, after eighty minutes; a Hoddle, who, perversely, had been obliged to play wide on the right. That was the measure of Bobby Robson's mistrust of him.

In Mexico, where England now played in a pre-World Cup tournament, the other England players actually conspired to see to it that Hoddle could move into the middle. The games were played under the deep shadow of the Heysel Disaster, where thirty-nine (mostly Italian) fans had died, after a charge by drunken Liverpool supporters caused a wall to collapse, before the European Cup final at the crumbling deathtrap of a stadium in Brussels. One found the Italian players and Enzo Bearzot, due to play England, astonishingly tolerant and sympathetic. Mexico City's altitude and pollution made conditions oppressive, compounded by the television-induced need to play in the heat of day. English clubs, meanwhile, would be banned from Europe for the next five years, with the inevitable consequences of isolation.

In the first game, Italy beat England 2–1 on a somewhat doubtful penalty. Hateley headed a typical goal and thought he should have had a penalty when pushed by Giuseppe Bergomi. Worryingly, he found it insufferably hot and difficult to breathe. That the World Cup finals would be played in Mexico was clearly scandalous, but clearly inevitable when, after the 1982 World Cup final in Madrid, Joao Havelange, the serpentine President of FIFA, flew out of Madrid to Mexico in the private plane of Emilio Azcarraga, owner of Televisa Mexicana, the Mexican plutocrat. Did Hateley get tired, one asked? 'Only in the last eighty minutes.' Hoddle came on as substitute, showed casual skills, set up Hateley's goal, prompting Bobby Robson to say he wished he'd play for ninety minutes as he did in those twenty. As if, in the conditions, anybody could without acclimatisation. The Germans, who arrived later than the other teams, didn't begin to adjust and lost 3–0 to England in the latter's third game, two goals being scored by a newcomer, the tall, blond Chelsea centre forward Kerry Dixon with Lineker in fine form for an hour. As indeed had been Trevor Francis in the previous game, lost 1–0 to the Mexican hosts.

Dixon said he loved playing with Hoddle whom Bobby Robson, one felt, would gladly drop again, given half a chance. Francis, lamenting the difficulties of adjustment, said you had to make yourself time to recover after every burst. By turns sullen and euphoric, Bobby Robson remarked in a euphoric moment that, 'We'll play Italy any time.' He hadn't met the real Italy at all. Heading home, England easily dispatched the USA 5–0 in Los Angeles. Reasonable optimism seemed justified.

The return game at Wembley against Romania came as early as 11 September and it was another draw, this time 1–1. Glenn Hoddle scored for England in the first half, Rodion Camataru broke through to equalise, with a suspicion of handball at the start of his run, in the second. Lucescu said Camataru had 'taken the ball with the outside of his chest'. But undeniably Camataru had exposed the fragility of England's central defence, composed this time of Terry Fenwick and the mobile but erratic Mark Wright. Only Sansom, in the England back four, looked truly adequate.

But in October, Northern Ireland went to Bucharest and gave England their passport to Mexico, winning the game 1–0. Meanwhile at Wembley, England were thrashing Turkey, 5–0 this time, with a hat trick for Lineker. When Northern Ireland came to Wembley the following month it was a goalless draw, to the outrage of Lucescu, who cried, 'Foul!' There was no evidence of collusion, though certain England players certainly preferred to see the Irish rather than the Communist Romanians go through and may at some preconscious level have masked their batteries.

What rough beast is this, one might have asked, parodying W. B. Yeats, slouching towards Monterrey, to be born? Bobby Robson continued on his glum, unpredictable, occasionally euphoric way. When a below-strength England won 4–0 in Cairo against Egypt, he celebrated the fact that the current side gave so few goals away, wholly overlooking the embarrassment of a first half in which only four stupendous saves by Peter Shilton averted goals. Later, in an appalling display in Tel Aviv against Israel, won by a mere 2–1 margin, his problems seemed larger than ever. Trevor Francis, so often injured, fell out with his club, Sampdoria of Genoa, and was relegated to the bench. Tony Woodcock was in and out of the Arsenal side. Villa's Gordon Cowans, however, showed bright promise as a playmaker, but he would not be seen in Mexico.

'*Butcher, sempre Butcher!*' Enzo Bearzot would joke. Butcher, always Butcher – Bobby Robson seemed to regard his old Ipswich centre half, however vulnerable, as a perpetual talisman. There was some consol-ation, however, in the bright form of the little Newcastle United forward, Peter Beardsley. Overall, however, one had to conclude that Bobby Robson had found the switch from the hectic, populous world of club management to the colder, isolated world of the international manager a difficult one. He seemed to change his mind a lot, to be easily dejected and upset.

Things did look up in Tblisi a month after the poor show in Israel, when England comfortably beat the USSR 1–0, with their two Italian-based playmakers, Wilkins and Cowans, on song, Hoddle majestic, Chris Waddle, so fast and so inconsistent, scoring the excellent goal. Eduard Malafeev, manager of Russia, doomed to dismissal, pronounced that 'England will be among the strongest in Mexico.' Yet who could predict anything with certainty?

In May in Los Angeles, they crushed Mexico, their future hosts, 3–0, but there was an ominous undertone to the match. Bryan Robson, essential fulcrum of the midfield, whose shoulder had for some time been liable to dislocation, collapsed and had to leave the field. Bobby Robson announced that no dislocation had occurred, which was a lie. A white lie, he insisted, in his subsequent, abysmal World Cup diary – Hoddle's, after the 1998 tournament, would be equally and expensively dire. The consequence was that Bryan would play in Mexico when palpably unfit, Bobby declaring fatuously and disingenuously, after all his years as player and manager, that when a shoulder went out easily, it went back easily. He knew better than anyone that, in such circumstances, an operation to pin it was the sole solution.

Why the lie? It was hard to get a straight answer out of him even when, some years later, I had a face-to-face interview with him in Lancaster Gate. But if Bobby's luck was out when his key man was injured it was emphatically in when Bryan dislocated the shoulder again playing against Morocco. At last forced to drop out, as was the expelled Ray Wilkins, it thus obliged Bobby to change his team radically for the better.

A week later in Vancouver, England had yet another of their dreary 1–0 wins, against the humble Canadians, despite fielding a team full of first choices. Lineker, alarmingly, left the field with his arm in a sling with a suspected double fracture, but here Bobby's luck was emphatically in; he would recover in time to excel in Mexico.

Not, alas, in the opening game against Portugal in Monterrey, but then nor did anybody else. Portugal's players had been rebellious, accusing their officials of treating them as though they were 'without a head and a heart', but they showed more heart than England on this occasion. The weather was hot and humid, the grass too long. Glenn Hoddle played, but couldn't save England. Yet when the squad was in training in Colorado Springs, Bobby Robson suddenly and surprisingly went into small ecstasies about him, declaring that he'd never thought he'd find a player to equal Johnny Haynes, with whom he'd played for Fulham and England. So we learned that the Road to Damascus passed through Colorado Springs.

Maradona Hands England Defeat in the Sun: World Cup, Argentina 1986

Robson's men made a shocking start to their campaign, losing by a cataclysmic goal. First Kenny Sansom, England's experienced left back, allowed Diamantino to slip past him, almost on the goal line. Butcher failed to cover, Gary Stevens the right back was absent at the far post, Carlos Manuel scored.

England on the same ground were no better against Morocco, when they lost both Bryan Robson and a now increasingly negative Ray Wilkins, untypically guilty of throwing the ball at the referee. Going in at half time, with Wilkins sent off, the players turned on the coach, Don Howe, who reportedly had been working them too hard in training. 'You're always telling us what to do!' they assailed him. 'What the fuck do we do now?' It was England's good fortune that the Moroccans, though they had several accomplished players, seemingly thought England too bad to be true, failed to exploit their one-man advantage and allowed the English off the hook, with a goalless draw.

In the team's hotel high up at Santillo, Bryan Robson, wearing a harness, wanted to go on. Wilkins, insisting he never intended the ball to strike the referee, thought he should. But not even Bobby Robson concurred and now the players had their way. In the vital third group game against Poland, they saw to it that Trevor Steven should play on the right flank, busy, tough little Peter Reid and Steve Hodge in midfield. It was a team transformed.

Gary Lineker, exceptionally fast but an erratic finisher, now became the unerring marksman, scoring all three English goals, splendidly and unselfishly supported now by the returning Peter Beardsley, inexplicably left out of the first two games. Lineker, always the essence of long-suffering sportsmanship whatever the provocation, scored twice in the first fourteen minutes, got a third when the Polish keeper, Jozef Mlynarczyk, dropped the ball: 3–0. A transformation.

So to the Azteca Stadium in Mexico City and another 3–0 victory, this time over a cynical Paraguay. Things might have been different but for two fine saves by Shilton, following blunders by his centre backs, first Martin, then Butcher. Scarcely had Shilton made his second save than England broke and scored, Hoddle and Hodge enabling Lineker to find the empty goal. In the second half, when the violent Paraguayans were indulged by a feeble Syrian referee, Lineker was brutally chopped across the throat by Rogelio Delgado, the centre back. Characteristically ironic, he afterwards observed, 'It was an accident. At least, I hope it was.' While he was off the field, Peter Beardsley scored a second and he himself had the satisfaction of getting the third.

Now, in the quarter-final at the Azteca, it would be Argentina, with all the looming aftermath of the Falklands War. Open, decent Jose Luis Brown, the Argentine centre back, clubless at the time, observed, 'We all had cousins, fathers, nephews in the Falklands, and some of them didn't come back. Lamentable things, but we shan't be thinking of them.'

Bobby Robson gave another of his gloomy press conferences, disputing the perfectly justified suggestion that England had started slowly. As to the menace of Maradona, 'I've got twenty-four hours to devise a way to stop Maradona. It won't be easy. Other teams have already tried everything. They've assigned one man to mark him, they've closed down space, they've let him go while attempting to cut off his service. To no avail. Let's just say that without Maradona, Argentina would have no chance of winning the World Cup. That's how great he is.' But who could anticipate the Hand of God?

The first half was somewhat placid, even Maradona seldom emerging. On fifty minutes, however, Maradona raced into the heart of the England defence, but lost the ball. Jorge Valdano, the tall attacker, failed to retain it, whereupon Steve Hodge, in a bizarre moment of aberration, kicked it over his head back into his own penalty box. It should have been Shilton's ball, but little Maradona jumped with him, stretched up a hand, and punched it into the net.

The inexperienced referee, the Tunisian, Ali Ben Naceur, appointed no doubt in an excess of political correctness, saw no evil, neither did his bemused linesman, and the goal was scandalously given. Scored, Maradona would afterwards provocatively maintain, by the Hand of God.

His second goal was altogether different, product of an astonishing slalom as he came in from the right, wrong-footing and leaving behind Stevens, Butcher and Fenwick, before he beat Shilton. After the game, the Roman journalist Gianni Melidoni opined that at that point, England were still in a state of shock, like a man who has just had his wallet stolen.

It was on seventy-four minutes that John Barnes arrived on the left wing and all but transformed the game with a superb exhibition of pace, power and control, far too much, against Argentina's new formation, a sweeper behind five others, for the right-sided Giusti, who was no real full back. Since his phenomenal goal in Rio, Barnes had been disappointingly erratic, though some blamed Bobby Robson for allegedly insisting that he play too close to his own left back. Now, however, ten minutes from time, five minutes after his inclusion, he escaped past Giusti and Lineker headed in his immaculate cross. On eighty-seven minutes, Barnes did it again, and for a fleeting moment it looked as if Lineker had scored. This time, however, it was Lineker, and not the ball, who ended in the net. England were beaten 2–1, Lineker was top scorer of the tournament with half a dozen goals, and was now en route to Barcelona. Good luck, bad luck? If Bobby Robson had been lucky when forced to remodel his team, the Hand of God had brought him no luck at all.

This should have been the start of something good. Alas, Bobby and his team were hell bent towards the monumental disappointments and humiliations of the European Championship finals, in which every game was lost and Bobby himself was pilloried. As indeed he had been when his wretched World Cup diary was published shortly before the 1986–87 season began. Interrogated in Stockholm, where England played and lost their first friendly of the new season, over Bryan Robson and his shoulder, Bobby's explanation was laughable. He was 'protecting' Bryan, he declared, at the players' request, in his anxiety not to let the football world know what was wrong with him. A deeply unhappy start to the new campaign to reach the European finals.

The opposition consisted of Yugoslavia, clearly the chief challenger, Northern Ireland and recent World Cup victims Turkey. The Irish were comfortably beaten 3–0 at Wembley with two goals for Lineker (one of them dazzling), bright performances from Hoddle, Beardsley and Hodge. It was a different proposition when the Yugoslavs visited Wembley in November. The game was won 2–0 with goals by Mabbutt and an enterprising Anderson, but the England defence was chaotic, affording the Yugoslav striker, Zlatko Vukovic, four spurned chances to score. The central defenders – Butcher, too slow, and Wright, too erratic – were alarmingly vulnerable.

Hope lay in the increasingly resilient form of the twenty-year-old Arsenal centre back, Tony Adams, though little did any of us know that he was well on the way to alcoholism. He made a reassuring debut against Spain in a Madrid friendly the following February, notable for the fact that Lineker, in lethal form, got all England's goals in a 4–2 win.

Adams admitted that he had to concentrate so much more than in a club game that by the end he had a headache. Lineker praised him. Miguel Munoz, the manager of Spain, praised Lineker: 'Lineker was the best on the field. He found space very well, but you must realise that this is one of the virtues that good players possess.' It must have been especially satisfying for an inspired Hoddle, who had been omitted when the teams last met in Madrid, in that fatal 1982 World Cup game.

From the sublime to the ridiculous. Or, if you prefer it, snakes and ladders. In Izmir, Turkey, who'd lost 8–0 to England on the previous occasion the teams had met on Turkish soil, set about the English team with a ferocity largely unchecked by Valeri Butenko, a feeble Russian referee. Bryan Robson was plainly unfit, Clive Allen of Spurs unfitted to lead the attack, which looked dangerous only when he was replaced by Hateley. For much of the game, played in a strong, bitter wind, England were under siege, but – Robson's luck, again – the Turks were without their two best forwards.

Still, qualification seemed feasible, the November trip to Belgrade being the cloud on the horizon. Predict Robson's England at your peril. In Dusseldorf, opening the new season with a September friendly, the central defence made a plethora of mistakes, some fourteen in all, five of them by Adams, Germany winning 3–1 in a canter. Yet when Turkey came to Wembley the following month, England thrashed them 8–0 again with Hoddle, coming on as a sub to play deep on the right, supreme where he'd been suppressed in Germany, Neil Webb showing international promise in midfield which, alas, would not endure. This, said Bobby Robson, was a team for a home match – with wingers, one assumed he meant. But the defence, even on a night like this, still looked fragile under pressure.

On a raw, rainy afternoon in Belgrade, England went ahead in four minutes, Peter Beardsley exploiting a weak header back to the Yugoslav keeper, and the Yugoslavs were stunned. Two goals in a minute followed in the twelfth and thirteenth, the first from a free kick in the box. Surprisingly Lineker, in the doldrums at Barcelona, did little, as Bobby Robson observed. Beardsley was the main man in a 4–1 victory. 'The best philosophy,' said Bobby, in his euphoria, 'is always to go for a win, wherever you are.'

England Slaughtered in Euro 88

Those words would ring horribly hollow when the European finals took place in West Germany, the following summer. The opening game was as big a blow to Bobby Robson as it was a vindication for Jackie Charlton, now the Republic of Ireland's manager, having been churlishly ignored by the Football Association. In Stuttgart, after a comedy of defensive errors, little Ray Houghton, a Glaswegian Scot – Jackie Charlton cast his net far and wide for players of Irish descent whatever their provenance – headed the game's only goal.

Bobby Robson himself seemed curiously confused; his team talks were reportedly prone to odd errors. Against Holland, in their second game, England were simply brushed aside. Marco Van Basten, who'd been used in Holland's first match only as a substitute, was irrepressible, scoring all his team's goals in a 3–1 win. Hoddle, who'd himself come on as a lively substitute against Ireland, was ineffectual. Fabio

Capello, scorer of that historic winning goal at Wembley and later a top club coach, remarked, 'I didn't see any reaction in the team. That was the thing that left me amazed; there wasn't the *rage* you expect from an England team that's losing.'

Rage, rage against the dying of the light; which definitively died in England's third and last game, when a Soviet team full of Dynamo Kiev players, managed by the Ukraine club's father figure, Valeri Lobanovski, cut through the English defence at will. Hoddle gave the ball away ineptly on the first Soviet goal, though his own free kick enabled Tony Adams to equalise against the run of play. Trevor Steven sent a bouncing header against the bar when he should have scored, but the Soviets then won 3–1 in a canter.

Sandrino Mazzola, a star attacker with Italy and Inter not long since, was quite astonished. 'This is incredible. What future can England have now? If they go on with him [Bobby Robson] it means that they won't win anything. I don't think he'll change his tactics. A team with Bryan Robson, Lineker and Barnes has players few other sides have. The last few years, English players have technically been getting better, but they don't combine it with the drive they used to have and I think that depends on the manager.'

Robson himself asserted that the Soviet defeat was 'England's one bad game, and the team were slaughtered for it'. The root problem was bad finishing. He sought to defend Lineker on the grounds he had been afflicted by incipient jaundice. He qualified those views the following year, when, to my huge surprise, he consented to that *tête-à-tête* in his Lancaster Gate office: he told another journalist that he didn't know whether to 'kick me in the balls' or accept the invitation, unaware that I was as reluctant about it as he, but under pressure from my sports editor.

In reply to Mazzola, he said that he respected the player, 'But that's just his opinion. I agree he mentioned three outstanding players, but that's three out of eleven. At the end of the Championship, Lineker wasn't a fit man. I knew he maybe could last sixty minutes against Russia and I was happy to take the chance.' As to his peculiar response to that defeat, when he made no reference to some wretched defending, he rejoined, 'Yes, but what I can't do is pan the players in public, can

I? You can, I can't. I have got people who have to play for me the next day. I can't do that. I've got to go into the next room and work with these players.'

How to recover from the nadir in Germany? England's next season, with World Cup qualification again in view, was one of strange paradox. It was initially hard to regard Robson as anything but a busted flush, a mere survivor, so badly exposed in Euro 88 that there was no logical case for his remaining. I even found myself at one point suggesting that Brian Clough be brought in, if only on a brief and temporary basis, to give the team a stimulus. Yet England, after vertiginous ups and downs, finished the season unbeaten, although they had touched the depths in November with a desperate draw in Saudi Arabia.

Sweden, favourites in a group which also included Poland and Albania, fell out of form, came to Wembley in October for the first World Cup qualifier in evident decline, and were held to a draw. Lip service was paid by Bobby Robson to Hoddle, whose midfield skills were badly missed, but he clearly had no intention of recalling him. Paul Gascoigne, maverick of mavericks, superbly skilled but wildly unpredictable, was used only in fits and starts during the season, beginning with an absurd five-minute appearance against Denmark in the opening September friendly at Wembley, quintessentially the kind of player who would beat against the long tradition of English conformism. But at least, in Nottingham Forest's Des Walker, Bobby Robson at last found and used a centre back with the pace so badly lacking in the middle.

The Swedish game was a goalless draw, accompanied by the now habitual Cockney chant of 'What a load of rubbish.' Yet the cries of 'Robson out!' came, illogically, at the very moment when England seemed likely to win the game and would have done were it not for two glaring and untypical misses by, of all people, Gary Lineker, clearly not match fit. Yet at least this gave England breathing space until the following March during which, after the horrors of Riyadh, they beat Greece in Athens in a February friendly, Barnes and Bryan Robson scoring.

Next it was Albania in Tirana, then a bizarre timewarp of a city, where white painted bicycles without lamps whirled through the darkness, storks nested on roofs, and Communism still ruled with an iron hand. Rather as in Cairo, it was one of those odd games in which England were initially outplayed, saved time and again by Shilton, only to run out winners 2–0, with Barnes and Robson on the mark again. When Albania came to Wembley the following month, it was to be thrashed 5–0, with Gascoigne, on for thirty-four minutes, a scorer. But the sight of Butcher, lumbering back into defence like a man looking for a taxi while Albania all but scored, was worryingly significant. Beardsley, back at last, scored twice that evening.

Then, in early June, after another redundant Rous Cup – curiously contested by Chile, who drew a paralysingly dull game at Wembley while England won in Glasgow – came a crucial 3–0 win at home to Poland in the World Cup. Yet the score was somewhat illusory. Time and again Walker's pace bailed out the English defence, though Poland looked a slipshod, nervous, demoralised team on the whole.

Before the last match of the season, a friendly drawn 1–1 in Copenhagen against a Denmark lacking several stars, Bobby Robson gave one of his morose press conferences, accusing the press of having been unfair to England after the Polish victory. England, he said, had made eighteen chances; it was natural they'd given a few away. Yet only in the final stages had two of those chances been taken and the defence had looked alarmingly vulnerable to crosses to the far post. Nevertheless, this was the first season since 1974–75 in which England had finished unbeaten. Lies, damn lies, statistics? Perhaps, but at least Bobby Robson had escaped liquidation.

The return against Sweden in Stockholm came very early in the 1989–90 season. Swedish form of late had been poor (though ultimately they did just enough to win the group), but England's was hardly any better, while outside the stadium their violent hooligan supporters would disgrace themselves once again. The Swedes had latterly given six away to Denmark, four away to the French, but this was a goalless draw. Things might have been different when, in the opening minutes, Liverpool's Steve McMahon made a clear chance for Gary Lineker, only for someone to blow a whistle in the crowd and Lineker to stop. 'I'm a bit annoyed,' he'd say, mildly. Shilton was again the hero, as was Butcher who, bandaged head and shirt derenched in his own blood from a wound to the brow, stood firm against wave after wave of Swedish attacks.

Robson's luck. There was a temptation to compare him with the apocryphal man who fell into a septic tank and came up smelling of eau de cologne. He was even publicly criticised by his own deputy, Don Howe, who stressed the need for a more sophisticated, flexible approach.

The subsequent trip to Katowice was yet one more occasion when Peter Shilton's superlative goalkeeping saved England from disaster, but even he was fortunate when, almost at the end, a fierce shot from distance by the Polish midfielder Ryszard Tarasiewicz beat him and twanged against the crossbar. The point-blank save he made from the incisive Polish striker Darius Dziekanowski, who had already run rings round Terry Butcher when playing for Celtic against Rangers, almost beggared belief. Modestly, Shilton reflected, 'He probably should have scored. It was a powerful header. At the end of the day, he should have given me no chance, but as it was, he gave me a chance, and I managed to get it away.' Acrobatically. So with another goalless draw, England scraped into the World Cup finals with the second best record of the group runners-up.

Tears of a Clown: World Cup, Italy 1990

England would be based in Cagliari, capital of Sardinia, where it was hoped the hooligans could be contained. Alas, there would be at least one bloody pre-match confrontation in which the English fans, by and large, were more sinned against than sinning.

Gazza would go although, given his fragile character, it was distressing to see how insensitively Bobby Robson treated him. 'Daft as a brush,' Robson called him, but, with the definitive exclusion of Hoddle, he was plainly England's one real hope of invention and surprise in midfield, with his supreme technique, his powerful right foot, his instant ability to sum up situations. Yet Robson stuck him on the left wing in a B-team international in Brighton and, shortly before the squad for Italy was announced, put him under ferocious pressure. Picking him for a friendly against the Czechs at Wembley, Robson insensitively announced that this was Gascoigne's last chance.

In the tunnel before the start, Gascoigne was kicking a ball against the wall in his anxiety, but he went out, played superbly, had a hand in three goals and got one himself, with a glorious solo.

Holland, Egypt and the Republic of Ireland, still led by Jackie Charlton, would be England's group opponents in Cagliari. The opening match against the Irish was of a blinding sterility, which led one Italian paper to head its match report, 'No Football Please, We're British'. In a harsh wind, even Gascoigne found life difficult. Lineker scored a characteristically opportunist goal in eight minutes, taking the ball past the Irish keeper Packy Bonner with his chest, running on to score. McMahon, on as a substitute, ineptly gave the ball away to Kevin Sheedy, who shot the left-footed equaliser.

Holland came next but this was a diminished Dutch team, beset by quarrels within the camp. Previously, in press conferences, Bobby Robson had insisted that the sweeper defence was utterly foreign to English footballers, and a four-in-line defence would be maintained. England's senior professionals now persuaded him otherwise, though in the event their caution proved excessive. Mark Wright, rehabilitated after his blunders against the Yugoslavs in 1986, filled the role capably but Terry Butcher found himself virtually playing at right back. The dynamic pace of Des Walker closed any gaps, though Bobby Robson had constantly criticised him for being reluctant to cross the halfway line. Further invaluable pace was given to the defence by little Paul Parker. In Katowice, Jacek Ziober and Roman Kosecki, the long-haired little Polish wingers, had overrun the English backs.

It was yet another goalless draw but England deserved to win, making far the greater number of chances, with Lineker, paired up front with John Barnes hitting the keeper's body and missing a clear opportunity later. Gascoigne now was emphatically up and running. This was a revitalised England.

Press relations meanwhile were at rock bottom, the consequence of those tabloid 'revelations' about the two Robsons. Naïvely, Bobby gave free run of the England camp to a novelist called Pete Davies who rewarded him in his subsequent book with a string of indiscretions; many, such as Gascoigne's telephone rant at his girlfriend, of the kind which any professional sports journalist would have excluded. The news media's lack of reticence, however, appeared to have no obvious effect on the team's performance.

Against Egypt, England reverted to a four-in-line defence. Ultra cautious, the Egyptians hardly deserved the praise afforded them by Bobby Robson after the game. Mark Wright headed the only goal from a searching free kick by Gascoigne and England were through to the next round.

Their opponents would be Belgium in Bologna, where, after 119 minutes England prevailed with a goal superbly and gymnastically struck by substitute David Platt, a late-developing attacker, discarded by Manchester United, groomed by Crewe Alexandra, burnished by Aston Villa. It was Gazza's free kick – again – from the left which enabled Platt to swivel and volley his goal. Once again, England played with a sweeper, which seemed somewhat redundant, since the Belgians used only one striker. Belgium twice hit the post. Barnes, after a splendid move, had a goal contentiously ruled out for a dubious offside.

Next, to Naples, where the opposition was the tournament's surprise package, Cameroon, none more so than their astonishing centre forward Roger Milla, aged (at least) thirty-eight, who was wont to come on and score as a second-half substitute. Cameroon had shocked Argentina by beating the holders in the curtain-raising game.

They very nearly beat England, too. 'A flat back four saved us,' said Bobby Robson, the following day. The point being that England had again started with a sweeper, in the shape of Wright. In the event, the three English centre backs served only to confuse one another. Though the abrasive Cameroon team had no fewer than four players suspended, they were vigorously effective, all the more so when the veteran Milla made his usual entry at half time. Without Bryan Robson, injured yet again and back in Blighty, and with David Platt starting for the first time, England took the lead when Platt headed in a left-flank cross from an adventurous Stuart Pearce. But yet again, only the defiance of Peter Shilton kept England's goal intact.

An erratic Mexican referee, Codesal, gave anomalous decisions in the second half, above all on penalties. Platt should have had one when brought down by the keeper, Thomas N'Kono, Cameroon got one when Gascoigne, fitfully inspired, felled Milla; Emmanuel Kunde scored. Eugene Ekeke, served by Milla, made it 2–1, whereupon Bobby Robson jettisoned the sweeper system which was never natural to him, taking off Butcher and finally putting on Trevor Steven. It was hard to know why Steven, who would now excel, had been out in the cold so long, but now he transformed the right flank, while Paul Parker subdued Milla.

Eight minutes before time, Gary Lineker was brought down and equalised from the spot. Mark Wright, colliding with Milla, poured blood from a cut above his right eye and had to move out of central defence; it meant England played extra time with ten fit men. On 105 minutes, however, they won the game when an inspired pass by Gascoigne put Lineker through. N'Kono brought him down, but this time he would not escape. Another penalty, and Lineker converted it. So England were in the semi-final. 'We pulled it out of the fire,' exulted Bobby Robson. 'I don't know how, sometimes. We were depleted. Wright, Walker [both had injuries]. But the two midfield players [Gascoigne and Platt] worked marvellously hard, they ran for miles . . . Parker and Trevor Steven did very, very well. Parker jumped like a salmon, tackled like a ferret. We were told to go home after the first match. Well, I believe the country back home is dancing in the streets, now . . . because we're in the top four in the world in 1990 . . . and I'm proud of that, because I stand up for our football.'

Now he said he would go to bed for two days. 'Then come and ask. We're going to enjoy it. We'll worry about Germany in good time. They're very good, we know what confronts us and they know what confronts them.'

Sad to reflect that what awaited England was the meaningless anti-climax of a third place match in Bari, which they'd lose to Italy. 'We've got here,' reflected Bobby Robson later, before the semi-final. 'I don't know how.'

Robson's luck? It certainly ran out in Turin against Germany, when England succumbed on penalties after extra time. And there was arguably ill luck when the Germans led, on the hour – a shot by the

German full back Andy Brehme hit Parker, curling into the air, over Shilton's head and into the net.

England, who again used Terry Butcher as sweeper but again replaced him in the second half with Trevor Steven, equalised ten minutes from time, when Parker crossed from the right; Jurgen Kohler and Klaus Augenthaler, central defenders, clumsily confused one another, allowing the unmarked Lineker to score. And, in an iconic moment much analysed in the years since, Gascoigne was cautioned and promptly wept when he realised it would mean suspension from the next match – possibly the final. Tears that touched so many. The daft brush had become the sad clown.

Overall, the German team looked tired, but it held out into extra time, during which each team hit the post: Chris Waddle for England, Guido Buchwald for Germany, while Shilton made glorious saves from Lothar Matthaus and Jurgen Klinsmann. But when it came to penalties, Pearce shot into the keeper Illgner's flying body, Waddle shot over the bar, and England were out.

In a moment of utter fatuity Peter Swales, Manchester City's chairman, and leading member of the Senior International Committee, announced that he would rather England lost the World Cup than Bobby Robson remain. Doubly fatuous, in that Robson had already announced before the tournament that he would not be continuing. So ended a stewardship hardly remarkable for its consistency, yet successful enough in two World Cups.

6 DO I NOT LIKE THAT

Graham Taylor 1990–94
Key Game: Norway v England, June 1993

'YOU'RE A LIAR, YOU WRITE LIES! YOU'RE A LIAR, YOU WRITE LIES!' Thus Graham Taylor, then manager of Watford, when he refused to shake hands with me ('I can't, I can't!') after a match against Queens Park Rangers at Shepherd's Bush. What was he talking about? I wondered, as the tirade continued, and we continued to argue in the corridor outside the press room. Gradually, as the smoke cleared, I realised he was talking about a criticism I'd made of him fully three years before in *World Soccer* magazine, when, during a youth international in Tel Aviv, he substituted a young full back who'd disagreed with his tactics.

My informant, a *Sunday Times* colleague, had sat next to Graham Taylor on the bench. Since, on examination, several other players had been substituted, perhaps Taylor had a case of sorts; other substitutions had been made, but his outburst was surely excessive. 'I couldn't understand it,' said QPR's manager Jim Smith, when I returned to Loftus Road a few days later. 'It was nothing to do with you.'

Well, it was; even if it seemed a classical Freudian instance of displacement; unconsciously transposing emotion from one subject on to another. In this case, my sustained criticism of Taylor's long-ball tactics, which seemed to me to be tainting the essence of English football, precisely because Watford initially made such positive use of them.

As we know, Taylor's guru was Wing Commander Charles Reep with his obsolescent Match Analysis. Leaving Watford, Taylor moderated his tactics at Aston Villa with some success. Once he came into the press box after a match at Millwall and asked me, 'Shall we start again?' On this occasion we did shake hands. I'd never disliked him personally, but when he was appointed to manage England, it bewildered me. Nor, in the ensuing years, did I ever understand the logic of it.

Tactically, he would always be compromised. His natural penchant for the long ball could hardly be indulged at this level, yet when it was not deployed there was a tactical void, a situation of neither fish nor fowl, which in retrospect made Bobby Robson seem almost a model of consistency.

True, Taylor took England, however uneasily, to the finals of the 1992 European Championship in Sweden where, though he was slightly unlucky to be eliminated by the Swedish hosts, he hardly assisted his cause with the bizarre substitution of Gary Lineker, on the verge of establishing a new England goalscoring record, with the assiduous but far less dynamic Alan Smith, supposedly to 'hold up the ball', at the very moment when England were desperate for a goal.

When it came to the qualifiers for the 1994 World Cup, it was scarcely a surprise when England fell by the wayside, Taylor's tactics in a crucial game in Norway defying rationality. And if Paul Gascoigne could be a trial to three successive England managers, Taylor unquestionably made a clumsy and ill-considered beginning, leaving him out of a qualifying game in Dublin on grounds that, given the Irish style, the ball would be often in the air, only to pick, in Gordon Cowans, a man who was shorter than Gascoigne. Ringing down the years is his agonised cry of 'Do I not like that!' when he sat on the bench in Holland, watching England's World Cup hopes being destroyed.

Yet till that third game of his reign against Ireland, he had made quite a promising start. A 'friendly' victory at Wembley over a weakened Hungary side was unimpressive, but when Poland arrived there for the first of the European qualifiers – admittedly without the incisive Dziekanowski – a 2–0 victory raised optimism.

To sweep or not to sweep, that was the question. True, Terry Butcher had at last proved a resourceful *libero* for England in their doomed semi-final against the Germans, but Taylor's attempt to use the system against the pallid Hungarians looked a snare and a delusion. It was right when the attacking sweeper, essential to Total Football, could have had free reign, but against a team which managed one shot throughout the game, the watchword was caution. A winger, in Waddle, was sacrificed till late in the game, and the full backs didn't overlap. Gary Lineker, captain for the first time, scored the one meagre goal.

Next, Poland, who had just contrived to lose humiliatingly in Warsaw to the USA. England won 2–0 despite the system rather than because of it. In a good humoured and plausible press conference next day, Taylor admitted he'd been thinking of changing the strategy at half time, though you couldn't help wondering whether this was an implicit apology for tactics which didn't work. He also admitted, in Thatcherite parlance, that England had been 'rather swamped' in midfield because the defenders were slow and reluctant to push up. But the midfield itself seemed undermanned. So Lineker was forced to drop into midfield, Gascoigne, splendid in flashes, similarly to lie deeper than he wished. Taylor was surely right to say that, before judging Gazza as a person, we should exhaust all possibilities of assessing him in football terms. Lineker, from a penalty and Peter Beardsley, in the last minute, scored in a 2–0 win.

The Republic of Ireland, then, was the first real test, and on a bumpy Lansdowne Road pitch, in a high wind, England without Gascoigne survived Jackie Charlton's long-ball bombardment. There seemed no logic in Taylor's preferring Cowans, who'd been out of the England team for four years. In leaving Gazza out, one reflected, Taylor was making a statement: that he was as wary of this gifted maverick as selectors and managers of England had been of others like him down the years.

It was a wretched game and, in the early phases England's sweeper defence struggled in the wind against the towering Niall Quinn, not least by a now erratic Tony Adams who within days was to begin three ignominious months in prison for crashing his car when drunk. It was ironic that Ireland's equalising goal should be headed by Tony

Cascarino, the player bought by Taylor for Aston Villa late the previous season when, you might say, the cloven hoof of long-ball theory was showing again. David Platt started and energetically finished the move which brought England the opening goal. But the omens were somewhat bleak.

So to the winter hiatus, activity resuming in February at Wembley with a friendly against a Milla-less Cameroon team, vastly different from the one which had so exuberantly tested England in Naples. Milla demanded too much money, the team as a whole demanded cash before they played. This time, Taylor seemed to get things right: at last a flat back four, with Trevor Steven belatedly on the right wing. Gazza, alas, pulled a groin in the second half; Bryan Robson returned, but diminished.

Ian Wright got his first chance in this game. A striker of dynamic pace, he had excelled the previous year at Wembley for Crystal Palace, in the Cup final against Manchester United. Wright had played till his early twenties in non-League football for London's Greenwich Borough. The case for his inclusion on this occasion was not proven, likewise whether he and Lineker – scorer of both goals, one a spot kick, in the 2–0 win – could co-exist. Indeed, he would never quite convince Taylor, though his opportunism would on occasion be invaluable.

In March, the Irish came to Wembley and drew, irrepressible where England were pitiful. True there was no Gazza, Steven, Waddle or McMahon, but England's ninth-minute goal, from the right back Lee Dixon, was a freak. England's three centre backs, with no designated sweeper, criminally left Niall Quinn quite unmarked to head in a cross by the outstanding Paul McGrath. Ray Houghton, whose goal had beaten England in Stuttgart in the previous European Championship, disastrously missed an easy chance to score the winner. 'Back to the drawing board,' was the headline writer's message for the England manager.

Turkey were the other team in the group, a bit of a basket case, thrashed 5–0 in Dublin. England, without Gascoigne, Steven and McMahon, and with Bryan Robson and Chris Waddle culpably ignored, squeezed through 1–0 in Izmir with a goal on his debut by

Chelsea's peppery little Dennis Wise. That Taylor should have preferred as pedestrian a player as the Crystal Palace midfielder, Geoff Thomas, was a worrying indication of his penchant for the less inspired. Speaking on television, his skin seemed perilously and not untypically thin. Still, on a dreadful pitch in Dublin, the Irish could only draw 0–0 with the Poles, and the road to Sweden still beckoned.

Gascoigne proceeded impetuously to smash up his knee in the Cup final, thus putting himself out for a year. So when Argentina came to Wembley later in May the midfield was a world made safe for Thomas and the abrasive Batty, of Leeds. Yet had England, going 2–0 ahead through Lineker and Platt, not given away two embarrassing goals from corners, they would deservedly have won. Four days earlier they had beaten a USSR side far better than a Maradona-less Argentina, 3–1, with two goals – one a penalty – for David Platt, one for Alan Smith.

June saw a meaningless, arduous tour to far-flung soccer outposts in which an England team containing numerous second-line players could win only 1–0 in Australia, 1–0 and 2–0 in New Zealand, concluding with a 4–2 victory in Malaysia in which Lineker got all the goals. Even Taylor was sceptical of the value of this exercise in accumulating air miles at the end of a long season.

The 1991–92 season began ominously with a 1–0 defeat by Germany in a friendly at Wembley in which invention, like Gascoigne, was conspicuous by its absence, players such as Gary Pallister, the ponderous Manchester United centre half, clearly inadequate, Trevor Steven wasted centrally.

Pessimism was all too fully justified when modest Turkey came to Wembley in October for their return European game and this time succumbed only 1–0. The most worrying aspect of the game was the way it exposed the evident bankruptcy of Taylor's thinking. Faced by the numb ineptitude of his team, he seemed paralysed by his problems. When substitutes were needed, none went on, Taylor strangely claiming, 'We weren't in the right mood.' Who on past experience could have predicted the tactical and technical superiority of the Turks? The former Denmark coach Sepp Piontek, now the manager of

Turkey, had called the England team predictable, and with reason. Chris Woods' alert goalkeeping saved them, the only goal coming from an error by his counterpart, Hayrettin, missing Pearce's cross, enabling Alan Smith to head home. Chris Waddle we were told would be given a roving commission. Instead, he spent the first half on the right wing, the second on the left. But Taylor could hardly be blamed for the anonymity of the returning Bryan Robson. Clearly a light of former days, this was his muted last international.

So, yet again, the crucial opposition would come from Poland, not this time in Chorzow or Katowice, but in the historic little city of Poznan. Persisting with his strange penchant for second-class players, Taylor had the Crystal Palace pair Andy Gray and Geoff Thomas in midfield, and Andy Sinton of Queens Park Rangers on the wing. Gray, all nerves, made a horrible hash of the fine chance made for him by the excellent David Platt, Gary Mabbutt scored a bizarre own goal, but headed to Lineker, playing with calm confidence, the ball with which he deftly hooked the equaliser.

Since Ireland, arguably the best team in the group, had thrown away their chances by drawing twice against Poland, England had qualified for the European finals in Sweden. Neither Taylor nor his sidekick, Lawrie McMenemy, a shrewd domestic manager at Southampton, but all at sea in European football, seemed likely to lead England to success. 'Remember your pride, lads!' McMenemy would tell the team, 'Remember the lion on your pockets!' Taylor jokingly announced that McMenemy, a broad former Guardsman, offered a good shoulder to cry on.

What did seem established was that Taylor was a lucky manager, muddling through after so signally failing to produce any kind of consistent policy, either in tactics or team selection; he still gave the impression of an international manager lurching uneasily from expedient to expedient. The learning curve grew steeper and steeper.

Yet hopes rose again when France came to Wembley in February and were comfortably beaten, 2–0. Lineker, coming on only as a second-half substitute, transformed the game with his talents. His was the second goal, the fruit of young Alan Shearer's cross. In a coruscating debut, Shearer's splendid opportunism had brought him the first goal. It was strange though, to see Lineker on the bench throughout the first half, with a spearhead of two youngsters in Shearer and David Hirst – both, as Taylor remarked, moving out too early to the flanks. But it was the first defeat for over three years for Michel Platini's French team, due to play in England's group in Sweden. Taylor modestly and tactfully insisted that the victory would have no bearing on what happened then.

One step forward, two steps back. Fluent, charming, utterly confusing, Taylor in March went to Prague with a team which made no sense at all, deploying players almost wantonly out of position. (Taylor gave the fatuous reason that he needed to mask his batteries like other teams, in a friendly. Except that on this very day, no other major team did.) David Rocastle, Arsenal's right winger, was at right back. In central midfield were striker John Barnes and Forest's clever but utterly one-paced centre forward, Nigel Clough. A late goal by Arsenal's centre back Martin Keown gave England a lucky 2–2 draw, but one was reminded that when Taylor played for Grimsby Town, he once had the task, on behalf of his chairman, of selling bottles of fresh air to tourists.

Luck, luck, luck. Were it not for a couple of dreadful errors by Packy Bonner, Ireland's goalkeeper, in Poznan, it would have been Ireland rather than England who would be going to Sweden. Yet by the time England got there, they had lost but a single game under Taylor. You can't argue with statistics – can you?

Things improved again, leading one to speculate whether Taylor's remit was an illustration of Chaos Theory. Tony Daley, a winger of skill, speed but erratic form, carefully nurtured by Taylor at Aston Villa, came into the team in Moscow, where England drew 2–2, and played again in a 1–0 win against Hungary in Budapest, each time doing well. When Taylor said of him that since Daley never knew what he was going to do, neither did the opposition, he might almost have been speaking about himself. And alas, when push came to shove in Stockholm, versus Sweden, it was Daley who'd become Taylor's nemesis.

In Budapest, Neil Webb scored the only goal, and there was time for a 1–1 draw at Wembley against a depleted Brazilian side, Gary

Lineker agonisingly missing a penalty on his last game for England at Wembley, a chance to draw level with Bobby Charlton's record goal tally; he'd announced he would retire after the European Championship.

Out of his League: European Championship, Sweden 1992

There was time for a 2–1 win in Finland en route to Sweden. 'We must only hope,' I wrote, 'that Taylor's secret weapon, his extraordinary luck, will hold.' It held in Helsinki where England won, with two goals from David Platt, but there was still no place up front for Tony Hateley, whose head could be so useful, or the precocious Alan Shearer. John Barnes had withdrawn, injured, but as against that, Denmark's Michael Laudrup, so formidable a forward, would not appear in the opening game – refusing to play for the Danes as long as Kurt Nielsen was the manager.

In Malmo, England and Denmark drew a dull goalless game. Hard to believe, then, that the Danes had virtually come straight off the beaches when at the last moment their team was summoned to replace Yugoslavia, embroiled in civil war and banished from the tournament. Bobby Charlton emerged from the match shaking his head in despair. 'Whatever happened to football?' he asked. 'Whatever happened to passing, and that sort of thing?' England began brightly, and could well have scored the opening goal, but things subsequently fell apart. After a brisk Danish breakaway had shredded England's left flank, John 'Faxe' Jensen shot against the inside of a post. Without Mark Wright, injured in the untidy display against Finland, pronounced unfit by a UEFA doctor after he'd actually flown to Sweden (Liverpool had concealed the injury for two days), England had to remodel their defence. Taylor had talked about playing 3–5–2, but in the event it was 4–4–2.

Not surprisingly, Denmark found it hard at first to get into their stride. Arsenal's Paul Merson showed initial pace on the left wing, but he was destined to be injured, too. Peter Schmeichel, the giant Denmark and Manchester United keeper, thwarted a point-blank, twelfth-minute shot from Platt, but the second half saw Denmark gaining control.

France under Michel Platini would prove a major, strangely negative, disappointment, their cautious style the very reverse of all that Platini had shown as a player. He would resign at the end of the tournament. In Malmo, again, after English hooligans had rioted round the beer tent so recklessly provided by the hosts, another dreary goalless draw ensued, England's fans emoting their customary chorus of 'What a load of rubbish!' Shorter than ever of fit players, Taylor at last gave Alan Shearer another chance. Stuart Pearce, forced off the field for attention to a cut inflicted by Basile Boli in the closing minutes, raced on again, to hit the bar with a free kick.

In Stockholm, England took the lead against the hosts, playing by far their best football of the tournament in a bright first half. After just three minutes, Gary Lineker's right wing centre was volleyed in by Platt. Twice Tony Daley wasted palpable chances to make it 2–0 which, in all probability, would have given England the game. As it was, Sweden revived, ran the second half, equalised with a header from a corner by their centre back Jan Eriksson, and won the match eight minutes from time with a fine goal by Thomas Brolin, after two wall passes.

Then Lineker was catastrophically substituted. Bemused, still one short of Charlton's record, he walked off into international retirement. After the game, Taylor made as little sense when he attributed the Swedish win to their physical superiority, leading many of us to assume that he was planning to institute the Old Watford tactics of long-ball biff and bang. It was suggested to him at the press conference that a more cogent analysis might focus on Daley's two expensive misses.

Though injuries had undermined him, there was little doubt that Taylor had been out of his league. But there was no talk or hope of replacing him, as the World Cup qualifiers approached, nor of flanking him with a resourceful assistant. The very symbol of his failure had been the crass substitution of Gary Lineker.

Late in August, Taylor flew to Rome to talk to Lazio about Paul Gascoigne's recovery from injury, saying how much better England might have done had he played in Sweden, and calling him 'one of the last superstars of world football'. Repenting, you might say, at leisure. Gazza was not ready for the first England game of the season, a depressing 1–0 defeat by Spain in Santander, and there was still no sign of ending the stand-off with Chris Waddle, who had matured in Marseille into a vastly more effective player. Instead, a debut on the right wing was offered to Manchester City's David White who threw away a splendid chance made for him by David Platt, and was never picked again. A flagrant error by Des Walker cost the Spanish goal.

England's World Cup qualifying group ominously included the might of Holland, plus the inevitable Poland, tiny San Marino and seemingly modest Norway. Taylor meanwhile seemed to be staggering from one strategy to another, too cautious to use the long-ball tactics implicit in his strange remarks in Sweden. Now he used a sweeper, a dated 4–2–4 for which he simply didn't have the players.

In October 1992 at Wembley, Gazza at last returned to the team, but the Norwegians embarrassingly held England to a 1–1 draw in this first World Cup eliminator. Gazza in fact played well, though characteristically blotting his copybook when he was booked for elbowing an opponent in the face – a fate which awaited him when England subsequently played Holland. He was, however, much helped by the way that David Batty filled the midfield gaps behind him, a strategy which excluded the use of wingers. David Platt got his usual goal for England, Kjetil Rekdal equalised.

Turkey were less of a problem at Wembley in November, least of all to a vibrant Gascoigne who scored two of England's four goals, Shearer and Pearce getting the others. Somewhat ominously, though, only 42,984 turned up to watch this; the fans were manifestly disenchanted.

February's 6–0 win against San Marino at Wembley was mere formality, a cakewalk against a team whose admission to the tournament emphasised the fiasco that international football had become. Continuing his hot streak of form, David Platt scored four of the goals, the striker Les Ferdinand, marking his debut with the last of the six.

Bryan Robson had faded, but the advent of the forceful, versatile young Londoner Paul Ince, largely made up for that. Gazza was the persisting problem; would he be good or would he be bad? So much depended on his invention. Strangely anonymous even against feeble San Marino at Wembley, he was mediocre when England next beat Turkey 2–0 in Izmir, even though he scored one of England's two goals. In Rome, some blamed his inconsistency on the fact that he had been out of the game so long, others on his relationship with Sheryl, his girlfriend. Another problem was the decline in form of Des Walker, ironically, just at the time he'd made a lucrative move from Nottingham Forest to Sampdoria of Genoa. Alarmingly, his famous pace had gone, perhaps because of the operation he'd had shortly before he left for Genoa. Talking of lack of confidence seemed to beg the question. His confidence had lapsed because his pace had gone. And this would prove fatal when Holland came to Wembley.

It was a game England should have won. They were a goal up through John Barnes in the very first minute, doubled their lead through David Platt, only for two factors to destroy it. One was the elbow from Holland's tough midfielder Jan Wouters, allegedly provoked by Gazza's taunts, forcing Gascoigne off at half time; the other, Walker's diminished speed, enabling little Marc Overmars to outpace him on the right, Walker bringing him down to give away the penalty from which Peter Jacobus Van Vossen equalised, five minutes from time. Dennis Bergkamp had scored the earlier Dutch goal, in the first half.

This left England with two vital away matches in the close season, against Poland in Chorzow and Norway in Oslo. For much of the game, the Poles were rampant but somehow contrived to score just once, through Darius Adamczuk, before half time. Gascoigne's performances here and in Norway were bordering on the inept. It was left to Ian Wright, a very late substitute, to save the game, and Taylor's face, with a remarkable half-volleyed 84th-minute goal, ingeniously fashioned from the left.

In Oslo, four days later, Taylor seemed to lose all contact with tactical reality. Obsessed by the danger that the big Norwegian right winger Jostein Flo could cut in from the flank to score, he utterly and fatally remodelled his defence, inexplicably using the big, heavy centre half Gary Pallister to mark Flo and throwing the whole team off balance. Despite his goal in Poland, Wright did not appear until after half time. Scoring just before and just after the break, with Walker again the guilty party on one goal, England lost 2–0, which, given the fact that they still had to play Holland away, made qualification a hazard.

Distressed by Gascoigne's decline, Taylor, perhaps somewhat tactlessly, announced that there had been a problem with Gazza's 'refuelling'; the euphemism was plain enough. He also said, quite cogently, of a player who had been seen sucking his thumb during the game, 'Gifted players find hard things easy and easy things very difficult, and the easy thing is to get fit.'

One yearned for Taylor to go; one knew that he would stay. Now he took his team, minus Gascoigne, withdrawn by Lazio, to the United States for a three-team tournament, and proceeded to lose the first match 2–0 in Boston, humiliatingly, against the hosts. It wasn't quite as traumatic as the 1950 World Cup defeat, since this American team had a number of players operating in Europe. One of them, Thomas Dooley, who enterprisingly got the first American goal, spoke English with a German accent, having lived most of his life in that country. The second goal arrived when the flamboyant Alexi Lalas rushed in at a corner and the ball rebounded from him into the net. Stubbornly, Taylor kept the obviously waning John Barnes, short of speed by his own admission, on the pitch throughout, Ian Wright beginning on the bench.

A 1–1 draw with Brazil in Washington was far more encouraging, Platt (who else?) putting England ahead, Tim Flowers, on his debut in goal, keeping them in the game with a string of saves. And a 2–1 defeat by Germany in the greenhouse-like Detroit Silverdome, with Ince in buoyant form, came about through a wretched error by Barnes, who dribbled across midfield before square passing to Andy Sinton, Christian Ziege intercepting.

Hope of change rose when, at one of Taylor's Boston press conferences, Bert 'The Inert' Millichip, the FA Chairman, appeared at the back of the room, fixed Taylor with what looked a minatory stare, and marched out as soon as the rambling discourse was over. But nothing, of course, was done.

Hope of qualification fitfully glimmered. While Taylor and McMenemy tried farcically to blame 'lack of passion' rather than inept selection and tactics for England's failures, Gazza was seemingly finding passion again. When a strangely abject Poland came to Wembley in early September, Gascoigne excelled – a display, alas, overshadowed by his being booked for the second time, and thus excluded from the crucial match in Holland. Ferdinand put England one up in seven minutes, Gazza, with a fine right footer, and Pearce, with a scorching left footer, making it 3–0 in the second half.

Gazza-less in Rotterdam, Taylor compounded his problems with another strange selection, choosing the lanky midfield player, Carlton Palmer, to play wide on the right. Holland themselves were without two of their brightest stars, Marco Van Basten, still injured, and Ruud Gullit, who had refused to play after clashing with Dick Advocaat, the manager.

Taylor was entitled to say that luck deserted him and England that evening, though he compounded his miseries by rashly allowing himself to be filmed on the bench for a television documentary. His confused cry of 'Do I not like that' has rung down the years. Certainly an erratic German referee, Karl Josef Assenmacher, did England few favours. True, he did disallow, five minutes from half time, what seemed a good goal by Frank Rijkaard for a doubtful offside. But when Ronald Koeman, the hefty blond Dutch centre back, curled in his team's first goal from a free kick, it was five minutes after he had surely deserved to be sent off, bringing down David Platt on the edge of the penalty box when he was through to score.

Koeman received only a yellow card rather than red and when the England left back, Tony Dorigo, took the resulting free kick, the referee allowed the Dutch defence to encroach. And when Koeman took his own free kick, and England charged it down, Assenmacher allowed him to take it again, this time to score. So England were out of the World Cup with the slight consolation of a 'stab in the back' excuse. And Taylor's haphazard regime at last was over.

7 TERRY TOO LATE

Terry Venables 1994–96
Key Game: England v Germany, June 1996

THERE WAS NEVER ANY DOUBT ABOUT TERRY VENABLES'
talents. They were abundant; perhaps, in the last analysis, superabundant, betraying him into areas where they functioned less well. He
was an excellent footballer, inside forward turned wing half, capped
at every level, including England amateur, a member of a fine young
Chelsea team, later successful at Spurs.

While at Chelsea, as a teenager, he astonished his future co-writer,
Gordon Williams, deputed to teach the club's youngsters English
language classes. Asked to write a short story, Terry alone complied,
and came back with a tale reminiscent of the famous American writer,
Damon Runyon. When Williams evoked the comparison Venables
replied that he had never heard of Runyon. Later, they would collaborate on novels and television plays, featuring a detective called Hazell.
Williams would readily admit that, when Terry became too busy to
continue, he could no longer go on.

Terry Venables was brought up in a Dagenham very different from
Alf Ramsey's rural days indeed, in a new and different, less class-
conscious, England, he never sought to disguise his Cockney accent.
On retiring as a player, he became a highly effective coach, managing
in due course Crystal Palace, Queens Park Rangers, Barcelona and
Tottenham. In Spain, where he quickly acquired the language, he
made a dramatic beginning with Barcelona, endearing himself to their

huge following by almost at once winning sensationally on the ground of their most bitter, traditional rivals, Real Madrid.

A notable humourist, busily speculating in shares and property, he seemed, when Bobby Robson completed his unpredictable tenure, an obvious candidate for the succession as manager of England. Perhaps a little too obvious and altogether too brisk and bright for the old dullards of the International Committee. The choice fell, disastrously, on Graham Taylor.

By the time Venables was elevated to the purple, it was arguably too late. Eventually losing his touch and his job with Barcelona, where patience was never a virtue, he had taken over Tottenham with mixed success. His tactics could sometimes be puzzling, but beyond that, his activities off the field were controversial. It beggared belief that he should appoint, as his right-hand man in the Tottenham office, the many-times bankrupt Eddie Ashby, who would ultimately go to prison. Meanwhile, Terry's activities away from football were such as to prompt not one but two *Panorama* investigations on BBC television, in which they accused him of various misdemeanours in his business career.

There were strange tales of fixtures and fittings bought by a now defunct company, Landhurst, for a million pounds from four pubs, one of which proved not to exist, items allegedly worth no more than a tenth of the price. While at Spurs, Venables fell foul of the wealthy entrepreneur and owner, Alan Sugar, he of the Amstrad computer, who now owned a club which he had saved from bankruptcy. Badly over-reaching himself, Venables challenged Sugar for the ownership of Spurs, and inevitably came a cropper.

'Alan Sugar said to people he'd dance on my grave,' Terry told me on an October afternoon in his Kensington club, Scribes West, 'and he's done it.' There, I spent an hour and a half talking to Venables and Ashby while they showed me a host of bank statements to prove their integrity. Not only was Terry forced out of Spurs, but a judge in the High Court suspended him for seven years from being a company director.

When his name was put forward as Taylor's successor, Bert 'The Inert' Millichip was quoted as saying, 'Over my dead body.' But when the smoke cleared after weeks of indecision, the FA finally announced that Venables had the job, with Millichip still seemingly alive.

Just as Ramsey, when he took over, faced four years of friendly matches, since England were prequalified as hosts of the 1966 World Cup, so Venables would be involved in nothing but friendlies till England staged the European Championship, in 1996. He would ultimately go out with a bang rather than a whimper, when England at Wembley lost another semi-final to Germany on penalties. But though there was much regret and dispute over his going – which in fact had already been decided – England's prowess in those finals had been somewhat illusory; while much of the football they had previously played had been disappointingly sterile.

As for Graham Taylor, he had gone out, if hardly with a bang, at least with an irrelevant fusillade of seven goals against poor, pathetic San Marino – a team with no right to be in such a competition – in Bologna in November 1993. This, however, after a gloriously farcical beginning. The game had hardly kicked off when a criminally inept back pass underhit by Stuart Pearce enabled the San Marino striker Davide Gaultieri to run on to score a goal in a record 8.3 seconds. The press box, largely occupied by English journalists, erupted in incredulous laughter.

Taylor resigned six days later and Venables fielded his first England team at Wembley in March 1994 in a friendly, won 1–0 against Denmark. Paul Gascoigne played, though he'd be substituted in the second half by another of the few gifted English mavericks, Matthew Le Tissier of Southampton: tall, powerful, a superb ball player, well capable, in the Italian expression, of 'inventing the game'. But under Venables, he would get only walk-on parts as a substitute, never the chance to establish himself and his talents in the side. So even under Terry, the age-old English bias against brilliance survived, even if in his case at least it did not include his protégé, Gascoigne.

Not that Gazza would be available to him for long. In another typically perverse piece of self-destruction, he would again ludicrously put himself out of the game for months, this time with a broken leg. It happened in the context of a Lazio training game. Just as the then young reserve defender, Alessandro Nesta, later to captain Italy, was about to kick the ball, Gazza attempted idiotically to tackle him from behind, was kicked in consequence, and seriously injured. Yet Lazio's turbulent fans loved him for his very excesses.

Against the Danes, Platt had a superlative game, seeming the very personification of Total Football in his versatility, taking his goal spectacularly, quite outshining Gascoigne, who in fact had not been fit enough to play.

It was an adequate beginning, which continued when in the next game a flabby Greek team with an inept third choice keeper – responsible for three of the goals – was overwhelmed 5–0. The first goal was scored by a lively new right winger in Darren Anderton, who'd played for Venables at Tottenham. But less impressive, five days later, at Wembley again, was a goalless draw with Norway, England's recent and embarrassing conquerors in Oslo.

The 1994–95 season began with a 2–0 win against a USA team which seemed far from match fit and scarcely at any time threatened to attack, let alone to score. Alan Shearer got both the goals. The subsequent Wembley friendly in October, against Romania, raised serious, previously unsuspected, doubts about Venables' tactical wisdom. It seemed almost perverse to put Le Tissier, for once getting a full game but a deeply frustrating one, out on the right wing rather than in his natural role behind the strikers, while Ian Wright, a striker par excellence, was marooned out on the left wing. Alan Shearer, largely left to his own devices but always resilient, made England's goal for Newcastle's Robert Lee, equalizing Ilie Dumitrescu's for Romania, when Tony Adams' obsession with the offside game let him through alone. Romania's was far the more sophisticated football, though they lacked punch.

Next up at Wembley, Nigeria, whose precocious little midfielder Jay Jay Okocha, years later to come to Bolton, profited from the fact that England – an old old story – lacking Ince, had no tackler to oppose him. But a fine goal by Platt won the day and Nigeria faded after that.

Fast forward to February, and the horrors of a night of violence in Dublin where neo-fascist English thugs ran riot and caused the abandonment of the game after twenty-seven minutes with Ireland a goal ahead. Warnings of what might happen had been ignored, the Irish police were shamefully slow and inept; and when their riot squad did belatedly arrive, it was to set about supporters regardless of whether they were among the perpetrators.

With its diet of non-competitive football, the England season limped on. Uruguay – shades of 1966 – ground out a goalless draw at Wembley where their manager derided England's performance; though his own weary-looking team seldom bothered to attack. At least there was the encouragement of the bright form of Anderton and of another talented winger in Liverpool's Steve McManaman, his second outing, when he came on at half time. But once again, mediocrity ruled, and Venables' attempt to defend the display was mere clutching at straws. Not least when he commended an anonymous John Barnes, who constantly gave the ball away, for his courage against close marking. Where was the Terry Venables of yesteryear, the manager who would revitalise England? Why such dire caution?

There was scant encouragement from the half-baked Umbro Cup, a mini tournament tacked on to the end of the season in June, when Venables' strategies, after more than a year in office, were less convincing than ever. He did at least have Gascoigne back for the three games, but decided to show him only in brief appearances as a substitute, which were the only periods in which the England attack had any real cohesion.

A narrow and unconvincing win at Wembley against a lively Japanese team, in which the little attacker Kazuyoshi Miura was never subdued, was followed by a truly dreadful performance at Leeds against what was virtually a Swedish reserve team. Two goals down at one point, England somehow scrambled to an unmerited 3–3 draw. Their defence was inept, not least with Pallister and Colin Cooper in the middle, while Warren Barton, at that time England's most costly defender, was a disastrous right back, constantly out of position. Finally came a comprehensive 3–1 defeat at Wembley by a gifted, far superior, Brazilian side in which the little inside forward – relevant term – Juninho, due eventually to play for Middlesbrough, was irrepressible. He was shamefully fouled by David Batty, who was lucky indeed not to be sent off. Even Tim Flowers, guilty on all three Swedish goals, was a liability.

'If I try to win every game,' said a beleaguered and diminished Terry Venables, 'and don't learn anything, what a waste of time that's been.' Yet in the midst of catastrophe, hope remained. So far as Europe and the eventual finals were concerned, none of the potential opposition looked invincible. Yet it seemed indisputable that Terry had flagrantly wasted time, and that if he were indeed on a learning curve, then it was advancing at the speed of a glacier. Nor would matters subsequently be helped by Alan Shearer, *goleador*-in-chief, who was entering a period of bleak sterility. He was the shadow of himself in the Umbro tournament.

Then there was the question of Paul Ince, essential to the England midfield. Traumatised by the horrid affair of Eric Cantona and the thug whom he karate kicked at Selhurst Park, Ince had withdrawn from the Umbro Cup, whereupon Terry omitted him from the uninspiring Wembley friendly against Colombia, which would open the new international season. A pure piece, so it seemed, of self-destruction. The match itself ended in a goalless draw which hardly reflected the reality. A young England team made copious chances, hitting the woodwork three times, but Colombia, standing in for the far stronger Croatians, might themselves have had several goals against a porous English defence. Clever Carlos Valderrama, the first Colombian ever to play club football in Europe, was given far too much room. This time, Terry essayed a five-man midfield, ever chopping and changing, which left Shearer a somewhat lonely figure. But Gazza was in inspiring form.

England, one felt, could still win the European title; if only by default. But when it next came to playing Norway in Oslo, Gazza had broken down once more, and Venables was still excluding Ince on the spurious grounds that he had not yet settled down after his move to Inter in Milan. Lo and behold, there was Ince having a fine game against Torino.

In Oslo, England and Norway bored each other to bits in another tedious draw, the Norwegians looking as if they'd based their tactics on the outmoded long-ball philosophy. Not a goal in sight. The following month, at Wembley, England did manage three against a limp Swiss team, which would provide immensely tougher competition when it came to the first match of the European finals. Only 29,874 bothered to turn up for the game, which told its own bleak tale. Venables, meanwhile, continued to be locked in a plethora of law suits.

When, in December, a below-strength Portugal team drew 1–1 at Wembley with a patched-up England team, the crowd was still lower – 28,592 – and Gascoigne, admittedly used too deep, was ominously out of form, despite a couple of recent bravura performances with his latest club, Rangers.

Late in March 1996, when Bulgaria were the visitors, Venables at last abandoned his silly, self-defeating feud with Paul Ince, who'd been excelling with Inter ever since the Englishman Roy Hodgson had taken over the side and put him in the middle. Venables by now had announced that he would not be continuing as manager when his contract ran out at the season's end, being overwhelmed by his legal problems. By May, it was known that Glenn Hoddle would be his successor.

This time, just 29,708 watched England scrape home 1–0 with a seventh-minute goal by Les Ferdinand, against a Bulgarian team lacking its two main attackers, and hardly at full stretch. Yet only a glorious late save by David Seaman robbed Emil Kostadinov of an equaliser. In April, it was the turn of Croatia to come to Wembley, draw 0–0, and expose England's mediocrity. Again it was a team shorn of two stars, and though Venables insisted, 'We suffocated them in the midfield,' it was chiefly because he put an extra man there, thus restraining the forays of Ince. In an about-turn, Venables now praised him, but he hardly got the best out of him.

For what seemed no good reason, England flew to the Far East in early June, beating China 3–0 in Beijing, Hong Kong only 1–0. It was there, notoriously, that several England players, Gazza inevitably among them, indulged in something called the Dentist's Chair, whereby its occupant leaned back and had alcohol poured down his throat. There were high jinks, smashed screens, Gazza involved again, on the plane flying home.

Football's Coming Home – Almost: Euro 96

The superfluous Far Eastern jaunt, and the tabloid fodder it provided, was not the ideal preparation for the European Championship finals soon to follow.

Nor, indeed, did England begin them well, held at Wembley, where they'd play all their games, by a Swiss team easily worth its 1–1 draw. Having previously deployed a five-man midfield with wingers, Venables abruptly and unsuccessfully reverted to 4–3–3. At least Alan Shearer at last scored his first goal of the season midway through the first half, courtesy of Paul Ince and an arguably indulgent linesman, for he looked offside. But the English defence was troubled throughout by the sheer pace of Kubilay Turkyilmaz, who equalised from a penalty.

Scotland came next, and after a dull first half, Steve McManaman, belatedly switched from the left flank to the right, and on to his own right foot, had ten dazzling minutes, in which he was materially responsible for setting up the first goal, headed by Shearer from Gary Neville's cross. But the half, and the game itself, was memorable for an astonishing goal by the newly peroxide-blond Gascoigne. Anonymous in the first half, he hooked the ball away from the big Scottish centre back Colin Hendry and with sublime technique, drove it home with his right foot. A moment of glorious impertinence.

Yet when Scotland at last mustered the will to attack, England's defence looked deficient. Gordon Durie headed against a post and David Seaman saved a penalty by Gary McAllister.

The following Tuesday saw England at last flourish and convince under Venables' aegis, with a rousing 4–1 win against the Dutch. It must be said that the Dutch team, traditionally riven by conflict, was at odds with itself, the black players and the whites bitterly opposed. It resulted in the tough little midfielder, Edgar Davids, being packed off home. Without him, England's own midfield was dominant and the double spearhead of Alan Shearer, on target at last, and Teddy Sheringham, slow perhaps in movement but so swift in thought, was devastatingly effective. They shared the four goals between them, Shearer scoring the first from a 23rd-minute penalty. Three more goals followed in the second half and England were 4–0 up before Holland scored.

Euphoria surged, and Wembley reverberated to the fans chorusing, 'Football's coming home'. But the ensuing quarter-final against Spain was a dismal, if fortuitous, anticlimax. Venables' luck just held, you might well say, a substantial part of which was the indomitable goal-keeping of David Seaman, though refereeing decisions played their undoubted part. The Spaniards were denied what looked a perfectly good goal for offside in the first half, when the overlapping of their left back Sergi time and again embarrassed England till a foul by Gary Neville slowed him down.

Without the suspended Paul Ince, England's midfield seemed made of cardboard, Platt failing utterly to replace him, while Gazza was subdued and Sheringham largely ineffective. Seaman made a string of fine saves, notably when Javier Manjarin was clean through and when, in the eventual penalty shoot-out, he saved the crucial spot kick by Nadal, England prevailing 4–2 after a goalless draw.

So, in the semi-final, it was Germany again; and once more, penalties would fatally decide. Had the electric Jurgen Klinsmann been fit to face England's suspect defence, one doubts whether England would have survived into extra time.

Surprisingly changing his tactics again, in the absence of the suspended right back, Gary Neville, Terry Venables deployed a three-man defence with 'retractable' wingers. Shearer put England ahead in a mere three minutes, Stefan Kuntz quickly equalised, but three minutes into extra time, a splendid move, involving five players, concluded when McManaman flew clear up the right flank, enabling Darren Anderton to shoot, and hit the near post. Alas, poor Southgate. With the penalty shoot-out level at 5–5, the defender had the moral courage to take that vital penalty, only to have it saved by the German keeper, Andreas Koepke.

So Terry Venables' reign ended on a note of tantalising anticlimax. Those, like myself, who had long been convinced that England could win the tournament, if only by default, were almost vindicated. Defeat on penalties, after all, is hardly true defeat. So Terry would depart, one might say, in the relative odour of sanctity. Much had been forgotten and forgiven.

8 HODDLE AND THE HEREAFTER

Glenn Hoddle 1996–99
Key Game: Italy v England, October 1997

GLENN HODDLE, TERRY VENABLES' SUCCESSOR, HAD BEEN PERHAPS the most talented English player of his era, though never wholly accepted; the traditional fate of the English maverick. Bobby Robson, in particular, had taken years until the Damascene conversion which preceded the 1986 World Cup, grudgingly and wastefully consigning Hoddle to the right flank before at last placing him where he belonged, in the middle. Hoddle's technique was matched by his strategic flair; there was no better British purveyor of the long, searching pass, and his right-footed shot was formidable. As shown on his debut against Bulgaria, when Ron Greenwood, then the England manager, promptly excluded him from the next game.

Playing successfully in France for Monaco, where he was hugely appreciated, he became player-manager of Swindon Town, whom he guided to an unprecedented promotion. He then became player-manager, then manager, of Chelsea, with reasonable results, before being chosen to lead England. There would inevitably be tactical changes, since Hoddle, rather than favouring wingers, preferred a system which deployed attacking full backs. It remained to be seen whether he was temperamentally suited to his demanding new role since, unlike the invariably ebullient Venables, he tended to be down-cast by press criticism when things went wrong.

Then as we shall see there was the matter of Mrs Eileen Drewery.

For many years, Hoddle had relied on her powers as a healer, and now he brought her into the England entourage. This was unquestionably with the best intentions, but it was always going to be hazardous policy, given the somewhat conservative instincts of the average professional footballer. Indeed, when Mrs Drewery stood, hands extended, above the seated Ray Parlour, Arsenal's right winger, he responded, 'Short back and sides, please!'

Such flippancy was ill judged but inevitable, as indeed was the division in the camp between those who accepted Mrs Drewery's value, and those who were simply sceptical. Nor was the situation improved by Mrs Drewery's penchant, however effective her ministrations, to court publicity. This tendency reached farcical dimensions when, claiming a direct connection with the Almighty, she maintained after Ian Wright had missed an easy chance to score against Italy in Rome, that she had been responsible – for fear of a violent response by the crowd. She made no mention of the fact that Italy promptly missed an open goal at the other end.

Eventually, Hoddle's spiritual beliefs would lead to his abrupt and deeply controversial dismissal. But not before he had taken England to the World Cup finals of 1998 in France, and a more than honourable defeat on penalties by Argentina. In due course, certain players, notably Gareth Southgate, would criticise what they considered his self-indulgence when showing off his exceptional skills in training sessions, and impatience with those less skilful than him. For the rest of that year, however, the beginning was bright and promising. All three World Cup qualifiers were duly won.

The most difficult of them was the second, against what one might call the inevitable Poland, at Wembley in October 1996. An England team with Southgate as its only recognised centre back and with Everton's left back, Andy Hinchcliffe, playing wide on the left were a goal down in seven minutes to Marek Citko. But Alan Shearer replied twice before half time and England retained the lead.

Moldova, in the opening qualifier, had proved undemanding enough, in Chisinau, where England cruised home 3–0, with David Beckham making his debut on the right wing, deploying a right foot remarkable both for its power and accuracy. A lack of pace was compensated by the sheer accuracy of his crosses from the right, while his free kicks swerved formidably.

In November, there was something of a contretemps when Hoddle insisted on putting Paul Gascoigne in the team, despite the fact that he had just been accused of brutally beating up his bride of fourteen weeks, Sheryl. Hoddle insisted that counselling rather than condemnation was the answer, actually attending one of Gazza's counselling sessions. So Gazza duly played in Tbilisi against Georgia in a 2–0 victory, which saw Sol Campbell powerful in central defence, though Alan Shearer was absent after an operation on his groin. Meanwhile, a contrite Gascoigne had escaped proceedings. Sheryl had declined to give evidence against him.

Early in December, Italy, England's chief rivals in the group, who had made an uneven start, sacked their manager, little Arrigo Sacchi, never a very popular figure, replacing him with the manager of the Under-21 team, former international centre half and 65-year-old father of the outstanding Paolo Maldini, Cesare. He would bring Italy to Wembley in February. Interesting, in retrospect, to recall that this was the first appearance for Italy, other than eighteen minutes as a substitute, for Fabio Cannavaro, destined in 2006 to captain his country to success in the World Cup, and to be voted European footballer of the year. Small for a centre back, he nevertheless dominated the dangerous Alan Shearer, while 'Billy' Costacurta, who had been in shaky form with Milan, was a faultless sweeper. He even provided the long pass which little Giancarlo Zola snapped up to glide past Pearce and beat the hapless keeper Ian Walker inside his near post, for the game's only goal.

Cesare Maldini had clearly got things right, though he insisted that he never thought he was gambling on Cannavaro, who had played so often and so well for his Under-21 team. Hoddle, by contrast, surprisingly gambled on Matthew Le Tissier – and lost. So often ignored by Terry Venables, Le Tissier had, in fact, had nine final minutes on the field as a substitute against Moldova, but he never began to function, let alone surprise the Italians: as indeed he had not surprised Maldini with his inclusion.

Hoddle was also criticised, when David Seaman dropped out, for using in goal neither Nigel Martyn nor Tim Flowers, both experienced internationals, but the inexperienced Ian Walker, much blamed for Zola's goal. Blamed, too, was Stuart Pearce in that episode, for alleged ball watching. Hoddle himself insisted he had been right to choose Le Tissier as a player capable of winning matches, and that he could well play again; which he didn't. It was a defeat, he said, not a disaster, he had said before the game that qualification did not depend just on this result; in that at least he would be proved right. But there was no doubt that on the night, Hoddle had erred and had been comprehensively outmanoeuvred.

Things improved, even if, in late March 1997, a 2–0 friendly win at Wembley against Mexico was unconvincing. The penalty given England on nineteen minutes looked less justifiable than the one denied Mexico early in the second half. Lacking several first choices, England scored through Teddy Sheringham, from the spot, and Robbie Fowler, but Nicky Butt's resourceful debut as a substitute in midfield was encouraging.

Georgia came to Wembley a month later and were again despatched 2–0, Shearer and Sheringham scoring. That same evening, however, in Naples, I saw Italy, in the image of the returning Roberto 'The Divine Ponytail' Baggio, dispose of Poland with ominous ease. 'Did you see how England struggled to beat Georgia?' demanded Cesare Maldini, his *catenaccio* defence working well again. 'First [we must take on] the Georgians, then England at home, but there's time for all that.' As for Piotr Nowak, the Polish player who had given England much trouble at Wembley, he remarked of the return to come, 'We'll have to play differently against England.'

On the last day of May, in Katowice, he would play for only fifty-seven minutes. Gascoigne, violently fouled and carried off on a stretcher in a previous Old Trafford 'friendly' versus South Africa, would be carried off again, early in the game. Shearer scored in six minutes but missed a penalty, and Sheringham got a last-minute goal.

Early in June, Hoddle took his team to the Tournoi de France, a World Cup rehearsal; in Nantes gaining a psychologically important and encouraging win over Italy, where there was much wailing and gnashing of teeth. Maldini, who'd said darkly before the tournament that rather than himself, 'other people wanted [Italy to take part in] it', and declared of what was virtually an England reserve team, 'The English showed themselves clearly the stronger, both from the physical and from the athletic point of view. At this stage we have nothing to spend but small change and our opponents have not spared us. But don't talk to me about lack of concentration or unsuitable approach. That's just literature. The truth is that at the end of our championship, certain reactions are missing, both automatically and physiologically.' Shades of his successful predecessor, Enzo Bearzot who, before each World Cup, embarked on a process of what he called 'disintoxicating' his players from the traumas of their League.

For Hoddle, however, it was a major triumph, not least because his bold choice of Manchester United's 22-year-old Paul Scholes, as an attacking midfielder, proved splendidly inspired. Even the Italian press eulogised the redhead's performance, one paper calling him 'the protagonist of the evening'. He scored England's second goal, just before half time, Ian Wright got the first, helped by an error from Italy's goalkeeper, Angelo Peruzzi. Three days later, in Montpellier, England recorded another encouraging victory beating the hosts, France, with a late goal by Shearer. Yet the three-man defence had seldom looked safe and was embarrassed by the incursions of Alain Dugarry, the incisive French striker. A glorious one-handed tip-over by David Seaman from a drive by the French left back Bixente Lizarazu was crucial.

In their final match, in Paris, against Brazil, England went down to a supremely well worked goal, scored by Romario, star of the 1994 World Cup. It was the only goal England conceded in the tournament, but Hoddle's words that England's Premier League had some of the worst defending and the worst defenders to be seen could hardly be forgotten. This was Brazil's only win.

There was no doubt that England's victory in Nantes had traumatised Cesare Maldini and the *azzurri*, no matter how marginal the occasion. Maldini, just as he had lamented the fact that the game in France came at the close of the season, now bewailed the early-season, September, date of his team's visit to Georgia. There, as in France, such was his state of mind that he even abandoned his *catenaccio* tactics, and reverted to the 4–4–2 strategy dear to Arrigo Sacchi. And in Tiblisi, Italy could only draw 0–0!

Predictably, Maldini was savaged by the media for his supposedly excessive caution. With England, Gascoigne in high fettle, strolling home the same day at Wembley against feeble Moldova, it meant that Italy had now fallen a point behind England, and all would depend on the return in Rome in October, when England now needed only a draw to finish top of the group. Italy would be anxious, and moreover would be without the fluent talents in midfield of Roberto Di Matteo, yellow carded for the second time in Tbilisi.

In Rome, England would have Paul Ince, absent against Moldova, back again, to give cover to Gascoigne, but would sorely miss the injured and essential Alan Shearer. Even against Moldova, Les Ferdinand had fired blanks. Wright had scored two of the four goals, and in Rome he would be partnered by Sheringham.

Gianfranco Zola, now a Chelsea player, sounded a warning: 'The English have improved on a tactical level. They are more crafty, now. Since we beat them the last time, they have been piling up points, always winning. You say they aren't so good away from home? But the only points they've dropped have been at Wembley. Let's forget the old England. Their club teams, too, have been getting important results away from home, in the European cups.' As it transpired, Cesare Maldini would oblige him to play deeper, in midfield rather than in his preferred role up front where he admitted he 'found himself running after Batty like a madman'. It was a tactical blunder. Hoddle had decided that were Zola to play farther up, Paul Ince would be used to mark him. As it was, Ince was free to play a crucially brave and forceful role in midfield.

Hoddle's strategy had been a resplendent success, while poor Cesare Maldini was covered with obloquy by an incandescent Italian press. He was blamed, *inter alia*, for using the inexperienced 'Pippo' Inzaghi in attack, and for his alleged fearfulness. 'Cesare Maldini's Italy,' wrote one journalist, 'chose the most timorous way, giving England the draw that the Masters fully deserved . . . For Glenn Hoddle's team, then, the World Cup has been a brilliantly accomplished mission.' A headline in the daily *Tuttosport* read, 'Zola A Ghost, Ince Heroic', while according to Rome's *Corriere Dello Sport*, 'We got out, moreover, without ever really having risked trying to win, against a real team, much better organised than ours, which finished coming closer to a goal than ever Italy did in the ninety minutes.'

Ian Wright, indeed, could hardly have come closer, near the end, when he struck the near, left-hand post, though as against that, of course, Christian Vieri proceeded to miss the simplest of chances at the other end. Alas, the occasion was blemished by shocking violence in the streets, English hooligans running amok, while in the stadium itself it was police who ran amok, belabouring wholly innocent English fans. For Paul Gascoigne, it was a happy and impressive return to the Olympic Stadium, where he had been so popular as a player with Lazio.

Meanwhile, Hoddle would be blessed with the emergence of a sparkling young talent, a striker at that, in the shape of the eighteen-year-old Liverpool prodigy, Michael Owen. Those of us fortunate enough to see this dynamic attacker make his debut as a substitute the previous year at Selhurst Park, against Wimbledon, quickly scoring a typically electric goal, would not easily forget the experience. Yet as the World Cup finals approached, with England's prospects clearly brightened by Owen's sparkling emergence, Hoddle was strangely negative about him. To say as he did that Owen was not a natural goalscorer was rather like saying that the sun set in the East. To declare that Owen still had much to learn was axiomatic, given his age. But also to imply that Owen should improve his behaviour seemed wholly gratuitous. Not least when, on the eve of the World Cup finals, it was reported that Teddy Sheringham –initially and inexplicably preferred to Owen – had indulged in some louche behaviour in a Portuguese night club; which Hoddle himself condemned. Not to mention the sporadic backsliding of Gascoigne which, indeed, would end in disaster.

Owen, in fact, was brave as well as gifted, though he would demonstrate in the World Cup a certain penchant for diving in the box. After the dramas and the thousand natural shocks of Rome, England embarked on a varied programme of seven 'friendly' matches – and with varying success. Paul Gascoigne figured in four of them, but his was a helter-skelter season for him, dropped at one point by Rangers, warned by Hoddle over his behaviour, transferred eventually to Middlesbrough. It was perhaps significant that, even without him, England had their best victory of the series when they beat Portugal 3–0 at Wembley in April 1998, Shearer and Sheringham sharing the goals.

Far more alarming was the performance in February at Wembley, where Chile humbled England with a 2–0 win, both goals, one a penalty, going to their clever captain, Marcelo Salas. No Gascoigne, but a lively debut by Owen. The team that drew, again minus Gascoigne – censured in Scotland for provocatively miming an Ulster fifer in the Old Firm game against Celtic a week earlier – was deemed 'experimental'. Execrable would be a better description of the side which, Owen-less, drew 0–0 at Wembley in May with the World Cup minnows of Saudi Arabia. England very properly were booed off the field.

Only a few days later, England flew from their training camp in La Manga, Spain, to play twice in a mini-tournament in Casablanca. In the first game, against Morocco, Wright came off with a pulled hamstring which would put him out of the World Cup. Young Owen, replacing him, received a fearful, if unintentional, kick in the face from Driss Benzakri, the Moroccan goalkeeper, but was allowed, most controversially, to return to the field, where he still contrived to score the only goal. The second game, against Belgium, was drawn 0–0.

Back in La Manga, Terry Sheringham did public penance for his excesses; and Paul Gascoigne was sent home. The day before the England squad was to be announced, Hoddle declared on television that Gascoigne's physical condition was most satisfactory. Yet the very next day, after he had been drunk on the golf course, Gazza was called to Hoddle's room and told he would be cut from the squad. His reaction was, perhaps predictably, explosive. He smashed a lamp, kicked the furniture, and momentarily seemed as if he would attack Hoddle.

Whatever the merits of his decision, Hoddle was met with obloquy when he subsequently described Gazza's violent reaction in detail, in his ill-judged *World Cup Diary*, while David Beckham wasn't spared.

The abiding mystery was that it had actually been 'ghosted' for him by none other than David Davies, a senior official at the Football Association with a brief to preside over communications – indeed it was Davies who, far from writing Hoddle's disastrous memoir, should have been the very man to oversee and possibly censor it. In its own way this World Cup diary did its supposed author more damage than Bobby Robson's wretched publication after the 1990 World Cup.

Hoddle Pays the Penalty: World Cup, France 1998

England began their qualifying group with a comfortable enough 2–0 win over a moderate Tunisian side. Next in Toulouse came Romania. Hoddle, almost perversely, preferred initially the one-paced Sheringham to the electric young Owen, and stuttered accordingly. Against Tunisia in Marseille, Owen had gone on for Sheringham only in the last half-dozen minutes. Now in Toulouse he had to wait seventy-three minutes before he replaced an ineffectual Sheringham, with England a goal down to Viorel Moldovan. Owen instantly transformed the England attack, used his pace to score a spectacular equalising goal, only for a bizarrely inept piece of defending by Graeme Le Saux to let in his Chelsea colleague, Dan Petrescu, to score the winner for Romania.

Owen duly started the third qualifying game in Lens against Colombia, won 2–0 with goals from Darren Anderton and David Beckham. But the defeat by Romania condemned England to second place, and a second-round confrontation with Argentina.

Who knows how that game might have ended had it not been for a moment of disastrous petulance by David Beckham. In Saint Etienne, the battle was titanic, the resistance of an England team reduced after forty-seven minutes to ten men by Beckham's expulsion and obliged to play on through half-an-hour's extra time, was phenomenal. Brought down by the wily Diego Simeone, Beckham, lying on the ground, swung out a foot at him and was promptly expelled by the Danish referee, Kim Milton Nielsen.

The match could scarcely have had a more explosive beginning, each side scoring from a somewhat contentious penalty in the first ten minutes. When Simeone burst through the English defence, David

Seaman rushed out and brought him down. There were two questions: first was it necessary to do so, secondly, was the fall excessively dramatic? In any event, Batistuta was secure with his spot kick. Much the same could be asked of Owen's tumble in the box when he sprawled at full pelt over a challenge by the opposing centre back, Roberto Ayala. Shearer scored the penalty. Six minutes more and with superb acceleration, Owen went past both Ayala and another defender, to give England the lead.

Alas, at a traditionally crucial moment just before half time, England conceded the equaliser. Under orders from manager Daniel Passarella, once the World Cup winning captain, from the bench, Argentina executed a cleverly conceived free kick, which found England's defence lacking in awareness. The strategy was consummated when Veron found Zanetti who scored.

But then, to the fury of Hoddle, who had constantly warned Beckham to curb his impetuosity, the Manchester United forward was sent off, and it became for England an inevitable war of attrition. Their defence, with Tony Adams and Sol Campbell defiant in the middle, held the Argentines at bay. Campbell even had the ball in the net, but the goal was disallowed since Shearer's elbow had previously connected with the face of Roa, Argentina's keeper. As against that, Gabriel Batistuta, Argentina's prolific centre forward, for once eluded Adams, but only to head wide.

So the game ground on into extra time, with no foreshortening Golden Goal, an experiment then in force, to abbreviate it. Penalties, that superfluous abomination, would thus decide. Berti converted the first for Argentina; Alan Shearer replied. Seaman then saved from the striker Hernan Crespo, but Roa did the same from Paul Ince. Veron now scored, as did Paul Merson, on as a substitute. Ayala made it 4–3, and then the lot fell on David Batty, who had never taken a spot kick before. Roa saved, England were out; with honour.

Hoddle published his notorious diary, but nemesis awaited him. In an interview with the football correspondent of *The Times*, he was unwise enough to declare his belief, well enough known in Buddhist lore, that disabled people were being punished for their sins in a previous life. He had apparently said as much before, without consequences, in a radio interview, but now there was outrage. Even the Prime Minister, Tony Blair, gratuitously agreed with the hosts of a morning television show that Hoddle deserved to be dismissed. Which he was. Naive as it may well have been, it hardly seemed a hanging offence. It was tempting to see it as what Freudians would call a displacement; he was actually, if belatedly, being punished for the indiscretions of his deplorable diary.

It still seemed harsh, not least because whatever the indiscretions of the diary, the charges of alleged arrogance, the strange ambivalence towards the emergent Owen, Hoddle's record was surely the best since that of Ramsey, who, after all, had never had to qualify for the World Cup. And in the last analysis, England's gallant performance against the odds could be seen as a moral victory.

In an ideal world, perhaps Hoddle should have resigned immediately after the World Cup, for the worst was emphatically to come, both on and off the field. With what might be called the usual indecent haste, the qualifiers for the now swollen European Championship were upon teams and players. England in Stockholm, against the ever-problematic Swedes, would make a dismal and somewhat shabby beginning.

It hardly looked likely to happen when, on 5 September, Alan Shearer put England ahead in a mere seventy-five seconds. It would prove an illusory goal. By half time, Sweden had gone into a 2–1 lead which they would keep; an England team including most of its World Cup complement had badly lost its way. Even the usually disciplined Michael Owen was booked while in the 67th minute Paul Ince was sent off, making matters worse with his oafish behaviour as he went.

The 0–0 draw at Wembley against weakened Bulgaria was abysmal, and things were little better in Luxembourg, where winning seemed a formality. The home team actually missed a penalty after five minutes, enabling England to recover and win 3–0, but with no kind of style or panache. One of England's goals, the second, was itself a penalty, converted by Alan Shearer, though at least there was a promising and adventurous show by young Rio Ferdinand in the unaccustomed position of right back. Both Hoddle and Shearer angrily denied that Shearer had harsh words for him after the match. But the news that Hoddle was hoping to recover Paul Gascoigne, who was then tackling his alcoholism in a clinic, seemed a true sign of desperation.

Nearly 73,000 had come, seen and been appalled by the display against the Bulgarians. Throughout the frustrating game, an England attack which included Shearer, Owen and Sheringham as a substitute, contrived but a single shot on goal. Hoddle, eulogised after the World Cup, had now become the familiar managerial whipping boy. Doubts long nurtured about his defensive formation seemed valid. Yet how could he make a silk purse out of a sow's ear?

Not that he would long be confronted with the problem. On 30 November, *The Times* published the article which gave his views on reincarnation; and the flak flew. On 2 February 1999, it was announced that his contract was being ended; the massive irony was that the announcement should be made by none other than David Davies, who had so controversially ghosted the World Cup diary which had initially got him into trouble, and was thought by some to be a stronger reason for dismissal than his religious views.

9 THE HIGHS AND LOWS OF KEVIN KEEGAN

Kevin Keegan 1999–2000
Key Game: England v Germany, October 2000

HODDLE'S SUCCESSOR WOULD BE KEVIN KEEGAN, AT THAT TIME the Chief Operations Officer – virtually the senior manager – at Fulham, to whom he insisted he would return after a mere four games. It seemed a bizarre arrangement, and would not be adhered to. As a footballer, Keegan was an inspiring example of the self-made star, largely discouraged in his early efforts to break through, but by dint of sheer application and endless hard work, becoming a major star with Liverpool, Hamburg and England, twice winning the title of European Footballer of the Year.

Originally an outside right, he had graduated into a vigorously effective all-purpose striker, playing a vital role in Liverpool's first ever victory in a European Cup final when, in Rome in 1977, he ran rings around Borussia Moenchengladbach's formidable Berti Vogts.

Retiring from the game and taking residence in Spain, where he played a lot of golf, he was eventually tempted back to England to manage Newcastle United. Though he'd had no managerial experience, he galvanised the team, and so nearly took them to the premier title in 1996, only to be demoralised by the mind games of Manchester United's Alex Ferguson, Newcastle failing to exploit what was at one stage a twelve-point advantage. An indication, perhaps, that for all his splendid ebullience, he could be susceptible to pressure.

Off the field, he was equally vivacious and engaging, a splendid public speaker who could hold an audience fascinated for an hour or more with his humour and his range of anecdotes. His appointment was generally popular, and he announced that supporters, somewhat unexpectedly, would see not only a passionate approach to performance on the field but also to the singing of the national anthem. As passionate, he doubtless hoped, as the chorus of hateful jeering with which England's rowdier fans greeted the playing of any other country's anthem at Wembley.

At least on his debut, when England, for the umpteenth time, played Poland at Wembley in the European context, his promise was made good. In the interim, an England team managed by caretaker Howard Wilkinson, former manager of Leeds United but now a senior coach at the Football Association, had lost 2–0 at Wembley to a France team inspired by the pace and irresistible thrust of the young, ever recalcitrant, Nicolas Anelka, who scored both goals and had another dubiously disallowed.

Against Poland, however, England reflected Keegan's own exuberance. They won 3–1, all goals scored by an ebullient Paul Scholes, albeit if one was hand assisted. At the time, one was tempted to say that Wembley seemed always to galvanise him, but in prospect, alas, was his red card the following June in the European match against Sweden. Ecstatic chants broke out from the fans, after such a promising debut, of, 'Keegan, Keegan!' Michael Owen was absent, and the following month would drop out of the game with hamstring and tendon injuries; which, alas, would become an all too constant affliction.

In late April, Keegan took advantage of a poorly attended friendly in Budapest against Hungary to field an experimental team with five new players, while giving Rio Ferdinand another cap. The result was a 1–1 draw, Shearer scoring his twenty-third goal for England from a penalty. After the match Keegan, who'd hinted a change of heart following the defeat of Poland, announced, 'It's time to stop playing games, I want the job,' and committed himself to England.

Not till June did his team play again, European qualifiers in swift succession against Sweden and Bulgaria. Alas, euphoria would die.

At Wembley, Sweden yet again looked to be England's nemesis, and this time Scholes had a dismal day. Lucky not to be sent off in the very first minute for a lunging challenge, he did indeed depart early in the second half for a reckless foul. With a malfunctioning midfield England were held to another of their goalless draws. Of the five debutants in Hungary only Sunderland's Michael Gray was playing, and only as a substitute.

Next to Sofia, to confront Bulgaria, themselves having forced a goalless draw at Wembley. This time, each team did score, Shearer first for England, Georgi Markov for Bulgaria, the equaliser. A pedestrian England couldn't even exploit the fact that the Bulgarians were down to ten men for most of the second half. Only a few days earlier, Keegan had admitted that he had been fairly criticised by the press. Now England were obliged to beat Luxembourg at home, no real test, but also the Poles, in Warsaw, to survive.

Luxembourg, at Wembley in early September, were duly thrashed 6–0 with twenty-year-old Kieron Dyer of Newcastle making an exuberant debut as an attacking right back. But in Warsaw, dullness descended again. England had yet another of those wretched goalless draws against the Poles, David Batty being sent off five minutes from time. So it all depended on Sweden beating Poland, and Keegan sent the Swedes 'a thousand thanks' for beating the Poles 2–0 in Stockholm.

But now came, as second-placed team in the group, the play-offs, and who should be the opposition but the first historically and traditionally of all England's opponents: Scotland. This, the first international fixture of all, had lately fallen into desuetude, but now it would be revived in perhaps its most important context.

The two matches took place in the space of four mid-November days, with sharply contrasting results. First, at Hampden Park, England won with some ease. Paul Scholes scored both goals in a 2–0 win and was booked for his excessive celebration of the first. Scotland were presumed down and out. Instead they came to Wembley and won with adventurous, fluent football. Their enterprise was rewarded with a fine headed goal on thirty-nine minutes by Don Hutchison, born, like Paul Gascoigne in Gateshead, but qualified for Scotland. Playing with no width – Ray Parlour, Arsenal's right winger, appeared only in the 90th minute – England were indebted to a glorious save by David Seaman from Christian Dailly in the second half which kept the score down to 1–0 and enabled England to qualify for the finals.

In the interim, various friendlies were played by a team in oscillating form, metamorphosing from a three-man defence to the more orthodox 4–4–2, which would be used in the finals. Dyer played against Belgium, uneasily beaten 2–1 at Sunderland, in a goalless draw against Argentina at Wembley, the following February, but missed the 1–1 draw at Wembley versus Brazil, when Franca equalised Owen's first-half goal, and got on only as a substitute four days later against Ukraine, beaten 2–0 at Wembley. There would, debatably, be no place for him in the finals in Holland and Belgium.

There was time for a disastrous performance in Valletta against little Malta in early June, a 2–1 victory, after which Keegan admitted that if England went on to play like that in the Low Countries, there was no hope for them. As it was, they did little of consequence.

European Championship, Holland/Belgium 2000
The opening group game, versus Portugal in Eindhoven, saw them surrender a two-goal lead for the first time since losing to West Germany in the 1970 World Cup quarter-finals. It was in only the third minute that Scholes headed in a right-wing cross from David Beckham. Another cross by Beckham, in a breakaway, was driven home by Steve McManaman. But with their midfield largely overrun, their rearguard conceding too much space, the lead was not held long.

A 25-yard shot by Luis Figo flew home off the heel of the backpedalling Tony Adams, David Seaman in goal was found wanting when a cross by Rui Costa, in exuberant form, was headed in by the diving Joao Pinto, while the same player split England's defence in the second half with a pass which enabled Nuno Gomes to get the winner.

Hope revived when in Charleroi, where their hooligan fans ran riot. England won 1–0 against a German team still less impressive than themselves. Beckham, giving his attack good service from the right, was awarded the free kick from which Alan Shearer headed the only goal, when the ball bounced its way to him. Afterwards, he was impulsively defended by Kevin Keegan: 'He has been knocked and pummelled by the media, who have questioned his right to be in the side and questioned his right to be captain. But once again, he has come in and got his goal. He is a man among men.'

Shearer got another goal, a penalty, against Romania, in what proved the third and final game in Charleroi. Romania themselves would get a very late winner from a penalty, clumsily conceded by Phil Neville. David Seaman, hurt in the warm-up, gave way in goal to Nigel Martyn, who conceded the opening goal when a cross hit the far post and bounced back over the line. Shearer's penalty equalised, after Christian Chivu tripped Paul Ince, and in first-half injury time, seemingly under pressure, England broke for a typical goal by Owen, beating the offside trap. All in vain. Three minutes after the break, Martin punched Dan Petrescu's cross straight to Dorinel Munteanu, who promptly equalised. And when Phil Neville felled Moldovan, Ioan Ganea converted the penalty.

'You have to ask,' said Keegan, in confessional mood, 'if we can pass the ball better and control the game. The answer in this tournament is, sadly, we couldn't. You cannot spend sixty minutes chasing the game and expect to succeed at this level.'

For Martin Keown, the Arsenal centre back, mistaken tactics caused England's failure. It was arguable that there was nothing basically wrong with the 4–4–2 system, merely with Keegan's mistaken use of it. The choice of the Neville brothers was greatly disputable. Gary might go on to win an infinity of England caps and become the Fred Kite, the shop steward, of his team, but he'd had a dismal season, not least in Brazil in the misbegotten Club World Cup, not to mention an erratic European game at Old Trafford for Manchester United against Real Madrid, while his brother Phil had been no more than third-choice left back for the club.

Keegan, it could be argued, had shown neither intelligence nor moral courage. He should surely have taken two younger players of the promise of Kieron Dyer and Rio Ferdinand, while he made minimal use of the lively midfielder, Nick Barmby, who, coming on as substitute on that occasion, too, had transformed the match against Ukraine at Wembley.

*　　*　　*

Keegan's writ would not run much longer, even though the opening match of the new season, early in September 2000, promised brighter things. An England team reverting to a three-man defence and with Andy Cole and Michael Owen – a late substitute – each incisive, was well worth a 1–1 draw in Paris with the world and European champions, France. Keegan's team, shorn of Neville brothers, looked far more sensibly selected and better balanced than the sides which had laboured through the European finals.

The twenty-year-old Gareth Barry made an excellent first start at left back – yet would still be looking for a place in England's teams six years later. Barmby played eighty-three minutes, Dyer came on after sixty-nine, and made the spectacular equaliser by a buoyant Owen four minutes from the end. 'I don't think anyone can ever fault the English pride,' said Owen. 'You have to go into the dressing room and hear some of the talking that goes on. Afterwards, the room is always full of blood and sweat.'

It was too good to last. Had Keegan only left well alone, perhaps the subsequent opening World Cup qualifier against Germany the following month – the last international to be played at dear old Wembley before the bulldozers went in – might have had a different story. Who, to this day, can know what possessed Keegan in a 4–4–2 system to place the one-paced central defender, Gareth Southgate, in central midfield? It was a disaster waiting to happen and it did, compounded by David Seaman's distraction on the quarter-hour when he allowed a quickly taken and far from irresistible free kick by Dietmar Hamann to find its way past him.

Booed off the field, tearful in the toilets, a fragile Kevin Keegan instantly resigned, saying, 'I have no complaints. I have not been quite good enough. I blame no one but myself.' Poor Southgate, who had already missed that penalty against the Germans, declared that he was as surprised as anybody else at being cast in midfield.

To make matters worse, a second qualifying match, away to Finland, was due only four days away. The team was entrusted, as it had been before that Wembley defeat by France, to Howard Wilkinson, who was no more convincing than Keegan. For if Keegan had ludicrously used Southgate in midfield, then Wilkinson proceeded to drop Owen.

Though the Finns were fortunate when, after just six minutes, their keeper Antii Niemi escaped punishment after bringing down Teddy Sheringham in the box, and when, three minutes from time, Ray Parlour's shot against the underside of the bar unquestionably came down behind the line, England were again mediocre. Wilkinson, Cassandra-like, compounded the situation by gloomily announcing that they should forget about qualifying for the ensuing 2002 World Cup and think about 2006.

Wilkinson then blessedly stood aside, enabling Peter Taylor to assume temporary control for the ensuing friendly in Italy. There was a certain irony here, since Wilkinson, when installed at the FA, had abruptly and high handedly replaced Taylor as manager of the England Under-21 team, which he had been running with such success, embarking on a series of negative results which prevented the side from qualifying for the eventual finals.

If this was Taylor's first time in charge, so it was for an infinitely more experienced club manager and former international, Gianni Trapattoni. Bringing back Dyer, Barmby and Rio Ferdinand, capping the gifted but unpredictable David James in goal, Taylor drew a more spirited performance from England in Turin, where only 22,000 bothered to watch, and a hard-hit goal by the midfielder Gennaro Gattuso decided the game.

Meanwhile, on 30 October, Sven-Goran Eriksson, the Swedish manager of Lazio in Rome, agreed to become the first foreigner to manage England. He would, it was announced, arrive the following July, but in fact he would take up his post seven months earlier, in January.

10 ERIKSSON: THE QUARTER-FINAL YEARS

Sven-Goran Eriksson 2001–06
Key Game: Germany v England, September 2001

THE APPOINTMENT OF SVEN-GORAN ERIKSSON PROVOKED THE inevitable outburst of xenophobia, never wholly allayed, though to those of us who had followed his European career in Portugal and all over Italy, the choice, initially at least, seemed a shrewd one. A footballer of limited talent, he had cut his teeth on the modest Degerfors club in his native Sweden, gone on with much success to manage Gothenburg, and from there gone south to achieve success in Lisbon during two spells with Benfica, and to give a good account of himself in Italy with Roma, Fiorentina, Sampdoria and Lazio, with whom he eventually won the *scudetto*, though at massive expense.

I had often come across him in Italy and been impressed, not least with his ability to survive the ferocious pressures of football in Rome. I remembered in particular being there just after his Roma team had lost passively away to Milan. Gianni Melidoni, chief football writer and sports editor of the Roman daily *Il Messaggero*, had boldly criticised the Roma players for deliberately trying to get Eriksson dismissed. Attending the subsequent press conference at Roma's head-quarters, I was impressed by Eriksson's calm demeanour.

When he was appointed, the controversial Chief Executive of the Football Association, Adam Crozier, had praised Eriksson as a man who always adhered to his contracts. At this point in time, the words indeed may have a hollow ring, but even then they were hardly convincing to those who knew Eriksson's record. Happy in Florence, he had tried to avoid a contractual obligation to return to Lisbon to manage Benfica, but the Portuguese club had insisted he fulfil his commitment. Subsequently, he had actually agreed to manage Blackburn Rovers when Lazio offered him their managerial role. This time, however, he found Blackburn more forgiving than Benfica.

Episodes such as these in retrospect may have adumbrated his behaviour. In subsequent years, while manager of England, he had surreptitious negotiations once with Manchester United and twice with Chelsea. Each time, however, he would find the Football Association as permissive as Blackburn, and it was only when he and his equally credulous agent were duped into similar aspirations by a reporter in Dubai posing as a sheikh, but working for the *News of the World*, that the FA finally decided that enough was enough. Even then, they were committed to continuing to pay his ludicrously rewarding contract of £5 million a year till he deigned to find other employment.

Yet after the feebleness of Keegan and the pessimism of Wilkinson, there is no doubt that Eriksson's initial impact was positive. He could hardly have made a brighter beginning. On the last day of February, Spain were brushed aside 3–0 in a friendly at Villa Park. With Tord Grip, once his team mate and mentor in Swedish football as his assistant, Eriksson made light of several absences, deploying a 4–4–2 system which included a veteran left back in Chris Powell. After a slightly shaky beginning, Nick Barmby put England ahead and the Spaniards seemed to lose heart. Eriksson, in a foreshadowing of the future, used seven substitutes in the second half, but this time, at least the effect was not negative. Emile Heskey and the centre back Ugo Ehiogu scored the other goals. His press conference, typically, was amiably bland.

In March, within the space of four days, came two World Cup qualifying matches which had to be won; and they were. During training sessions, the players had noted that Eriksson stood quietly on the sidelines, but when it came to the games themselves, his briefing was comprehensive. But the victory against the Finns, at Anfield, was anything but facile. Finland, indeed, took a first-half lead with a goal of embarrassing dimensions; chaos at a corner, the ball rebounding from Gary Neville's knee past David Seaman. Owen equalised, Beckham scored the winner on fifty minutes, Andy Cole, who found it so hard to score for England, wasted a sitter. And the clever Finnish attacker Jari Litmanen was thwarted only by a providential save from Seaman.

In Tirana, Norman Wisdom, bizarrely, a celebrity in Albania, cavorted with the local police around the ground. Ashley Cole received his first cap at left back and was knocked down by a lipstick. But England, scoring three times in the last eighteen minutes, with Andy Cole getting one at last, prevailed 3–1. Germany, however, retained their group lead. 'I'm here,' said Eriksson, 'and I am not going away.' Not for a long time. Sceptics began to change their tune, Bobby Charlton among them. David James, whose future antics in goal would hardly help Eriksson sleep after games, praised the Swede's 'devotion to being prepared'.

Early in June, after a week's preparation in the sunshine of La Manga, England played their last World Cup qualifier of the season against Greece in a roasting hot Athens. Effective rather than brilliant, England went ahead through Paul Scholes nineteen minutes into the second half and doubled their lead through one of David Beckham's insidious free kicks. Eriksson praised Beckham's captaincy. The Germans still had a six-point group lead, but qualification was no longer a mere mirage. After all, England had a game in hand, and Eriksson expressed his own optimism.

A mid-August friendly against Holland at White Hart Lane was hardly encouraging, though half the team was missing, and the League season had yet to begin. Once again, in deference to club managers concerned about exposing their players with so little preparation, there were mass substitutions. You felt sorry for the promising young midfielder, Owen Hargreaves, who, unusually, had come straight from Canadian football to Bayern Munich, without kicking a ball in England. Stuck out on the unfamiliar left wing, he looked a lonely figure. Sad, too, for David James, who had scarcely come on as a second-half substitute when, colliding with Martin Keown, he severely damaged his knee. One remembers the brave face he put on it after-wards in the Tottenham car park.

In little more than a fortnight, England were due to play their crucial game in Munich. Germany had only once ever lost a World Cup qualifying game, a fact about which Eriksson was characteristic-ally phlegmatic.

It was a match which would end for England in total and sensa-tional triumph, arguably one of the most remarkable victories in the history of the national team, a game after which Eriksson, if only temporarily, became an heroic figure. But the foremost hero of the hour was an irresistible Michael Owen, author of a hat trick and scourge of a bewildered and flat-footed German defence.

Eriksson deployed Heskey as strike partner to Owen, with Barmby back on the left flank, a position he was well used to filling though a naturally right-footed player. Eriksson said that he knew Heskey wanted to play up front and knew he would give his best there. 'I know we can do it,' he told the press, but even he could hardly have anticipated how sensationally. Yet after a mere six minutes, Germany had gone ahead against an England team found wanting in defence. Michael Ballack's centre from the left sailed between Rio Ferdinand and Ashley Cole, enabling the clever little winger Oliver Neuville to head the ball down to the big striker Carsten Jancker, who knocked it in from close range. It could have been traumatic for England, yet in another seven minutes they were level. One of David Beckham's ever-productive free kicks from the right was met by the head of Gary Neville, flicked on by Barmby to Owen, who duly equalised.

It might well be said, however, that the watershed of the match came when Germany's talented young midfielder, Sebastian Deisler, all alone, eight yards out with only David Seaman to beat, and dead centre, shot over the bar. Seaman himself made a resilient save from Jorg Bohme. So it was that, exploiting a pass from Ferdinand, Liverpool's powerful young midfielder, Steven Gerrard, beat Oliver Kahn with a fearsome right-footed drive, giving England a 2–1 half-time lead. In the dressing room, Eriksson simply told his team 'just to keep playing'. They were highly responsive to him.

From the moment Owen had scored his first goal, it became increasingly clear that the heavy-footed, confused German defence had no answer to him. Just a couple of minutes into the second half, Heskey nodded the ball on, Owen pursued it, Kahn anxiously got it away. The reprieve was brief. When Heskey nodded down Beckham's left-footed cross, Owen swept in England's third with his right foot. His hat trick came when, receiving from Gerrard, he surged through the scattered and demoralised German defence to score again. Ferdinand and Scholes sent the powerful Heskey through, leaving Mark Rehmer in his wake, to get the astonishing fifth with a fulminating drive. The final score, 5–1. The stuff that dreams are made on.

Eriksson took it all with his trademark calm; he didn't, he said, yet know what this meant for England; indeed there were a couple of games to come. He admitted 'a little luck' in scoring before half time, though this could hardly be seen as luck in any definitive sense. Recovery, he pursued, was ensured by the players' belief that 'we can achieve big things'. The country was beginning to believe too.

Four days later, Albania visited Newcastle, and were beaten 2–0 with goals by Owen and Robbie Fowler, who had not figured in Munich. Home matches now would be played away from Wembley, mired in an endless saga of bickering and frustration. This was the very result which Eriksson said he had been seeking. At St James' Park, the team's arrival was greeted with almost hysterical acclaim which would not, said Eriksson, happen in any other country. Inevitably the performance was something of an anticlimax. Owen said he had never felt so tired, though mentally, rather than physically. 'We cannot afford to drop the pace,' admitted Eriksson, 'we have to play a high tempo game.' He eulogised David Beckham's captaincy, calling him 'the complete player'; one sniffed hyperbole in the air.

The final, vital, qualifying game took place at Old Trafford without Michael Owen, betrayed by a hamstring which would plague him indefinitely and entail visits to an unorthodox specialist in Germany. Greece had been thrashed 5–1 in Finland on the night England won by the same score in Munich, but Eriksson carefully played down any sense of euphoria; and as events unfolded was proved all too wise.

Automatic qualification was still not assured. The match had to be won – it was assumed the Germans were likely to get three points in Finland – and it was so nearly lost.

With Martyn, Keown and Fowler replacing Seaman, Campbell and Owen, all injured, England were manifestly second best in the opening half. The Greek striker, Angelos Charisteas, destined to become a hero of Greece's phenomenal triumph in the 2004 European Championship, beat Martyn with a strong, diagonal shot after the Greek attacking right back showed up the vulnerability of Ashley Cole as a defensive rather than an overlapping left back, going past him to deliver the cross.

Eriksson put on Andy Cole to replace Barmby, but only a fine save by Martyn avoided a second Greek goal by the forceful Theo Zagorakis. Greeks, these, who were assuredly bearing no gifts. Martyn proceeded to make another essential save from the right winger, Giorgos Karagounis, and Beckham, in his urgency, became the Total Footballer, ubiquitous in his desperate desire to turn the tide.

Turned it was after Eriksson midway through the second half made what proved an inspired substitution, the 35-year-old Teddy Sheringham, saver of lost causes, coming on for Fowler. He had been on the field just a couple of minutes when another of those invaluable Beckham free kicks gave him the chance of a back header which brought the English equaliser.

Yet within a mere minute, a resilient Greece had taken the lead again, when Themis Nikolaidis spun to shoot past Martyn from well inside the box. Defeat and disaster once more, but Beckham and Sheringham would again come to the rescue, however debatably. In the very last minute, Sheringham ingeniously obtained a free kick, when surely backing into Kostas Konstantinidis. Sheringham himself wanted to try his luck, but Beckham, who had tried unsuccessfully with half a dozen such chances, prevailed, and sent his exquisitely swerved free kick into the top right-hand corner of the goal. In Gelsenkirchen, Germany had already been held to a draw by the Finns. Prematurely celebrating, they were devastated when England, too, gained their draw, and pipped them on goal difference for first place in the group, with automatic qualification. Germany had to qualfy via the play-offs for the finals in 2002, in which they were to make a major impact.

If we are talking about luck, then certainly Eriksson, like his team, had it in spades. In Stockholm he was being celebrated as his country's Personality of the Year; the hype was cranking up, more so now that England knew their tough World Cup group would include Argentina, Nigeria and, perhaps inevitably, Sweden.

Previously amicable relations between Eriksson and the press were strained when strong rumours circulated that he had been in contact with Manchester United, with a view to succeeding Alex Ferguson, who had announced he would retire as manager. Made aware of the rumours Ferguson, who appeared to have been playing a deliberate game, abruptly announced he would stay.

As the build-up to the finals in Japan and Korea continued, England turned out for a series of meaningless friendlies, blemished by the plethora of withdrawals and substitutions that were agreed as a sop to club managers reluctant to release their prize assets. It was hard to develop any tactical coherence when the team that finished the game was completely different from the one that kicked off. But it was in this context that Eriksson unveiled some promising newcomers, such as the precocious West Ham inside forward – hardly your average midfielder – and Owen Hargreaves, who unusually had gone straight from Canadian football to Bayern Munich, without kicking a ball in England.

Early in April came the grim news that David Beckham had been seriously injured playing for Manchester United at Old Trafford in the Champions League against Deportivo La Coruna. A foul from the abrasive Argentine, Aldo Duscher, had broken the metatarsal bone in his foot. He would recover sufficiently to play in the World Cup finals, but the persisting injury was surely responsible for the way he jumped out of a tackle in England's eventual quarter-final in Japan, facilitating Brazil's equalising goal.

Almost concurrently, what might euphemistically be termed Eriksson's romantic life became a cause célèbre. He had arrived in London accompanied by a flamboyant and volatile 37-year-old Italian lawyer, Nancy Dell'Olio, whom, when managing Lazio in Rome, he had prised away from her elderly husband. Eriksson's own first marriage had ended in divorce, and his liaison with Nancy had ended a long relationship with a Swedish woman.

But now, a joyful tabloid press announced, he was passionately involved with still another Swede, the blonde TV 'personality' Ulrika Jonsson, noted chiefly for her endless thirst for publicity. Her earlier liaison with the English international centre forward, Stan Collymore, had ended with his knocking her down and kicking her, some four years earlier, in a Parisian bar. The tabloids made great sport of the story that Eriksson, according to Ulrika's nanny, had left his built-up shoes outside the door of her bedroom, at once a warning and an admission. What surprised was not so much any moral aspect of the affair, but the light it cast on Eriksson's reckless lack of judgement. If he was going to choose a new lover, why should it be one so notoriously insatiable to be in the public eye?

If he was now seen as libidinous, he was also to be perceived as greedy. Reportedly making £2.5 million a year from his England role, he became involved in a multiplicity of commercial deals, varying from the promotion of PlayStation to pasta sauce to a so-called classical collection of music on CD, to which one had to presume he had listened. Nancy meanwhile insisted loudly that their romance was far from dead, while the impression increased that those built-up shoes might be containing feet of clay. The years to come would bring still more lurid sequels.

The days before setting off for South-east Asia seemed to be peppered with medical bulletins on injured potential squad members. There was captain Beckham, of course, and the metatarsal saga which gripped the nation for weeks. Kieron Dyer had suffered a shocking foul when playing for Newcastle at Southampton which would presumably put him out of contention with injured knee ligaments. Bobby Robson, Newcastle's manager, pleaded Dyer's cause and Eriksson, generously but unwisely, chose him for the squad, but his physical condition would prevent him from functioning at full capacity, and made just three appearances as substitute. Just before the squad was due to leave, Eriksson was told by Liverpool that the dynamic Steven Gerrard was unfit to go. And before the quarter-finals, Michael

Owen, too, was destined to be hurt, straining a groin, even if he did continue to play. One could hardly, in such circumstances, continue to call Eriksson a lucky manager.

But to choose a plainly suspect Dyer while overlooking Steve McManaman, so recently in dazzling form for Real Madrid in the final of the European Cup, seemed almost perverse. McManaman had not been used since he came on as a substitute in the draw with Greece. And it was all too predictable that Owen would miss the splendid service of penetrating long passes from his Liverpool team mate Gerrard, on which he and his electric pace thrived.

After a training spell in Dubai, from which football journalists were unwisely banned, opening the door to the news reporters whom Ted Croker had nicknamed 'the Rotters', the England party moved for a week to the idyllic Korean island of Jeju, where a friendly was played against the South Koreans themselves. Adopting a 4–3–3 formation, England led by a goal from Owen in the first half, but instituted eight subs in the second, fell apart, and were held 1–1. Trevor Sinclair, the winger, a late call-up, on the fringe of the final squad, had a dreadful game and, confessing that he 'couldn't do it', went home, demoralised. But he would, somewhat farcically, be recalled, after Danny Murphy was injured.

After another farcical friendly (adopting a 4–3–3 formation), this time against Cameroon, which was of no value at all as eight substitutions totally disrupted any team shape they might have had, the squad flew to Japan, where a huge, ecstatic crowd greeted them like pop stars at Osaka airport. England played a final, preparatory game, this time, well below strength and reverted to 4–4–2 against powerful Cameroon. Eriksson sought solace after a fortunate draw, in reflecting that the senior players had been saving their legs, though youngsters Owen Hargreaves and the energetic goalscorer Darius Vassell had impressed him.

Quarter-finals again: World Cup, Japan and Korea 2002

Sweden, the eternal bogey team, were ominously the first opponents, in Saitama. Another poor performance, another lucky draw. Sol Campbell headed England into the lead from David Beckham's corner, jumping majestically above the defence. But after almost an hour, Danny Mills, the right back replacing injured Gary Neville, clumsily enabled Niclas Alexandersson, the Swedish winger, to shoot left footed past David Seaman. Sweden dominated the rest of the game against an increasingly desperate English defence. There were trenchant words afterwards from the Swedish goalkeeper, Magnus Hedman: 'You put up the long ball and hope for the knock on to Owen, but that way of playing is dependent on chance.'

The auguries, then, for the second match, against the old, abrasive foe, Argentina under the roof at Sapporo, were anything but encouraging. Yet in the event, England would win, taking joyous revenge for the bitter defeat four years earlier in Saint Etienne. And while this would be achieved through a penalty, it would not, by contrast, be won *on* penalties.

England, indeed, surpassed themselves, and none more so than the previously unsung Manchester United midfielder, Nicky Butt, who would win the admiration of Pele himself. Not only did he nullify his United team mate, the designated Argentine playmaker, Juan Sebastian Veron, who was eventually substituted, but he supplied, midway through the first half, the pass from which Owen, dashing through, shot between the legs of his marker, Walter Samuel, only to hit the post. He had clearly taken to heart Eriksson's instructions to be more mobile. And this time there would be no Roberto Ayala, injured, to oppose him. Not that Ayala had been able to subdue him in Saint Etienne.

On nineteen minutes, Hargreaves, who had not been having the best of times, came off with an injury, which proved a blessing in disguise. Trevor Sinclair, now much improved, came on to the left flank, enabling Scholes to move off it and play a far more influential role. Four minutes into the second half, his splendid volley forced an equally spectacular save from the opposing keeper, Pablo Cavallero.

By that time, England, a minute before half time, had scored what proved the decisive goal. Owen, in dynamic form, raced past Mauricio Pochettino, who desperately brought him down. Refusing to be put off by the Argentinians' delaying tactics, Beckham drove home the penalty. Revenge was sweet. England were playing scintillating football. A move of no fewer than seventeen passes concluded with a fierce volley by Sheringham, a substitute, which Cavallero soared to turn over the bar. But with just ten minutes left, Eriksson seemed perilously to lose his nerve. He took off Owen, who had been stretching and tormenting the Argentinian defence, to put on not another striker, but a second left back, in the shape of Wayne Bridge, fielded in front of Ashley Cole. Thus gratuitously handed over the initiative, Argentina surged into attack, and Pochettino's header from a corner produced a fine save from Seaman. So England, deservedly, hung on.

The third and final group game was against Nigeria in Osaka; a goalless anticlimax, but enough to qualify England for the second round. The fierce heat and humidity, plus a possible reaction from the game against Argentina, may well have had something to do with the display. Bar the one mistake he seemed to make in every match, which nearly gave Julius Aghahowa a goal, Rio Ferdinand had an impeccable game. Sheringham missed a palpable chance, Scholes had a shot tipped over the bar but Owen, at least, was vivacious.

In Niigata, England were fortunate enough to find the usually competent Danish goalkeeper, Thomas Sorensen, on a disastrous day. After a mere four minutes, Beckham took a corner from the left, Sorensen fumbled what looked an easy ball, when Ferdinand put in a far post header, and the ball sputtered over the line. Twenty minutes later, with the Danes seemingly demoralised, Sinclair centred, Butt forced the ball through the legs of Thomas Gravesen and Owen swooped to make it 2–0. He was subsequently forced off, injured, but another blunder by the hapless Sorensen allowed what looked an unthreatening shot by Heskey to go past him. An excellent game for Butt, a Danish fiasco.

Six days later, in Shizuoka, it might be said that both England and Eriksson met their moment of truth. England would go out of the tournament, and for a passive Eriksson, it would never be bright, confident morning again. Yet things began so well, and so badly for Brazil. Midway through the first half, an unforced, inexplicable error by the Brazilian centre back, Lucio, had Owen racing through to score the gift of a goal. But the effervescent Ronaldinho would prove to be England's nemesis, even if he wasn't destined to finish the match.

In first-half injury time, he set off on a run which a fit Beckham might have nipped in the bud. But Beckham jumped out of the way of a tackle, clearly mindful of his vulnerable foot, and Ronaldinho ran irresistibly on, brushing off a challenge by Paul Scholes, cleverly eluding another by Ashley Cole, before unselfishly giving Rivaldo the easiest of chances.

With Owen clearly far from being fully fit, and with little inspiration coming from midfield, England lost the plot, and Eriksson was of scant help to them. Gareth Southgate famously remarked later that at half time, England needed Winston Churchill, but they got Iain Duncan Smith.

Five minutes into the second half, Ronaldinho, from a diabolic free kick, scored the goal which would put England out of the running. A shot which swerved tantalisingly over the head of a stranded and ultimately tearful David Seaman, to end in the net and make it 2–1. There were those afterwards who dismissed the goal as a fluke. But Ronaldinho insisted that he meant it and, given his flair for scoring with remarkable shots before and since this game, and given Seaman's known vulnerability to shots from afar, he has claims to be believed.

England needed the inventiveness of a Gascoigne to break down the opposition defence, even when, with half an hour still to play, the Brazilians were reduced to ten men when Ronaldinho – of all people – was sent off for a reckless tackle on Danny Mills.

Should Eriksson, as the minutes ebbed by and the numerical advantage went for nothing, at least have risked bringing on Joe Cole, whose natural flair might have produced chances? Owen came off with twenty minutes left, giving way to Vassell, while Dyer replaced Sinclair on the hour but predictably, given his lack of match practice, made little impact. If ifs and ans were pots and pans . . . Or if what had been interpreted as Eriksson's supposed sangfroid had not been so plainly exposed as ineffectuality. At least Ronaldinho generously expressed his sympathy for Seaman.

'It was terrible to see England play like that,' said Guus Hiddink, Holland's coach for the South Korean team, whose own Dutch side had been thrashed in Euro 96 at Wembley. Yet to call them 'the worst of all the negative European teams' was surely excessive. They had unquestionably had their moments as well as their miseries.

There would be little to celebrate in the ensuing season, the irony being that the worse his England teams performed, the better the backing Eriksson received from a strangely deluded Football Association. Notably from the Chief Executive, Mark Palios, a former Tranmere Rovers footballer who'd gone successfully into the City, whose once warm relationship with Eriksson would end in squalor and scandal.

England began their competitive programme in October 2002 with the opening European Championship qualifier against Slovakia in Bratislava; a dull laborious performance, even though they managed eventually to eke out a 2–1 win, second-half goals from Beckham and Owen cancelling the goal Szilard Nemeth scored for the Slovaks in the first half. Four days later, in Southampton, a disastrous display against the modest Macedonians, personified by Seaman's vulner-ability in goal, resulted in a 2–2 draw, the keeper giving away one embarrassing goal straight from a right-wing corner. Though Seaman might plausibly have asked why Paul Scholes ducked on the goal line, as the ball flew in.

Still there was no place for Steve McManaman, and it was outra-geous, midway through the season, to hear Tord Grip, once Eriksson's mentor, now his assistant, gratuitously state, 'Steve McManaman has never really played a good match for England and at the moment isn't up for selection for the national team. He needs to be a regular in the Real Madrid line-up before he can come up for discussion.' What of Euro 96, when McManaman, used on the right rather than the left, had such scintillating moments?

Eriksson and England, however, were to have an immense piece of luck, potentially cataclysmic: the precocious emergence of the teenaged Wayne Rooney, the first major English talent to appear since the dazzling but doomed Paul Gascoigne, now reduced to picking up the pieces of his career with this club and that, while fighting his alcoholism.

Born into a tough working-class Liverpudlian family, in which boxing had been more evident than football, Rooney's natural gifts, his supreme self-confidence, were quite phenomenal. At age sixteen, he scored, as a substitute at Goodison Park, a goal of fantastic power, accuracy and surprise, to give Everton victory over Arsenal. To the strength of a square and stalwart frame, he added unusual ball skills, pace, and that peripheral vision which enabled him to make the right pass, find the right man, without hesitation.

Eriksson, understandably, had doubts about launching him, still a mere seventeen-year-old, in a major international game, but fortunately for the England team that played Turkey in a European qualifier at Sunderland in April 2003, he changed his mind: and was rewarded by a glorious, match-saving display against a Turkish team which threatened to win the day. Rooney had gone on to the field for the last ten minutes in a dire English exhibition in tiny Liechtenstein; a meagre 2–0 win. Four days later came the test against Turkey.

Eriksson finally ignored the over-cautious pleas from Rooney's manager at Everton, David Moyes, who insisted that Rooney still had a lot to learn. It seemed more pertinent to say that Rooney had a lot to teach. Having scored that stupendous goal in the previous season, he had recently taken Arsenal's flailing defence apart in a match at Highbury. Now he would come to the rescue of an England team initially outplayed by a technically superior Turkey, several times threatening to take the lead. England's so-called diamond formation, which, not for the last time, exiled the right-footed Steven Gerrard to the left flank and prevented him serving Owen with his raking passes, was ineffective. It was the boy Rooney who took the bull by the horns.

With astonishing maturity and enterprise, he began dropping into midfield to look for the ball, sometimes coolly juggling it past opponents, then hit the kind of crossfield and through-passes of which any playmaker would be proud. Until his supreme confidence began to course its way through the team, England had looked a sadly uneasy side. There had been plenty for David James, now in goal, to do. Luckily, Rooney's confidence would prove contagious. Gradually England, with Nicky Butt giving Rooney solid support in midfield, gained a hold on the game. Darius Vassell, who had substituted Owen, gave England the lead after seventy-six minutes. David Beckham, in the last minute, doubled the score from a penalty, just one minute after Rooney himself had left the field to great acclaim.

February had seen a fiasco of a friendly at West Ham against Australia, and a further blow to Eriksson's reputation. True, the fixture came at a very delicate time both for Arsenal and Manchester United, due to meet in the FA Cup at Old Trafford the previous Saturday and to play Champions League matches the following week. But it was surely a craven dereliction of responsibility to announce in advance that the first-choice England team would play only in the first half to be replaced in toto in the second by a bunch of youngsters. Again, in June, in a friendly against Serbia and Montenegro at the Walkers Stadium in Leicester, England made ten substitutions, Serbia made all eleven.

Subsequently Eriksson tried to make the best of a bad job by suggesting that all friendlies be played at the end of the season. A notion which made scant sense, given that the early summer, aside from the year immediately following participation in the World Cup, was the time when England teams toured abroad.

In June came the return European fixture against Slovakia at Middlesbrough's Riverside, which it was essential to win. And they did, by 2–1, of course. Owen scored both goals, the first from a penalty procured by one of his deceptive dives, the second a header, after fine work by the now centrally located Gerrard. An ebullient second-half display erased the memory of a poor English first half and an embarrassing goal conceded from a bouncing free kick. Though the margin was narrow, this was by far England's best display of the season. The European finals now seemed well within their grasp. 'We didn't start too well,' said Owen, 'but the manager told us to keep calm because our class would tell.' And he insisted he'd been fouled for the penalty. But Rooney for once disappointed.

July saw Eriksson caught off guard when a photographer snapped him entering the Russian oligarch Roman Abramovich's London house, in the inevitable company of the super fixer, the Israeli agent Pini Zuhavi. Eriksson, through the FA, emitted an explanation which explained nothing. Or rather nothing that wasn't clear enough already.

He didn't deny that the Chelsea managerial job then filled by the Italian Claudio Ranieri had been under discussion. But the following month, after England had beaten Croatia 3–1 in a friendly at Ipswich – with the usual plethora of substitutes, some bright attacking but some shaky defending – it appeared that the FA wanted to extend Eriksson's contract provided England qualified for the European finals. The extension could reportedly last till 2008. Logic went out of the window.

The three remaining European qualifiers followed, the clincher always likely to be the third, in Istanbul. In Skopje, against Macedonia, England were welcomed by the burning of a St George's Cross flag, and monkey chanting at Emile Heskey. Nor was Beckham immune from abuse, but he had emphatically the last laugh, consistently influential, first producing the cross on fifty-three minutes which Heskey, a substitute, headed down for Rooney to sweep home his first England goal, and then winning the game from the penalty spot after John Terry, chasing Beckham's chip, had been fouled in the box.

Macedonia were in front at half time, when Ashley Cole failed to cut out a cross from the right, Campbell stumbled trying to head clear, enabling Goran Pandev to find Georgi Hristov who scored. Gerrard was missed. Hargreaves, not for the first time, looked lost on the left.

Next, little Liechtenstein at a surprisingly packed Old Trafford, and a pedestrian 2–0 victory. Just as well that Wayne Rooney, playing behind the front two, was in such ubiquitous and dynamic form. With the score embarrassingly at 0–0 at the break, England scored twice in quick succession in the second half, a spectacular header from Owen off Gerrard's fine cross, a thunderbolt from Rooney, from Gerrard's precise headed pass. Eriksson won praise for his half-time team talk, demanding quicker tempo, fewer touches, but against such fragile opposition, it should hardly have been relevant.

So in October to Istanbul, where a draw would now be enough for automatic qualification. But would England be there at all? In a ludicrous episode at their training headquarters in St Albans, the England players, whipped up by Gary 'Fred Kite' Neville, masquerading as a kind of shop steward – and thus evoking memories of Peter Sellers' comic creation in the film *I'm All Right Jack* – threatened to strike unless Rio Ferdinand was restored to the squad.

Guilty of evading a drugs test at the Manchester United training ground, driving out of the gates after twice being reminded of the commitment, allegedly to buy bed linen in town, Ferdinand was properly excluded from the squad. Later, having failed in an appeal, he would be suspended for eight months, which was a great deal less than the mandatory two years imposed on athletes who similarly offended. Ferdinand moreover never offered the ghost of a valid excuse, even when he published his obnoxious autobiography after the 2006 World Cup. He had, we were to believe, simply forgotten. Or do people simply forget what they do not want to remember? As it transpired, Terry and Campbell gave rock-like central defence performances in Istanbul, while Ferdinand, for all his undoubted talents, had just given away an embarrassing goal, playing in the Champions League for Manchester United in Stuttgart, further evidence of his odd penchant for error.

Neville and the England players, shamefully egged on by Gordon Taylor, of the Professional Footballers' Association, and tacitly supported by Eriksson, seemed initially to believe that England could duck out of the Istanbul game and remain in the tournament. It was quickly made clear to them that they were more likely to be thrown out. To his credit, David Beckham, as captain, advised against the move, and the players meekly backed down. Willing to wound and yet afraid to strike, you might say. But Beckham blotted his own copybook after the goalless draw which qualified the team by ludicrously dedicating the result to Ferdinand!

Overall, it was a solid if hardly brilliant performance against a Turkish team with nerves on edge. None more so than Alpay, the Aston Villa centre half who, when Beckham skied a penalty over the bar in the first half, yelled insults into his face. The confrontation continued down the tunnel at the break, when Rooney punched Alpay on the nose, Alpay having insulted Beckham's mother. Beckham had manifestly slipped as he ran up to take the kick, awarded when Gerrard was felled by Tugay. Alas, though this was the first spot kick which Beckham had ever missed for England, there would be more missed penalties to come. Much to his credit, Pierluigi Collina, the authoritative Italian referee, took Beckham and Alpay into his dressing room, defusing the situation by telling them that if things thus continued they'd both be sent off.

So England, deprived of Michael Owen, achieved their draw and their survival. But Eriksson had anything but a cordial reception from English journalists after the game. Having evaded questions at the pre-match media conference, he was now assailed with demands about his future intentions; would he stay or would he go? Under extreme pressure, he eventually asserted that he would indeed manage England in the forthcoming European Championship finals. But whatever the various romances in his life, the romance with the press was emphatically dead, and there was much worse to come.

Friendlies against Denmark, Portugal, Sweden, Japan and Iceland followed, vitiated by their multiple substitutions (eight, nine, eight, eight and eleven respectively), though Sepp Blatter, for once coming up with a relevant idea instead of the fifty-one bad ideas a day with which he was once credited, was pressing for the substitutions to be limited to six. Meanwhile, this was hardly the way to mould a team together.

The month after the Sweden game, Eriksson had been caught on camera once again. This time, again in London, he was visiting the house of the recently appointed Chief Executive at Chelsea, Peter Kenyon, acquired from Manchester United. Far from dismissing or berating him, the FA's Mark Palios raised Eriksson's salary to over £4 million, confirming him in office despite the fact that not a ball had been kicked in the European finals. Again, a tell-tale photograph of Eriksson's arrival was taken and published, but by now any relation between logic and the decisions emanating from Soho Square – where the previous Chief Executive, Adam Crozier, had expensively moved the FA's offices despite, reportedly, not having gained the necessary support – seemed minimal. Kenyon talked unconvincingly about 'informal discussions' and Eriksson's 'enormous loyalty to the England job.'

More Shoot-out Misery: European Championship, Portugal 2004

This was a tournament which would be won, astonishingly, by the utterly unfancied Greek team, managed by the shrewd German veteran, Otto Rehhagel, a team without real stars which nonetheless humiliated teams allegedly full of them. Of England's team, only Wayne Rooney gave an outstanding account of himself, and it was, alas, his injury in the first half of the quarter-final against Portugal in Lisbon which surely cost England further progress.

'Here against France,' said Eriksson, 'we should have won that game and we did some stupid mistakes.' Among them, tactically, his own, the evident product of excessive caution. 'We had to defend deep,' he averred, after the opening match against France. The holders in Lisbon had slipped from England's grasp in injury time, 'because if you defend on the halfway line and Henry gets away, then you will never catch him'. This seemed the essence of defeatism, not least against a French team which would prove anything but irresistible in the tournament.

This obsession with Thierry Henry, who in fact would have an indifferent competition, inevitably gave more space to David Trezeguet and Zinedine Zidane. England's emphasis on counter-attacking caution meant that when they did go ahead on thirty-eight minutes, it was a bolt from the blue, one of Beckham's famous right-wing free kicks enabling Frank Lampard to score. But when Mikael Silvestre fouled Rooney in the second half, Beckham – with no excuse this time about slipping – had his spot kick saved by Fabien Barthez.

So France called the tune against a tiring English side, and grabbed two goals in added time. Heskey's crude foul on the edge of the box – his days of international grace by then a mere memory – enabled Zidane to equalise from an ingenious free kick. Two minutes later Gerrard, of all unlikely people, culpably underhit a back pass to David James, who consequently brought down Henry. Zidane showed Beckham how spot kicks should be taken.

Four days later, things were looking up when Switzerland in Coimbra were brushed aside 3–0 after an uneasy first twenty minutes. With Rooney rampant, as indeed he had been against the French, England led when he headed in after a four-man move, making him at the time the youngest player (at eighteen years and seven months) to score in the European Championship finals. The die was cast when Bernt Haas of Switzerland was expelled on the hour for a second yellow card. Vassell, at great pace, won a tackle, played the ball out to Rooney, who hit a fierce shot which flew home off the post and the head of the horizontal goalkeeper. Steven Gerrard, in commanding form, struck the third. Rooney said modestly, 'I just go out looking to do well for the team.'

Croatia, who had drawn with France, were expected to be a tougher test, but England subdued them impressively, 4–2, in Lisbon's Stadium of Light. Rooney, with two of the four goals, was in dynamic form, an undoubted international star. Yet Niko Kovac gave the Croatians the lead, ominously, after a mere five minutes, Ashley Cole, later to flourish on the overlap, knocking a Croatian free kick into his own goalmouth. A surprised James could only block the ball, Kovac darting in to score.

Eriksson, who had warned his players about Croatian free kicks, remarked, 'I cannot tell you what I was thinking at the time. They were not very nice words.' But on forty minutes Paul Scholes scored his first international goal for three years, when Rooney nodded a loose ball to him – keeper Tomislav Butina having saved from Owen – and Rooney himself just on half time made it 2–1 with a fizzing 25-yard drive.

In the second half, Rooney swopped passes with Owen to score his second, Igor Tudor – who was supposed to be a major menace – got one back for Croatia, Lampard struck England's fourth. Somewhat ungraciously, the Croatian coach Otto Baric called Rooney 'a very good player but not a phenomenon; there are at least ten players in Europe who can stop him'.

'I don't know who they are,' responded Eriksson, hoping Portugal in the quarter-finals wouldn't have one of them. Alas they did, all too painfully and disastrously.

Yet the match, in Lisbon, could hardly have begun more auspiciously for England. After only three minutes, Costinha culpably missed a ball from Gerrard, which thus became a devastating through-pass to Owen who, with typical opportunism, whirled on the chance and shot home. After twenty-four more minutes, however, for England the die was virtually cast. Wayne Rooney, who had already shown his huge all-round value to the team, not only up front but when dropping back to reinforce the midfield, took a kick in a challenge with

Jorge Andrade and limped off the field with a broken bone in his foot. It was as great a psychological blow to England as it was a fillip to Portugal.

Eriksson brought on Vassell, doomed alas to miss the vital penalty, in place of Rooney but caution again became the negative watchword for the English team. Early in the second half, Eriksson took off Scholes, replacing him with the pedestrian Phil Neville. Eight minutes from time he would bring on another prosaic figure in Owen Hargreaves – destined to come to life only in the German World Cup of 2006 – in place of Gerrard. As in Japan, it was surely a moment that cried out for a gamble on Joe Cole and his ability to do the unexpected, but just as in Japan, gambling was not for Eriksson.

So it was, a mere minute after Gerrard had gone off, and with the England team perhaps still trying to readjust, when Portugal equalised through the last player you'd have expected to get on the field, let alone to score. And to get on for none other than the mighty Luis Figo, who had been trying too hard to do too much on his own. Replacing him was the young striker Helder Postiga, almost a figure of fun the previous season with Tottenham Hotspur and, back in Portugal, a surprising selection even for the squad by coach Luiz Felipe 'Big Phil' Scolari.

Yet when another sub, the clever, elusive Simao, crossed from the left, Postiga found himself criminally unmarked and headed the equaliser. A goal which had long been imminent. So the game went into extra time and on 110 minutes, the Portuguese went ahead through another far better known substitute, elegant Rui Costa, whose powerful shot flew in off the bar.

Much to their credit, England rose from the canvas. Five minutes later, John Terry nodded down a corner from Beckham, Frank Lampard spun to score. Yet should the game have gone to extra time at all? The question is still tormenting. On ninety minutes, Sol Campbell leaped to head the ball past Ricardo, the Portuguese keeper, only for the Swiss referee Urs Meier to disallow the goal for an alleged foul on the keeper by John Terry's flailing arm. 'Sitting on the bench,' said Eriksson, afterwards, 'I thought it was a goal, and looking on TV I still think it was a goal. But you can't do anything about it.'

Some referees may well have given the goal; others, like Meier, would not. It was hardly an excuse which got the unimaginative Eriksson off the hook; he had again appeared prosaic and inflexible, and in a tournament in which so many wingers sparkled, England had none – David Beckham was revealed as a one-paced, one-trick pony with a superb right foot who had to do damage from afar.

And it was Beckham who would lamentably miss the first of England's penalties when the game was still drawn after extra time. That Eriksson should have deputed him to go first after his recent failures from the spot was criticised even by the illustrious Franz Beckenbauer. This time, Beckham's shot soared abysmally over the bar. Subsequently, he blamed it on the condition of the pitch, though ten other players succeeded in scoring. Rui Costa alone missed, surprisingly, for Portugal. Owen, Lampard, Terry and Hargreaves all scored for England. So the match went to sudden death, enabling Ricardo, initially a criticised choice, to become doubly his team's hero. He pushed out Vassell's penalty, then proceeded to score the winner himself.

Penalties, penalties. Would England ever get the hang of them? A vicious tabloid campaign provoked a stream of threatening messages to the hapless Urs Meier. Talk of an anti-English conspiracy was surely an excuse for failure. 'To get over this,' declared Eriksson, 'will take more than twenty-four hours, much longer.'

Eriksson could console himself that his annual £4 million-plus job was still safe. Sacking him would be so vastly expensive that it would take a fake sheikh and his own foolish greed to bring that finally about. What might politely be described as his extracurricular activity might, in the meantime, have ended his reign in some ignominy. But since the behaviour of the FA's Chief Executive Mark Palios was even more squalid, perhaps that allowed the Swede to go on his Teflon way.

Both men behaved recklessly beyond belief. Again, as in the case of Eriksson's fling with Ulrika Jonsson, perhaps still more so, the matter of morality, however germane, seemed overshadowed by the question of sheer common sense. Both men, first Palios then Eriksson, had an affair with Faria Alam, the assistant at the Football Association to David Davies. When Palios withdrew from the relationship, Eriksson, giving new meaning to the image of a hands-on manager, stepped into the breach. And Faria Alam, when that affair ended too – with poor Nancy Dell'Olio clinging on like grim death to a knob-stick – took her tale to the *News of the World*.

It was at this point that Palios, the man who had so controversially supported Eriksson after his flirtation with Chelsea, who had given him what amounted to a massive disloyalty bonus, now treacherously set out to betray him. He persuaded Colin Gibson, the former sports editor of the *Daily Mail*, now in charge of the FA's press relations, to approach the *News of the World* and offer them Palios's co-operation if they would keep him out of the picture and confine their revelations to Eriksson. The paper refused, published the whole story, and gave chapter and verse on Gibson's rejected approach. There was plainly no way Palios·could stay in office and out he went, but why the FA should decide in such sordid circumstances to pay him a £650,000 bonus was inexplicable. Eriksson stayed. His team wilted.

The following year, Alam had the temerity to go to a tribunal, alleging that she had also been propositioned by David Davies, who denied it furiously. With similar emphasis, he gave a press conference outside FA headquarters defending Eriksson – to the best of his ability – and extolling his virtues. Alam's claim for wrongful dismissal was properly thrown out, and Davies was wholly exonerated.

Meanwhile, back on the pitch, an August 2004 friendly in Newcastle against Ukraine was won 3–0 and brightened by an exciting debut by the young Manchester City right winger, Shaun Wright-Phillips, adopted son of Ian Wright. Coming on early in the second half, he showed electric pace, the classic winger's ability to beat his full back on the outside – qualities denied to Beckham, who scored the first England goal, but moved inside. Wright-Phillips crowned his performance on seventy-two minutes with a spectacular solo goal, cutting in to score. But his chances would be only sporadic, and his eventual move at a colossal fee to Chelsea would erode his confidence and stunt his promising career as Chelsea, too, with their superfluity of stars, gave him only occasional games.

As for Beckham, he was by now, after his bitter falling out with Alex Ferguson, his original mentor, selling shirts in massive quantities for Real Madrid, his marriage supposedly tottering. The same might be said about his international form. It was increasingly clear that for all his dangerous free kicks and his long-range crosses, he was an encumbrance on the team's attack. But for Eriksson, he was untouchable; even if, the following season, it meant moving him into a position which impeded the whole working of the team. And so, illogically, it would go on; right the way into the 2006 World Cup finals despite the emergence of another fine young natural right winger in the shape of Tottenham's Aaron Lennon.

England's World Cup qualifying group seemed hardly formidable. True, there was the inevitable Poland yet again. But Austria looked a modest team and the group was made up merely by the limited local opposition of Wales and Northern Ireland, and by the weak Azerbaijan. But form would be confounded.

As soon as early September came the first qualifier in Vienna, a game which England seemed to have in their pockets but ultimately might even have lost. It was, alas, another of those awful games for the goalkeeper nicknamed, for all his manifest talents, 'Calamity' James. Asked on television what he thought of James as an England keeper, Gordon Banks, once such a distinguished incumbent, somewhat damningly replied that a prerequisite was not to make mistakes. There had been times, as we have seen, when even Gordon made them himself, to the ire of Alf Ramsey, but James' errors were . . . more calamitous.

Eriksson hardly made matters better by trying once again to use Wayne Bridge, an out-and-out left back, in left midfield, in front of Ashley Cole. It hadn't worked at home to Macedonia, it had risked throwing away that World Cup game in Sapporo against Argentina, and it looked no more logical in Vienna.

Austria, who had recently lost 5–1 at home to Denmark, looked down and out when England went 2–0 ahead, even if the first goal was a study in self-destruction. When Alex Manninger, Austria's keeper, dropped a cross by Gary Neville, his left back Martin Stranzl distractedly passed the ball back to him. Manninger, equally distracted, picked the ball up, thus conceding a free kick well inside the box. Lampard, set up by Beckham and Smith, scored from four yards.

This hardly galvanised England, but they scored again on sixty-four minutes with a fine shot by Gerrard. Five minutes earlier, the erratic James had almost given a goal away when, racing out of his goal, he was eluded on the right by Mario Haas, whose shot was squeezed off the line by the covering John Terry. Then two Austrian goals within two minutes gave them a wholly unexpected draw. First on seventy-one minutes the substitute Roland Kollmann curled a perfectly executed free kick past James. Then, as the England defence retreated before a burst by Andreas Ivanschitz, James allowed his twenty-yard shot, slightly defected off Terry, to run under his body. And so the match was drawn.

Things went better four days later against Poland in Katowice, where Paul Robinson capably replaced James in goal and Jermain Defoe of Spurs proved a lively presence up front, giving England a first-half lead with a brisk piece of opportunism. Maciej Zurawski equalised for Poland on forty-eight minutes, but England's luck was in when Arkadiusz Glowacki put through his own goal. In neither game could Rooney play, while Owen was still in the protracted and finally unsuccessful process of settling in at Real Madrid, where his arrival had been greeted with none of the ecstatic delight met by the far less gifted zeitgeist figure, David Beckham.

Eriksson won praise for his decisive dropping of both James and Alan Smith, who had both been expecting to play, in favour of two such internationally inexperienced players. Defoe spun splendidly to score his goal and was generally effervescent, but by 2006 and the World Cup finals, his form with Spurs had been erratic, though to omit him in favour of the seventeen-year-old Theo Walcott, who had never played a game for Arsenal in the Premiership, and had made just one substitute appearance for England, was the stuff of folly.

Piqued by the fusillade of criticism which had followed their poor display in Vienna, the England players left the stadium refusing to give press interviews. Shades of St Albans. For his part, Eriksson praised Defoe: 'I am impressed by him, he's very hungry, a big, big talent,' but the impression would not last. Yet once again England, having taken the lead, had gone into their familiar shell, and nearly paid for it, needing that own goal to achieve eventual victory.

Next at Old Trafford, England, with Rooney (now a Manchester United player) back in a 4–3–3 formation, easily beat a strangely passive Wales 2–0. Andy Melville, the Welsh centre back, was hurt in the warm up, necessitating a reshuffle of the team, but, not for the first time, the manager Mark Hughes was oddly reluctant to deploy the elusive Robert Earnshaw up front, till far too late in the game. Left alone, John Hartson could accomplish little; the Welsh dragons had no fire to breathe.

Worse still, England scored a somewhat fortuitous goal in only four minutes when Frank Lampard's shot flew in off the heel of a Michael Owen surely glad of a brief escape from his frustrations in Madrid. The second goal was superbly curled home by Beckham out on the left, but he ended the match with a yellow card and a broken rib, both the result of clashes with the Welsh left back, Ben Thatcher. There was, in police parlance, reason to believe that Beckham invited the yellow card, so that he would miss the match in Azerbaijan four days later rather than the more demanding match to come, but he certainly did not invite the broken rib. Eriksson, who had warned him before the game to stay calm and not incur a yellow card, with consequent suspension, was displeased, but the matter became academic after Beckham's injury. So back went Beckham to Madrid for treatment, and the continuing squalls engendered by the disclosures of his romantic life.

Without him in Baku, appalling weather made the match against Azerbaijan something of a lottery, against a team managed by the former Brazilian World Cup captain Carlos Alberto. A goal by Owen midway through the first half proved sufficient, in a hectic game which saw three England players booked.

After that tough encounter, the ease with which they accounted in March for Northern Ireland – who would take dramatic revenge in Belfast – was something of a relief, netting four goals without reply. Beckham was in every sense a marginal figure out on the right, doing little but take dead-ball kicks. Joe Cole and Wayne Rooney, however, were ebullient and it was Cole just after the break who scored the first English goal.

Four days later, in Newcastle, Azerbaijan were beaten 2–0, with second-half goals by Gerrard and Beckham. May saw a brief tour of the United States with a mixed bag of players. Two odd-goal victories, the USA being beaten, not without difficulty, 2–1 in Chicago, both goals beautifully struck from either flank by the Manchester United reserve Kieran Richardson; Colombia in New Jersey defeated 3–2 in an entertaining game distinguished by a fine hat trick from Michael Owen, who was now rapidly climbing towards the top of the England goalscorers' list. Had he only stayed fit the following season, rather than missing much of it at Newcastle United, how much better might England have done in Germany. Not to mention the deeply vexed question of whether Wayne Rooney should have been allowed to play there at all.

In the 2005–06 season, the Beckham problem became acute, Eriksson's seeming desire to use him at all costs in whatever unsuitable position distorting the tactics of the team both in Cardiff and, disastrously, in Belfast. This was presaged by a truly disgraceful 4–1 defeat in an August friendly in Copenhagen against a Danish team, which was hardly a European power. James, who had yet another of his abysmal games, was arguably at fault with three of the goals.

Early in September, England squeezed through 1–0 in Cardiff in the return match with Wales, deploying a formation which made little sense, but testified to Eriksson's determination to keep Beckham in the team come what may. Giving a genuine winger in Wright-Phillips another game on the flank, he fielded Beckham as what could only be described as a kind of quarter back, floating about in the midfield, confusing friend rather than foe. He did have a couple of impressive moments: once when, in the first half, he made a saving tackle on the overlapping right back, Richard Duffy, once in the second when his fine long pass to the right enabled Wright-Phillips to cross and Joe Cole to score with a shot which flew in off the head of the Welsh centre back, Danny Gabbidon.

But England's unaccustomed 4–5–1 formation never flowed and Rooney, forced to toil alone up front for much of the match, was plainly frustrated when Defoe came on and the Manchester United man was told to play first on one flank, then on the other; which made no tactical sense. Still, if England could win their last three games, they would be clear of Poland.

Easier said than done. They lost in the most humiliating manner in Belfast to a Northern Ireland team which, till it at last won 2–0 against Azerbaijan in their previous match, had found goalscoring the merest mirage. But they scored against England; and they won. Now not even Paul Robinson, whose superb one-handed save from John Hartson's header had protected them in Cardiff, could rescue them. Owen, missing in Cardiff, was back, but he could not help them either.

Eriksson had four days to change his misbegotten Beckham-as-play-maker policy but he did not use it. It was a match in which England who had not lost in Northern Ireland for seventy-eight years, never got off the ground, with their clumsy 4–5–1 formation. Wayne Rooney was at his most turbulent. You could, to vary an old saying, take the boy out of the backstreets, but you couldn't take the backstreets out of the boy. When the Swiss referee admonished and yellow carded him for a crude foul on Keith Gillespie, Rooney swore at him, just as he did at Beckham, when the captain urged him to calm down. In the dressing room the two nearly came to blows and had to be separated.

Yet it was surely specious of Eriksson after the game to blame his team's dismal defeat on Rooney, rather than on his own fallacious strategies. Rooney, he said, made 'a stupid challenge and he could have been sent off'. After which, said Eriksson, 'We lost our spirit totally.' This of an England team.

The winning goal came when little Steven Davis, the clever young Aston Villa strategist, sent the Leeds striker David Healy – suddenly a prolific goalscorer in internationals – racing through with a perfectly calibrated pass, to beat Robinson with his right-footed shot. Protracted delirium. Much credit went to the Northern Ireland manager Lawrie Sanchez, who had scored the goal whereby Wimbledon beat Liverpool in the 1988 FA Cup final.

So England's qualification hung in the balance. Austria and Poland – the chief rivals – would have to be beaten, at home, or it would come to the play-offs. And beaten Austria were at Old Trafford, but most ingloriously. A match in which Beckham got himself sent off, this time for two yellow cards, for the second time in his international career.

Losing recently to Poland 3–2 in Chorzow, where they had thrown caution to the wind, brought Roland Linz into attack and almost saved the game, Austria came to Manchester with no ambition, and without their manager and former star centre forward Hans Krankl who had resigned over a contractual dispute. They made scant effort to score and England's back four – where Rio Ferdinand, dropped after Belfast, returned as substitute for Campbell – seemed over-manned. Frank Lampard scored the only goal on twenty-five minutes from a penalty.

Back to Old Trafford four days later, and the make-or-break game with Poland. Deploying a 4–1–3–1–1 formation, England scraped through, though the excellent goalkeeping by Poland's Artur Boruc, destined to play for Celtic, several times frustrated them. Both sides scored in the very last minute of the first half. When Lampard's corner was deflected to Joe Cole, his shot was knocked in by Owen. Back, suddenly and alarmingly, came the Poles, Kamil Kusowski surging down the right flank to cross, for the lamentably unmarked Tomasz Frankowski to volley home.

The game was eighty minutes old when England at last achieved the winner. Joe Cole sent Owen away, and his precise cross was met by Frank Lampard with a spectacular volley which even Boruc couldn't stop. So England, by the skin of their teeth, had reached the World Cup finals again.

Far more promising was the 3–2 victory in a friendly in November played, untypically, in Zurich against Argentina, a game notable both for the crisp opportunism of a Michael Owen at his best, which won the match for England, and for a supreme performance by the Argentine playmaker, Juan Roman Riquelme. England's attempts to man-mark him out of the game with the Tottenham centre back, Ledley King, were ridiculed. King could hardly find him and indeed it was only when he had left the field with six minutes remaining that Owen scored his two decisive goals. The match however, furnished another example of Eriksson's confused selection, when he chose at left back Wayne Bridge who was far from match fit, having had only an hour's first team football. His error was central to Crespo's 34th-minute goal from which Argentina took the lead.

Early in the New Year, Eriksson was unmasked again, and this time there was no Mark Palios to save him. It seems astonishing that anyone as widely experienced as Eriksson, not to mention his agent, the former swimmer and opera singer Athol Still, and an accompanying lawyer, should have been duped by the *News of the World*'s resident impersonator, masquerading as an Arab sheikh. Lured to Dubai, they were seemingly enticed by the prospect of Eriksson, whose contract, however contentiously, had still to run to 2008, taking over as manager of Aston Villa, should Villa first be taken over. Eriksson also put the cat among the pigeons by talking of how much corruption there was over transfers in the English game.

Even the Football Association could not put up with that, and Eriksson was told that he would no longer be in charge of England's team after the World Cup finals. It would have made sense to sack him immediately; I wrote in the *Sunday Times* that I couldn't see any England team under Eriksson going further than the quarter-finals. Nor did they, despite a ludicrous outburst of media optimism before the tournament. In any event, he would have to be paid a salary now estimated at a hyperbolic £5 million a year until he found another managerial job, which unsurprisingly he would prove in no hurry to do.

Manifestly jumping the gun, the Football Association went in search of a successor to Eriksson before May was out, failed to get 'Big Phil' Scolari and contentiously settled for Steve McClaren. Appoint in haste, regret at leisure. In charge, if that be the word, of the search was the recently appointed Chief Executive of the FA, Brian Barwick, previously the head of ITV Sport, and giving ominous signs from the first of being out of his depth. His first interview, given it seemed more from a desire to be heard than from any real reason to speak, assured us that he had good relations with Eriksson, which was supposedly 'significant'. He also took the opportunity for publicly criticising Manchester United's Alan Smith for supposedly refusing an England call-up, adding, with clumsy superfluity, that he himself had never played for England. The following day Eriksson helpfully pointed out that the injured Smith had dropped out with his blessing.

So Barwick embarked on a fruitless pursuit of Scolari, the Brazilian manager of Portugal, across Europe, only for Scolari eventually to announce that he had no intention of accepting, his assertion that pressure on his family played a part in his refusal seeming somewhat unlikely. Whereupon the job was offered to Eriksson's assistant, Steve McClaren, the manager of Middlesbrough.

The fact that McClaren had been Eriksson's coach both at the last European Championship and the previous World Cup seemed a good reason for avoiding him, rather than appointing him. Early in the year, according to the Middlesbrough captain and future manager, Gareth Southgate, McClaren had seemed so depressed that senior players had to take over the running of the team for a while. And though Boro had reached the final of the UEFA Cup, they were tactically naïve and were annihilated 4–0 by Seville.

Common sense suggested the FA should wait till after the tournament when, indeed, so many countries involved would change their coaches. As it was, McClaren arrived as a club manager of no special distinction, while any potential plea of 'Not me, Guv!' after the latest of Eriksson's and England's disappointments would hardly convince.

You could certainly say, however, that Eriksson had no luck at all when it came to the fitness of his star turn. Owen was back and playing again, but he had been fit enough to play only ten full League games for Newcastle United, scoring seven goals. Now he was notionally fit again, but inevitably the sharpness had gone from his game. As for Rooney he, like David Beckham four years earlier, had fallen foul of what might be called the curse of the metatarsal. It was no surprise that his manager at Manchester United did not want him to play at all, nor that Eriksson was keen to use him at all costs. With medical opinion oscillating as the days passed, an uneasy compromise was reached between Alex Ferguson and Eriksson, but in the event Eriksson did not adhere to that. Worse still, he even condemned the far from match-fit Rooney to toil alone in attack.

Big Phil Penalises Sven: World Cup, Germany 2006
England, initially without Rooney, made a truly wretched start to the group qualifiers, labouring to beat first Paraguay and then the

remarkable Trinidad and Tobago team, whose band of largely obscure players, reinforced by an astonishing veteran keeper in Shaka Hislop who wasn't expected to play at all and the ex-Aston Villa striker Dwight Yorke, bewildered the Swedes in their first game.

Opening against Paraguay in Frankfurt, England had the encouragement of a third-minute goal when Paraguay's experienced centre back and skipper, Carlos Gamarra, headed Beckham's free kick – England's solitary reliable weapon – into his own goal. Eriksson blamed the intense heat for his team's subsequent deficiencies. Far from going on to sweep Paraguay aside, even when they had to replace their injured keeper, England, with a dreary proliferation of long balls towards the towering Peter Crouch, who ended absurdly as a one-man strike force, were lucky not to concede an equaliser when Paul Robinson, all too typically, pawed at a cross but Carlos Paredes shot too high.

An evidently worried Eriksson now, controversially if not irresponsibly, picked Wayne Rooney for the next game, in Nuremberg, against Trinidad. It had been assumed, not least by Alex Ferguson, that if Rooney were to play at all, it would not be before the second stage of the competition when his metatarsal injury – which Owen too had suffered – might have sufficiently healed.

Long balls to Crouch were again a depressing feature of England's play. He missed an easy chance and when he did head a late goal it should arguably have been annulled since he'd helped himself upwards by grasping Brent Sancho's dreadlocks. Gerrard, effective but obliged to play too deep, scored a still later second, a strong shot with his lesser left foot. Rooney, on for the last half hour, looked understandably short of fitness. But things had improved when the dynamic Spurs right winger Aaron Lennon arrived, Beckham dropping diplomatically to right back, whence it was his cross which gave Crouch his goal.

Sweden in Cologne were the third opponents. The game started badly when poor Michael Owen, after just four minutes, took a heavy fall and caused such damage to his knee that he would be out not only of the World Cup but from football itself for the forseeable future. He was replaced by Crouch, which again meant dependence on the long ball. With Rooney showing sporadic flashes of his terrific talents, Joe Cole put England ahead with a superbly executed goal, chesting a clearance from a corner, to volley a superb topspun right-foot shot which curled and dipped past the goalkeeper, Andreas Isaksson.

Laborious in open play, Sweden were all too dangerous as the game went on from any kind of corner, free kick or throw in especially from the left– the kind of balls which English defences from time immemorial were expected to deal with all day long. Not now. Robinson, in goal, looked as vulnerable as the usually solid John Terry, Sol Campbell and Ashley Cole. You could hardly blame Eriksson for that.

It was, embarrassingly, a Swedish bombardment. A corner from the left by Tobias Linderoth was met not by an English head but that of the striker Marcus Allback, eluding both Robinson, no dominator of his area, and on the far post, Ashley Cole. The aerial assault continued, Sweden twice striking the bar, from Henrik Larsson's header and a shot by the centre back, Olof Mellberg.

Rooney came off after sixty-nine largely frustrated minutes, Gerrard made a belated appearance, and it was his shot five minutes from time which somewhat flatteringly restored England's lead. They could not keep it, nor did they deserve to. The game was in its final minute when another long throw from the left was culpably allowed to bounce in the box, and Larsson made just sufficient contact to score. So Sweden remained unbeaten by England since 1968.

Still, one way or another, England had limped into the second, knock-out, round. Meanwhile no one was enjoying himself, or herself, more than the raucous so-called Wags, the wives and girlfriends of the England players, unwisely allowed to stay in a hotel not far from the team's headquarters. Eliciting Groucho Marx's old adage, 'better nouveau than never', they spent their days shopping, their evenings and nights in noisy conviviality, though it was reported that Relatively Posh Spice kept her distance.

The second round saw another meagre England victory, this time 1–0 against Ecuador. Lennon, who had not even been used in the previous match, this time would get a measly last three minutes, substituting Beckham who had been in no physical condition to play, having been taken ill before the game. But yet another of his deceptive free kicks won it against an Ecuador team which had begun the tournament brightly, but fallen apart in their final group game against Germany. Eriksson's fear of the counterattack led to his using the defensive Michael Carrick in midfield in another of his 4–1–4–1 formations, while though Rooney was once again obliged to play alone up front, he not only lasted the full ninety minutes but was at his electrifying best in the latter stages. Indeed, when he skilfully got to the left byline and pulled the ball back to Lampard, the Chelsea man, in dismal form throughout the tournament, should surely have scored rather than hoof the ball high.

Beckham's decisive goal came on the hour, the ball so skilfully placed as to fall tantalisingly just inside the left-hand post. Even the Ecuador coach, Suarez, called it, 'Perfect . . . a great free kick.' But by and large England's wheels had failed yet again to turn; indeed, only a glorious last-ditch interception by Ashley Cole prevented a disastrous early goal. John Terry ineptly headed the ball backwards, sending Carlos Tenorio clean through, but just as he shot, Cole, who had heroically made up the ground, stretched out a foot to deflect the ball against the top of the bar and out.

And so, as one had rather surmised, England one way or another had reached the quarter-final which was fated to be their regular nemesis under Sven-Goran Eriksson. The opponents, just as in the last European Championship, would be Portugal, under 'Big Phil' Scolari, and it would go to penalties again. In Gelsenkirchen, England, now deploying a 4–5–1 formation, were as pedestrian, Lampard as ineffectual, as ever. The revelation was the previously much-disparaged Owen Hargreaves, butt of the England fans, who gave a sterling and commanding performance in midfield.

Perhaps it was all too forseeable that Wayne Rooney, so manifestly exploited, should ultimately explode. This he did around the hour, stamping on the groin of the Portuguese centre back Ricardo Carvalho, who'd fouled him. It hardly needed the antics of Rooney's Manchester United team mate, Cristiano Ronaldo, to have him sent off. There was no moral justification for Rooney's violence, yet in context his frustration was all too understandable. There was every reason to believe that he had been sacrificed by Eriksson in a desperate attempt to save his own strategic skin.

Beckham, laborious and outpaced, went off, replaced by Lennon early in the second half. Twice, with typical bursts of pace, skill and courage, the Spurs youngster made palpable chances to score, once again leaving one to wonder what he might have accomplished had Eriksson not continued his Beckham fixation, however hard he might insist that it was no kind of a 'marriage'. Gift horses, and all that. Owen himself would later decry Eriksson's policies, yet in the none too distant past he had been a supporter. Easy and understandable enough to be wise after the event, but by and large international footballers support the managers who pick them.

Goalless at full time, the match remained tense and disjointed through the extra period, both sides seemingly and inexorably settling for penalties. With their dismal record it was a mystery that England saw their salvation in the Russian roulette of the shoot-out. This time, having apparently practised for this in training, they contrived to miss three of their four spot kicks. The era of Eriksson and Beckham was over.

11 AND AFTER

Steve McClaren 2006–present
Key Game: Croatia v England, October 2006

SO NOW, UNPROMISINGLY, IT WOULD COME TO STEVE McCLAREN, and the early results were no better than one could logically expect them to be. From the first it seemed a clear case of Buggins' turn. 'Scribble, scribble, Mr Gibbon,' said a scornful Royal to the author of *The Decline and Fall of the Roman Empire*, and scribble, scribble went McClaren on the touchline as he made his infinity of notes on the game he was watching. In this case, alas, no masterpieces would emerge.

A veritable entourage surrounded him. No Alf Ramsey, he, determined to go it alone without even a coach to assist him. McClaren's right hand would be Terry Venables, something of a blast from the past, his own tactics as England manager, as we have seen, often subject to criticism; in recent years the saviour of McClaren's former club Middlesbrough when called in to coach; sometime manager of Australia; brusquely ejected from his office at Leeds. And then, bizarrely, there was the egregious Max Clifford, expert in enabling the Faria Alams of this world to grow rich on the proceeds of their own or others' indiscretions. Clifford, it appeared, had helped McClaren avoid bad publicity when, separated at the time from his wife, he had had – surprise, surprise – an affair with his secretary. But Clifford, after eulogising McClaren and his supposed qualities, did not stay around for long.

It was surely the ultimate humiliation, one wrote at the time, when even Max Clifford left the sinking ship. But at least McClaren had had the courage to drop the previously untouchable David Beckham, even if his penchant was for using his former protégé at Middlesbrough, Stewart Downing, a winger seriously short of pace and ball skills.

McClaren's England had a deceptively positive beginning. First an unadventurous Greek team showed little resistance in a friendly. Then Andorra, who surely had scant right to be in the European Championship at all, were casually annihilated in the first qualifier for 2008. But then it came to Macedonia, ever the bogey team since that dreadful day at Southampton and David Seaman's blunder. England managed a 1–0 win in Skopje, Peter Crouch scoring with a half-bicycle kick. But John Terry had to be at his most defiant and dominating to keep the Macedonians out, though he was lucky not to concede a penalty for handling, and Ashley Cole once had to clear off the line.

To keep Downing on for the whole game and bring on Lennon only after seventy-six minutes was baffling. But the narrowness of the victory was symbolised by the fact that even Crouch's shot was pushed by the keeper Nikolovski on to the underside of the bar and only just crossed the line. Macedonia then came to England and drew, just as they had done in Southampton; except that this time, neither side could score.

If this seemed the nadir for McClaren's England, much worse was to follow. In Zagreb, where his 3–5–2 formation looked completely misconceived, England would lose 2–0. The whole disastrous evening was surely summed up when Paul Robinson, attempting to kick a back pass clear, missed the ball totally as it hit a divot, and ran on past him, into his goal.

Not only to dispense with wingers, but to assume that his right back, Phil Neville, now and then an overlapper with Manchester United, could at this level do not only his defensive job but what a winger should, was to plumb the very depths of illogicality. It was rumoured that Venables had favoured such a formation but with different personnel. You began to understand why a psychologist played a seemingly crucial role in McClaren's entourage, just as he had – seemingly with mixed success – at Middlesbrough. 'I take the blame,' he said.

There was a glimmer of light when, in November, England went to Amsterdam and drew 1–1 in a friendly with a technically superior Holland. McClaren certainly deserved applause for his bold and successful decision to give a debut at right back to the big precocious Manchester City defender, Micah Richards, who rewarded him with a buoyant performance. But using the speedy Everton striker, Andy Johnson, on the right flank seemed perverse. Nor, in fact, had Johnson been in recent form for Everton.

Still, Wayne Rooney, cleverly served by Joe Cole from the right, snapped up his goal well, even if the Dutch manager, Marco Van Basten, once the hammer of the England defence, was surprised the English should concede the late equaliser from a throw in. Arjen Robben took it from the right, Jan Vennegoor of Hesselink preceded Rio Ferdinand to flick the ball on, Robinson did not intervene, Rafael Van der Vaart scored. McClaren professed his undimmed optimism.

After another wretched performance in a friendly against Spain, England now faced a European qualifier in Israel against a team, in Tel Aviv, who ordinarily would seem to pose no great problem. But Israel of late had dramatically improved, McClaren's England were in turmoil, and there could be no certainty of success. From being something of a formality – the away games against the more formidable Russia and Croatia still lay ahead – the match had now become crucial to the success of the McClaren regime. Emitting gung-ho platitudes, McClaren ignored the fact that if England were in a state of potential crisis, then he himself was largely to blame.

Manifestly out of his depth, the very embodiment of the Peter Principle, whereby people are constantly promoted one step above their capacities, McClaren notably failed to confront the dualism between Frank Lampard – who had a wretched World Cup but improved as the new season went on – and Steven Gerrard, his obvious superior, in central midfield.

He picked another cack-handed team, with not a left footer in sight, fatuously ignoring one such in Gareth Barry, in splendid form for the 'unfashionable' Aston Villa; though Ashley Cole was suspended, the manager preferred the right-footed centre back, Jamie Carragher. Meanwhile the right-footed Aaron Lennon, who in fact had a vibrant first half, was used on the left flank, ensuring that most of his crosses curled in towards the defence. This compromise was largely determined by the fact that again McClaren stuck Gerrard on the right flank rather than dynamically in the centre, where Lampard had another poor game. The system paradoxically ensures that you get the best out of neither player.

Result: failure to score again in a drab goalless draw, though McClaren could scarcely be blamed for the dismal form of his supposedly best player, Wayne Rooney, who looked temperamentally unable to cope with the role assigned to him in McClaren's myopic game plan.

Panglossian as ever, McClaren told us how well England had played in Tel Aviv. Against minuscule, spiteful Andorra in Barcelona, what seemed to be a diplomatic injury to Lampard's wrist at least enabled him to deploy Gerrard successfully in central midfield, whence he scored two of England's three goals. But the first-half display, jeered by the contemptuous England fans, was abysmal, and McClaren himself, abused throughout, flounced out of the press conference in less than a couple of minutes. On the day of the match, it transpired that the selection committee had wanted to give him only a two-year contract, but that the birdbrains of the FA board had voted for four.

If McClaren were the *reductio ad absurdum* of England managers, a worse choice even than Graham Taylor, Alf Ramsey was the finest by a nautical mile. Yet even his once-triumphant career ended in cruel anticlimax, as did his own life. In retrospect, it seems astounding that Walter Winterbottom, his predecessor, should have survived for sixteen years, despite the two humiliations by Hungary. Defeat by the USA in the 1950 World Cup could be regarded as a freak.

But Winterbottom, who might, as we have seen, have been replaced by Jesse Carver, owed his longevity to the formidable patronage of Stanley Rous, and his complete dominance of the Football Association.

Among other incumbents, Bobby Robson so nearly got his England team to the 1990 World Cup final, but emphatically rode his luck.

Don Revie was a greedy disaster, Ron Greenwood called to the colours well after he had reached his meridian. Glenn Hoddle talked himself out of the role. Terry Venables juggled his job with his prolix business life, but at least attained a European semi-final.

Have England reached the nadir with McClaren? Or would it not be fairer to demand who was responsible for putting him there? The buck surely stops with Barwick.

A black, bleak immediate future seems to loom.

ENGLAND TEAM RESULTS 1946–2007

The following pages include details of every official match played under the managers since Walter Winterbottom took up the post in 1946. The number of caps attained by each player follows his name in brackets, the captain is in bold type and any player who was sent off is in italics. A player's name in brackets denotes he substituted the preceding player. Dates, venue, result and goalscorers are also featured, and attendance figures are compiled from official and unofficial sources.

1946

MANAGER: WALTER WINTERBOTTOM

Home International Championship

DATE	VENUE	OPPONENTS	SCORE	GOALSCORERS	ATTENDANCE	TEAM
Sep 28	Windsor Park, Belfast	N. IRELAND	W 7-2	Carter H, Mannion 3, Finney, Lawton, Langton	57,111	Swift (1), Scott (1), **Hardwick** (1), Wright W (1), Franklin (1), Cockburn (1), Finney (1), Carter H (7), Lawton (9), Mannion (1), Langton (1)

Friendly

DATE	VENUE	OPPONENTS	SCORE	GOALSCORERS	ATTENDANCE	TEAM
Sep 30	Dalymount Park, Dublin	R. of IRELAND	W 1-0	Finney	32,000	Swift (2), Scott (2), **Hardwick** (2), Wright W (2), Franklin (2), Cockburn (2), Finney (2), Carter H (8), Lawton (10), Mannion (2), Langton (2)

Home International Championship

DATE	VENUE	OPPONENTS	SCORE	GOALSCORERS	ATTENDANCE	TEAM
Nov 13	Maine Road, Manchester	WALES	W 3-0	Mannion 2, Lawton	59,121	Swift (3), Scott (3), **Hardwick** (3), Wright W (3), Franklin (3), Cockburn (3), Finney (3), Carter H (9), Lawton (11), Mannion (3), Langton (3)

Friendly

DATE	VENUE	OPPONENTS	SCORE	GOALSCORERS	ATTENDANCE	TEAM
Nov 27	Leeds Road, Huddersfield	HOLLAND	W 8-2	Lawton 4, Carter H 2, Mannion, Finney	32,435	Swift (4), Scott (4), **Hardwick** (4), Wright W (4), Franklin (4), Johnston (1), Finney (4), Carter H (10), Lawton (12), Mannion (4), Langton (4)

1947

Home International Championship

DATE	VENUE	OPPONENTS	SCORE	GOALSCORERS	ATTENDANCE	TEAM
Apr 12	Wembley, London	SCOTLAND	D 1-1	Carter H	98,200	Swift (5), Scott (5), **Hardwick** (5), Wright W (5), Franklin (5), Johnston (2), Matthews (18), Carter H (11), Lawton (13), Mannion (5), Mullen (1)

Friendlies

DATE	VENUE	OPPONENTS	SCORE	GOALSCORERS	ATTENDANCE	TEAM
May 3	Highbury, London	FRANCE	W 3-0	Finney, Mannion, Carter H	54,389	Swift (6), Scott (6), **Hardwick** (6), Wright W (6), Franklin (6), Lowe (1), Finney (5), Carter H (12), Lawton (14), Mannion (6), Langton (5)
May 18	Zurich	SWITZERLAND	L 0-1		34,000	Swift (7), Scott (7), **Hardwick** (7), Wright W (7), Franklin (7), Lowe (2), Matthews (19), Carter H (13), Lawton (15), Mannion (7), Langton (6)
May 25	Lisbon	PORTUGAL	W 10-0	Lawton 4, Mortensen 4, Finney, Matthews	65,000	Swift (8), Scott (8), **Hardwick** (8), Wright W (8), Franklin (8), Lowe (3), Matthews (20), Mortensen (1), Lawton (16), Mannion (8), Finney (6)
Sep 21	Brussels	BELGIUM	W 5-2	Lawton 2, Mortensen Finney 2	54,326	Swift (9), Scott (9), **Hardwick** (9), Ward (1), Franklin (9), Wright W (9), Matthews (21), Mortensen (2), Lawton (17), Mannion (9), Finney (7)

Home International Championship

DATE	VENUE	OPPONENTS	SCORE	GOALSCORERS	ATTENDANCE	TEAM
Oct 18	Ninian Park, Cardiff	WALES	W 3-0	Finney, Mortensen, Lawton	55,000	Swift (10), Scott (10), **Hardwick** (10), Taylor P (1), Franklin (10), Wright W (10), Matthews (22), Mortensen (3), Lawton (18), Mannion (10), Finney (8)
Nov 5	Goodison Park, Liverpool	N. IRELAND	D 2-2	Mannion, Lawton	67,980	Swift (11), Scott (11), **Hardwick** (11), Taylor P (2), Franklin (11), Wright W (11), Matthews (23), Mortensen (4), Lawton (19), Mannion (11), Finney (9)

Friendly

DATE	VENUE	OPPONENTS	SCORE	GOALSCORERS	ATTENDANCE	TEAM
Nov 19	Highbury, London	SWEDEN	W 4-2	Mortensen 3, Lawton (pen)	44,282	Swift (12), Scott (12), **Hardwick** (12), Taylor P (3), Franklin (12), Wright W (12), Finney (10), Mortensen (5), Lawton (20), Mannion (12), Langton (7)

1948

Home International Championship

DATE	VENUE	OPPONENTS	SCORE	GOALSCORERS	ATTENDANCE	TEAM
Apr 10	Hampden Park, Glasgow	SCOTLAND	W 2-0	Finney, Mortensen	135,376	Swift (13), Scott (13), **Hardwick** (13), Wright W (13), Franklin (13), Cockburn (4), Matthews (24), Mortensen (6), Lawton (21), Pearson (1), Finney (11)

Friendlies

DATE	VENUE	OPPONENTS	SCORE	GOALSCORERS	ATTENDANCE	TEAM
May 16	Turin	ITALY	W 4-0	Mortensen, Lawton, Finney 2	58,000	**Swift** (14), Scott (14), Howe (1), Wright W (14), Franklin (14), Cockburn (5), Matthews (25), Mortensen (7), Lawton (22), Mannion (13), Finney (12)
Sep 26	Copenhagen	DENMARK	D 0-0		41,000	**Swift** (15), Scott (15), Aston (1), Wright W (15), Franklin (15), Cockburn (6), Matthews (26), Hagan (1), Lawton (23), Shackleton (1), Langton (8)

Home International Championship

DATE	VENUE	OPPONENTS	SCORE	GOALSCORERS	ATTENDANCE	TEAM
Oct 9	Windsor Park, Belfast	N. IRELAND	W 6-2	Matthews, Mortensen 3, Milburn, Pearson	53,629	Swift (16), Scott (16), Howe (2), **Wright W** (16), Franklin (16), Cockburn (7), Matthews (27), Mortensen (8), Milburn (1), Pearson (2), Finney (13)
Nov 10	Villa Park, Birmingham	WALES	W 1-0	Finney	67,770	Swift (17), Scott (17), Aston (2), Ward (2), Franklin (17), **Wright W** (17), Matthews (28), Mortensen (9), Milburn (2), Shackleton (2), Finney (14)

Friendly

DATE	VENUE	OPPONENTS	SCORE	GOALSCORERS	ATTENDANCE	TEAM
Dec 2	Highbury, London	SWITZERLAND	W 6-0	Haines 2, Hancocks 2, Rowley, Milburn	48,000	Ditchburn (1), Ramsey (1), Aston (3), **Wright W** (18), Franklin (18), Cockburn (8), Matthews (29), Rowley (1), Milburn (3), Haines (1), Hancocks (1)

1949

Home International Championship

DATE	VENUE	OPPONENTS	SCORE	GOALSCORERS	ATTENDANCE	TEAM
Apr 9	Wembley, London	SCOTLAND	L 1-3	Milburn	98,188	Swift (18), Aston (4), Howe (3), **Wright W** (19), Franklin (19), Cockburn (9), Matthews (30), Mortensen (10), Milburn (4), Pearson (3), Finney (15)

Friendlies

DATE	VENUE	OPPONENTS	SCORE	GOALSCORERS	ATTENDANCE	TEAM
May 13	Stockholm	SWEDEN	L 1-3	Finney	37,500	Ditchburn (2), Shimwell (1), Aston (5), **Wright W** (20), Franklin (20), Cockburn (10), Finney (16), Mortensen (11), Bentley (1), Rowley J (2), Langton (9)
May 18	Oslo	NORWAY	W 4-1	Mullen, Finney, Morris, own goal	36,000	Swift (19), Ellerington (1), Aston (6), **Wright W** (21), Franklin (21), Dickinson (1), Finney (17), Morris (1), Mortensen (12), Mannion (14), Mullen (2)7
May 22	Paris	FRANCE	W 3-1	Morris 2, Wright W	61,308	Williams (1), Ellerington (2), Aston (7), **Wright W** (22), Franklin (22), Dickinson (2), Finney (18), Morris (2), Rowley J (3), Mannion (15), Mullen (3)
Sep 21	Goodison Park, Liverpool	R. of IRELAND	L 0-2		51,487	Williams (2), Mozley (1), Aston (8), **Wright W** (23), Franklin (23), Dickinson (3), Harris P (1), Morris (3), Pye (1), Mannion (16), Finney (19)

Home International Championship/World Cup Qualifiers

DATE	VENUE	OPPONENTS	SCORE	GOALSCORERS	ATTENDANCE	TEAM
Oct 15	Ninian Park, Cardiff	WALES	W 4-1	Mortensen, Milburn 3	61,079	Williams (3), Mozley (2), Aston (9), **Wright W** (24), Franklin (24), Dickinson (4), Finney (20), Mortensen (13), Milburn (5), Shackleton (3), Hancocks (2)
Nov 16	Maine Road, Manchester	N. IRELAND	W 9-2	Rowley J 4, Froggatt J, Pearson 2, Mortensen 2	69,762	Streten (1), Mozley (3), Aston (10), Watson (1), Franklin (25), **Wright W** (25), Finney (21), Mortensen (14), Rowley J (4), Pearson (4), Froggatt J (1)

Friendly

DATE	VENUE	OPPONENTS	SCORE	GOALSCORERS	ATTENDANCE	TEAM
Nov 30	White Hart Lane, London	ITALY	W 2-0	Rowley J, Wright W	71,797	Williams (4), Ramsey (2), Aston (11), Watson (2), Franklin (26), **Wright W** (26), Finney (22), Mortensen (15), Rowley (5), Pearson (5), Froggatt J (2)

1950

Home International Championship/World Cup Qualifiers

DATE	VENUE	OPPONENTS	SCORE	GOALSCORERS	ATTENDANCE	TEAM
Apr 15	Hampden Park, Glasgow	SCOTLAND	W 1-0	Bentley	133,300	Williams (5), Ramsey (3), Aston (12), **Wright W** (27), Franklin (27), Dickinson (5), Finney (23), Mannion (17), Mortensen (16), Bentley (2), Langton (10)

Friendlies

DATE	VENUE	OPPONENTS	SCORE	GOALSCORERS	ATTENDANCE	TEAM
May 14	Lisbon	PORTUGAL	W 5-3	Finney 4 (2 pens), Mortensen	65,000	Williams (6), Ramsey (4), Aston (13), **Wright W** (28), Jones WH (1), Dickinson (6), Milburn (6), Mortensen (17), Bentley (3), Mannion (18), Finney (24)
May 18	Brussels	BELGIUM	W 4-1	Mullen, Mortensen, Mannion, Bentley	55,854	Williams (7), Ramsey (5), Aston (14), **Wright W** (29), Jones WH (2), Dickinson (7), Milburn (7), (Mullen) (4), Mortensen (18), Bentley (4), Mannion (19), Finney (25)

THE WORLD CUP FINALS 1950 (BRAZIL)

Group Stage – Pool 2

DATE	VENUE	OPPONENTS	SCORE	GOALSCORERS	ATTENDANCE	TEAM
Jun 25	Rio	CHILE	W 2-0	Mortensen, Mannion	29,703	Williams (8), Ramsey (6), Aston (15), **Wright W** (30), Hughes L (1), Dickinson (8), Finney (26), Mannion (20), Bentley (5), Mortensen (19), Mullen (5)
Jun 29	Belo Horizonte	USA	L 0-1		10,151	Williams (9), Ramsey (7), Aston (16), **Wright W** (31), Hughes L (2), Dickinson (9), Finney (27), Mannion (21), Bentley (6), Mortensen (20), Mullen (6)
July 2	Rio	SPAIN	L 0-1		74,462	Williams (10), Ramsey (8), Eckersley (1), **Wright W** (32), Hughes L (3), Dickinson (10), Matthews (31), Mortensen (21), Milburn (8), Baily E (1), Finney (28)

POOL 2	P	W	D	L	F	A	Pts
SPAIN	3	3	0	0	6	1	6
ENGLAND	3	1	0	2	2	2	2
CHILE	3	1	0	2	5	6	2
USA	3	1	0	2	4	8	2

1950 (continued)

Home International Championship

DATE	VENUE	OPPONENTS	SCORE	GOALSCORERS	ATTENDANCE	TEAM
Oct 7	Windsor Park, Belfast	N. IRELAND	W 4-1	Baily E 2, Lee J, Wright W	50,000	Williams (11), Ramsey (9), Aston (17), **Wright W** (33), Chilton (1), Dickinson (11), Matthews (32), Mannion (22),
Nov 15	Roker Park, Sunderland	WALES	W 4-2	Baily E 2, Mannion, Milburn	59,137	Williams (12), **Ramsey** (10), Smith L (1), Watson (3), Compton L (1), Dickinson (12), Finney (29), Mannion (23), Milburn (9), Baily E (3), Medley (1)

Friendly

DATE	VENUE	OPPONENTS	SCORE	GOALSCORERS	ATTENDANCE	TEAM
Nov 22	Highbury, London	YUGOSLAVIA	D 2-2	Lofthouse 2	61,454	Williams (13), **Ramsey** (11), Eckersley (2), Watson (4), Compton L (2), Dickinson (13), Hancocks (3), Mannion (24), Lofthouse (1), Baily E (4), Medley (2)

1951

Home International Championship

DATE	VENUE	OPPONENTS	SCORE	GOALSCORERS	ATTENDANCE	TEAM
Apr 14	Wembley, London	SCOTLAND	L 2-3	Hassall, Finney	98,000	Williams (14), Ramsey (12), Eckersley (3), Johnston (3), Froggatt J (3), **Wright W** (34), Matthews (33), Mannion (25), Mortensen (22), Hassall (1), Finney (30)

Friendlies

DATE	VENUE	OPPONENTS	SCORE	GOALSCORERS	ATTENDANCE	TEAM
May 9	Wembley, London	ARGENTINA	W 2-1	Mortensen, Milburn	60,000	Williams (15), Ramsey (13), Eckersley (4), **Wright W** (35), Taylor J (1), Cockburn (11), Finney (31), Mortensen (23), Milburn (10), Hassall (2), Metcalfe (1)
May 19	Goodison Park, Liverpool	PORTUGAL	W 5-2	Nicholson, Milburn 2, Finney, Hassall	52,686	Williams (16), **Ramsey** (14), Eckersley (5), Nicholson (1), Taylor J (2), Cockburn (12), Finney (32), Pearson (6), Milburn (11), Hassall (3), Metcalfe (2)
Oct 3	Highbury, London	FRANCE	D 2-2	Medley, own goal	57,603	Williams (17), Ramsey (15), Willis (1), **Wright W** (36), Chilton (2), Cockburn (13), Finney (33), Mannion (26), Milburn (12), Hassall (4), Medley (3)

Home International Championship

DATE	VENUE	OPPONENTS	SCORE	GOALSCORERS	ATTENDANCE	TEAM
Oct 20	Ninian Park, Cardiff	WALES	D 1-1	Baily E	60,000	Williams (18), Ramsey (16), Smith L (2), **Wright W** (37), Barrass (1), Dickinson (14), Finney (34), Thompson T (1), Lofthouse (2), Baily E (5), Medley (4)
Nov 14	Villa Park, Birmingham	N. IRELAND	W 2-0	Lofthouse 2	57,889	Merrick (1), Ramsey (17), Smith L (3), **Wright W** (38), Barrass (2), Dickinson (15), Finney (35), Sewell (1), Lofthouse (3), Phillips (1), Medley (5)

Friendly

DATE	VENUE	OPPONENTS	SCORE	GOALSCORERS	ATTENDANCE	TEAM
Nov 28	Wembley, London	AUSTRIA	D 2-2	Ramsey (pen), Lofthouse	100,000	Merrick (2), Ramsey (18), Eckersley (6), **Wright W** (39), Froggatt J (4), Dickinson (16), Milton (1), Broadis (1), Lofthouse (4), Baily E (6), Medley (6)

1952

Home International Championship

DATE	VENUE	OPPONENTS	SCORE	GOALSCORERS	ATTENDANCE	TEAM
Apr 5	Hampden Park, Glasgow	SCOTLAND	W 2-1	Pearson 2	133,991	Merrick (3), Ramsey (19), Garrett (1), **Wright W** (40), Froggatt J (5), Dickinson (17), Finney (36), Broadis (2), Lofthouse (5), Pearson (7), Rowley J (6)

Friendlies

DATE	VENUE	OPPONENTS	SCORE	GOALSCORERS	ATTENDANCE	TEAM
May 18	Florence	ITALY	D 1-1	Broadis	93,000	Merrick (4), Ramsey (20), Garrett (2), **Wright W** (41), Froggatt J (6), Dickinson (18), Finney (37), Broadis (3), Lofthouse (6), Pearson (8), Elliott (1)
May 25	Vienna	AUSTRIA	W 3-2	Lofthouse 2, Sewell	65,000	Merrick (5), Ramsey (21), Eckersley (7), **Wright W** (42), Froggatt J (7), Dickinson (19), Finney (38), Sewell (2), Lofthouse (7), Baily E (7), Elliott (2)
May 28	Zurich	SWITZERLAND	W 3-0	Sewell, Lofthouse 2	33,000	Merrick (6), Ramsey (22), Eckersley (8), **Wright W** (43), Froggatt J (8), Dickinson (20), Allen R (1), Sewell (3), Lofthouse (8), Baily E (8), Finney (39)

Home International Championship

DATE	VENUE	OPPONENTS	SCORE	GOALSCORERS	ATTENDANCE	TEAM
Oct 4	Windsor Park, Belfast	N. IRELAND	D 2-2	Lofthouse, Elliott	58,000	Merrick (7), Ramsey (23), Eckersley (9), **Wright W** (44), Froggatt J (9), Dickinson (21), Finney (40), Sewell (4), Lofthouse (9), Baily E (9), Elliott (3)
Nov 12	Wembley, London	WALES	W 5-2	Finney, Lofthouse 2, Froggatt J, Bentley	94,094	Merrick (8), Ramsey (24), Smith L (4), **Wright W** (45), Froggatt J (10), Dickinson (22), Finney (41), Froggatt R (1), Lofthouse (10), Bentley (7), Elliott (4)

Friendly

DATE	VENUE	OPPONENTS	SCORE	GOALSCORERS	ATTENDANCE	TEAM
Nov 26	Wembley, London	BELGIUM	W 5-0	Elliott 2, Lofthouse 2, Froggatt R	68,333	Merrick (9), Ramsey (25), Smith L (5), **Wright W** (46), Froggatt J (11), Dickinson (23), Finney (42), Bentley (8), Lofthouse (11), Froggatt R (2), Elliott (5)

1953

Home International Championship

DATE	VENUE	OPPONENTS	SCORE	GOALSCORERS	ATTENDANCE	TEAM
Apr 18	Wembley, London	SCOTLAND	D 2-2	Broadis 2	97,000	Merrick (10), Ramsey (26), Smith L (6), **Wright W** (47), Barrass (3), Dickinson (24), Finney (43), Broadis (4), Lofthouse (12), Froggatt R (3), Froggatt J (12)

Friendlies

DATE	VENUE	OPPONENTS	SCORE	GOALSCORERS	ATTENDANCE	TEAM
May 17	Buenos Aires	ARGENTINA	D 0-0	(abandoned after 23 mins; waterlogged pitch)	80,000	Merrick (11), Ramsey (27), Eckersley (10), **Wright W** (48), Johnston (4), Dickinson (25), Finney (44), Broadis (5), Lofthouse (13), Taylor T (1), Berry (1)
May 24	Santiago	CHILE	W 2-1	Taylor T, Lofthouse	56,398	Merrick (12), Ramsey (28), Eckersley (11), **Wright W** (49), Johnston (5), Dickinson (26), Finney (45), Broadis (6), Lofthouse (14), Taylor T (2), Berry (2)
May 31	Montevideo	URUGUAY	L 1-2	Taylor T	66,072	Merrick (13), Ramsey (29), Eckersley (12), **Wright W** (50), Johnston (6), Dickinson (27), Finney (46), Broadis (7), Lofthouse (15), Taylor T (3), Berry (3)
Jun 8	New York	USA	W 6-3	Broadis, Finney 2, Lofthouse 2, Froggatt R	7,271	Ditchburn (3), Ramsey (30), Eckersley (13), **Wright W** (51), Johnston (7), Dickinson (28), Finney (47), Broadis (8), Lofthouse (16), Froggatt R (4), Froggatt J (13)

Home International Championship/World Cup Qualifier

DATE	VENUE	OPPONENTS	SCORE	GOALSCORERS	ATTENDANCE	TEAM
Oct 10	Ninian Park, Cardiff	WALES	W 4-1	Wilshaw 2, Lofthouse 2	61,000	Merrick (14), Garrett (3), Eckersley (14), **Wright W** (52), Johnston (8), Dickinson (29), Finney (48), Quixall (1), Lofthouse (17), Wilshaw (1), Mullen (7)

Friendly

DATE	VENUE	OPPONENTS	SCORE	GOALSCORERS	ATTENDANCE	TEAM
Oct 21	Wembley, London	REST OF EUROPE	D 4-4	Mullen 2, Mortensen, Ramsey (pen)	96,000	Merrick (15), Ramsey (31), Eckersley (15), **Wright W** (53), Ufton (1), Dickinson (30), Matthews (34), Mortensen (24), Lofthouse (18), Quixall (2), Mullen (8)

Home International Championship/World Cup Qualifier

DATE	VENUE	OPPONENTS	SCORE	GOALSCORERS	ATTENDANCE	TEAM
Nov 11	Goodison Park, Liverpool	N. IRELAND	W 3-1	Hassall 2, Lofthouse	70,000	Merrick (16), Rickaby (1), Eckersley (16), **Wright W** (54), Johnston (9), Dickinson (31), Matthews (35), Quixall (3), Lofthouse (19), Hassall (5), Mullen (9)

Friendly

DATE	VENUE	OPPONENTS	SCORE	GOALSCORERS	ATTENDANCE	TEAM
Nov 25	Wembley, London	HUNGARY	L 3-6	Sewell, Mortensen, Ramsey (pen)	100,000	Merrick (17), Ramsey (32), Eckersley (17), **Wright W** (55), Johnston (10), Dickinson (32), Matthews (36), Taylor E (1), Mortensen (25), Sewell (5), Robb (1),

1954

Home International Championship/World Cup Qualifier

DATE	VENUE	OPPONENTS	SCORE	GOALSCORERS	ATTENDANCE	TEAM
Apr 3	Hampden Park, Glasgow	SCOTLAND	W 4-2	Broadis, Nicholls, Allen, Mullen	134,544	Merrick (18), Staniforth (1), Byrne R (1), **Wright W** (56), Clarke H (1), Dickinson (33), Finney (49), Broadis (9), Allen R (2), Nicholls (1), Mullen (10),

Friendlies

DATE	VENUE	OPPONENTS	SCORE	GOALSCORERS	ATTENDANCE	TEAM
May 16	Belgrade	YUGOSLAVIA	L 0-1		60,000	Merrick (19), Staniforth (2), Byrne R (2), **Wright W** (57), Owen (1), Dickinson (34), Finney (50), Broadis (10), Allen R (3), Nicholls (2), Mullen (11)
May 23	Budapest	HUNGARY	L 1-7	Broadis	92,000	Merrick (20), Staniforth (3), Byrne R (3), **Wright W** (58), Owen (2), Dickinson (35), Harris P (2), Sewell (6), Jezzard (1), Broadis (11), Finney (51)

THE WORLD CUP FINALS 1954 (SWITZERLAND)

Group Stage – Pool 4

DATE	VENUE	OPPONENTS	SCORE	GOALSCORERS	ATTENDANCE	TEAM
Jun 17	Basle	BELGIUM	D 4-4	Broadis 2, Lofthouse 2	14,000	Merrick (21), Staniforth (4), Byrne R (4), **Wright W** (59), Owen (3), Dickinson (36), Matthews (37), Broadis (12), Lofthouse (20), Taylor T (4), Finney (52)
Jun 20	Berne	SWITZERLAND	W 2-0	Wilshaw, Mullen	30,000	Merrick (22), Staniforth (5), Byrne R (5), McGarry (1), **Wright W** (60), Dickinson (37), Finney (53), Broadis (13), Taylor T (5), Wilshaw (2), Mullen (12)

Quarter-final

DATE	VENUE	OPPONENTS	SCORE	GOALSCORERS	ATTENDANCE	TEAM
Jun 26	Basle	URUGUAY	L 2-4	Lofthouse, Finney	35,000	Merrick (23), Staniforth (6), Byrne R (6), McGarry (2), **Wright W** (61), Dickinson (38), Matthews (38), Broadis (14), Lofthouse (21), Wilshaw (3), Finney (54)

Pool 4

	P	W	D	L	F	A	Pts
ENGLAND	2	1	1	0	6	4	3
ITALY	2	1	0	1	5	3	2
SWITZERLAND	2	1	0	1	2	3	2
BELGIUM	2	0	1	1	5	8	1

1954 (continued)

Home International Championship

DATE	VENUE	OPPONENTS	SCORE	GOALSCORERS	ATTENDANCE	TEAM
Oct 2	Windsor Park, Belfast	N. IRELAND	W 2-0	Haynes, Revie	59,000	Wood (1), Foulkes (1), Byrne R (7), Wheeler (1), **Wright W** (62), Barlow (1), Matthews (39), Revie (1), Lofthouse (22), Haynes (1), Pilkington (1)
Nov 10	Wembley, London	WALES	W 3-2	Bentley 3	89,789	Wood (2), Staniforth (7), Byrne R (8), Phillips (2), **Wright W** (63), Slater (1), Matthews (40), Bentley (9), Allen R (4), Shackleton (4), Blunstone (1)

Friendly

DATE	VENUE	OPPONENTS	SCORE	GOALSCORERS	ATTENDANCE	TEAM
Dec 1	Wembley, London	W. GERMANY	W 3-1	Bentley, Allen R, Shackleton	100,000	Williams (19), Staniforth (8), Byrne R (9), Phillips (3), **Wright W** (64), Slater (2), Matthews (41), Bentley (10), Allen R (5), Shackleton (5), Finney (55)

1955

Home International Championship

DATE	VENUE	OPPONENTS	SCORE	GOALSCORERS	ATTENDANCE	TEAM
Apr 2	Wembley, London	SCOTLAND	W 7-2	Wilshaw 4, Lofthouse 2, Revie	96,847	Williams (20), Meadows (1), Byrne R (10), Armstrong (1), **Wright W** (65), Edwards (1), Matthews (42), Revie (2), Lofthouse (23), Wilshaw (4), Blunstone (2)

Friendlies

DATE	VENUE	OPPONENTS	SCORE	GOALSCORERS	ATTENDANCE	TEAM
May 15	Paris	FRANCE	L 0-1		54,696	Williams (21), Sillett P (1), Byrne R (11), Flowers (1), **Wright W** (66), Edwards (2), Matthews (43), Revie (3), Lofthouse (24), Wilshaw (5), Blunstone (3)
May 18	Madrid	SPAIN	D 1-1	Bentley	125,000	Williams (22), Sillett P (2), Byrne R (12), Dickinson (39), **Wright W** (67), Edwards (3), Matthews (44), Bentley (11), Lofthouse (25), Wilshaw (6), Quixall (4)
May 22	Oporto	PORTUGAL	L 1-3	Bentley	52,000	Williams (23), Sillett P (3), Byrne R (13), Dickinson (40), **Wright W** (68), Edwards (4), Matthews (45), Bentley (12), Lofthouse (26), (Quixall 5), Wilshaw (7), Blunstone (4)
Oct 2	Copenhagen	DENMARK	W 5-1	Revie 2 (1 pen), Lofthouse 2, Bradford	53,000	Baynham (1), Hall (1), Byrne R (14), McGarry (3), **Wright W** (69), Dickinson (41), Milburn (13), Revie (4), Lofthouse (27), Bradford (1), Finney (56)

Home International Championship

DATE	VENUE	OPPONENTS	SCORE	GOALSCORERS	ATTENDANCE	TEAM
Oct 22	Ninian Park, Cardiff	WALES	L 1-2	own goal	60,000	Williams (24), Hall (2), Byrne R (15), McGarry (4), **Wright W** (70), Dickinson (42), Matthews (46), Revie (5), Lofthouse (28), Wilshaw (8), Finney (57)
Nov 2	Wembley, London	N. IRELAND	W 3-0	Wilshaw 2, Finney	60,000	Baynham (2), Hall (3), Byrne R (16), Clayton (1), **Wright W** (71), Dickinson (43), Finney (58), Haynes (2), Jezzard (2), Wilshaw (9), Perry (1)

Friendly

DATE	VENUE	OPPONENTS	SCORE	GOALSCORERS	ATTENDANCE	TEAM
Nov 30	Wembley, London	SPAIN	W 4-1	Atyeo, Perry 2, Finney	95,550	Baynham (3), Hall (4), Byrne R (17), Clayton (2), **Wright W** (72), Dickinson (44), Finney (59), Atyeo (1), Lofthouse (29), Haynes (3), Perry (2)

1956

Home International Championship

DATE	VENUE	OPPONENTS	SCORE	GOALSCORERS	ATTENDANCE	TEAM
Apr 14	Hampden Park, Glasgow	SCOTLAND	D 1-1	Haynes	132,817	Matthews R (1), Hall (5), Byrne R (18), Dickinson (45), **Wright W** (73), Edwards (5), Finney (60), Taylor T (6), Lofthouse (30), Haynes (4), Perry (3)

Friendlies

DATE	VENUE	OPPONENTS	SCORE	GOALSCORERS	ATTENDANCE	TEAM
May 9	Wembley, London	BRAZIL	W 4-2	Taylor T 2, Grainger 2	97,000	Matthews R (2), Hall (6), Byrne R (19), Clayton (3), **Wright W** (74), Edwards (6), Matthews S (47), Atyeo (2), Taylor T (7), Haynes (5), Grainger (1)
May 16	Stockholm	SWEDEN	D 0-0		35,000	Matthews R (3), Hall (7), Byrne R (20), Clayton (4), **Wright W** (75), Edwards (7), Berry (4), Atyeo (3), Taylor T (8), Haynes (6), Grainger (2)
May 20	Helsinki	FINLAND	W 5-1	Wilshaw, Haynes, Astall, Lofthouse 2	20,177	Wood (3), Hall (8), Byrne R (21), Clayton (5), **Wright W** (76), Edwards (8), Astall (1), Haynes (7), Taylor T (9), (Lofthouse 31), Wilshaw (10), Grainger (3)
May 26	Berlin	W. GERMANY	W 3-1	Edwards, Grainger, Haynes	90,000	Matthews R (4), Hall (9), Byrne R (22), Clayton (6), **Wright W** (77), Edwards (9), Astall (2), Haynes (8), Taylor T (10), Wilshaw (11), Grainger (4)

Home International Championship

DATE	VENUE	OPPONENTS	SCORE	GOALSCORERS	ATTENDANCE	TEAM
Oct 6	Windsor Park, Belfast	N. IRELAND	D 1-1	Matthews S	58,420	Matthews R (5), Hall (10), Byrne R (23), Clayton (7), **Wright W** (78), Edwards (10), Matthews S (48), Revie (6), Taylor T (11), Wilshaw (12), Grainger (5)
Nov 14	Wembley, London	WALES	W 3-1	Haynes, Brooks, Finney	93,796	Ditchburn (4), Hall (11), Byrne R (24), Clayton (8), **Wright W** (79), Dickinson (46), Matthews S (49), Brooks (1), Finney (61), Haynes (9), Grainger (6)

Friendly

DATE	VENUE	OPPONENTS	SCORE	GOALSCORERS	ATTENDANCE	TEAM
Nov 28	Wembley, London	YUGOSLAVIA	W 3-0	Brooks, Taylor T 2	75,000	Ditchburn (5), Hall (12), Byrne R (25), Clayton (9), **Wright W** (80), Dickinson (47), Matthews S (50), Brooks (2), Finney (62), Haynes (10), (Taylor T 12), Blunstone (5)

World Cup Qualifier

DATE	VENUE	OPPONENTS	SCORE	GOALSCORERS	ATTENDANCE	TEAM
Dec 5	Molineux, Wolverhampton	DENMARK	W 5-2	Taylor T 3, Edwards 2	54,083	Ditchburn (6), Hall (13), Byrne R (26), Clayton (10), **Wright W** (81), Dickinson (48), Matthews S (51), Brooks (3), Taylor T (13), Edwards (11), Finney (63)

1957

Home International Championship

DATE	VENUE	OPPONENTS	SCORE	GOALSCORERS	ATTENDANCE	TEAM
Apr 6	Wembley, London	SCOTLAND	W 2-1	Kevan, Edwards	97,520	Hodgkinson (1), Hall (14), Byrne R (27), Clayton (11), **Wright W** (82), Edwards (12), Matthews S (52), Thompson T (2), Finney (64), Kevan (1), Grainger (7)

World Cup Qualifiers

DATE	VENUE	OPPONENTS	SCORE	GOALSCORERS	ATTENDANCE	TEAM
May 8	Wembley, London	R. of IRELAND	W 5-1	Taylor T 3, Atyeo 2,	52,000	Hodgkinson (2), Hall (15), Byrne R (28), Clayton (12), **Wright W** (83), Edwards (13), Matthews S (53), Atyeo (4), Taylor T (14), Haynes (11), Finney (65)
May 15	Copenhagen	DENMARK	W 4-1	Haynes, Taylor T 2, Atyeo	35,000	Hodgkinson (3), Hall (16), Byrne R (29), Clayton (13), **Wright W** (84), Edwards (14), Matthews S (54), Atyeo (5), Taylor T (15), Haynes (12), Finney (66)
May 19	Dalymount Park, Dublin	R. of IRELAND	D 1-1	Atyeo	47,000	Hodgkinson (4), Hall (17), Byrne R (30), Clayton (14), **Wright W** (85), Edwards (15), Finney (67), Atyeo (6), Taylor T (16), Haynes (13), Pegg (1)

Home International Championship

DATE	VENUE	OPPONENTS	SCORE	GOALSCORERS	ATTENDANCE	TEAM
Oct 19	Ninian Park, Cardiff	WALES	W 4-0	Haynes 2, Finney, own goal	58,000	Hopkinson (1), Howe D (1), Byrne R (31), Clayton (15), **Wright W** (86), Edwards (16), Douglas (1), Kevan (2), Taylor T (17), Haynes (14), Finney (68)
Nov 6	Wembley, London	N. IRELAND	L 2-3	A'Court, Edwards	40,000	Hopkinson (2), Howe D (2), Byrne R (32), Clayton (16), **Wright W** (87), Edwards (17), Douglas (2), Kevan (3), Taylor T (18), Haynes (15), A'Court (1)

Friendly

DATE	VENUE	OPPONENTS	SCORE	GOALSCORERS	ATTENDANCE	TEAM
Nov 27	Wembley, London	FRANCE	W 4-0	Taylor T 2, Robson R 2	64,349	Hopkinson (3), Howe D (3), Byrne R (33), Clayton (17), **Wright W** (88), Edwards (18), Douglas (3), Robson R (1), Taylor T (19), Haynes (16), Finney (69)

1958

Home International Championship

DATE	VENUE	OPPONENTS	SCORE	GOALSCORERS	ATTENDANCE	TEAM
Apr 19	Hampden Park, Glasgow	SCOTLAND	W 4-0	Douglas, Kevan 2, Charlton R	127,874	Hopkinson (4), Howe D (4), Langley (1), Clayton (18), **Wright W** (89), Slater (3), Douglas (4), Charlton R (1), Kevan (4), Haynes (17), Finney (70)

Friendlies

DATE	VENUE	OPPONENTS	SCORE	GOALSCORERS	ATTENDANCE	TEAM
May 7	Wembley, London	PORTUGAL	W 2-1	Charlton R 2	72,000	Hopkinson (5), Howe D (5), Langley (2), Clayton (19), **Wright W** (90), Slater (4), Douglas (5), Charlton R (2), Kevan (5), Haynes (18), Finney (71)
May 11	Belgrade	YUGOSLAVIA	L 0-5		55,000	Hopkinson (6), Howe D (6), Langley (3), Clayton (20), **Wright W** (91), Slater (5), Douglas (6), Charlton R (3), Kevan (6), Haynes (19), Finney (72)
May 18	Moscow	USSR	D 1-1	Kevan	102,000	McDonald (1), Howe D (7), Banks T (1), Clamp (1), **Wright W** (92), Slater (6), Douglas (7), Robson R (2), Kevan (7), Haynes (20), Finney (73)

THE WORLD CUP FINALS 1958 (SWEDEN)

Group Stage – Pool 2

DATE	VENUE	OPPONENTS	SCORE	GOALSCORERS	ATTENDANCE	TEAM
Jun 8	Gothenburg	USSR	D 2-2	Kevan, Finney (pen)	49,348	McDonald (2), Howe D (8), Banks T (2), Clamp (2), **Wright W** (93), Slater (7), Douglas (8), Robson R (3), Kevan (8), Haynes (21), Finney (74)
Jun 11	Gothenburg	BRAZIL	D 0-0		40,895	McDonald (3), Howe D (9), Banks T (3), Clamp (3), **Wright W** (94), Slater (8), Douglas (9), Robson R (4), Kevan (9), Haynes (22), A'Court (2)
Jun 15	Boras	AUSTRIA	D 2-2	Haynes, Kevan	16,800	McDonald (4), Howe D (10), Banks T (4), Clamp (4), **Wright W** (95), Slater (9), Douglas (10), Robson R (5), Kevan (10), Haynes (23), A'Court (3)

Play-off

DATE	VENUE	OPPONENTS	SCORE	GOALSCORERS	ATTENDANCE	TEAM
Jun 17	Gothenburg	USSR	L 0-1		23,182	McDonald (5), Howe D (11), Banks T (5), Clayton (21), **Wright W** (96), Slater (10), Brabrook (1), Broadbent (1), Kevan (11), Haynes (24), A'Court (4)

Pool 2

	P	W	D	L	F	A	Pts
BRAZIL	3	2	1	0	5	0	5
ENGLAND	3	0	3	0	4	4	3
SOVIET UNION	3	1	1	1	4	4	3
AUSTRIA	3	0	1	2	2	7	1

1958 (continued)

Home International Championship

DATE	VENUE	OPPONENTS	SCORE	GOALSCORERS	ATTENDANCE	TEAM
Oct 4	Windsor Park, Belfast	N. IRELAND	D 3-3	Charlton R 2, Finney	58,000	McDonald (6), Howe D (12), Banks T (6), Clayton (22), **Wright W** (97), McGuinness (1), Brabrook (2), Broadbent (2), Charlton R (4), Haynes (25), Finney (75)

Friendly

DATE	VENUE	OPPONENTS	SCORE	GOALSCORERS	ATTENDANCE	TEAM
Oct 22	Wembley, London	USSR	W 5-0	Haynes 3, Charlton R (pen), Lofthouse	100,000	McDonald (7), Howe D (13), Shaw G (1), Clayton (23), **Wright W** (98), Slater (11), Douglas (11), Charlton R (5), Lofthouse (32), Haynes (26), Finney (76)

Home International Championship

DATE	VENUE	OPPONENTS	SCORE	GOALSCORERS	ATTENDANCE	TEAM
Nov 26	Villa Park, Birmingham	WALES	D 2-2	Broadbent 2	41,581	McDonald (8), Howe D (14), Shaw G (2), Clayton (24), **Wright W** (99), Flowers (2), Clapton (1), Broadbent (3), Lofthouse (33), Charlton R (6), A'Court (5)

1959

Home International Championship

DATE	VENUE	OPPONENTS	SCORE	GOALSCORERS	ATTENDANCE	TEAM
Apr 11	Wembley, London	SCOTLAND	W 1-0	Charlton R	98,329	Hopkinson (7), Howe D (15), Shaw G (3), Clayton (25), **Wright W** (100), Flowers (3), Douglas (12), Broadbent (4), Charlton R (7), Haynes (27), Holden (1)

Friendlies

DATE	VENUE	OPPONENTS	SCORE	GOALSCORERS	ATTENDANCE	TEAM
May 6	Wembley, London	ITALY	D 2-2	Charlton R, Bradley	92,000	Hopkinson (8), Howe D (16), Shaw G (4), Clayton (26), **Wright W** (101), Flowers (4), Bradley (1), Broadbent (5), Charlton R (8), Haynes (28), Holden (2)
May 13	Rio	BRAZIL	L 0-2		160,000	Hopkinson (9), Howe D (17), Armfield (1), Clayton (27), **Wright W** (102), Flowers (5), Deeley (1), Broadbent (6), Charlton R (9), Haynes (29), Holden (3)
May 17	Lima	PERU	L 1-4	Greaves	50,306	Hopkinson (10), Howe D (18), Armfield (2), Clayton (28), **Wright W** (103), Flowers (6), Deeley (2), Greaves (1), Charlton R (10), Haynes (30), Holden (4)
May 24	Mexico City	MEXICO	L 1-2	Kevan	83,000	Hopkinson (11), Howe D (19), Armfield (3), Clayton (29), **Wright W** (104), McGuinness (2), (Flowers 7), Holden (5), (Bradley 2), Greaves (2), Kevan (12), Haynes (31), Charlton R (11)

1959 (continued)

Friendly

DATE	VENUE	OPPONENTS	SCORE	GOALSCORERS	ATTENDANCE	TEAM
May 28	Los Angeles	USA	W 8-1	Charlton R 3 (1 pen), Flowers 2, Bradley, Kevan, Haynes	14,000	Hopkinson (12), Howe D (20), Armfield (4), Clayton (30), **Wright W** (105), Flowers (8), Bradley (3), Greaves (3), Kevan (13), Haynes (32), Charlton R (12)

Home International Championship

DATE	VENUE	OPPONENTS	SCORE	GOALSCORERS	ATTENDANCE	TEAM
Oct 17	Ninian Park, Cardiff	WALES	D 1-1	Greaves	62,000	Hopkinson (13), Howe D (21), Allen A (1), Clayton (31), Smith T (1), Flowers (9), Connelly (1), Greaves (4), Clough (1), Charlton R (13), Holliday (1)

Friendly

DATE	VENUE	OPPONENTS	SCORE	GOALSCORERS	ATTENDANCE	TEAM
Oct 28	Wembley, London	SWEDEN	L 2-3	Connelly, Charlton R	80,000	Hopkinson (14), Howe D (22), Allen A (2), Clayton (32), Smith T (2), Flowers (10), Connelly (2), Greaves (5), Clough (2), Charlton R (14), Holliday (2)

Home International Championship

DATE	VENUE	OPPONENTS	SCORE	GOALSCORERS	ATTENDANCE	TEAM
Nov 18	Wembley, London	N. IRELAND	W 2-1	Baker, Parry	60,000	Springett R (1), Howe D (23), Allen A (3), Clayton (33), Brown (1), Flowers (11), Connelly (3), Haynes (33), Baker (1), Parry (1), Holliday (3)

1960

Home International Championship

DATE	VENUE	OPPONENTS	SCORE	GOALSCORERS	ATTENDANCE	TEAM
Apr 9	Hampden Park, Glasgow	SCOTLAND	D 1-1	Charlton R (pen)	129,193	Springett R (2), Armfield (5), Wilson (1), **Clayton** (34), Slater (12), Flowers (12), Connelly (4), Broadbent (7), Baker (2), Parry (2), Charlton R (15)

Friendlies

DATE	VENUE	OPPONENTS	SCORE	GOALSCORERS	ATTENDANCE	TEAM
May 11	Wembley, London	YUGOSLAVIA	D 3-3	Douglas, Greaves, Haynes	60,000	Springett R (3), Armfield (6), Wilson (2), **Clayton** (35), Swan (1), Flowers (13), Douglas (13), Haynes (34), Baker (3), Greaves (6), Charlton R (16)
May 15	Madrid	SPAIN	L 0-3		77,000	Springett R (4), Armfield (7), Wilson (3), Robson R (6), Swan (2), Flowers (14), Brabrook (3), **Haynes** (35), Baker (4), Greaves (7), Charlton R (17)
May 22	Budapest	HUNGARY	L 0-2		90,000	Springett R (5), Armfield (8), Wilson (4), Robson R (7), Swan (3), Flowers (15), Douglas (14), **Haynes** (36), Baker (5), Viollet (1), Charlton R (18)

Home International Championship

DATE	VENUE	OPPONENTS	SCORE	GOALSCORERS	ATTENDANCE	TEAM
Oct 8	Windsor Park, Belfast	N. IRELAND	W 5-2	Smith R, Greaves 2, Charlton R, Douglas	60,000	Springett R (6), Armfield (9), McNeil (1), Robson R (8), Swan (4), Flowers (16), Douglas (15), Greaves (8), Smith R (1), **Haynes** (37), Charlton R (19)

World Cup Qualifier

DATE	VENUE	OPPONENTS	SCORE	GOALSCORERS	ATTENDANCE	TEAM
Oct 19	Luxembourg	LUXEMBOURG	W 9-0	Greaves 3, Charlton R 3, Smith R 2, Haynes	5,500	Springett R (7), Armfield (10), McNeil (2), Robson R (9), Swan (5), Flowers (17), Douglas (16), Greaves (9), Smith R (2), **Haynes** (38), Charlton R (20)

Friendly

DATE	VENUE	OPPONENTS	SCORE	GOALSCORERS	ATTENDANCE	TEAM
Oct 26	Wembley, London	SPAIN	W 4-2	Greaves, Douglas, Smith R (2),	80,000	Springett R (8), Armfield (11), McNeil (3), Robson R (10), Swan (6), Flowers (18), Douglas (17), Greaves (10), Smith R (3), **Haynes** (39), Charlton R (21)

Home International Championship

DATE	VENUE	OPPONENTS	SCORE	GOALSCORERS	ATTENDANCE	TEAM
Nov 23	Wembley, London	WALES	W 5-1	Greaves 2, Charlton R, Smith R, Haynes	65,000	Hodgkinson (5), Armfield (12), McNeil (4), Robson R (11), Swan (7), Flowers (19), Douglas (18), Greaves (11), Smith R (4), **Haynes** (40), Charlton R (22)

1961

Home International Championship

DATE	VENUE	OPPONENTS	SCORE	GOALSCORERS	ATTENDANCE	TEAM
Apr 15	Wembley, London	SCOTLAND	W 9-3	Robson R, Greaves 3, Douglas, Smith R 2, Haynes 2	97,350	Springett R (9), Armfield (13), McNeil (5), Robson R (12), Swan (8), Flowers (20), Douglas (19), Greaves (12), Smith R (5), **Haynes** (41), Charlton R (23)

Friendly

DATE	VENUE	OPPONENTS	SCORE	GOALSCORERS	ATTENDANCE	TEAM
May 10	Wembley, London	MEXICO	W 8-0	Hitchens, Charlton R 3, Robson R, Douglas 2, Flowers (pen)	77,000	Springett R (10), Armfield (14), McNeil (6), Robson R (13), Swan (9), Flowers (21), Douglas (20), Kevan (14), Hitchens (1), **Haynes** (42), Charlton R (24)

1961 (continued)

World Cup Qualifier

DATE	VENUE	OPPONENTS	SCORE	GOALSCORERS	ATTENDANCE	TEAM
May 21	Lisbon	PORTUGAL	D 1-1	Flowers	65,000	Springett R (11), Armfield (15), McNeil (7), Robson R (14), Swan (10), Flowers (22), Douglas (21), Greaves (13), Smith R (6), **Haynes** (43), Charlton R (25)

Friendlies

DATE	VENUE	OPPONENTS	SCORE	GOALSCORERS	ATTENDANCE	TEAM
May 24	Rome	ITALY	W 3-2	Hitchens 2, Greaves	90,000	Springett R (12), Armfield (16), McNeil (8), Robson R (15), Swan (11), Flowers (23), Douglas (22), Greaves (14), Hitchens (2), **Haynes** (44), Charlton R (26)
May 27	Vienna	AUSTRIA	L 1-3	Greaves	90,000	Springett R (13), Armfield (17), Angus (1), Miller (1), Swan (12), Flowers (24), Douglas (23), Greaves (15), Hitchens (3), **Haynes** (45), Charlton R (27)

World Cup Qualifier

DATE	VENUE	OPPONENTS	SCORE	GOALSCORERS	ATTENDANCE	TEAM
Sep 28	Highbury, London	LUXEMBOURG	W 4-1	Pointer, Viollet, Charlton R (2),	33,409	Springett R (14), **Armfield** (18), McNeil (9), Robson R (16), Swan (13), Flowers (25), Douglas (24), Fantham (1), Pointer (1), Viollet (2), Charlton R (28)

Home International Championship

DATE	VENUE	OPPONENTS	SCORE	GOALSCORERS	ATTENDANCE	TEAM
Oct 14	Ninian Park, Cardiff	WALES	D 1-1	Douglas	61,566	Springett R (15), Armfield (19), Wilson (5), Robson R (17), Swan (14), Flowers (26), Connelly (5), Douglas (25), Pointer (2), **Haynes** (46), Charlton R (29)

World Cup Qualifier

DATE	VENUE	OPPONENTS	SCORE	GOALSCORERS	ATTENDANCE	TEAM
Oct 25	Wembley, London	PORTUGAL	W 2-0	Connelly, Pointer	100,000	Springett R (16), Armfield (20), Wilson (6), Robson R (18), Swan (15), Flowers (27), Connelly (6), Douglas (26), Pointer (3), **Haynes** (47), Charlton R (30)

Home International Championship

DATE	VENUE	OPPONENTS	SCORE	GOALSCORERS	ATTENDANCE	TEAM
Nov 22	Wembley, London	N. IRELAND	D 1-1	Charlton R	30,000	Springett R (17), Armfield (21), Wilson (7), Robson R (19), Swan (16), Flowers (28), Douglas (27), Byrne J (1), Crawford (1), **Haynes** (48), Charlton R (31)

1962

Friendly

DATE	VENUE	OPPONENTS	SCORE	GOALSCORERS	ATTENDANCE	TEAM
Apr 4	Wembley, London	AUSTRIA	W 3-1	Crawford, Flowers (pen), Hunt	50,000	Springett R (18), Armfield (22), Wilson (8), Anderson (1), Swan (17), Flowers (29), Connelly (7), Hunt (1), Crawford (2), **Haynes** (49), Charlton R (32)

Home International Championship

DATE	VENUE	OPPONENTS	SCORE	GOALSCORERS	ATTENDANCE	TEAM
Apr 14	Hampden Park, Glasgow	SCOTLAND	L 0-2		132,441	Springett R (19), Armfield (23), Wilson (9), Anderson (2), Swan (18), Flowers (30), Douglas (28), Greaves (16), Smith R (7), **Haynes** (50), Charlton R (33)

Friendlies

DATE	VENUE	OPPONENTS	SCORE	GOALSCORERS	ATTENDANCE	TEAM
May 9	Wembley, London	SWITZERLAND	W 3-1	Flowers, Hitchens, Connelly	35,000	Springett R (20), Armfield (24), Wilson (10), Robson R (20), Swan (19), Flowers (31), Connelly (8), Greaves (17), Hitchens (4), **Haynes** (51), Charlton R (34)
May 20	Lima	PERU	W 4-0	Flowers (pen), Greaves 3	32,565	Springett R (21), Armfield (25), Wilson (11), Moore (1), Norman (1), Flowers (32), Douglas (29), Greaves (18), Hitchens (5), **Haynes** (52), Charlton R (35)

THE WORLD CUP FINALS 1962 (CHILE)

Group Stage – Group 4

DATE	VENUE	OPPONENTS	SCORE	GOALSCORERS	ATTENDANCE	TEAM
May 31	Rancagua	HUNGARY	L 1-2	Flowers (pen)	7,938	Springett R (22), Armfield (26), Wilson (12), Moore (2), Norman (2), Flowers (33), Douglas (30), Greaves (19), Hitchens (6), **Haynes** (53), Charlton R (36)
Jun 2	Rancagua	ARGENTINA	W 3-1	Flowers (pen), Charlton R, Greaves	9,794	Springett R (23), Armfield (27), Wilson (13), Moore (3), Norman (3), Flowers (34), Douglas (31), Greaves (20), Peacock (1), **Haynes** (54), Charlton R (37)
Jun 7	Rancagua	BULGARIA	D 0-0		5,700	Springett R (24), Armfield (28), Wilson (14), Moore (4), Norman (4), Flowers (35), Douglas (32), Greaves (21), Peacock (2), **Haynes** (55), Charlton R (38)

Quarter-final

DATE	VENUE	OPPONENTS	SCORE	GOALSCORERS	ATTENDANCE	TEAM
Jun 10	Vina del Mar	BRAZIL	L 1-3	Hitchens	17,736	Springett R (25), Armfield (29), Wilson (15), Moore (5), Norman (5), Flowers (36), Douglas (33), Greaves (22), Hitchens (7), **Haynes** (56), Charlton R (39)

Group 4

	P	W	D	L	F	A	Pts
HUNGARY	3	2	1	0	8	2	5
ENGLAND	3	1	1	1	4	3	3
ARGENTINA	3	1	1	1	2	3	3
BULGARIA	3	0	1	2	1	7	1

1962 (continued)

European Nations Cup Qualifier

DATE	VENUE	OPPONENTS	SCORE	GOALSCORERS	ATTENDANCE	TEAM
Oct 3	Hillsborough, Sheffield	FRANCE	D 1-1	Flowers (pen)	35,380	Springett R (26), **Armfield** (30), Wilson (16), Moore (6), Norman (6), Flowers (37), Hellawell (1), Crowe (1), Charnley (1), Greaves (23), Hinton A (1)

Home International Championship

DATE	VENUE	OPPONENTS	SCORE	GOALSCORERS	ATTENDANCE	TEAM
Oct 20	Windsor Park, Belfast	N. IRELAND	W 3-1	Greaves, O'Grady 2	55,000	Springett R (27), **Armfield** (31), Wilson (17), Moore (7), Labone (1), Flowers (38), Hellawell (2), Hill F (1), Peacock (3), Greaves (24), O'Grady (1)
Nov 21	Wembley, London	WALES	W 4-0	Connelly, Peacock 2, Greaves	27,500	Springett R (28), **Armfield** (32), Shaw G (5), Moore (8), Labone (2), Flowers (39), Connelly (9), Hill F (2), Peacock (4), Greaves (25), Tambling (1)

1963

MANAGER CHANGED TO: ALF RAMSEY

European Nations Cup Qualifier

DATE	VENUE	OPPONENTS	SCORE	GOALSCORERS	ATTENDANCE	TEAM
Feb 27	Paris	FRANCE	L 2-5	Smith R, Tambling	23,986	Springett R (29), **Armfield** (33), Henry (1), Moore (9), Labone (3), Flowers (40), Connelly (10), Tambling (2), Smith R (8), Greaves (26), Charlton R (40)

Home International Championship

DATE	VENUE	OPPONENTS	SCORE	GOALSCORERS	ATTENDANCE	TEAM
Apr 6	Wembley, London	SCOTLAND	L 1-2	Douglas	98,606	Banks (1), **Armfield** (34), Byrne G (1), Moore (10), Norman (7), Flowers (41), Douglas (34), Greaves (27), Smith R (9), Melia (1), Charlton R (41)

Friendlies

DATE	VENUE	OPPONENTS	SCORE	GOALSCORERS	ATTENDANCE	TEAM
May 8	Wembley, London	BRAZIL	D 1-1	Douglas	92,000	Banks (2), **Armfield** (35), Wilson (18), Milne (1), Norman (8), Moore (11), Douglas (35), Greaves (28), Smith R (10), Eastham (1), Charlton R (42)
May 29	Bratislava	CZECHOSLOVAKIA	W 4-2	Greaves 2, Smith R, Charlton R	50,000	Banks (3), Shellito (1), Wilson (19), Milne (2), Norman (9), **Moore** (12), Paine (1), Greaves (29), Smith R (11), Eastham (2), Charlton R (43)

1963 (continued)

Friendlies

DATE	VENUE	OPPONENTS	SCORE	GOALSCORERS	ATTENDANCE	TEAM
Jun 2	Leipzig	E. GERMANY	W 2-1	Hunt, Charlton R	90,000	Banks (4), **Armfield** (36), Wilson (20), Milne (3), Norman (10), Moore (13), Paine (2), Hunt (2), Smith R (12), Eastham (3), Charlton R (44)
Jun 5	Basle	SWITZERLAND	W 8-1	Charlton R 3, Byrne J 2, Douglas, Kay, Melia	49,800	Springett R (30), **Armfield** (37), Wilson (21), Kay (1), Moore (14), Flowers (42), Douglas (36), Greaves (30), Byrne J (2), Melia (2), Charlton R (45)

Home International Championship

| Oct 12 | Ninian Park, Cardiff | WALES | W 4-0 | Smith R 2, Greaves, Charlton R | 48,350 | Banks (5), **Armfield** (38), Wilson (22), Milne (4), Norman (11), Moore (15), Paine (3), Greaves (31), Smith R (13), Eastham (4), Charlton R (46) |

Friendly

| Oct 23 | Wembley, London | REST OF WORLD | W 2-1 | Paine, Greaves | 100,000 | Banks (6), **Armfield** (39), Wilson (23), Milne (5), Norman (12), Moore (16), Paine (4), Greaves (32), Smith R (14), Eastham (5), Charlton R (47) |

Home International Championship

| Nov 20 | Wembley, London | N. IRELAND | W 8-3 | Greaves 4, Paine 3, Smith R | 55,000 | Banks (7), **Armfield** (40), Thomson R (1), Milne (6), Norman (13), Moore (17), Paine (5), Greaves (33), Smith R (15), Eastham (6), Charlton R (48) |

1964

Home International Championship

DATE	VENUE	OPPONENTS	SCORE	GOALSCORERS	ATTENDANCE	TEAM
Apr 11	Hampden Park, Glasgow	SCOTLAND	L 0-1		133,245	Banks (8), **Armfield** (41), Wilson (24), Milne (7), Norman (14), Moore (18), Paine (6), Hunt (3), Byrne J (3), Eastham (7), Charlton R (49)

Friendlies

May 6	Wembley, London	URUGUAY	W 2-1	Byrne J 2	55,000	Banks (9), Cohen (1), Wilson (25), Milne (8), Norman (15), **Moore** (19), Paine (7), Greaves (34), Byrne J (4), Eastham (8), Charlton R (50)
May 17	Lisbon	PORTUGAL	W 4-3	Byrne J 3, Charlton R	40,000	Banks (10), Cohen (2), Wilson (26), Milne (9), Norman (16), **Moore** (20), Thompson P (1), Greaves (35), Byrne J (5), Eastham (9), Charlton R (51)
May 24	Dalymount Park, Dublin	R. of IRELAND	W 3-1	Eastham, Byrne J, Greaves	45,000	Waiters (1), Cohen (3), Wilson (27), Milne (10), Flowers (43), **Moore** (21), Thompson P (2), Greaves (36), Byrne J (6), Eastham (10), Charlton R (52)
May 27	New York	USA	W 10-0	Hunt 4, Pickering 3, Paine 2, Charlton R	5,000	Banks (11), Cohen (4), Thomson R (2), Bailey M (1), Norman (17), **Flowers** (44), Paine (8), Hunt (4), Pickering (1), Eastham (11), (Charlton R 53), Thompson P (3)

Brazilian Jubilee Tournament

May 30	Rio	BRAZIL	L 1-5	Greaves	77,000	Waiters (2), Cohen (5), Wilson (28), Milne (11), Norman (18), **Moore** (22), Thompson P (4), Greaves (37), Byrne J (7), Eastham (12), Charlton R (54)
Jun 4	Sao Paulo	PORTUGAL	D 1-1	Hunt	25,000	Banks (12), Thomson R (3), Wilson (29), Flowers (45), Norman (19), **Moore** (23), Paine (9), Greaves (38), Byrne J (8), Hunt (5), Thompson P (5)
Jun 6	Rio	ARGENTINA	L 0-1		15,000	Banks (13), Thomson R (4), Wilson (30), Milne (12), Norman (20), **Moore** (24), Thompson P (6), Greaves (39), Byrne J (9), Eastham (13), Charlton R (55)

Home International Championship

| Oct 3 | Windsor Park, Belfast | N. IRELAND | W 4-3 | Pickering, Greaves 3 | 58,000 | Banks (14), Cohen (6), Thomson R (5), Milne (13), Norman (21), **Moore** (25), Paine (10), Greaves (40), Pickering (2), Charlton R (56), Thompson P (7) |

Friendly

| Oct 21 | Wembley, London | BELGIUM | D 2-2 | Pickering, Hinton | 55,000 | Waiters (3), Cohen (7), Thomson R (6), Milne (14), Norman (22), **Moore** (26), Thompson P (8), Greaves (41), Pickering (3), Venables (1), Hinton A (2) |

Home International Championship

| Nov 18 | Wembley, London | WALES | W 2-1 | Wignall 2 | 40,000 | Waiters (4), Cohen (8), Thomson R (7), Bailey M (2), **Flowers** (46), Young (1), Thompson P (9), Hunt (6), Wignall (1), Byrne J (10), Hinton A (3) |

Friendly

| Dec 9 | Amsterdam | HOLLAND | D 1-1 | Greaves | 60,000 | Waiters (5), Cohen (9), Thomson R (8), Mullery (1), Norman (23), **Flowers** (47), Thompson P (10), Greaves (42), Wignall (2), Venables (2), Charlton R (57) |

1965

Home International Championship

DATE	VENUE	OPPONENTS	SCORE	GOALSCORERS	ATTENDANCE	TEAM
Apr 10	Wembley, London	SCOTLAND	D 2-2	Charlton R, Greaves	98,199	Banks (15), Cohen (10), Wilson (31), Stiles (1), Charlton J (1), **Moore** (27), Thompson P (11), Greaves (43), Bridges (1), Byrne J (11), Charlton R (58)

Friendlies

DATE	VENUE	OPPONENTS	SCORE	GOALSCORERS	ATTENDANCE	TEAM
May 5	Wembley, London	HUNGARY	W 1-0	Greaves	70,000	Banks (16), Cohen (11), Wilson (32), Stiles (2), Charlton J (2), **Moore** (28), Paine (11), Greaves (44), Bridges (2), Eastham (14), Connelly (11)
May 9	Belgrade	YUGOSLAVIA	D 1-1	Bridges	70,000	Banks (17), Cohen (12), Wilson (33), Stiles (3), Charlton J (3), **Moore** (29), Paine (12), Greaves (45), Bridges (3), Ball (1), Connelly (12)
May 12	Nuremberg	W. GERMANY	W 1-0	Paine	70,000	Banks (18), Cohen (13), Wilson (34), Flowers (48), Charlton J (4), **Moore** (30), Paine (13), Ball (2), Jones M (1), Eastham (15), Temple (1)
May 16	Gothenburg	SWEDEN	W 2-1	Ball, Connelly	18,975	Banks (19), Cohen (14), Wilson (35), Stiles (4), Charlton J (5), **Moore** (31), Paine (14), Ball (3), Jones M (2), Eastham (16), Connelly (13)

Home International Championship

DATE	VENUE	OPPONENTS	SCORE	GOALSCORERS	ATTENDANCE	TEAM
Oct 2	Ninian Park, Cardiff	WALES	D 0-0		30,000	Springett (31), Cohen (15), Wilson (36), Stiles (5), Charlton J (6), **Moore** (32), Paine (15), Greaves (46), Peacock (5), Charlton R (59), Connelly (14)

Friendly

DATE	VENUE	OPPONENTS	SCORE	GOALSCORERS	ATTENDANCE	TEAM
Oct 20	Wembley, London	AUSTRIA	L 2-3	Charlton R, Connelly	65,000	Springett R (32), Cohen (16), Wilson (37), Stiles (6), Charlton J (7), **Moore** (33), Paine (16), Greaves (47), Bridges (4), Charlton R (60), Connelly (15)

Home International Championship

DATE	VENUE	OPPONENTS	SCORE	GOALSCORERS	ATTENDANCE	TEAM
Nov 10	Wembley, London	N. IRELAND	W 2-1	Baker, Peacock	70,000	Banks (20), Cohen (17), Wilson (38), Stiles (7), Charlton J (8), **Moore** (34), Thompson P (12), Baker (6), Peacock (6), Charlton R (61), Connelly (16)

Friendly

DATE	VENUE	OPPONENTS	SCORE	GOALSCORERS	ATTENDANCE	TEAM
Dec 8	Madrid	SPAIN	W 2-0	Baker, Hunt	30,000	Banks (21), Cohen (18), Wilson (39), Stiles (8), Charlton J (9), **Moore** (35), Ball (4), Hunt (7), Baker (7), (Hunter (1), Eastham (17), Charlton R (62)

1966

Friendlies

DATE	VENUE	OPPONENTS	SCORE	GOALSCORERS	ATTENDANCE	TEAM
Jan 5	Goodison Park, Liverpool	POLAND	D 1-1	Moore	47,839	Banks (22), Cohen (19), Wilson (40), Stiles (9), Charlton J (10), **Moore** (36), Ball (5), Hunt (8), Baker (8), Eastham (18), Harris G (1)
Feb 23	Wembley, London	W. GERMANY	W 1-0	Stiles	75,000	Banks (23), Cohen (20), Newton K (1), (Wilson 41), **Moore** (37), Charlton J (11), Hunter (2), Ball (6), Hunt (9), Stiles (10), Hurst (1), Charlton R (63)

Home International Championship

DATE	VENUE	OPPONENTS	SCORE	GOALSCORERS	ATTENDANCE	TEAM
Apr 2	Hampden Park, Glasgow	SCOTLAND	W 4-3	Hurst, Hunt 2, Charlton R	123,052	Banks (24), Cohen (21), Newton K (2), Stiles (11), Charlton J (12), **Moore** (38), Ball (7), Hunt (10), Charlton R (64), Hurst (2), Connelly (17)

Friendlies

DATE	VENUE	OPPONENTS	SCORE	GOALSCORERS	ATTENDANCE	TEAM
May 4	Wembley, London	YUGOSLAVIA	W 2-0	Greaves, Charlton R	55,000	Banks (25), **Armfield** (42), Wilson (42), Peters (1), Charlton J (13), Hunter (3), Paine (17), Greaves (48), Charlton R (65), Hurst (3), Tambling (3)
Jun 26	Helsinki	FINLAND	W 3-0	Peters, Hunt, Charlton J	12,899	Banks (26), **Armfield** (43), Wilson (43), Peters (2), Charlton J (14), Hunter (4), Callaghan (1), Hunt (11), Charlton R (66), Hurst (4), Ball (8)
Jun 29	Oslo	NORWAY	W 6-1	Greaves 4, Connelly, Moore	29,534	Springett R (33), Cohen (22), Byrne G (2), Stiles (12), Flowers (49), **Moore** (39), Paine (18), Greaves (49), Charlton R (67), Hunt (12), Connelly (18)
July 3	Copenhagen	DENMARK	W 2-0	Charlton J, Eastham	32,000	Bonetti (1), Cohen (23), Wilson (44), Stiles (13), Charlton J (15), **Moore** (40), Ball (9), Greaves (50), Hurst (5), Eastham (19), Connelly (19)
July 5	Chorzow	POLAND	W 1-0	Hunt	93,000	Banks (27), Cohen (24), Wilson (45), Stiles (14), Charlton J (16), **Moore** (41), Ball (10), Greaves (51), Charlton R (68), Hunt (13), Peters (3)

THE WORLD CUP FINALS 1966 (ENGLAND)

Group Stage – Group 1   England qualified as hosts

DATE	VENUE	OPPONENTS	SCORE	GOALSCORERS	ATTENDANCE	TEAM
Jul 11	Wembley, London	URUGUAY	D 0-0		87,148	Banks (28), Cohen (25), Wilson (46), Stiles (15), Charlton J (17), **Moore** (42), Ball (11), Greaves (52), Charlton R (69), Hunt (14), Connelly (20)
Jul 16	Wembley, London	MEXICO	W 2-0	Charlton R, Hunt	92,570	Banks (29), Cohen (26), Wilson (47), Stiles (16), Charlton J (18), **Moore** (43), Paine (19), Greaves (53), Charlton R (70), Hunt (15), Peters (4)
Jul 20	Wembley, London	FRANCE	W 2-0	Hunt 2	98,270	Banks (30), Cohen (27), Wilson (48), Stiles (17), Charlton J (19), **Moore** (44), Callaghan (2), Greaves (54), Charlton R (71), Hunt (16), Peters (5)

GROUP 1	P	W	D	L	F	A	Pts
ENGLAND	3	2	1	0	4	0	5
URUGUAY	3	1	2	0	2	1	4
MEXICO	3	0	2	1	1	3	2
FRANCE	3	0	1	2	2	5	1

Quarter-final

DATE	VENUE	OPPONENTS	SCORE	GOALSCORERS	ATTENDANCE	TEAM
Jul 23	Wembley, London	ARGENTINA	W 1-0	Hurst	90,584	Banks (31), Cohen (28), Wilson (49), Stiles (18), Charlton J (20), **Moore** (45), Ball (12), Hurst (6), Charlton R (72), Hunt (17), Peters (6)

Semi-final

DATE	VENUE	OPPONENTS	SCORE	GOALSCORERS	ATTENDANCE	TEAM
Jul 26	Wembley, London	PORTUGAL	W 2-1	Charlton R. 2	94,493	Banks (32), Cohen (29), Wilson (50), Stiles (19), Charlton J (21), **Moore** (46), Ball (13), Hurst (7), Charlton R (73), Hunt (18), Peters (7)

Final

DATE	VENUE	OPPONENTS	SCORE	GOALSCORERS	ATTENDANCE	TEAM
Jul 30	Wembley, London	W. GERMANY	W 4-2	Hurst 3, Peters	96,924	Banks (33), Cohen (30), Wilson (51), Stiles (20), Charlton J (22), **Moore** (47), Ball (14), Hurst (8), Charlton R (74), Hunt (19), Peters (8)

1966 (continued)

Home International Championship/European Nations Cup Qualifier

DATE	VENUE	OPPONENTS	SCORE	GOALSCORERS	ATTENDANCE	TEAM
Oct 22	Windsor Park, Belfast	N. IRELAND	W 2-0	Hunt, Peters	48,600	Banks (34), Cohen (31), Wilson (52), Stiles (21), Charlton J (23), **Moore** (48), Ball (15), Hurst (9), Charlton R (75), Hunt (20), Peters (9)

Friendly

DATE	VENUE	OPPONENTS	SCORE	GOALSCORERS	ATTENDANCE	TEAM
Nov 2	Wembley, London	CZECHOSLOVAKIA	D 0-0		75,000	Banks (35), Cohen (32), Wilson (53), Stiles (22), Charlton J (24), **Moore** (49), Ball (16), Hurst (10), Charlton R (76), Hunt (21), Peters (10)

Home International Championship/European Nations Cup Qualifier

DATE	VENUE	OPPONENTS	SCORE	GOALSCORERS	ATTENDANCE	TEAM
Nov 16	Wembley, London	WALES	W 5-1	Hurst 2, Charlton R, Charlton J, own goal	75,380	Banks (36), Cohen (33), Wilson (54), Stiles (23), Charlton J (25), **Moore** (50), Ball (17), Hurst (11), Charlton R (77), Hunt (22), Peters (11)

1967

Home International Championship/European Nations Cup Qualifiers

DATE	VENUE	OPPONENTS	SCORE	GOALSCORERS	ATTENDANCE	TEAM
Apr 15	Wembley, London	SCOTLAND	L 2-3	Charlton J, Hurst	99,063	Banks (37), Cohen (34), Wilson (55), Stiles (24), Charlton J (26), **Moore** (51), Ball (18), Greaves (55), Charlton R (78), Hurst (12), Peters (12)

1967 (continued)

Friendlies

DATE	VENUE	OPPONENTS	SCORE	GOALSCORERS	ATTENDANCE	TEAM
May 24	Wembley, London	SPAIN	W 2-0	Greaves, Hunt	97,500	Bonetti (2), Cohen (35), Newton K (3), Mullery (2), Labone (4), **Moore** (52), Ball (19), Greaves (56), Hurst (13), Hunt (23), Hollins (1)
May 27	Vienna	AUSTRIA	W 1-0	Ball	50,000	Bonetti (3), Newton K (4), Wilson (56), Mullery (3), Labone (5), **Moore** (53), Ball (20), Greaves (57), Hurst (14), Hunt (24), Hunter (5)

Home International Championship/European Nations Cup Qualifiers

DATE	VENUE	OPPONENTS	SCORE	GOALSCORERS	ATTENDANCE	TEAM
Oct 21	Ninian Park, Cardiff	WALES	W 3-0	Peters, Charlton R, Ball (pen)	44,960	Banks (38), Cohen (36), Newton K (5), Mullery (4), Charlton J (27), **Moore** (54), Ball (21), Hunt (25), Charlton R (79), Hurst (15), Peters (13)
Nov 22	Wembley, London	N. IRELAND	W 2-0	Hurst, Charlton R	85,000	Banks (39), Cohen (37), Wilson (57), Mullery (5), Sadler (1), **Moore** (55), Thompson P (13), Hunt (26), Charlton R (80), Hurst (16), Peters (14)

Friendly

DATE	VENUE	OPPONENTS	SCORE	GOALSCORERS	ATTENDANCE	TEAM
Dec 6	Wembley, London	USSR	D 2-2	Ball, Peters	93,000	Banks (40), Knowles (1), Wilson (58), Mullery (6), Sadler (2), **Moore** (56), Ball (22), Hunt (27), Charlton R (81), Hurst (17), Peters (15)

1968

Home International Championship/European Nations Cup Qualifier

DATE	VENUE	OPPONENTS	SCORE	GOALSCORERS	ATTENDANCE	TEAM
Feb 24	Hampden Park, Glasgow	SCOTLAND	D 1-1	Peters	134,000	Banks (41), Newton K (6), Wilson (59), Mullery (7), Labone (6), **Moore** (57), Ball (23), Hurst (18), Summerbee (1), Charlton R (82), Peters (16)

European Nations Cup Quarter-final

DATE	VENUE	OPPONENTS	SCORE	GOALSCORERS	ATTENDANCE	TEAM
Apr 3	Wembley, London	SPAIN	W 1-0	Charlton R	100,000	Banks (42), Knowles (2), Wilson (60), Mullery (8), Charlton J (28), **Moore** (58), Ball (24), Hunt (28), Summerbee (2), Charlton R (83), Peters (17)
May 8	Madrid	SPAIN	W 2-1	Peters, Hunter	120,000	Bonetti (4), Newton K (7), Wilson (61), Mullery (9), Labone (7), **Moore** (59), Ball (25), Peters (18), Charlton R (84), Hunt (29), Hunter (6)

Friendlies

DATE	VENUE	OPPONENTS	SCORE	GOALSCORERS	ATTENDANCE	TEAM
May 22	Wembley, London	SWEDEN	W 3-1	Peters, Charlton R, Hunt	72,500	Stepney (1), Newton K (8), Knowles (3), Mullery (10), Labone (8), **Moore** (60), Bell (1), Peters (19), Charlton R (85), (Hurst 19), Hunt (30), Hunter (7)
Jun 1	Hanover	W. GERMANY	L 0-1		79,124	Banks (43), Newton K (9), Knowles (4), Hunter (8), Labone (9), **Moore** (61), Ball (26), Bell (2), Summerbee (3), Hurst (20), Thompson P (14)

European Nations Cup Semi-final

DATE	VENUE	OPPONENTS	SCORE	GOALSCORERS	ATTENDANCE	TEAM
Jun 5	Florence	YUGOSLAVIA	L 0-1		60,000	Banks (44), Newton K (10), Wilson (62), *Mullery* (11), Labone (10), **Moore** (62), Ball (27), Peters (20), Charlton R (86), Hunt (31), Hunter (9)

European Nations Cup Third Place Match

DATE	VENUE	OPPONENTS	SCORE	GOALSCORERS	ATTENDANCE	TEAM
Jun 8	Rome	USSR	W 2-0	Charlton R, Hurst	80,000	Banks (45), Wright T (1), Wilson (63), Stiles (25), Labone (11), **Moore** (63), Hunter (10), Hunt (32), Charlton R (87), Hurst (21), Peters (21)

Friendlies

DATE	VENUE	OPPONENTS	SCORE	GOALSCORERS	ATTENDANCE	TEAM
Nov 6	Bucharest	ROMANIA	D 0-0		80,000	Banks (46), Wright T (2), (McNab 1), Newton K (11), Mullery (12), Labone (12), **Moore** (64), Ball (28), Hunt (33), Charlton R (88), Hurst (22), Peters (22)
Dec 11	Wembley, London	BULGARIA	D 1-1	Hurst	80,000	West (1), Newton K (12), (Reaney 1), McNab (2), Mullery (13), Labone (13), **Moore** (65), Lee F (1), Bell (3), Charlton R (89), Hurst (23), Peters (23)

1969

Friendlies

DATE	VENUE	OPPONENTS	SCORE	GOALSCORERS	ATTENDANCE	TEAM
Jan 15	Wembley, London	ROMANIA	D 1-1	Charlton J	80,000	Banks (47), Wright T (3), McNab (3), Stiles (26), Charlton J (29), Hunter (11), Radford (1), Hunt (34), **Charlton R** (90), Hurst (24), Ball (29)
Mar 12	Wembley, London	FRANCE	W 5-0	Hurst 3 (2 pens), O'Grady, Lee F	85,000	Banks (48), Newton K (13), Cooper (1), Mullery (14), Charlton J (30), **Moore** (66), Lee F (2), Bell (4), Hurst (25), Peters (24), O'Grady (2)

Home International Championship

DATE	VENUE	OPPONENTS	SCORE	GOALSCORERS	ATTENDANCE	TEAM
May 3	Windsor Park, Belfast	N. IRELAND	W 3-1	Peters, Lee F, Hurst (pen)	23,000	Banks (49), Newton K (14), McNab (4), Mullery (15), Labone (14), **Moore** (67), Ball (30), Lee F (3), Charlton R (91), Hurst (26), Peters (25)
May 7	Wembley, London	WALES	W 2-1	Charlton R, Lee F	70,000	West (2), Newton K (15), Cooper (2), **Moore** (68), Charlton J (31), Hunter (12), Lee F (4), Bell (5), Astle (1), Charlton R (92), Ball (31)
May 10	Wembley, London	SCOTLAND	W 4-1	Peters 2, Hurst 2 (1 pen)	89,902	Banks (50), Newton K (16), Cooper (3), Mullery (16), Labone (15), **Moore** (69), Lee F (5), Ball (32), Charlton R (93), Hurst (27), Peters (26)

Friendlies

DATE	VENUE	OPPONENTS	SCORE	GOALSCORERS	ATTENDANCE	TEAM
Jun 1	Mexico City	MEXICO	D 0-0		105,000	West (3), Newton K (17), (Wright T 4), Cooper (4), Mullery (17), Labone (16), **Moore** (70), Lee F (6), Ball (33), Charlton R (94), Hurst (28), Peters (27)
Jun 8	Montevideo	URUGUAY	W 2-1	Lee F, Hurst	54,161	Banks (51), Wright T (5), Newton K (18), Mullery (18), Labone (17), **Moore** (71), Lee F (7), Bell (6), Hurst (29), Ball (34), Peters (28)
Jun 12	Rio	BRAZIL	L 1-2	Bell	135,000	Banks (52), Wright T (6), Newton K (19), Mullery (19), Labone (18), **Moore** (72), Ball (35), Bell (7), Charlton R (95), Hurst (30), Peters (29)
Nov 5	Amsterdam	HOLLAND	W 1-0	Bell	33,000	Bonetti (5), Wright T (7), Hughes (1), Mullery (20), Charlton J (32), **Moore** (73), Lee F (8), (Thompson P 15), Bell (8), Charlton R (96), Hurst (31), Peters (30)
Dec 10	Wembley, London	PORTUGAL	W 1-0	Charlton J	100,000	Bonetti (6), Reaney (2), Hughes (2), Mullery (21), Charlton J (33), **Moore** (74), Lee F (9), Bell (9), (Peters 31), Astle (2), Charlton R (97), Ball (36)

1970

Friendlies

DATE	VENUE	OPPONENTS	SCORE	GOALSCORERS	ATTENDANCE	TEAM
Jan 14	Wembley	HOLLAND	D 0-0		75,000	Banks (53), Newton K (20), Cooper (5), Peters (32), Charlton J (34), Hunter (13), Lee F (10), (Mullery 22), Bell (10), Jones M (3), (Hurst 32), **Charlton R** (98), Moore (1)
Feb 25	Brussels	BELGIUM	W 3-1	Ball 2, Hurst	20,594	Banks (54), Wright T (8), Cooper (6), **Moore** (75), Labone (19), Hughes (3), Lee F (11), Ball (37), Osgood (1), Hurst (33), Peters (33)

Home International Championship

DATE	VENUE	OPPONENTS	SCORE	GOALSCORERS	ATTENDANCE	TEAM
Apr 18	Ninian Park, Cardiff	WALES	D 1-1	Lee F	50,000	Banks (55), Wright T (9), Hughes (4), Mullery (23), Labone (20), **Moore** (76), Lee F (12), Ball (38), Charlton R (99), Hurst (34), Peters (34)
Apr 21	Wembley	N. IRELAND	W 3-1	Peters, Hurst, Charlton R	100,000	Banks (56), Newton K (21), (Bell 11), Hughes (5), Mullery (24), Moore (77), Stiles (27), Coates (1), Kidd (1), **Charlton R** (100), Hurst (35), Peters (35)
Apr 25	Hampden Park, Glasgow	SCOTLAND	D 0-0		137,438	Banks (57), Newton K (22), Hughes (6), Stiles (28), Labone (21), **Moore** (78), Thompson P (16), (Mullery 25), Ball (39), Astle (3), Hurst (36), Peters (36)

Friendlies

DATE	VENUE	OPPONENTS	SCORE	GOALSCORERS	ATTENDANCE	TEAM
May 20	Bogota	COLOMBIA	W 4-0	Peters 2, Charlton R, Ball	36,000	Banks (58), Newton K (23), Cooper (7), Mullery (26), Labone (22), **Moore** (79), Lee F (13), Ball (40), Charlton R (101), Hurst (37), Peters (37)
May 24	Quito	ECUADOR	W 2-0	Lee F, Kidd	36,000	Banks (59), Newton K (24), Cooper (8), Mullery (27), Labone (23), **Moore** (80), Lee F (14), (Kidd 2), Ball (41), Charlton R (102), (Sadler 3), Hurst (38), Peters (38)

THE WORLD CUP FINALS 1970 (MEXICO)

Group Stage – Group 3

England qualified as holders

DATE	VENUE	OPPONENTS	SCORE	GOALSCORERS	ATTENDANCE	TEAM
Jun 2	Guadalajara	ROMANIA	W 1-0	Hurst	50,000	Banks (60), Newton K (25), (Wright T 10), Cooper (9), Mullery (28), Labone (24), **Moore** (81), Lee F (15), (Osgood 2), Ball (42), Charlton R (103), Hurst (39), Peters (39)
Jun 7	Guadalajara	BRAZIL	L 0-1		70,950	Banks (61), Wright T (11), Cooper (10), Mullery (29), Labone (25), **Moore** (82), Lee F (16), (Astle 4), Ball (43), Charlton R (104), (Bell 12), Hurst (40), Peters (40)
Jun 11	Guadalajara	CZECHOSLOVAKIA	W 1-0	Clarke A (pen)	49,000	Banks (62), Newton K (26), Cooper (11), Mullery (30), Charlton J (35), **Moore** (83), Bell (13), Charlton R (105), (Ball 44), Astle (5), (Osgood 3), Clarke A (1), Peters (41)

Quarter-final

DATE	VENUE	OPPONENTS	SCORE	GOALSCORERS	ATTENDANCE	TEAM
Jun 14	Leon	W. GERMANY	L 2-3	Mullery, Peters	32,000	Bonetti (7), Newton K (27), Cooper (12), Mullery (31), Labone (26), **Moore** (84), Lee F (17), Ball (45), Charlton R (106), (Bell 14), Hurst (41), Peters (42), (Hunter 14)

Group 3

	P	W	D	L	F	A	Pts
BRAZIL	3	3	0	0	8	3	6
ENGLAND	3	2	0	1	2	1	4
ROMANIA	3	1	0	2	4	5	2
CZECHOSLOVAKIA	3	0	0	3	2	7	0

1970 (continued)

Friendly

DATE	VENUE	OPPONENTS	SCORE	GOALSCORERS	ATTENDANCE	TEAM
Nov 25	Wembley, London	E. GERMANY	W 3-1	Lee F, Peters, Clarke A	93,000	Shilton (1), Hughes (7), Cooper (13), Mullery (32), Sadler (4), **Moore** (85), Lee F (18), Ball (46), Hurst (42), Clarke A (2), Peters (43)

1971

European Championship Qualifiers

DATE	VENUE	OPPONENTS	SCORE	GOALSCORERS	ATTENDANCE	TEAM
Feb 3	Valletta	MALTA	W 1-0	Peters	29,751	Banks (63), Reaney (3), Hughes (8), **Mullery** (33), McFarland (1), Hunter (15), Ball (47), Chivers (1), Royle (1), Harvey (1), Peters (44)
Apr 21	Wembley, London	GREECE	W 3-0	Chivers, Hurst, Lee F	55,123	Banks (64), Storey (1), Hughes (9), Mullery (34), McFarland (2), **Moore** (86), Lee F (19), Ball (48), (Coates 2), Chivers (2), Hurst (43), Peters (45)
May 12	Wembley, London	MALTA	W 5-0	Chivers 2, Lee F, Clarke A (pen), Lawler	41,534	Banks (65), Lawler (1), Cooper (14), **Moore** (87), McFarland (3), Hughes (10), Lee F (20), Coates (3), Chivers (3), Clarke A (3), Peters (46), (Ball 49)

Home International Championship

DATE	VENUE	OPPONENTS	SCORE	GOALSCORERS	ATTENDANCE	TEAM
May 15	Windsor Park, Belfast	N. IRELAND	W 1-0	Clarke A	33,000	Banks (66), Madeley (1), Cooper (15), Storey (2), McFarland (4), **Moore** (88), Lee F (21), Ball (50), Chivers (4), Clarke A (4), Peters (47)
May 19	Wembley, London	WALES	D 0-0		70,000	Shilton (2), Lawler (2), Cooper (16), Smith (1), Lloyd (1), Hughes (11), Lee F (22), Coates (4), (Clarke A 5), Hurst (44), Brown A (1), **Peters** (48)
May 22	Wembley, London	SCOTLAND	W 3-1	Peters, Chivers 2	91,469	Banks (67), Lawler (3), Cooper (17), Storey (3), McFarland (5), **Moore** (89), Lee F (23), (Clarke A 6), Ball (51), Chivers (5), Hurst (45), Peters (49)

European Championship Qualifiers

DATE	VENUE	OPPONENTS	SCORE	GOALSCORERS	ATTENDANCE	TEAM
Oct 13	Basle	SWITZERLAND	W 3-2	Hurst, Chivers, own goal	47,877	Banks (68), Lawler (4), Cooper (18), Mullery (35), McFarland (6), **Moore** (90), Lee F (24), Madeley (2), Chivers (6), Hurst (46), (Radford 2), Peters (50)
Nov 10	Wembley, London	SWITZERLAND	D 1-1	Summerbee	90,423	Shilton (3), Madeley (3), Cooper (19), Storey (4), Lloyd (2), **Moore** (91), Summerbee (4), (Chivers 7), Ball (52), Hurst (47), Lee F (25), (Marsh 1), Hughes (12)
Dec 1	Piraeus	GREECE	W 2-0	Hurst, Chivers	34,014	Banks (69), Madeley (4), Hughes (13), Bell (15), McFarland (7), **Moore** (92), Lee F (26), Ball (53), Chivers (8), Hurst (48), Peters (51)

1972

European Championship Qualifiers

DATE	VENUE	OPPONENTS	SCORE	GOALSCORERS	ATTENDANCE	TEAM
Apr 29	Wembley, London	W. GERMANY	L 1-3	Lee F	100,000	Banks (70), Madeley (5), Hughes (14), Bell (16), **Moore** (93), Hunter (16), Lee F (27), Ball (54), Chivers (9), Hurst (49), (Marsh 2), Peters (52)
May 13	Berlin	W. GERMANY	D 0-0		76,200	Banks (71), Madeley (6), Hughes (15), Storey (5), McFarland (8), **Moore** (94), Ball (55), Bell (17), Chivers (10), Marsh (3), (Summerbee 5), Hunter (17), (Peters 53)

Home International Championship

DATE	VENUE	OPPONENTS	SCORE	GOALSCORERS	ATTENDANCE	TEAM
May 20	Ninian Park, Cardiff	WALES	W 3-0	Hughes, Bell, Marsh	34,000	Banks (72), Madeley (7), Hughes (16), Storey (6), McFarland (9), **Moore** (95), Summerbee (6), Bell (18), Macdonald (1), Marsh (4), Hunter (18)
May 23	Wembley, London	N. IRELAND	L 0-1		64,000	Shilton (4), Todd (1), Hughes (17), Storey (7), Lloyd (3), Hunter (19), Summerbee (7), **Bell** (19), Macdonald (2), (Chivers 11), Marsh (5), Currie (1), (Peters 54)
May 27	Hampden Park, Glasgow	SCOTLAND	W 1-0	Ball	119,325	Banks (73), Madeley (8), Hughes (18), Storey (8), McFarland (10), **Moore** (96), Ball (56), Bell (20), Chivers (12), Marsh (6), (Macdonald 3), Hunter (20)

Friendly

DATE	VENUE	OPPONENTS	SCORE	GOALSCORERS	ATTENDANCE	TEAM
Oct 11	Wembley, London	YUGOSLAVIA	D 1-1	Royle	50,000	Shilton (5), Mills (1), Lampard (1), Storey (9), Blockley (1), **Moore** (97), Ball (57), Channon (1), Royle (2), Bell (21), Marsh (7)

World Cup Qualifier

DATE	VENUE	OPPONENTS	SCORE	GOALSCORERS	ATTENDANCE	TEAM
Nov 15	Ninian Park, Cardiff	WALES	W 1-0	Bell	36,384	Clemence (1), Storey (10), Hughes (19), Hunter (21), McFarland (11), **Moore** (98), Keegan (1), Marsh (8), Chivers (13), Bell (22), Ball (58)

1973

World Cup Qualifier

DATE	VENUE	OPPONENTS	SCORE	GOALSCORERS	ATTENDANCE	TEAM
Jan 24	Wembley, London	WALES	D 1-1	Hunter	62,273	Clemence (2), Storey (11), Hughes (20), Hunter (22), McFarland (12), **Moore** (99), Keegan (2), Bell (23), Chivers (14), Marsh (9), Ball (59)

Friendly

DATE	VENUE	OPPONENTS	SCORE	GOALSCORERS	ATTENDANCE	TEAM
Feb 14	Hampden Park, Glasgow	SCOTLAND	W 5-0	Clarke A 2, Channon, Chivers, own goal	48,470	Shilton (6), Storey (12), Hughes (21), Bell (24), Madeley (9), **Moore** (100), Ball (60), Channon (2), Chivers (15), Clarke A (7), Peters (55)

Home International Championship

DATE	VENUE	OPPONENTS	SCORE	GOALSCORERS	ATTENDANCE	TEAM
May 12	Goodison Park, Liverpool	N. IRELAND	W 2-1	Chivers 2	29,865	Shilton (7), Storey (13), Nish (1), Bell (25), McFarland (13), **Moore** (101), Ball (61), Channon (3), Chivers (16), Richards (1), Peters (56)
May 15	Wembley, London	WALES	W 3-0	Chivers, Channon, Peters	38,000	Shilton (8), Storey (14), Hughes (22), Bell (26), McFarland (14), **Moore** (102), Ball (62), Channon (4), Chivers (17), Clarke A (8), Peters (57)
May 19	Wembley, London	SCOTLAND	W 1-0	Peters	95,950	Shilton (9), Storey (15), Hughes (23), Bell (27), McFarland (15), **Moore** (103), Ball (63), Channon (5), Chivers (18), Clarke A (9), Peters (58)

Friendly

DATE	VENUE	OPPONENTS	SCORE	GOALSCORERS	ATTENDANCE	TEAM
May 27	Prague	CZECHOSLOVAKIA	D 1-1	Clarke A	25,000	Shilton (10), Madeley (10), Storey (16), Bell (28), McFarland (16), **Moore** (104), Ball (64), Channon (6), Chivers (19), Clarke A (10), Peters (59)

World Cup Qualifier

DATE	VENUE	OPPONENTS	SCORE	GOALSCORERS	ATTENDANCE	TEAM
Jun 6	Chorzow	POLAND	L 0-2		73,714	Shilton (11), Madeley (11), Hughes (24), Storey (17), McFarland (17), **Moore** (105), *Ball* (65), Bell (29), Chivers (20), Clarke A (11), Peters (60)

Friendlies

DATE	VENUE	OPPONENTS	SCORE	GOALSCORERS	ATTENDANCE	TEAM
Jun 10	Moscow	USSR	W 2-1	Chivers, own goal	85,000	Shilton (12), Madeley (12), Hughes (25), Storey (18), McFarland (18), **Moore** (106), Currie (2), Channon (7), (Summerbee 8), Chivers (21), Clarke A (12), (Macdonald 4), Peters (61), (Hunter 23)
Jun 14	Turin	ITALY	L 0-2		60,000	Shilton (13), Madeley (13), Hughes (26), Storey (19), McFarland (19), **Moore** (107), Currie (3), Channon (8), Chivers (22), Clarke A (13), Peters (62)

1973 (continued)

Friendly

DATE	VENUE	OPPONENTS	SCORE	GOALSCORERS	ATTENDANCE	TEAM
Sep 26	Wembley, London	AUSTRIA	W 7-0	Channon 2, Clarke A 2, Chivers, Currie, Bell	48,000	Shilton (14), Madeley (14), Hughes (27), Bell (30), McFarland (20), Hunter (24), Currie (4), Channon (9), Chivers (23), Clarke A (14), **Peters** (63)

World Cup Qualifier

Oct 17	Wembley, London	POLAND	D 1-1	Clarke A (pen)	100,000	Shilton (15), Madeley (15), Hughes (28), Bell (31), McFarland (21), Hunter (25), Currie (5), Channon (10), Chivers (24), (Hector 1), Clarke A (15), **Peters** (64)

Friendly

Nov 14	Wembley, London	ITALY	L 0-1		88,000	Shilton (16), Madeley (16), Hughes (29), Bell (32), McFarland (22), **Moore** (108), Currie (6), Channon (11), Osgood (4), Clarke A (16), (Hector 2), Peters (65)

1974

Friendly

DATE	VENUE	OPPONENTS	SCORE	GOALSCORERS	ATTENDANCE	TEAM
Apr 3	Lisbon	PORTUGAL	D 0-0		20,000	Parkes (1), Nish (2), Pejic (1), Dobson (1), Watson (1), Todd (2), Bowles (1), Channon (12), Macdonald (5), (Ball 66), Brooking (1), **Peters** (66)

(CARETAKER-MANAGER: JOE MERCER)

Home International Championship

May 11	Ninian Park, Cardiff	WALES	W 2-0	Bowles, Keegan	25,734	Shilton (17), Nish (3), Pejic (2), **Hughes** (30), McFarland (23), Todd (3), Keegan (3), Bell (33), Channon (13), Weller (1), Bowles (2)
May 15	Wembley, London	N. IRELAND	W 1-0	Weller	45,500	Shilton (18), Nish (4), Pejic (3), **Hughes** (31), McFarland (24), (Hunter 26), Todd (4), Keegan (4), Weller (2), Channon (14), Bell (34), Bowles (3), (Worthington 1),
May 18	Hampden Park, Glasgow	SCOTLAND	L 0-2		94,487	Shilton (19), Nish (5), Pejic (4), **Hughes** (32), Hunter (27), (Watson 2), Todd (5), Channon (15), Bell (35), Worthington (2), (Macdonald 6), Weller (3), Peters (67)

Friendlies

May 22	Wembley, London	ARGENTINA	D 2-2	Channon, Worthington	68,000	Shilton (20), **Hughes** (33), Lindsay (1), Todd (6), Watson (3), Bell (36), Keegan (5), Channon (16), Worthington (3), Weller (4), Brooking (2)
May 29	Leipzig	E. GERMANY	D 1-1	Channon	95,000	Clemence (3), **Hughes** (34), Lindsay (2), Todd (7), Watson (4), Dobson (2), Keegan (6), Channon (17), Worthington (4), Bell (37), Brooking (3)
Jun 1	Sofia	BULGARIA	W 1-0	Worthington	60,000	Clemence (4), **Hughes** (35), Lindsay (3), Todd (8), Watson (5), Dobson (3), Keegan (7), Channon (18), Worthington (5), Bell (38), Brooking (4)
Jun 5	Belgrade	YUGOSLAVIA	D 2-2	Channon, Keegan	90,000	Clemence (5), **Hughes** (36), Lindsay (4), Todd (9), Watson (6), Dobson (4), Keegan (8), Channon (19), Worthington (6), (Macdonald 7), Bell (39), Brooking (5)

MANAGER CHANGED TO: DON REVIE

European Championship Qualifiers

Oct 30	Wembley, London	CZECHOSLOVAKIA	W 3-0	Channon, Bell 2	83,858	Clemence (6), Madeley (17), **Hughes** (37), Dobson (5), (Brooking 6), Watson (7), Hunter (28), Bell (40), Francis G (1), Worthington (7), (Thomas 1), Channon (20), Keegan (9)
Nov 20	Wembley, London	PORTUGAL	D 0-0		84,461	Clemence (7), Madeley (18), Cooper (20), (Todd 10), **Hughes** (38), Watson (8), Brooking (7), Bell (41), Francis G (2), Channon (21), Clarke A (17), (Worthington 8), Thomas (2)

1975

Friendly

DATE	VENUE	OPPONENTS	SCORE	GOALSCORERS	ATTENDANCE	TEAM
Mar 12	Wembley, London	W. GERMANY	W 2-0	Bell, Macdonald	100,000	Clemence (8), Whitworth (1), Gillard (1), Bell (42), Watson (9), Todd (11), **Ball** (67), Macdonald (8), Channon (22), Hudson (1), Keegan (10)

European Championship Qualifiers

Apr 16	Wembley, London	CYPRUS	W 5-0	Macdonald 5	68,245	Shilton (21), Madeley (19), Beattie (1), Todd (12), Watson (10), Bell (43), **Ball** (68), Macdonald (9), Channon (23), (Thomas 3), Hudson (2), Keegan (11)

1975 (continued)

European Championship Qualifiers

DATE	VENUE	OPPONENTS	SCORE	GOALSCORERS	ATTENDANCE	TEAM
May 11	Limassol	CYPRUS	W 1-0	Keegan	16,200	Clemence (9), Whitworth (2), Beattie (2), (Hughes 39), Todd (13), Watson (11), Bell (44), Thomas (4), (Tueart 1), Macdonald (10), Channon (24), **Ball** (69), Keegan (12)

Home International Championship

DATE	VENUE	OPPONENTS	SCORE	GOALSCORERS	ATTENDANCE	TEAM
May 17	Windsor Park, Belfast	N. IRELAND	D 0-0		36,500	Clemence (10), Whitworth (3), Hughes (40), Todd (14), Watson (12), Bell (45), **Ball** (70), Viljoen (1), Macdonald (11), (Channon 25), Keegan (13), Tueart (2)
May 21	Wembley, London	WALES	D 2-2	Johnson 2	53,000	Clemence (11), Whitworth (4), Gillard (2), Francis G (3), Watson (13), Todd (15), **Ball** (71), Channon (26), (Little 1), Johnson (1), Viljoen (2), Thomas (5)
May 24	Wembley, London	SCOTLAND	W 5-1	Francis G 2, Beattie, Bell, Johnson	98,241	Clemence (12), Whitworth (5), Beattie (3), Bell (46), Watson (14), Todd (16), **Ball** (72), Channon (27), Johnson (2), Francis G (4), Keegan (14), (Thomas 6)

Friendly

DATE	VENUE	OPPONENTS	SCORE	GOALSCORERS	ATTENDANCE	TEAM
Sep 3	Basle	SWITZERLAND	W 2-1	Keegan, Channon	30,000	Clemence (13), Whitworth (6), Beattie (4), Bell (47), Watson (15), Todd (17), Currie (7), Channon (28), Johnson (3), (Macdonald 12), **Francis G** (5), Keegan (15)

European Championship Qualifiers

DATE	VENUE	OPPONENTS	SCORE	GOALSCORERS	ATTENDANCE	TEAM
Oct 30	Bratislava	CZECHOSLOVAKIA	L 1-2	Channon	50,651	Clemence (14), Madeley (20), Gillard (3), **Francis G** (6), McFarland (25), (Watson 16), Todd (18), Keegan (16), Channon (29), (Thomas 7), Macdonald (13), Clarke A (18), Bell (48)
Nov 19	Lisbon	PORTUGAL	D 1-1	Channon	60,000	Clemence (15), Whitworth (7), Beattie (5), **Francis G** (7), Watson (17), Todd (19), Keegan (17), Channon (30), Macdonald (14), (Thomas 8), Brooking (8), Madeley (21), (Clarke A 19)

1976

Friendly

DATE	VENUE	OPPONENTS	SCORE	GOALSCORERS	ATTENDANCE	TEAM
Mar 24	Racecourse Ground, Wrexham	WALES	W 2-1	Kennedy, Taylor	20,927	Clemence (16), Cherry (1), (Clement 1), Mills (2), Neal (1), Thompson (1), Doyle (1), **Keegan** (18), Channon (31), (Taylor 1), Boyer (1), Brooking (9), Kennedy (1)

Home International Championship

DATE	VENUE	OPPONENTS	SCORE	GOALSCORERS	ATTENDANCE	TEAM
May 8	Ninian Park, Cardiff	WALES	W 1-0	Taylor	24,592	Clemence (17), Clement (2), Mills (3), Towers (1), Greenhoff (1), Thompson (2), Keegan (19), **Francis G** (8), Pearson (1), Kennedy (2), Taylor (2)
May 11	Wembley, London	N. IRELAND	W 4-0	Francis G, Channon 2 (1 pen), Pearson	48,000	Clemence (18), Todd (20), Mills (4), Thompson (3), Greenhoff (2), Kennedy (3), Keegan (20), (Royle 3), **Francis G** (9), Pearson (2), Channon (32), Taylor (3), (Towers 2)
May 15	Hampden Park, Glasgow	SCOTLAND	L 1-2	Channon	85,165	Clemence (19), Todd (21), Mills (5), Thompson (4), McFarland (26), (Doyle 2), Kennedy (4), Keegan (21), **Francis G** (10), Pearson (3), (Cherry 2), Channon (33), Taylor (4)

US Bicentennial Tournament

DATE	VENUE	OPPONENTS	SCORE	GOALSCORERS	ATTENDANCE	TEAM
May 23	Los Angeles	BRAZIL	L 0-1		32,900	Clemence (20), Todd (22), Mills (6), Thompson (5), Doyle (3), Cherry (3), Keegan (22), Brooking (10), Pearson (4), **Francis G** (11), Channon (34)
May 28	New York	ITALY	W 3-2	Channon 2, Thompson	40,650	Rimmer (1), (Corrigan 1), Clement (3), Neal (2), (Mills 7), Thompson (6), Doyle (4), Towers (3), Wilkins (1), **Channon** (35), Royle (4), Brooking (11), Hill (1)

World Cup Qualifier

DATE	VENUE	OPPONENTS	SCORE	GOALSCORERS	ATTENDANCE	TEAM
Jun 13	Helsinki	FINLAND	W 4-1	Keegan 2, Channon, Pearson	24,336	Clemence (21), Todd (23), Mills (8), Thompson (7), Madeley (22), Cherry (4), Keegan (23), Channon (36), Pearson (5), Brooking (12), **Francis G** (12)

Friendly

DATE	VENUE	OPPONENTS	SCORE	GOALSCORERS	ATTENDANCE	TEAM
Sep 8	Wembley, London	R. of IRELAND	D 1-1	Pearson	51,000	Clemence (22), Todd (24), Madeley (23), Greenhoff (3), McFarland (27), Cherry (5), **Keegan** (24), Wilkins (2), Pearson (6), Brooking (13), George (1), (Hill 2)

World Cup Qualifiers

DATE	VENUE	OPPONENTS	SCORE	GOALSCORERS	ATTENDANCE	TEAM
Oct 13	Wembley, London	FINLAND	W 2-1	Tueart, Royle	92,000	Clemence (23), Todd (25), Beattie (6), Thompson (8), Greenhoff (4), Wilkins (3), **Keegan** (25), Channon (37), Royle (5), Brooking (14), (Mills 9), Tueart (3), (Hill 3)
Nov 17	Rome	ITALY	L 0-2		70,718	Clemence (24), Clement (4), (Beattie 7), Mills (10), Greenhoff (5), McFarland (28), Hughes (41), **Keegan** (26), Cherry (6), Channon (38), Bowles (4), Brooking (15)

1977

Friendly

DATE	VENUE	OPPONENTS	SCORE	GOALSCORERS	ATTENDANCE	TEAM
Feb 9	Wembley, London	HOLLAND	L 0-2		90,260	Clemence (25), Clement (5), Beattie (8), Doyle (5), Watson (18), Madeley (24), (Pearson 7), **Keegan** (27), Greenhoff (6), (Todd 26), Francis T (1), Bowles (5), Brooking (16)

World Cup Qualifier

DATE	VENUE	OPPONENTS	SCORE	GOALSCORERS	ATTENDANCE	TEAM
Mar 30	Wembley, London	LUXEMBOURG	W 5-0	Keegan, Francis T, Kennedy, Channon 2 (1 pen)	81,718	Clemence (26), Gidman (1), Cherry (7), Kennedy (5), Watson (19), Hughes (42), **Keegan** (28), Channon (39), Royle (6), (Mariner 1), Francis T (2), Hill (4)

Home International Championship

DATE	VENUE	OPPONENTS	SCORE	GOALSCORERS	ATTENDANCE	TEAM
May 28	Windsor Park Belfast	N. IRELAND	W 2-1	Channon, Tueart	35,000	Shilton (22), Cherry (8), Mills (11), Greenhoff (7), Watson (20), Todd (27), Wilkins (4), (Talbot 1), **Channon** (40), Mariner (2), Brooking (17), Tueart (4)
May 31	Wembley, London	WALES	L 0-1		48,000	Shilton (23), Neal (3), Mills (12), Greenhoff (8), Watson (21), Hughes (43), **Keegan** (29), Channon (41), Pearson (8), Brooking (18), (Tueart 5), Kennedy (6)
Jun 4	Wembley, London	SCOTLAND	L 1-2	Channon (pen)	98,103	Clemence (27), Neal (4), Mills (13), Greenhoff (9), (Cherry 9), Watson (22), **Hughes** (44), Francis T (3), Channon (42), Pearson (9), Talbot (2), Kennedy (7), (Tueart 6)

Friendlies

DATE	VENUE	OPPONENTS	SCORE	GOALSCORERS	ATTENDANCE	TEAM
Jun 8	Rio	BRAZIL	D 0-0		77,000	Clemence (28), Neal (5), Cherry (10), Greenhoff (10), Watson (23), Hughes (45), **Keegan** (30), Francis T (4), Pearson (10), (Channon 43), Wilkins (5), (Kennedy 8), Talbot (3)
Jun 12	Buenos Aires	ARGENTINA	D 1-1	Pearson	60,000	Clemence (29), Neal (6), *Cherry* (11), Greenhoff (11), (Kennedy 9), Watson (24), Hughes (46), **Keegan** (31), Channon (44), Pearson (11), Wilkins (6), Talbot (4)
Jun 15	Montevideo	URUGUAY	D 0-0		25,000	Clemence (30), Neal (7), Cherry (12), Greenhoff (12), Watson (25), Hughes (47), **Keegan** (32), Channon (45), Pearson (12), Wilkins (7), Talbot (5)

MANAGER CHANGED TO: RON GREENWOOD

DATE	VENUE	OPPONENTS	SCORE	GOALSCORERS	ATTENDANCE	TEAM
Sep 7	Wembley, London	SWITZERLAND	D 0-0		42,000	Clemence (31), Neal (8), Cherry (13), McDermott (1), Watson (26), **Hughes** (48), Keegan (33), Channon (46), (Hill 5), Francis T (5), Kennedy (10), Callaghan (3), (Wilkins 8)

World Cup Qualifiers

DATE	VENUE	OPPONENTS	SCORE	GOALSCORERS	ATTENDANCE	TEAM
Oct 12	Luxembourg	LUXEMBOURG	W 2-0	Kennedy, Mariner	10,621	Clemence (32), Cherry (14), **Hughes** (49), McDermott (2), (Whymark 1), Watson (27), (Beattie 9), Kennedy (11), Wilkins (9), Francis T (6), Mariner (3), Hill (6), Callaghan (4)
Nov 16	Wembley, London	ITALY	W 2-0	Keegan, Brooking	92,000	Clemence (33), Neal (9), Cherry (15), Wilkins (10), Watson (28), **Hughes** (50), Keegan (34), (Francis T 7), Coppell (1), Latchford (1), (Pearson 13), Brooking (19), Barnes (1)

1978

Friendlies

DATE	VENUE	OPPONENTS	SCORE	GOALSCORERS	ATTENDANCE	TEAM
Feb 22	Munich	W. GERMANY	L 1-2	Pearson	77,850	Clemence (34), Neal (10), Mills (14), Wilkins (11), Watson (29), **Hughes** (51), Keegan (35), (Francis T 8), Coppell (2), Pearson (14), Brooking (20), Barnes (2)
Apr 19	Wembley, London	BRAZIL	D 1-1	Keegan	92,500	Corrigan (2), Mills (15), Cherry (16), Greenhoff (13), Watson (30), Currie (8), **Keegan** (36), Coppell (3), Latchford (2), Francis T (9), Barnes (3)

Home International Championship

DATE	VENUE	OPPONENTS	SCORE	GOALSCORERS	ATTENDANCE	TEAM
May 13	Ninian Park, Cardiff	WALES	W 3-1	Latchford, Currie, Barnes	17,698	Shilton (24), **Mills** (16), Cherry (17), (Currie 9), Greenhoff (14), Watson (31), Wilkins (12), Coppell (4), Francis T (10), Latchford (3), (Mariner 4), Brooking (21), Barnes (4)
May 16	Wembley, London	N. IRELAND	W 1-0	Neal	55,000	Clemence (35), Neal (11), Mills (17), Wilkins (13), Watson (32), **Hughes** (52), Currie (10), Coppell (5), Pearson (15), Woodcock (1), Greenhoff (15)
May 20	Hampden Park, Glasgow	SCOTLAND	W 1-0	Coppell	88,319	Clemence (36), Neal (12), Mills (18), Currie (11), Watson (33), **Hughes** (53), (Greenhoff 16), Wilkins (14), Coppell (6), Mariner (5), (Brooking 22), Francis T (11), Barnes (5)

1978 (continued)

Friendly

DATE	VENUE	OPPONENTS	SCORE	GOALSCORERS	ATTENDANCE	TEAM
May 24	Wembley, London	HUNGARY	W 4-1	Barnes, Neal (pen), Francis T, Currie	75,000	Shilton (25), Neal (13), Mills (19), Wilkins (15), Watson (34), (Greenhoff 17), **Hughes** (54), Keegan (37), Coppell (7), Francis T (12), Brooking (23), (Currie 12), Barnes (6)

European Championship Qualifiers

DATE	VENUE	OPPONENTS	SCORE	GOALSCORERS	ATTENDANCE	TEAM
Sep 20	Copenhagen	DENMARK	W 4-3	Keegan 2, Neal, Latchford	47,600	Clemence (37), Neal (14), Mills (20), Wilkins (16), Watson (35), **Hughes** (55), Keegan (38), Coppell (8), Latchford (4), Brooking (24), Barnes (7)
Oct 25	Lansdowne Road, Dublin	R. of IRELAND	D 1-1	Latchford	55,000	Clemence (38), Neal (15), Mills (21), Wilkins (17), Watson (36), (Thompson 9), **Hughes** (56), Keegan (39), Coppell (9), Latchford (5), Brooking (25), Barnes (8), (Woodcock 2)

Friendly

DATE	VENUE	OPPONENTS	SCORE	GOALSCORERS	ATTENDANCE	TEAM
Nov 29	Wembley, London	CZECHOSLOVAKIA	W 1-0	Coppell	92,000	Shilton (26), Anderson (1), Cherry (18), Thompson (10), Watson (37), Wilkins (18), **Keegan** (40), Coppell (10), Woodcock (3), (Latchford 6), Currie (13), Barnes (9)

1979

European Championship Qualifier

DATE	VENUE	OPPONENTS	SCORE	GOALSCORERS	ATTENDANCE	TEAM
Feb 7	Wembley, London	N. IRELAND	W 4-0	Keegan, Latchford 2, Watson	92,000	Clemence (39), Neal (16), Mills (22), Currie (14), Watson (38), **Hughes** (57), Keegan (41), Coppell (11), Latchford (7), Brooking (26), Barnes (10)

Home International Championship

DATE	VENUE	OPPONENTS	SCORE	GOALSCORERS	ATTENDANCE	TEAM
May 19	Windsor Park, Belfast	N. IRELAND	W 2-0	Watson, Coppell	35,000	Clemence (40), Neal (17), **Mills** (23), Thompson (11), Watson (39), Currie (15), Coppell (12), Wilkins (19), Latchford (8), McDermott (3), Barnes (11)
May 23	Wembley, London	WALES	D 0-0		70,220	Corrigan (3), Cherry (19), Sansom (1), Currie (16), Watson (40), **Hughes** (58), Keegan (42), (Coppell 13), Wilkins (20), (Brooking 27), Latchford (9), McDermott (4), Cunningham (1)
May 26	Wembley, London	SCOTLAND	W 3-1	Barnes, Coppell, Keegan	100,000	Clemence (41), Neal (18), Mills (24), Thompson (12), Watson (41), Wilkins (21), **Keegan** (43), Coppell (14), Latchford (10), Brooking (28), Barnes (12)

European Championship Qualifier

DATE	VENUE	OPPONENTS	SCORE	GOALSCORERS	ATTENDANCE	TEAM
Jun 6	Sofia	BULGARIA	W 3-0	Keegan, Watson, Barnes	47,500	Clemence (42), Neal (19), Mills (25), Thompson (13), Watson (42), Wilkins (22), **Keegan** (44), Coppell (15), Latchford (11), (Francis T 13), Brooking (29), Barnes (13), (Woodcock 4)

Friendlies

DATE	VENUE	OPPONENTS	SCORE	GOALSCORERS	ATTENDANCE	TEAM
Jun 10	Stockholm	SWEDEN	D 0-0		35,691	Shilton (27), Anderson (2), Cherry (20), McDermott (5), (Wilkins 23), Watson (43), (Thompson 14), **Hughes** (59), Keegan (45), Francis T (14), (Brooking 30), Woodcock (5), Currie (17), Cunningham (2)
Jun 13	Vienna	AUSTRIA	L 3-4	Keegan, Coppell, Wilkins	60,000	Shilton (28), (Clemence 43), Neal (20), Mills (26), Thompson (15), Watson (44), Wilkins (24), **Keegan** (46), Coppell (16), Latchford (12), (Francis T 15), Brooking (31), Barnes (14), (Cunningham 3)

European Championship Qualifiers

DATE	VENUE	OPPONENTS	SCORE	GOALSCORERS	ATTENDANCE	TEAM
Sep 12	Wembley, London	DENMARK	W 1-0	Keegan	85,000	Clemence (44), Neal (21), Mills (27), Thompson (16), Watson (45), Wilkins (25), McDermott (6), Coppell (17), **Keegan** (47), Brooking (32), Barnes (15)
Oct 17	Windsor Park, Belfast	N. IRELAND	W 5-1	Francis T 2, Woodcock 2, own goal	25,000	Shilton (29), Neal (22), Mills (28), Thompson (17), Watson (46), Wilkins (26), **Keegan** (48), Coppell (18), Francis T (16), Brooking (33), (McDermott 7), Woodcock (6)
Nov 22	Wembley, London	BULGARIA	W 2-0	Watson, Hoddle	71,491	Clemence (45), Anderson (3), Sansom (2), **Thompson** (18), Watson (47), Wilkins (27), Reeves (1), Hoddle (1), Francis T (17), Kennedy (12), Woodcock (7)

1980

European Championship Qualifiers

DATE	VENUE	OPPONENTS	SCORE	GOALSCORERS	ATTENDANCE	TEAM
Feb 6	Wembley, London	R. of IRELAND	W 2-0	Keegan 2	90,299	Clemence (46), Cherry (21), Sansom (3), Thompson (19), Watson (48), Robson (1), Keegan (49), McDermott (8), Johnson (4), (Coppell 19), Woodcock (8), Cunningham (4)

Friendlies

DATE	VENUE	OPPONENTS	SCORE	GOALSCORERS	ATTENDANCE	TEAM
Mar 26	Barcelona	SPAIN	W 2-0	Woodcock, Francis T	50,000	Shilton (30), Neal (23), (Hughes 60), Mills (29), Thompson (20), Watson (49), Wilkins (28), Keegan (50), Coppell (20), Francis T (18), (Cunningham 5), Kennedy (13), Woodcock (9)
May 13	Wembley, London	ARGENTINA	W 3-1	Johnson 2, Keegan	92,000	Clemence (47), Neal (24), (Cherry 22), Sansom (4), Thompson (21), Watson (50), Wilkins (29), Keegan (51), Coppell (21), Johnson (5), (Birtles 1), Kennedy (14), (Brooking 34), Woodcock (10)

Home International Championship

DATE	VENUE	OPPONENTS	SCORE	GOALSCORERS	ATTENDANCE	TEAM
May 17	Racecourse Ground, Wrexham	WALES	L 1-4	Mariner	24,386	Clemence (48), Neal (25), (Sansom 5), Cherry (23), Thompson (22), Lloyd (4), (Wilkins 30), Kennedy (15), Coppell (22), Hoddle (2), Mariner (6), Brooking (35), Barnes (16)
May 20	Wembley, London	N. IRELAND	D 1-1	Johnson	33,676	Corrigan (4), Cherry (24), Sansom (6), Wilkins (31), Watson (51), Hughes (61), Reeves (2), (Mariner 7), McDermott (9), Johnson (6), Brooking (36), Devonshire (1)
May 24	Hampden Park, Glasgow	SCOTLAND	W 2-0	Brooking, Coppell	85,000	Clemence (49), Cherry (25), Sansom (7), Thompson (23), Watson (52), Wilkins (32), Coppell (23), McDermott (10), Johnson (7), Brooking (37), Mariner (8), (Hughes 62)

Friendly

DATE	VENUE	OPPONENTS	SCORE	GOALSCORERS	ATTENDANCE	TEAM
May 31	Sydney	AUSTRALIA	W 2-1	Hoddle, Mariner	30,000	Corrigan (5), Cherry (26), Lampard (2), Talbot (6), Osman (1), Butcher (1), Robson (2), (Greenhoff 18), Sunderland (1), (Ward 1), Mariner (9), Hoddle (3), Armstrong (1), (Devonshire 2)

EUROPEAN CHAMPIONSHIP FINALS 1980

Group Stage – Group 2

DATE	VENUE	OPPONENTS	SCORE	GOALSCORERS	ATTENDANCE	TEAM
Jun 12	Turin	BELGIUM	D 1-1	Wilkins	15,186	Clemence (50), Neal (26), Sansom (8), Thompson (24), Watson (53), Wilkins (33), Keegan (52), Coppell (24), (McDermott 11), Johnson (8), (Kennedy 16), Brooking (38), Woodcock (11)
Jun 15	Turin	ITALY	L 0-1		59,649	Shilton (31), Neal (27), Sansom (9), Thompson (25), Watson (54), Wilkins (34), Keegan (53), Coppell (25), Birtles (2), (Mariner 10), Kennedy (17), Woodcock (12)
Jun 18	Naples	SPAIN	W 2-1	Brooking, Woodcock	14,440	Clemence (51), Anderson (4), (Cherry 27), Mills (30), Thompson (26), Watson (55), Wilkins (35), Keegan (54), McDermott (12), Woodcock (13), Brooking (39), Hoddle (4), (Mariner 11)

Group 2

	P	W	D	L	F	A	Pts
BELGIUM	3	1	2	0	3	2	4
ITALY	3	1	2	0	1	0	4
ENGLAND	3	1	1	1	3	3	3
SPAIN	3	0	1	2	2	4	1

1980 (continued)

World Cup Qualifiers

DATE	VENUE	OPPONENTS	SCORE	GOALSCORERS	ATTENDANCE	TEAM
Sep 10	Wembley, London	NORWAY	W 4-0	McDermott 2 (1 pen), Woodcock, Mariner	48,200	Shilton (32), Anderson (5), Sansom (10), **Thompson** (27), Watson (56), Robson (3), Gates (1), McDermott (13), Mariner (12), Woodcock (14), Rix (1)
Oct 15	Bucharest	ROMANIA	L 1-2	Woodcock	75,000	Clemence (52), Neal (28), Sansom (11), **Thompson** (28), Watson (57), Robson (4), Gates (2), (Coppell 26), McDermott (14), Birtles (3), (Cunningham 6), Woodcock (15), Rix (2)
Nov 19	Wembley, London	SWITZERLAND	W 2-1	Mariner, own goal	70,000	Shilton (33), Neal (29), Sansom (12), Robson (5), Watson (58), **Mills** (31), Coppell (27), McDermott (15), Mariner (13), Brooking (40), (Rix 3), Woodcock (16)

1981

Friendly

DATE	VENUE	OPPONENTS	SCORE	GOALSCORERS	ATTENDANCE	TEAM
Mar 25	Wembley, London	SPAIN	L 1-2	Hoddle	71,840	Clemence (53), Neal (30), Sansom (13), Robson (6), Osman (2), Butcher (2), **Keegan** (55), Francis T (19), (Barnes 17), Mariner (14), Brooking (41), (Wilkins 36), Hoddle (5)

World Cup Qualifier

DATE	VENUE	OPPONENTS	SCORE	GOALSCORERS	ATTENDANCE	TEAM
Apr 29	Wembley, London	ROMANIA	D 0-0		62,500	Shilton (34), Anderson (6), Sansom (14), Robson (7), **Watson** (59), Osman (3), Coppell (28), Wilkins (37), Francis T (20), Brooking (42), (McDermott 16), Woodcock (17)

Friendly

DATE	VENUE	OPPONENTS	SCORE	GOALSCORERS	ATTENDANCE	TEAM
May 12	Wembley, London	BRAZIL	L 0-1		75,000	**Clemence** (54), Neal (31), Sansom (15), Robson (8), Martin (1), Wilkins (38), Coppell (29), McDermott (17), Withe (1), Rix (4), Barnes (18)

Home International Championship

DATE	VENUE	OPPONENTS	SCORE	GOALSCORERS	ATTENDANCE	TEAM
May 20	Wembley, London	WALES	D 0-0		34,280	Corrigan (6), Anderson (7), Sansom (16), Robson (9), **Watson** (60), Wilkins (39), Coppell (30), Hoddle (6), Withe (2), (Woodcock 18), Rix (5), Barnes (19)
May 23	Wembley, London	SCOTLAND	L 0-1		90,000	Corrigan (7), Anderson (8), Sansom (17), Wilkins (40), **Watson** (61), (Martin 2) Robson (10), Coppell (31), Hoddle (7), Withe (3), Woodcock (19), (Francis T 21), Rix (6)

World Cup Qualifiers

DATE	VENUE	OPPONENTS	SCORE	GOALSCORERS	ATTENDANCE	TEAM
May 30	Basle	SWITZERLAND	L 1-2	McDermott	40,000	Clemence (55), Mills (32), Sansom (18), Wilkins (41), Watson (62), (Barnes 20), Osman (4), **Keegan** (56), Coppell (32), Mariner (15), Francis T (22), (McDermott 18), Robson (11)
Jun 6	Budapest	HUNGARY	W 3-1	Brooking 2, Keegan (pen)	68,000	Clemence (56), Neal (32), Mills (33), Thompson (29), Watson (63), Robson (12), **Keegan** (57), Coppell (33), Mariner (16), Brooking (43), (Wilkins 42), McDermott (19)
Sep 9	Oslo	NORWAY	L 1-2	Robson	28,500	Clemence (57), Neal (33), Mills (34), Thompson (30), Osman (5), Robson (13), **Keegan** (58), Francis T (23), Mariner (17), (Withe 4), Hoddle (8), (Barnes 21), McDermott (20)
Nov 18	Wembley, London	HUNGARY	W 1-0	Mariner	92,000	Shilton (35), Neal (34), Mills (35), Thompson (31), Martin (3), Robson (14), **Keegan** (59), Coppell (34), (Morley 1), Mariner (18), Brooking (44), McDermott (21)

1982

Home International Championship

DATE	VENUE	OPPONENTS	SCORE	GOALSCORERS	ATTENDANCE	TEAM
Feb 23	Wembley, London	N. IRELAND	W 4-0	Robson, Keegan, Hoddle, Wilkins	54,900	Clemence (58), Anderson (9), Sansom (19), Wilkins (43), Watson (64), Foster (1), **Keegan** (60), Robson (15), Francis T (24), (Regis 1), Hoddle (9), Morley (2), (Woodcock 20)
Apr 27	Ninian Park, Cardiff	WALES	W 1-0	Francis T	25,000	Corrigan (8), Neal (35), Sansom (20), **Thompson** (32), Butcher (3), Wilkins (44), Robson (16), Francis T (25), (Regis 2), Withe (5), Hoddle (10), (McDermott 22), Morley (3)

1982 (continued)

Friendly

DATE	VENUE	OPPONENTS	SCORE	GOALSCORERS	ATTENDANCE	TEAM
May 25	Wembley, London	HOLLAND	W 2-0	Mariner, Woodcock	69,000	**Shilton** (36), Neal (36), Sansom (21), Thompson (33), Foster (2), Wilkins (45), Robson (17), McDermott (23), Mariner (19), (Barnes 22), Woodcock (21), Devonshire (3), (Rix 7)

Home International Championship

DATE	VENUE	OPPONENTS	SCORE	GOALSCORERS	ATTENDANCE	TEAM
May 29	Hampden Park, Glasgow	SCOTLAND	W 1-0	Mariner	80,529	Shilton (37), Mills (36), Sansom (22), Thompson (34), Butcher (4), Wilkins (46), **Keegan** (61), (McDermott 24), Coppell (35), Mariner (20), (Francis T 26), Brooking (45), Robson (18)

Friendlies

DATE	VENUE	OPPONENTS	SCORE	GOALSCORERS	ATTENDANCE	TEAM
Jun 2	Reykjavik	ICELAND	D 1-1	Goddard	11,110	Corrigan (9), Anderson (10), **Neal** (37), McDermott (25), Watson (65), Osman (6), Morley (4), Hoddle (11), Withe (6), Regis (3), (Goddard 1), Devonshire (4), (Perryman 1)
Jun 3	Helsinki	FINLAND	W 4-1	Robson 2, Mariner 2	21,521	Clemence (59), Mills (37), Sansom (23), Thompson (35), Martin (4), Wilkins (47), **Keegan** (62), Coppell (36), (Francis T 27), Mariner (21), Brooking (46), (Woodcock 22), Robson (19), (Rix 8)

THE WORLD CUP FINALS 1982 (SPAIN)

Group Stage – Group 4

DATE	VENUE	OPPONENTS	SCORE	GOALSCORERS	ATTENDANCE	TEAM
Jun 16	Bilbao	FRANCE	W 3-1	Robson 2, Mariner	44,172	Shilton (38), **Mills** (38), Sansom (24), (Neal 38), Thompson (36), Butcher (5), Wilkins (48), Coppell (37), Francis T (28), Mariner (22), Rix (9), Robson (20)
Jun 20	Bilbao	CZECHOSLOVAKIA	W 2-0	Francis T, own goal	42,000	Shilton (39), **Mills** (39), Sansom (25), Thompson (37), Butcher (6), Wilkins (49), Coppell (38), Francis T (29), Mariner (23), Rix (10), Robson (21), (Hoddle 12)
Jun 25	Bilbao	KUWAIT	W 1-0	Francis T	39,700	Shilton (40), Neal (39), **Mills** (40), Thompson (38), Foster (3), Wilkins (50), Coppell (39), Francis T (30), Mariner (24), Rix (11), Hoddle (13)

Second Round – Group B

DATE	VENUE	OPPONENTS	SCORE	GOALSCORERS	ATTENDANCE	TEAM
Jun 29	Madrid	W. GERMANY	D 0-0		90,089	Shilton (41), **Mills** (41), Sansom (26), Thompson (39), Butcher (7), Wilkins (51), Coppell (40), Francis T (31), (Woodcock 23), Mariner (25), Rix (12), Robson (22)
July 5	Madrid	SPAIN	D 0-0		60,000	Shilton (42), **Mills** (42), Sansom (27), Thompson (40), Butcher (8), Wilkins (52), Robson (23), Francis T (32), Mariner (26), Woodcock (24), (Keegan 63), Rix (13), (Brooking 47)

Group 4

	P	W	D	L	F	A	Pts
ENGLAND	3	3	0	0	6	1	6
FRANCE	3	1	1	1	6	5	3
CZECHOSLOVAKIA	3	0	2	1	2	4	2
KUWAIT	3	0	1	2	2	6	1

Group B

	P	W	D	L	F	A	Pts
WEST GERMANY	2	1	1	0	2	1	3
ENGLAND	2	0	2	0	0	0	2
SPAIN	2	0	1	1	1	2	1

1982 (continued)

MANAGER CHANGED TO: BOBBY ROBSON

European Championship Qualifier

DATE	VENUE	OPPONENTS	SCORE	GOALSCORERS	ATTENDANCE	TEAM
Sep 22	Copenhagen	DENMARK	D 2-2	Francis T 2	44,300	Shilton (43), Neal (40), Sansom (28), **Wilkins** (53), Osman (7), Butcher (9), Morley (5), (Hill 1), Robson (24), Mariner (27), Francis T (33), Rix (14)

Friendly

| Oct 13 | Wembley, London | W. GERMANY | L 1-2 | Woodcock | 68,000 | Shilton (44), Mabbutt (1), Sansom (29), Thompson (41), Butcher (10), **Wilkins** (54), Hill (2), Regis (4), (Blissett 1), Mariner (28), (Woodcock 25), Armstrong (2), (Rix 15), Devonshire (5) |

European Championship Qualifiers

| Nov 17 | Salonika | GREECE | W 3-0 | Woodcock 2, Lee | 45,000 | Shilton (45), Neal (41), Sansom (30), Thompson (42), Martin (5), Mabbutt (2), **Robson** (25), Lee (1), Mariner (29), Woodcock (26), Morley (6) |
| Dec 15 | Wembley, London | LUXEMBOURG | W 9-0 | Blissett 3, Woodcock, Coppell, Hoddle, Chamberlain, Neal, own goal | 35,000 | Clemence (60), Neal (42), Sansom (31), Martin (6), Butcher (11), Mabbutt (3), (Hoddle 14), **Robson** (26), Lee (2), Blissett (2), Coppell (41), (Chamberlain 1), Woodcock (27) |

1983

Home International Championship

DATE	VENUE	OPPONENTS	SCORE	GOALSCORERS	ATTENDANCE	TEAM
Feb 23	Wembley, London	WALES	W 2-1	Butcher, Neal (pen)	24,000	**Shilton** (46), Neal (43), Statham (1), Mabbutt (4), Martin (7), Butcher (12), Lee (3), Blissett (3), Mariner (30), Cowans (1), Devonshire (6)

European Championship Qualifiers

| Mar 30 | Wembley, London | GREECE | D 0 0 | | 48,500 | **Shilton** (47), Neal (44), Sansom (32), Mabbutt (5), Martin (8), Butcher (13), Coppell (42), Lee (4), Francis T (34), Woodcock (28), (Blissett 4), Devonshire (7), (Rix 16) |
| Apr 27 | Wembley, London | HUNGARY | W 2-0 | Francis T, Withe | 55,000 | **Shilton** (48), Neal (45), Sansom (33), Mabbutt (6), Martin (9), Butcher (14), Lee (5), Francis T (35), Withe (7), Blissett (5), Cowans (2) |

Home International Championship

| May 28 | Windsor Park, Belfast | N. IRELAND | D 0-0 | | 22,000 | **Shilton** (49), Neal (46), Sansom (34), Mabbutt (7), Roberts (1), Butcher (15), Hoddle (15), Francis T (36), Withe (8), Blissett (6), (Barnes J 1), Cowans (3) |
| Jun 1 | Wembley, London | SCOTLAND | W 2-0 | Robson, Cowans | 84,000 | Shilton (50), Neal (47), Sansom (35), Lee (6), Roberts (2), Butcher (16), **Robson** (27), (Mabbutt 8), Francis T (37), Withe (9), (Blissett 7), Hoddle (16), Cowans (4) |

Friendlies

Jun 12	Sydney	AUSTRALIA	D 0-0		28,000	**Shilton** (51), Thomas (1), Statham (2), (Barnes J 2), Williams (1), Osman (8), Butcher (17), Barham (1), Gregory (1), Blissett (8), (Walsh 1), Francis T (38), Cowans (5)
Jun 15	Brisbane	AUSTRALIA	W 1-0	Walsh	10,000	**Shilton** (52), Neal (48), Statham (3), (Williams 2), Barham (2), Osman (9), Butcher (18), Gregory (2), Francis T (39), Walsh (2), Cowans (6), Barnes J (3)
Jun 19	Melbourne	AUSTRALIA	D 1-1	Francis T	20,000	**Shilton** (53), (Spink 1), Neal (49), (Thomas 2), Pickering (1), Lee (7), Osman (10), Butcher (19), Gregory (3), Francis T (40), Walsh (3), (Blissett 9), Cowans (7), Barnes J (4)

European Championship Qualifiers

Sep 21	Wembley, London	DENMARK	L 0-1		82,500	Shilton (54), Neal (50), Sansom (36), Lee (8), (Chamberlain 2), Osman (11), Butcher (20), **Wilkins** (55), Gregory (4), Mariner (31), Francis T (41), Barnes J (5), (Blissett 10)
Oct 12	Budapest	HUNGARY	W 3-0	Hoddle, Lee, Mariner	25,000	Shilton (55), Gregory (5), Sansom (37), Mabbutt (9), Martin (10), Butcher (21), **Robson** (28), Lee (9), Mariner (32), Hoddle (17), Blissett (11), (Withe 10)
Nov 16	Luxembourg	LUXEMBOURG	W 4-0	Robson 2, Mariner, Butcher	12,000	Clemence (61), Duxbury (1), Sansom (38), Lee (10), Martin (11), Butcher (22), **Robson** (29), Hoddle (18), Mariner (33), Woodcock (29), (Barnes J 6), Devonshire (8)

1984

Friendly

DATE	VENUE	OPPONENTS	SCORE	GOALSCORERS	ATTENDANCE	TEAM
Feb 29	Paris	FRANCE	L 0-2		45,554	Shilton (56), Duxbury (2), Sansom (39), Lee (11), (Barnes J 7), Roberts (3), Butcher (23), **Robson** (30), Stein (1), (Woodcock 30), Walsh (4), Hoddle (19), Williams (3)

Home International Championship

Apr 4	Wembley, London	N. IRELAND	W 1-0	Woodcock	24,000	Shilton (57), Anderson (11), Kennedy A (1), Lee (12), Roberts (4), Butcher (24), **Robson** (31), Wilkins (56), Woodcock (31), Francis T (42), Rix (17)
May 2	Racecourse Ground, Wrexham	WALES	L 0-1		14,250	Shilton (58), Duxbury (3), Kennedy A (2), Lee (13), Martin (12), (Fenwick 1), Wright (1), **Wilkins** (57), Gregory (6), Walsh (5), Woodcock (32), Armstrong (3), (Blissett 12)
May 26	Hampden Park, Glasgow	SCOTLAND	D 1-1	Woodcock	73,064	Shilton (59), Duxbury (4), Sansom (40), Wilkins (58), Roberts (5), Fenwick (2), Chamberlain (3), (Hunt 1), **Robson** (32), Woodcock (33), (Lineker 1), Blissett (13), Barnes J (8)

Friendlies

Jun 2	Wembley, London	USSR	L 0-2		38,125	Shilton (60), Duxbury (5), Sansom (41), Wilkins (59), Roberts (6), Fenwick (3), Chamberlain (4), **Robson** (33), Francis T (43), (Hateley 1), Blissett (14), Barnes J (9), (Hunt 2)
Jun 10	Rio	BRAZIL	W 2-0	Barnes J, Hateley	56,126	Shilton (61), Duxbury (6), Sansom (42), Wilkins (60), Watson (1), Fenwick (4), **Robson** (34), Chamberlain (5), Hateley (2), Woodcock (34), (Allen 1), Barnes J (10)
Jun 13	Montevideo	URUGUAY	L 0-2		34,500	Shilton (62), Duxbury (7), Sansom (43), Wilkins (61), Watson (2), Fenwick (5), **Robson** (35), Chamberlain (6), Hateley (3), Allen (2), (Woodcock 35), Barnes J (11)
Jun 17	Santiago	CHILE	D 0-0		9,876	Shilton (63), Duxbury (8), Sansom (44), Wilkins (62), Watson (3), Fenwick (6), **Robson** (36), Chamberlain (7), (Lee 14), Hateley (4), Allen (3), Barnes J (12)
Sep 12	Wembley, London	E. GERMANY	W 1-0	Robson	23,951	Shilton (64), Duxbury (9), Sansom (45), Williams (4), Wright (2), Butcher (25), **Robson** (37), Wilkins (63), Mariner (34), (Hateley 5), Woodcock (36), (Francis T 44), Barnes J (13)

World Cup Qualifiers

Oct 17	Wembley, London	FINLAND	W 5-0	Hateley 2, Woodcock, Robson, Sansom	47,234	Shilton (65), Duxbury (10), (Stevens G 1), Sansom (46), Williams (5), Wright (3), Butcher (26), **Robson** (38), (Chamberlain 8), Wilkins (64), Hateley (6), Woodcock (37), Barnes J (14)
Nov 14	Istanbul	TURKEY	W 8-0	Robson 3, Woodcock 2, Barnes J 2, Anderson	40,000	Shilton (66), Anderson (12), Sansom (47), Williams (6), (Stevens G 2), Wright (4), Butcher (27), **Robson** (39), Wilkins (65), Withe (11), (Francis T 45), Woodcock (38), Barnes J (15)

1985

World Cup Qualifier

DATE	VENUE	OPPONENTS	SCORE	GOALSCORERS	ATTENDANCE	TEAM
Feb 27	Windsor Park, Belfast	N. IRELAND	W 1-0	Hateley	28,500	Shilton (67), Anderson (13), Sansom (48), **Wilkins** (66), Martin (13), Butcher (28), Steven (1), Stevens G (3), Hateley (7), Woodcock (39), (Francis T 46), Barnes J (16)

Friendly

Mar 26	Wembley, London	R. of IRELAND	W 2-1	Steven, Lineker	34,793	Bailey (1), Anderson (14), Sansom (49), Steven (2), Wright (5), Butcher (29), **Robson** (40), (Hoddle 20), Wilkins (67), Hateley (8), (Davenport 1), Lineker (2), Waddle (1)

World Cup Qualifiers

May 1	Bucharest	ROMANIA	D 0-0		70,000	Shilton (68), Anderson (15), Sansom (50), Steven (3), Wright (6), Butcher (30), **Robson** (41), Wilkins (68), Mariner (35), (Lineker 3), Francis T (47), Barnes J (17), (Waddle 2)
May 22	Helsinki	FINLAND	D 1-1	Hateley	30,311	Shilton (69), Anderson (16), Sansom (51), Steven (4), (Waddle 3), Butcher (31), Fenwick (7), **Robson** (42), Wilkins (69), Hateley (9), Francis T (48), Barnes J (18)

Rous Cup

May 25	Hampden Park, Glasgow	SCOTLAND	L 0-1		66,489	Shilton (70), Anderson (17), Sansom (52), Hoddle (21), (Lineker 4), Butcher (32), Fenwick (8), **Robson** (43), Wilkins (70), Hateley (10), Francis T (49), Barnes J (19), (Waddle 4)

1985 (continued)

Mexico City Tournament

DATE	VENUE	OPPONENTS	SCORE	GOALSCORERS	ATTENDANCE	TEAM
Jun 6	Mexico City	ITALY	L 1-2	Hateley	8,000	Shilton (71), Stevens M (1), Sansom (53), Steven (5), (Hoddle 22), Wright (7), Butcher (33), **Robson** (44), Wilkins (71), Hateley (11), Francis T (50), (Lineker 5), Waddle (5), (Barnes J 20)
Jun 9	Mexico City	MEXICO	L 0-1		15,000	Bailey (2), Anderson (18), Sansom (54), Hoddle (23), (Dixon 1), Watson (4), Fenwick (9), **Robson** (45), Wilkins (72), (Reid 1), Hateley (12), Francis T (51), Barnes J (21), (Waddle 6)
Jun 12	Mexico City	W. GERMANY	W 3-0	Robson, Dixon 2	10,000	Shilton (72), Stevens M (2), Sansom (55), Hoddle (24), Wright (8), Butcher (34), **Robson** (46), (Bracewell 1), Reid (2), Dixon (2), Lineker (6), (Barnes J 22), Waddle (7)

Friendly

DATE	VENUE	OPPONENTS	SCORE	GOALSCORERS	ATTENDANCE	TEAM
Jun 16	Los Angeles	USA	W 5-0	Lineker 2, Dixon 2, Steven	10,145	Woods (1), Anderson (19), Sansom (56), (Watson 5), Hoddle (25), (Reid 3), Butcher (35), Fenwick (10), **Robson** (47), (Steven 6), Bracewell (2), Dixon (3), Lineker (7), Waddle (8), (Barnes J 23)

World Cup Qualifiers

DATE	VENUE	OPPONENTS	SCORE	GOALSCORERS	ATTENDANCE	TEAM
Sep 11	Wembley, London	ROMANIA	D 1-1	Hoddle	59,500	Shilton (73), Stevens M (3), Sansom (57), Hoddle (26), Wright (9), Fenwick (11), **Robson** (48), Reid (4), Hateley (13), Lineker (8), (Woodcock 40), Waddle (9), (Barnes J 24)
Oct 16	Wembley, London	TURKEY	W 5-0	Waddle, Lineker 3, Robson	52,500	Shilton (74), Stevens M (4), Sansom (58), Hoddle (27), Wright (10), Fenwick (12), **Robson** (49), (Steven 7), Wilkins (73), Hateley (14), (Woodcock 41), Lineker (9), Waddle (10)
Nov 13	Wembley, London	N. IRELAND	D 0-0		70,500	Shilton (75), Stevens M (5), Sansom (59), **Wilkins** (74), Wright (11), Fenwick (13), Hoddle (28), Bracewell (3), Dixon (4), Lineker (10), Waddle (11)

1986

Friendlies

DATE	VENUE	OPPONENTS	SCORE	GOALSCORERS	ATTENDANCE	TEAM
Jan 29	Cairo	EGYPT	W 4-0	Steven, Wallace, Cowans, own goal	20,000	Shilton (76), (Woods 2), Stevens M (6), Sansom (60), Cowans (8), Wright (12), Fenwick (14), Steven (8), (Hill 3), **Wilkins** (75), Hateley (15), Lineker (11), (Beardsley 1), Wallace (1)
Feb 26	Tel Aviv	ISRAEL	W 2-1	Robson 2 (1 pen)	15,000	Shilton (77), (Woods 3), Stevens M (7), Sansom (61), Wilkins (76), Martin (14), Butcher (36), **Robson** (50), Hoddle (29), Dixon (5), (Woodcock 42), Beardsley (2), Waddle (12), (Barnes J 25)
Mar 26	Tbilisi	USSR	W 1-0	Waddle	62,500	Shilton (78), Anderson (20), Sansom (62), **Wilkins** (77), Wright (13), Butcher (37), Hoddle (30), Cowans (9), (Hodge 1), Beardsley (3), Lineker (12), Waddle (13), (Steven 9)

Rous Cup

DATE	VENUE	OPPONENTS	SCORE	GOALSCORERS	ATTENDANCE	TEAM
Apr 23	Wembley, London	SCOTLAND	W 2-1	Butcher, Hoddle	68,357	Shilton (79), Stevens M (8), Sansom (63), Hoddle (31), Watson (6), Butcher (38), **Wilkins** (78), (Reid 5), Hodge (2), (Stevens G 4), Hateley (16), Francis T (52), Waddle (14)

Friendlies

DATE	VENUE	OPPONENTS	SCORE	GOALSCORERS	ATTENDANCE	TEAM
May 17	Los Angeles	MEXICO	W 3-0	Hateley 2, Beardsley	45,000	Shilton (80), Anderson (21), Sansom (64), Hoddle (32), Butcher (39), Fenwick (15), **Robson** (51), (Stevens G 5), Wilkins (79), (Steven 10), Hateley (17), (Dixon 6), Beardsley (4), Waddle (15), (Barnes J 26)
May 24	Vancouver	CANADA	W 1-0	Hateley	8,150	Shilton (81), (Woods 4), Stevens M (9), Sansom (65), Hoddle (33), Martin (15), Butcher (40), **Wilkins** (80), (Reid 6), Hodge (3), Hateley (18), Lineker (13), (Beardsley 5), Waddle (16), (Barnes J 27)

THE WORLD CUP FINALS 1986 (MEXICO)

Group Stage – Group F

DATE	VENUE	OPPONENTS	SCORE	GOALSCORERS	ATTENDANCE	TEAM
Jun 3	Monterrey	PORTUGAL	L 0-1		19,998	Shilton (82), Stevens M (10), Sansom (66), Hoddle (34), Butcher (41), Fenwick (16), **Robson** (52), (Hodge 4), Wilkins (81), Hateley (19), Lineker (14), Waddle (17), (Beardsley 6)
Jun 6	Monterrey	MOROCCO	D 0-0		20,200	Shilton (83), Stevens M (11), Sansom (67), Hoddle (35), Butcher (42), Fenwick (17), **Robson** (53), (Hodge 5), *Wilkins* (82), Hateley (20), (Stevens G 6), Lineker (15), Waddle (18)
Jun 11	Mexico City	POLAND	W 3-0	Lineker 3	22,700	**Shilton** (84), Stevens M (12), Sansom (68), Hoddle (36), Martin (16), Butcher (43), Hodge (6), Reid (7), Beardsley (7), (Waddle 19), Lineker (16), (Dixon 7), Steven (11)

Second Round

DATE	VENUE	OPPONENTS	SCORE	GOALSCORERS	ATTENDANCE	TEAM
Jun 18	Mexico City	PARAGUAY	W 3-0	Lineker 2, Beardsley	98,728	**Shilton** (85), Stevens M (13), Sansom (69), Hoddle (37), Martin (16), Butcher (44), Hodge (7), Reid (8), (Stevens G 7), Beardsley (8), (Hateley 21), Lineker (17), Steven (12)

Quarter-final

DATE	VENUE	OPPONENTS	SCORE	GOALSCORERS	ATTENDANCE	TEAM
Jun 22	Mexico City	ARGENTINA	L 1-2	Lineker	114,580	**Shilton** (86), Stevens M (14), Sansom (70), Hoddle (38), Butcher (45), Fenwick (19), Hodge (8), Reid (9), (Waddle 20), Beardsley (9), Lineker (18), Steven (13), (Barnes J 28)

Group F

	P	W	D	L	F	A	Pts
Morocco	3	1	2	0	3	1	4
England	3	1	1	1	3	1	3
Poland	3	1	1	1	1	3	3
Portugal	3	1	0	2	2	4	2

1986 (continued)

Friendly

DATE	VENUE	OPPONENTS	SCORE	GOALSCORERS	ATTENDANCE	TEAM
Sep 10	Stockholm	SWEDEN	L 0-1		15,646	**Shilton** (87), Anderson (22), Sansom (71), Steven (14), (Cottee 1), Martin (17), Butcher (46), Hodge (9), Wilkins (83), Dixon (8), Hoddle (39), Barnes J (29), (Waddle 21)

European Championship Qualifiers

DATE	VENUE	OPPONENTS	SCORE	GOALSCORERS	ATTENDANCE	TEAM
Oct 15	Wembley, London	N. IRELAND	W 3-0	Lineker 2, Waddle	35,300	Shilton (88), Anderson (23), Sansom (72), Hoddle (40), Watson (7), Butcher (47), **Robson** (54), Hodge (10), Beardsley (10), (Cottee 2), Lineker (19), Waddle (22)
Nov 12	Wembley, London	YUGOSLAVIA	W 2-0	Mabbutt, Anderson	60,000	Woods (5), Anderson (24), Sansom (73), Mabbutt (10), Wright (14), **Butcher** (48), Hoddle (41), Hodge (11), (Wilkins 84), Beardsley (11), Lineker (20), Waddle (23), (Steven 15)

1987

Friendly

DATE	VENUE	OPPONENTS	SCORE	GOALSCORERS	ATTENDANCE	TEAM
Feb 18	Madrid	SPAIN	W 4-2	Lineker 4	35,000	Shilton (89), (Woods 6), Anderson (25), Sansom (74), Hoddle (42), Butcher (49), Adams (1), **Robson** (55), Hodge (12), Beardsley (12), Lineker (21), Waddle (24), (Steven 16)

European Championship Qualifiers

DATE	VENUE	OPPONENTS	SCORE	GOALSCORERS	ATTENDANCE	TEAM
Apr 1	Windsor Park, Belfast	N. IRELAND	W 2-0	Robson, Waddle	20,578	Shilton (90), (Woods 7), Anderson (26), Sansom (75), Mabbutt (11), Wright (15), Butcher (50), **Robson** (56), Hodge (13), Beardsley (13), Lineker (22), Waddle (25)
Apr 29	Izmir	TURKEY	D 0-0		25,000	Woods (8), Anderson (27), Sansom (76), Hoddle (43), Adams (2), Mabbutt (12), **Robson** (57), Hodge (14), (Barnes J 30), Allen (4), (Hateley 22), Lineker (23), Waddle (26)

1987 (continued)

Rous Cup

DATE	VENUE	OPPONENTS	SCORE	GOALSCORERS	ATTENDANCE	TEAM
May 19	Wembley, London	BRAZIL	D 1-1	Lineker	92,000	Shilton (91), Stevens M (15), Pearce (1), Reid (10), Butcher (51), Adams (3), **Robson** (58), Barnes J (31), Beardsley (14), Lineker (24), (Hateley 23), Waddle (27)
May 23	Hampden Park, Glasgow	SCOTLAND	D 0-0		64,713	Woods (9), Stevens M (16), Pearce (2), Hoddle (44), Wright (16), Butcher (52), **Robson** (59), Hodge (15), Hateley (24), Beardsley (15), Waddle (28)

Friendly

DATE	VENUE	OPPONENTS	SCORE	GOALSCORERS	ATTENDANCE	TEAM
Sep 9	Dusseldorf	W. GERMANY	L 1-3	Lineker	50,000	**Shilton** (92), Anderson (28), Sansom (77), (Pearce 3), Hoddle (45), (Webb 1), Adams (4), Mabbutt (13), Reid (11), Barnes J (32), Beardsley (16), Lineker (25), Waddle (29), (Hateley 25)

European Championship Qualifiers

DATE	VENUE	OPPONENTS	SCORE	GOALSCORERS	ATTENDANCE	TEAM
Oct 14	Wembley, London	TURKEY	W 8-0	Lineker 3, Barnes J 2, Robson, Beardsley, Webb	45,528	Shilton (93), Stevens M (17), Sansom (78), Steven (17), (Hoddle 46), Butcher (53), Adams (5), **Robson** (60), Webb (2), Beardsley (17), (Regis 5), Lineker (26), Barnes J (33)
Nov 11	Belgrade	YUGOSLAVIA	W 4-1	Beardsley, Barnes J, Robson, Adams	70,000	Shilton (94), Stevens M (18), Sansom (79), Steven (18), Butcher (54), Adams (6), **Robson** (61), (Reid 12), Webb (3), (Hoddle 47), Beardsley (18), Lineker (27), Barnes J (34)

1988

Friendlies

DATE	VENUE	OPPONENTS	SCORE	GOALSCORERS	ATTENDANCE	TEAM
Feb 17	Tel Aviv	ISRAEL	D 0-0		6,000	Woods (10), Stevens M (19), Pearce (4), Webb (4), Watson (8), Wright (17), (Fenwick 20), Allen (5), (Harford 1), McMahon (1), **Beardsley** (19), Barnes J (35), Waddle (30)
Mar 23	Wembley, London	HOLLAND	D 2-2	Lineker, Adams	74,590	Shilton (95), Stevens M (20), Sansom (80), Steven (19), Watson (9), (Wright 18), Adams (7), **Robson** (62), Webb (5), (Hoddle 48), Beardsley (20), (Hateley 26), Lineker (28), Barnes J (36)
Apr 27	Budapest	HUNGARY	D 0-0		35,000	Woods (11), Anderson (29), Pearce (5), (Stevens M 21), Steven (20), Adams (8), Pallister (1), **Robson** (63), McMahon (2), Beardsley (21), (Hateley 27), Lineker (29), (Cottee 3), Waddle (31), (Hoddle 49)

Rous Cup

DATE	VENUE	OPPONENTS	SCORE	GOALSCORERS	ATTENDANCE	TEAM
May 21	Wembley, London	SCOTLAND	W 1-0	Beardsley	70,480	Shilton (96), Stevens M (22), Sansom (81), Webb (6), Watson (10), Adams (9), **Robson** (64), Steven (21), (Waddle 32), Beardsley (22), Lineker (30), Barnes J (37)
May 24	Wembley, London	COLOMBIA	D 1-1	Lineker	25,756	Shilton (97), Anderson (30), Sansom (82), McMahon (3), Wright (19), Adams (10), **Robson** (65), Waddle (33), (Hoddle 50), Beardsley (23), Lineker (31), Barnes J (38), (Hateley 28)

Friendly

DATE	VENUE	OPPONENTS	SCORE	GOALSCORERS	ATTENDANCE	TEAM
May 28	Lausanne	SWITZERLAND	W 1-0	Lineker	10,000	Shilton (98), (Woods 12), Stevens M (23), Sansom (83), Steven (22), (Waddle 34), Wright (20), Adams (11), (Watson 11), **Robson** (66), (Reid 13), Webb (7), Beardsley (24), Lineker (32), Barnes J (39)

EUROPEAN CHAMPIONSHIP FINALS 1988

Group Stage – Group 2

DATE	VENUE	OPPONENTS	SCORE	GOALSCORERS	ATTENDANCE	TEAM
Jun 12	Stuttgart	R. of IRELAND	L 0-1		53,000	Shilton (99), Stevens M (24), Sansom (84), Webb (8), (Hoddle 51), Wright (21), Adams (12), **Robson** (67), Waddle (35), Beardsley (25), (Hateley 29), Lineker (33), Barnes J (40)
Jun 15	Dusseldorf	HOLLAND	L 1-3	Robson	65,000	Shilton (100), Stevens M (25), Sansom (85), Steven (23), (Waddle 36), Wright (22), Adams (13), **Robson** (68), Hoddle (52), Beardsley (26), (Hateley 30), Lineker (34), Barnes J (41)
Jun 18	Frankfurt	USSR	L 1-3	Adams	53,000	Woods (13), Stevens M (26), Sansom (86), Hoddle (53), Watson (12), Adams (14), **Robson** (69), McMahon (4), (Webb 9), Lineker (35), (Hateley 31), Steven (24), Barnes J (42)

Group 2

	P	W	D	L	F	A	Pts
Soviet Union	3	2	1	0	5	2	5
Netherlands	3	2	0	1	4	2	4
Rep. of Ireland	3	1	1	1	2	2	3
England	3	0	0	3	2	7	0

1988 (continued)

Friendly

DATE	VENUE	OPPONENTS	SCORE	GOALSCORERS	ATTENDANCE	TEAM
Sep 14	Wembley, London	DENMARK	W 1-0	Webb	25,837	Shilton (101), (Woods 14), Stevens M (27), Pearce (6), Rocastle (1), Butcher (55), Adams (15), (Walker 1), **Robson** (70), Webb (10), Harford (2), (Cottee 4), Beardsley (27), (Gascoigne 1), Hodge (16)

World Cup Qualifier

DATE	VENUE	OPPONENTS	SCORE	GOALSCORERS	ATTENDANCE	TEAM
Oct 19	Wembley, London	SWEDEN	D 0-0		65,628	Shilton (102), Stevens M (28), Pearce (7), Webb (11), Butcher (56), Adams (16), (Walker 2), **Robson** (71), Waddle (37), Beardsley (28), Lineker (36), Barnes J (43), (Cottee 5)

Friendly

DATE	VENUE	OPPONENTS	SCORE	GOALSCORERS	ATTENDANCE	TEAM
Nov 16	Riyadh	SAUDI ARABIA	D 1-1	Adams	8,000	Seaman (1), Sterland (1), Pearce (8), Thomas M (1), (Gascoigne 2), Adams (17), Pallister (2), **Robson** (72), Rocastle (2), Beardsley (29), (Smith A 1), Lineker (37), Waddle (38), (Marwood 1)

1989

Friendly

DATE	VENUE	OPPONENTS	SCORE	GOALSCORERS	ATTENDANCE	TEAM
Feb 8	Athens	GREECE	W 2-1	Barnes J, Robson	6,000	Shilton (103), Stevens M (29), Pearce (9), Rocastle (3), Butcher (57), Walker (3), **Robson** (73), Webb (12), Smith A (2), (Beardsley 30), Lineker (38), Barnes J (44)

World Cup Qualifiers

DATE	VENUE	OPPONENTS	SCORE	GOALSCORERS	ATTENDANCE	TEAM
Mar 8	Tirana	ALBANIA	W 2-0	Barnes J, Robson	25,000	Shilton (104), Stevens M (30), Pearce (10), Rocastle (4), Butcher (58), Walker (4), **Robson** (74), Webb (13), Barnes J (45), Lineker (39), (Smith A 3), Waddle (39), (Beardsley 31)
Apr 26	Wembley, London	ALBANIA	W 5-0	Lineker, Beardsley 2, Waddle, Gascoigne	60,602	Shilton (105), Stevens M (31), (Parker 1), Pearce (11), Webb (14), Butcher (59), Walker (5), **Robson** (75), Rocastle (5), (Gascoigne 3), Beardsley (32), Lineker (40), Waddle (40)

Rous Cup

DATE	VENUE	OPPONENTS	SCORE	GOALSCORERS	ATTENDANCE	TEAM
May 23	Wembley, London	CHILE	D 0-0		15,628	Shilton (106), Parker (2), Pearce (12), Webb (15), Butcher (60), Walker (6), **Robson** (76), Gascoigne (4), Clough (1), Fashanu (1), (Cottee 6), Waddle (41)

1989 (continued)

Rous Cup

DATE	VENUE	OPPONENTS	SCORE	GOALSCORERS	ATTENDANCE	TEAM
May 27	Hampden Park, Glasgow	SCOTLAND	W 2-0	Waddle, Bull	63,282	Shilton (107), Stevens M (32), Pearce (13), Steven (25), Butcher (61), Walker (7), **Robson** (77), Webb (16), Fashanu (2), (Bull 1), Cottee (7), (Gascoigne 5), Waddle (42)

World Cup Qualifier

DATE	VENUE	OPPONENTS	SCORE	GOALSCORERS	ATTENDANCE	TEAM
Jun 3	Wembley, London	POLAND	W 3-0	Lineker, Barnes J, Webb	69,203	Shilton (108), Stevens M (33), Pearce (14), Webb (17), Butcher (62), Walker (8), **Robson** (78), Waddle (43), (Rocastle 6), Beardsley (33), (Smith A 4), Lineker (41), Barnes J (46)

Friendly

DATE	VENUE	OPPONENTS	SCORE	GOALSCORERS	ATTENDANCE	TEAM
Jun 7	Copenhagen	DENMARK	D 1-1	Lineker	18,400	Shilton (109), (Seaman 2), Parker (3), Pearce (15), Webb (18), (McMahon 5), Butcher (63), Walker (9), **Robson** (79), Rocastle (7), Beardsley (34), (Bull 2), Lineker (42), Barnes J (47), (Waddle 44)

World Cup Qualifiers

DATE	VENUE	OPPONENTS	SCORE	GOALSCORERS	ATTENDANCE	TEAM
Sep 6	Stockholm	SWEDEN	D 0-0		38,588	Shilton (110), Stevens M (34), Pearce (16), McMahon (6), **Butcher** (64), Walker (10), Waddle (45), Webb (19), (Gascoigne 6), Beardsley (35), Lineker (43), Barnes J (48), (Rocastle 8)
Oct 11	Katowice	POLAND	D 0-0		32,423	Shilton (111), Stevens M (35), Pearce (17), McMahon (7), Butcher (65), Walker (11), **Robson** (80), Rocastle (9), Beardsley (36), Lineker (44), Waddle (46)

Friendlies

DATE	VENUE	OPPONENTS	SCORE	GOALSCORERS	ATTENDANCE	TEAM
Nov 15	Wembley, London	ITALY	D 0-0		67,500	Shilton (112), (Beasant 1), Stevens M (36), Pearce (18), (Winterburn 1), McMahon (8), (Hodge 17), Butcher (66), Walker (12), **Robson** (81), (Phelan 1), Waddle (47), Beardsley (37), (Platt 1), Lineker (45), Barnes J (49)
Dec 13	Wembley, London	YUGOSLAVIA	W 2-1	Robson 2	34,796	Shilton (113), (Beasant 2), Parker (4), Pearce (19), (Dorigo 1), Thomas M (2), (Platt 2), Butcher (67), Walker (13), **Robson** (82), (McMahon 9), Rocastle (10), (Hodge 18), Bull (3), Lineker (46), Waddle (48)

1990

Friendlies

DATE	VENUE	OPPONENTS	SCORE	GOALSCORERS	ATTENDANCE	TEAM
Mar 28	Wembley, London	BRAZIL	W 1-0	Lineker	80,000	Shilton (114), (Woods 15), Stevens M (37), Pearce (20), McMahon (10), **Butcher** (68), Walker (14), Platt (3), Waddle (49), Beardsley (38), (Gascoigne 7), Lineker (47), Barnes J (50)
Apr 25	Wembley, London	CZECHOSLOVAKIA	W 4-2	Bull 2, Pearce, Gascoigne	21,342	Shilton (115), (Seaman 3), Dixon (1), Pearce (21), (Dorigo 2), Steven (26), Butcher (69), Walker (15), (Wright 23), **Robson** (83), (McMahon 11), Gascoigne (8), Bull (4), Lineker (48), Hodge (19)
May 15	Wembley, London	DENMARK	W 1-0	Lineker	27,643	Shilton 116, (Woods 16), Stevens M (38), Pearce (22), (Dorigo 3), McMahon (12), (Platt 4), **Butcher** (70), Walker (16), Hodge (20), Gascoigne (9), Waddle (50), (Rocastle 11), Lineker (49), (Bull 5), Barnes J (51)
May 22	Wembley, London	URUGUAY	L 1-2	Barnes J	38,751	Shilton (117), Parker (5), Pearce (23), Hodge (21), (Beardsley 39), Butcher (71), Walker (17), **Robson** (84), Gascoigne (10), Waddle (51), Lineker (50), (Bull 6), Barnes J (52)
Jun 2	Tunis	TUNISIA	D 1-1	Bull	25,000	Shilton (118), Stevens M (39), Pearce (24), Hodge (22), (Beardsley 40), Butcher (72), (Wright 24), Walker (18), **Robson** (85), Gascoigne (11), Waddle (52), (Platt 5), Lineker (51), (Bull 7), Barnes J (53)

THE WORLD CUP FINALS 1990 (ITALY)

Group Stage – Group F

DATE	VENUE	OPPONENTS	SCORE	GOALSCORERS	ATTENDANCE	TEAM
Jun 11	Cagliari	R. of IRELAND	D 1-1	Lineker	35,238	Shilton (119), Stevens M (40), Pearce (25), Gascoigne (12), Butcher (73), Walker (19), **Robson** (86), Beardsley (41), (McMahon 13), Waddle (53), Lineker (52), (Bull 8), Barnes J (54)
Jun 16	Cagliari	HOLLAND	D 0-0		35,267	Shilton (120), Parker (6), Pearce (26), Wright (25), Butcher (74), Walker (20), **Robson** (87), (Platt 6), Gascoigne (13), Waddle (54), (Bull 9), Lineker (53), Barnes J (55)
Jun 21	Cagliari	EGYPT	W 1-0	Wright	34,959	**Shilton** (121), Parker (7), Pearce (27), McMahon (14), Wright (26), Walker (21), Waddle (55), (Platt 7), Gascoigne (14), Bull (10), (Beardsley 42), Lineker (54), Barnes J (56)

Second Round

DATE	VENUE	OPPONENTS	SCORE	GOALSCORERS	ATTENDANCE	TEAM
Jun 26	Bologna	BELGIUM	W 1-0	Platt	34,520	Shilton (122), Parker (8), Pearce (28), Wright (27), **Butcher** (75), Walker (22), McMahon (15), (Platt 8), Gascoigne (15), Waddle (56), Lineker (55), Barnes J (57), (Bull 11)

Quarter-final

DATE	VENUE	OPPONENTS	SCORE	GOALSCORERS	ATTENDANCE	TEAM
July 1	Naples	CAMEROON	W 3-2	Platt, Lineker 2 (2 pens)	55,205	Shilton (123), Parker (9), Pearce (29), Wright (28), **Butcher** (76), (Steven 27), Walker (23), Platt (9), Gascoigne (16), Waddle (57), Lineker (56), Barnes J (58), (Beardsley 43)

Semi-final

DATE	VENUE	OPPONENTS	SCORE	GOALSCORERS	ATTENDANCE	TEAM
July 4	Turin	W. GERMANY	D 1-1	Lineker England lost 4-3 on penalties	62,628	Shilton (124), Parker (10), Pearce (30), Wright (29), **Butcher** (77), (Steven 28), Walker (24), Platt (10), Gascoigne (17), Beardsley (44), Lineker (57), Waddle (58)

Third Place Play-off

DATE	VENUE	OPPONENTS	SCORE	GOALSCORERS	ATTENDANCE	TEAM
July 7	Bari	ITALY	L 1-2	Platt	51,426	**Shilton** (125), Stevens M (41), Dorigo (4), Parker (11), Wright (30), Walker (25), Platt (11), McMahon (16), (Webb 20), Beardsley (45), Lineker (58), Steven (29), (Waddle 59)

Group F	P	W	D	L	F	A	Pts
ENGLAND	3	1	2	0	2	1	4
NETHERLANDS	3	0	3	0	2	2	3
REP. OF IRELAND	3	0	3	0	2	2	3
EGYPT	3	0	2	1	1	2	2

1990 (continued)

MANAGER CHANGED TO: GRAHAM TAYLOR

Friendly

DATE	VENUE	OPPONENTS	SCORE	GOALSCORERS	ATTENDANCE	TEAM
Sep 12	Wembley, London	HUNGARY	W 1-0	Lineker	51,459	Woods (17), Dixon (2), Pearce (31), (Dorigo 5), Parker (12), Wright (31), Walker (26), Platt (12), Gascoigne (18), Bull (12), (Waddle 60), **Lineker** (59), Barnes J (59)

European Championship Qualifiers

DATE	VENUE	OPPONENTS	SCORE	GOALSCORERS	ATTENDANCE	TEAM
Oct 17	Wembley, London	POLAND	W 2-0	Lineker (pen), Beardsley	77,040	Woods (18), Dixon (3), Pearce (32), Parker (13), Wright (32), Walker (27), Platt (13), Gascoigne (19), Bull (13), (Waddle 61), **Lineker** (60), (Beardsley 46), Barnes J (60)
Nov 14	Lansdowne Road, Dublin	R. of IRELAND	D 1-1	Platt	46,000	Woods (19), Dixon (4), Pearce (33), Adams (18), Wright (33), Walker (28), Platt (14), McMahon (17), Beardsley (47), **Lineker** (61), Cowans (10)

1991

Friendly

DATE	VENUE	OPPONENTS	SCORE	GOALSCORERS	ATTENDANCE	TEAM
Feb 6	Wembley, London	CAMEROON	W 2-0	Lineker 2 (1 pen)	61,075	Seaman (4), Dixon (5), Pearce (34), Steven (30), Wright (34), Walker (29), **Robson** (88), (Pallister 3), Gascoigne (20), (Hodge 23), Wright I (1), Lineker (62), Barnes J (61)

European Championship Qualifiers

DATE	VENUE	OPPONENTS	SCORE	GOALSCORERS	ATTENDANCE	TEAM
Mar 27	Wembley, London	R. of IRELAND	D 1-1	Dixon	77,753	Seaman (5), Dixon (6), Pearce (35), Adams (19), (Sharpe 1), Wright (35), Walker (30), **Robson** (89), Platt (15), Beardsley (48), Lineker (63), (Wright I 2), Barnes J (62)
May 1	Izmir	TURKEY	W 1-0	Wise	25,000	Seaman (6), Dixon (7), Pearce (36), Wise (1), Pallister (4), Walker (31), Platt (16), Thomas (1), (Hodge 24), Smith (5), **Lineker** (64), Barnes J (63)

England Challenge Cup

DATE	VENUE	OPPONENTS	SCORE	GOALSCORERS	ATTENDANCE	TEAM
May 21	Wembley, London	USSR	W 3-1	Smith, Platt 2 (1 pen)	23,789	Woods (20), Stevens M (42), Dorigo (6), Wise (2), (Batty 1), **Wright** (36), (Beardsley 49), Parker (14), Platt (17), Thomas (2), Smith (6), Wright I (3), Barnes J (64)
May 25	Wembley, London	ARGENTINA	D 2-2	Lineker, Platt	44,497	Seaman (7), Dixon (8), Pearce (37), Batty (2), Wright (37), Walker (32), Platt (18), Thomas (3), Smith (7), **Lineker** (65), Barnes J (65), (Clough 2)

Friendlies

DATE	VENUE	OPPONENTS	SCORE	GOALSCORERS	ATTENDANCE	TEAM
Jun 1	Sydney	AUSTRALIA	W 1-0	own goal	35,472	Woods (21), Parker (15), Pearce (38), Batty (3), Wright (38), Walker (33), Platt (19), Thomas (4), Clough (3), **Lineker** (66), (Wise 3), Hirst (1), (Salako 1)
Jun 3	Auckland	NEW ZEALAND	W 1-0	Lineker	17,520	Woods (22), Parker (16), Pearce (39), Batty (4), (Deane 1), Barrett (1), Walker (34), Platt (20), Thomas (5), Walters (1), (Salako 2), **Lineker** (67), Wise (4)
Jun 8	Wellington	NEW ZEALAND	W 2-0	Pearce, Hirst	12,000	Woods (23), Charles (1), **Pearce** (40), Wise (5), Wright (39), Walker (35), Platt (21), Thomas (6), Deane (2), (Hirst 2), Wright I (4), Salako (3)
Jun 12	Kuala Lumpur	MALAYSIA	W 4-2	Lineker 4	45,000	Woods (24), Charles (2), Pearce (41), Batty (5), Wright (40), Walker (36), Platt (22), Thomas (7), Clough (4), **Lineker** (68), Salako (4)
Sep 11	Wembley, London	GERMANY	L 0-1		59,493	Woods (25), Dixon (9), Dorigo (7), Batty (6), Parker (17), Pallister (5), Platt (23), Steven (31), (Merson 1), Smith (8), **Lineker** (69), Salako (5), (Stewart 1)

European Championship Qualifiers

DATE	VENUE	OPPONENTS	SCORE	GOALSCORERS	ATTENDANCE	TEAM
Oct 16	Wembley, London	TURKEY	W 1-0	Smith	50,896	Woods (26), Dixon (10), Pearce (42), Batty (7), Mabbutt (14), Walker (37), Robson (90), Platt (24), Smith (9), **Lineker** (70), Waddle (62)
Nov 13	Poznan	POLAND	D 1-1	Lineker	15,000	Woods (27), Dixon (11), Pearce (43), Gray (1), (Smith 10), Mabbutt (15), Walker (38), Platt (25), Thomas (8), Rocastle (12), **Lineker** (71), Sinton (1), (Daley 1)

1992

Friendlies

DATE	VENUE	OPPONENTS	SCORE	GOALSCORERS	ATTENDANCE	TEAM
Feb 19	Wembley, London	FRANCE	W 2-0	Shearer, Lineker	58,723	Woods (28), Jones (1), **Pearce** (44), Keown (1), Wright (41), Walker (39), Webb (21), Thomas (9), Clough (5), Shearer (1), Hirst (3), (Lineker 72)
Mar 25	Prague	CZECHOSLOVAKIA	D 2-2	Merson, Keown	6,000	Seaman (8), Keown (2), **Pearce** (45), Rocastle (13), (Dixon 12), Mabbutt (16), (Lineker 73), Walker (40), Platt (26), Merson (2), Clough (6), (Stewart 2), Hateley (32), Barnes J (66), (Dorigo 8)
Apr 29	Moscow	CIS	D 2-2	Lineker, Steven	25,000	Woods (29), (Martyn 1), Stevens M (43), Sinton (2), (Curle 1), Steven (32), (Stewart 3), Keown (3), Walker (41), Platt (27), Palmer (1), Shearer (2), (Clough 7), **Lineker** (74), Daley (2)
May 12	Budapest	HUNGARY	W 1-0	Webb	25,000	Martyn (2), (Seaman 9), Stevens M (44), Dorigo (9), Curle (2), (Sinton 3), Keown (4), Walker (42), Webb (22), (Batty 8), Palmer (2), Merson (3), (Smith 11), **Lineker** (75), Daley (3), (Wright I 5)
May 17	Wembley, London	BRAZIL	D 1-1	Platt	53,428	Woods (30), Stevens M (45), Dorigo (10), (Pearce 46), Steven (33), (Rocastle 14), Keown (5), Walker (43), Daley (4), (Merson 4), Palmer (3), Platt (28), **Lineker** (76), Sinton (4), (Webb 23)
Jun 3	Helsinki	FINLAND	W 2-1	Platt 2	16,101	Woods (31), Stevens M (46), (Palmer 4), Pearce (47), Keown (6), Wright (42), Walker (44), Platt (29), Steven (34), (Daley 5), Webb (24), **Lineker** (77), Barnes J (67), (Merson 5)

EUROPEAN CHAMPIONSHIP FINALS 1992

Group Stage – Pool 2

DATE	VENUE	OPPONENTS	SCORE	GOALSCORERS	ATTENDANCE	TEAM
Jun 11	Malmo	DENMARK	D 0-0		26,385	Woods (32), Keown (7), Pearce (48), Steven (35), Curle (3), (Daley 6), Walker (45), Platt (30), Palmer (5), Smith (12), **Lineker** (78), Merson (6), (Webb 25)
Jun 14	Malmo	FRANCE	D 0-0		26,535	Woods (33), Keown (8), Pearce (49), Batty (9), Palmer (6), Walker (46), Platt (31), Steven (36), Shearer (3), **Lineker** (79), Sinton (5)
Jun 17	Stockholm	SWEDEN	L 1-2	Platt	30,126	Woods (34), Keown (9), Pearce (50), Batty (10), Palmer (7), Walker (47), Daley (7), Webb (26), Platt (32), **Lineker** (80), (Smith 13), Sinton (6), (Merson 7)

POOL 2

	P	W	D	L	F	A	Pts
SWEDEN	3	2	1	0	4	2	5
DENMARK	3	1	1	1	2	2	3
FRANCE	3	0	2	1	2	3	2
ENGLAND	3	0	2	1	1	2	2

1992 (continued)

Friendly

DATE	VENUE	OPPONENTS	SCORE	GOALSCORERS	ATTENDANCE	TEAM
Sep 9	Santander	SPAIN	L 0-1		22,000	Woods (35), Dixon (13), (Bardsley 1), (Palmer 8), **Pearce** (51), Ince (1), Wright (43), Walker (48), White (1), (Merson 8), Platt (33), Clough (8), Shearer (4), Sinton (7), (Deane 3)

World Cup Qualifiers

DATE	VENUE	OPPONENTS	SCORE	GOALSCORERS	ATTENDANCE	TEAM
Oct 14	Wembley, London	NORWAY	D 1-1	Platt	51,441	Woods (36), Dixon (14), (Palmer 9), **Pearce** (52), Batty (11), Adams (20), Walker (49), Platt (34), Gascoigne (21), Shearer (5), Wright I (6), (Merson 9), Ince (2)
Nov 18	Wembley, London	TURKEY	W 4-0	Gascoigne 2, Shearer, Pearce	42,984	Woods (37), Dixon (15), **Pearce** (53), Palmer (10), Adams (21), Walker (50), Platt (35), Gascoigne (22), Shearer (6), Wright I (7), Ince (3)

1993

World Cup Qualifiers

DATE	VENUE	OPPONENTS	SCORE	GOALSCORERS	ATTENDANCE	TEAM
Feb 17	Wembley, London	SAN MARINO	W 6-0	Platt 4, Palmer, Ferdinand	51,154	Woods (38), Dixon (16), Dorigo (11), Palmer (11), Adams (22), Walker (51), **Platt** (36), Gascoigne (23), Ferdinand (1), Batty (12), Barnes J (68)
Mar 31	Izmir	TURKEY	W 2-0	Platt, Gascoigne	60,000	Woods (39), Dixon (17), (Clough 9), Sinton (8), Palmer (12), Adams (23), Walker (52), **Platt** (37), Gascoigne (24), Wright I (8), (Sharpe 2), Ince (4), Barnes J (69)
Apr 28	Wembley, London	HOLLAND	D 2-2	Barnes J, Platt	73,163	Woods (40), Dixon (18), Keown (10), Palmer (13), Adams (24), Walker (53), **Platt** (38), Gascoigne (25), (Merson 10), Ferdinand (2), Ince (5), Barnes J (70)
May 29	Katowice	POLAND	D 1-1	Wright I	60,000	Woods (41), Bardsley (2), Dorigo (12), Palmer (14), (Wright I 9), Adams (25), Walker (54), **Platt** (39), Gascoigne (26), (Clough 10), Sheringham (1), Ince (6), Barnes J (71)
Jun 2	Oslo	NORWAY	L 0-2		22,250	Woods (42), Dixon (19), Sharpe (3), Pallister (6), Adams (26), Walker (55), (Clough 11), **Platt** (40), Palmer (15), Ferdinand (3), Sheringham (2), (Wright I 10), Gascoigne (27)

1993 (continued)

US Cup

DATE	VENUE	OPPONENTS	SCORE	GOALSCORERS	ATTENDANCE	TEAM
Jun 9	Boston	USA	L 0-2		37,652	Woods (43), Dixon (20), Dorigo (13), Batty (13), Pallister (7), Palmer (16), (Walker 56), Ince (7), Clough (12), Ferdinand (4), (Wright I 11), Barnes J (72), Sharpe (4)
Jun 13	Washington	BRAZIL	D 1-1	Platt	54,118	Flowers (1), Barrett (2), Dorigo (14), Batty (14), (Platt 41), Pallister (8), Walker (57), Ince (8), (Palmer 17), Clough (13), (Merson 11), Wright I (12), Sinton (9), Sharpe (5)
Jun 19	Detroit	GERMANY	L 1-2	Platt	62,126	Martyn (3), Barrett (3), Sinton (10), Sharpe (6), (Winterburn 2), Pallister (9), (Keown 11), Walker (58), Platt (42), Ince (9), Clough (14), (Wright I 13), Merson (12), Barnes J (73)

World Cup Qualifiers

DATE	VENUE	OPPONENTS	SCORE	GOALSCORERS	ATTENDANCE	TEAM
Sep 8	Wembley, London	POLAND	W 3-0	Ferdinand, Gascoigne, Pearce,	71,220	Seaman (10), Jones (2), Pearce (54), Ince (10), Adams (27), Pallister (10), Platt (43), Gascoigne (28), Ferdinand (5), Wright I (14), Sharpe (7)
Oct 13	Rotterdam	HOLLAND	L 0-2		48,000	Seaman (11), Parker (18), Dorigo (15), Palmer (18), (Sinton 11), Adams (28), Pallister (11), Platt (44), Ince (11), Shearer (7), Merson (13), (Wright I 15), Sharpe (8)
Nov 17	Bologna	SAN MARINO	W 7-1	Ince 2, Wright I 4, Ferdinand	2,378	Seaman (12), Dixon (21), Pearce (55), Ince (12), Pallister (12), Walker (59), Ripley (1), Platt (45), Ferdinand (6), Wright I (16), Sinton (12)

1994

MANAGER CHANGED TO: TERRY VENABLES

Friendlies

DATE	VENUE	OPPONENTS	SCORE	GOALSCORERS	ATTENDANCE	TEAM
Mar 9	Wembley, London	DENMARK	W 1-0	Platt	71,970	Seaman (13), Parker (19), Le Saux (1), Ince (13), (Batty 15), Adams (29), Pallister (13), Anderton (1), Gascoigne (29), (Le Tissier 1), Shearer (8), Beardsley (50), Platt (46)
May 17	Wembley, London	GREECE	W 5-0	Anderton, Beardsley, Platt 2 (1 pen), Shearer	23,659	Flowers (2), Jones (3), (Pearce 56), Le Saux (2), Richardson (1), Bould (1), Adams (30), Anderton (2), (Le Tissier 2), Merson (14), Shearer (9), Beardsley (51), (Wright I 17), Platt (47)
May 22	Wembley, London	NORWAY	D 0-0		64,327	Seaman (14), Jones (4), Le Saux (3), Ince (14), (Wright I 18), Bould (2), Adams (31), Anderton (3), (Le Tissier 3), Platt (48), Shearer (10), Beardsley (52), Wise (6)
Sep 7	Wembley, London	USA	W 2-0	Shearer 2	38,629	Seaman (15), Jones (5), Le Saux (4), Venison (1), Adams (32), Pallister (14), Anderton (4), Platt (49), Shearer (11), (Wright I 19), Sheringham (3), (Ferdinand 7), Barnes J (74)
Oct 12	Wembley, London	ROMANIA	D 1-1	Lee	48,754	Seaman (16), Jones (6), (Pearce 57), Le Saux (5), Ince (15), Adams (33), Pallister (15), Le Tissier (4), Lee (1), (Wise 7), Shearer (12), Wright I (20), (Sheringham 4), Barnes J (75)
Nov 16	Wembley, London	NIGERIA	W 1-0	Platt	37,196	Flowers (3), Jones (7), Le Saux (6), Wise (8), Howey (1), Ruddock (1), Platt (50), Lee (2), (McManaman 1), Shearer (13), (Sheringham 5), Beardsley (53), (Le Tissier 5), Barnes J (76)

1995

Friendlies

DATE	VENUE	OPPONENTS	SCORE	GOALSCORERS	ATTENDANCE	TEAM
Feb 15	Lansdowne Road Dublin	R. of IRELAND	L 0-1	(Abandoned after 27 minutes due to crowd trouble)	46,000	Seaman (17), Barton (1), Le Saux (7), Ince (16), Adams (34), Pallister (16), Anderton (5), Platt (51), Shearer (14), Beardsley (54), Le Tissier (6)
Mar 29	Wembley, London	URUGUAY	D 0-0		34,849	Flowers (4), Jones (8), Le Saux (8), (McManaman 2), Venison (2), Adams (35), Pallister (17), Anderton (6), Platt (52), Beardsley (55), (Barmby 1), Sheringham (6), (Cole 1), Barnes J (77)

1995 (continued)

Umbro International Trophy

DATE	VENUE	OPPONENTS	SCORE	GOALSCORERS	ATTENDANCE	TEAM
Jun 3	Wembley, London	JAPAN	W 2-1	Anderton, Platt (pen)	21,142	Flowers (5), Neville G (1), Pearce (58), Batty (16), (Gascoigne 30), Scales (1), Unsworth (1), Anderton (7), Beardsley (56), (McManaman 3), Shearer (15), Collymore (1), (Sheringham 7), **Platt** (53)
Jun 8	Elland Road, Leeds	SWEDEN	D 3-3	Sheringham, Platt, Anderton	32,008	Flowers (6), Barton (2), Le Saux (9), **Platt** (54), Cooper (1), Pallister (18), (Scales 2), Anderton (8), Beardsley (57), (Barmby 2), Shearer (16), Sheringham (8), Barnes J (78), (Gascoigne 31)
Jun 11	Wembley, London	BRAZIL	L 1-3	Le Saux	67,318	Flowers (7), Neville G (2), Pearce (59), Batty (17), (Gascoigne 32), Cooper (2), Scales (3), (Barton 3), Anderton (9), **Platt** (55), Shearer (17), Sheringham (9), (Collymore 2), Le Saux (10)

Friendlies

DATE	VENUE	OPPONENTS	SCORE	GOALSCORERS	ATTENDANCE	TEAM
Sep 6	Wembley, London	COLOMBIA	D 0-0		20,038	Seaman (18), Neville G (3), Le Saux (11), Redknapp (1), (Lee 3), **Adams** (36), Howey (2), McManaman (4), Barmby (3), Shearer (18), (Sheringham 10), Gascoigne (33), (Barnes J 79), Wise (9)
Oct 11	Oslo	NORWAY	D 0-0		21,006	Seaman (19), Neville G (4), Pearce (60), Redknapp (2), **Adams** (37), Pallister (19), Lee (4), Barmby (4), (Sheringham 11), Shearer (19), McManaman (5), Wise (10), (Stone 1)
Nov 15	Wembley, London	SWITZERLAND	W 3-1	Pearce, Sheringham, Stone	29,874	Seaman (20), Neville G (5), Pearce (61), Redknapp (3), (Stone 2), **Adams** (38), Pallister (20), Lee (5), Gascoigne (34), Shearer (20), Sheringham (12), McManaman (6)
Dec 12	Wembley, London	PORTUGAL	D 1-1	Stone	28,592	Seaman (21), Neville G (6), Pearce (62), (Le Saux 12), Stone (3), **Adams** (39), Howey (3), Barmby (5), (McManaman 7), Gascoigne (35), Shearer (21), Ferdinand (8), (Beardsley 58), Wise (11), (Southgate 1)

1996

Friendlies

DATE	VENUE	OPPONENTS	SCORE	GOALSCORERS	ATTENDANCE	TEAM
Mar 27	Wembley, London	BULGARIA	W 1-0	Ferdinand	29,708	Seaman (22), Neville G (7), **Pearce** (63), Stone (4), Southgate (2), Howey (4), McManaman (8), Gascoigne (36), (Lee 6), Ferdinand (9), (Platt 56), Sheringham (13), (Fowler 1), Ince (17)
Apr 24	Wembley, London	CROATIA	D 0-0		33,650	Seaman (23), Neville G (8), Pearce (64), Stone (5), Wright (44), Ince (18), McManaman (9), Gascoigne (37), Fowler (2), Sheringham (14), **Platt** (57)
May 18	Wembley, London	HUNGARY	W 3-0	Anderton 2, Platt	34,184	Seaman (24), (Walker 1), Neville G (9), Pearce (65), **Platt** (58), (Wise 12), Wright (45), (Southgate 3), Ince (19), (Campbell 1), Anderton (10), Lee (7), Ferdinand (10), (Shearer 22), Sheringham (15), Wilcox (1)
May 23	Beijing	CHINA	W 3-0	Barmby 2, Gascoigne	65,000	Flowers (8), (Walker 2), Neville G (10), Neville P (1), Redknapp (4), **Adams** (40), (Ehiogu 1), Southgate (4), Anderton (11), Barmby (6), (Beardsley 59), Shearer (23), (Fowler 3), Gascoigne (38), McManaman (10), (Stone 6)

EUROPEAN CHAMPIONSHIP FINALS 1996

Group Stage – Group A

DATE	VENUE	OPPONENTS	SCORE	GOALSCORERS	ATTENDANCE	TEAM
Jun 8	Wembley, London	SWITZERLAND	D 1-1	Shearer	76,567	Seaman (25), Neville G (11), Pearce (66), Ince (20), **Adams** (41), Southgate (5), Anderton (12), Gascoigne (39), (Platt 59), Shearer (24), Sheringham (16), (Barmby 7), McManaman (11), (Stone 7)
Jun 15	Wembley, London	SCOTLAND	W 2-0	Shearer, Gascoigne	76,864	Seaman (26), Neville G (12), Pearce (67), (Redknapp 5), (Campbell 2), Ince (21), (Stone 8), **Adams** (42), Southgate (6), Anderton (13), Gascoigne (40), Shearer (25), Sheringham (17), McManaman (12)
Jun 18	Wembley, London	HOLLAND	W 4-1	Shearer 2 (1 pen), Sheringham 2	76,798	Seaman (27), Neville G (13), Pearce (68), Ince (22), (Platt 60), **Adams** (43), Southgate (7), Anderton (14), Gascoigne (41), Shearer (26), (Barmby 8), Sheringham (18), (Fowler 4), McManaman (13)

Quarter-final

DATE	VENUE	OPPONENTS	SCORE	GOALSCORERS	ATTENDANCE	TEAM
Jun 22	Wembley, London	SPAIN	D 0-0	(England won 4-2 on penalties)	75,440	Seaman (28), Neville G (14), Pearce (69), Platt (61), **Adams** (44), Southgate (8), Anderton (15), (Fowler 5), Gascoigne (42), Shearer (27), Sheringham (19), (Stone 9), McManaman (14), (Barmby 9)

Semi-final

DATE	VENUE	OPPONENTS	SCORE	GOALSCORERS	ATTENDANCE	TEAM
Jun 26	Wembley, London	GERMANY	D 1-1	Shearer (England lost 6-5 on penalties)	75,862	Seaman (29), Ince (23), Pearce (70), Platt (62), **Adams** (45), Southgate (9), Anderton (16), Gascoigne (43), Shearer (28), Sheringham (20), McManaman (15)

Group A

	P	W	D	L	F	A	Pts
ENGLAND	3	2	1	0	7	2	7
NETHERLANDS	3	1	1	1	3	4	4
SCOTLAND	3	1	1	1	1	2	4
SWITZERLAND	3	0	1	2	1	4	1

1996 (continued)

MANAGER CHANGED TO: GLENN HODDLE

World Cup Qualifiers

DATE	VENUE	OPPONENTS	SCORE	GOALSCORERS	ATTENDANCE	TEAM
Sep 1	Chisinau	MOLDOVA	W 3-0	Gascoigne, Shearer, Barmby	15,000	Seaman (30), Neville G (15), Pearce (71), Ince (24), Pallister (21), Southgate (10), Beckham (1), Gascoigne (44), (Batty 18), **Shearer** (29), Barmby (10), (Le Tissier 7), Hinchcliffe (1)
Oct 9	Wembley, London	POLAND	W 2-1	Shearer 2	74,663	Seaman (31), Neville G (16), Pearce (72), Ince (25), Southgate (11), (Pallister 22), Hinchcliffe (2), Beckham (2), Gascoigne (45), **Shearer** (30), Ferdinand (11), McManaman (16)
Nov 9	Tbilisi	GEORGIA	W 2-0	Ferdinand, Sheringham	48,000	Seaman (32), Campbell (3), Hinchcliffe (3), Ince (26), **Adams** (46), Southgate (12), Beckham (3), Gascoigne (46), Ferdinand (12), (Wright I 21), Sheringham (21), Batty (19)

1997

World Cup Qualifier

DATE	VENUE	OPPONENTS	SCORE	GOALSCORERS	ATTENDANCE	TEAM
Feb 12	Wembley, London	ITALY	L 0-1		75,055	Walker (3), Neville G (17), Pearce (73), Ince (27), Campbell (4), Le Saux (13), Beckham (4), Batty (20), (Wright I 22), **Shearer** (31), Le Tissier (8), (Ferdinand 13), McManaman (17), (Merson 15)

Friendly

DATE	VENUE	OPPONENTS	SCORE	GOALSCORERS	ATTENDANCE	TEAM
Mar 29	Wembley, London	MEXICO	W 2-0	Fowler, Sheringham (pen)	48,076	James (1), Keown (12), Pearce (74), Batty (21), (Redknapp 6), Southgate (13), Le Saux (14), Lee (8), Ince (28), Fowler (6), Sheringham (22), (Wright I 23), McManaman (18), (Butt 1)

1997 (continued)

World Cup Qualifier

DATE	VENUE	OPPONENTS	SCORE	GOALSCORERS	ATTENDANCE	TEAM
Apr 30	Wembley, London	GEORGIA	W 2-0	Shearer, Sheringham	71,206	Seaman (33), Neville G (18), Campbell (5), Batty (22), Adams (47), (Southgate 14), Le Saux (15), Beckham (5), Ince (29), (Redknapp 7), **Shearer** (32), Sheringham (23), Lee (9)

Friendly

DATE	VENUE	OPPONENTS	SCORE	GOALSCORERS	ATTENDANCE	TEAM
May 24	Old Trafford	SOUTH AFRICA	W 2-1	Wright I, Lee	52,676	Martyn (4), Neville P (2), **Pearce** (75), Keown (13), Southgate (15), Le Saux (16), (Beckham 6), Redknapp (8), (Batty 23), Gascoigne (47), (Campbell 6), Wright I (24), Sheringham (24), (Scholes 1), Lee (10), (Butt 2)

World Cup Qualifier

DATE	VENUE	OPPONENTS	SCORE	GOALSCORERS	ATTENDANCE	TEAM
May 31	Katowice	POLAND	W 2-0	Shearer, Sheringham	35,000	Seaman (34), Neville G (19), Campbell (7), Ince (30), Southgate (16), Le Saux (17), Beckham (7), (Neville P 3), Gascoigne (48), (Batty 24), **Shearer** (33), Sheringham (25), Lee (11)

Tournoi de France

DATE	VENUE	OPPONENTS	SCORE	GOALSCORERS	ATTENDANCE	TEAM
Jun 4	Nantes	ITALY	W 2-0	Wright I, Scholes	25,000	Flowers (9), Neville P (4), Pearce (76), Keown (14), Southgate (17), Le Saux (18), (Neville G 20), Beckham (8), **Ince** (31), Wright I (25), (Cole 2), Sheringham (26), (Gascoigne 49), Scholes (2)
Jun 7	Montpellier	FRANCE	W 1-0	Shearer	25,000	Seaman (35), Neville G (21), Campbell (8), Neville P (5), Southgate (18), Le Saux (19), Beckham (9), (Lee 12), Gascoigne (50), **Shearer** (34), Wright I (26), (Sheringham 27), Batty (25), (Ince 32)
Jun 10	Paris	BRAZIL	L 0-1		50,000	Seaman (36), Keown (15), (Neville G 22), Campbell (9), Ince (33), Southgate (19), Le Saux (20), Neville P (6), Gascoigne (51), **Shearer** (35), Sheringham (28), (Wright I 27), Scholes (3), (Lee 13)

World Cup Qualifiers

DATE	VENUE	OPPONENTS	SCORE	GOALSCORERS	ATTENDANCE	TEAM
Sep 10	Wembley, London	MOLDOVA	W 4-0	Scholes, Wright I 2, Gascoigne	74,102	**Seaman** (37), Neville G (23), Neville P (7), Batty (26), Southgate (20), Campbell (10), Beckham (10), (Ripley 2), (Butt 3), Gascoigne (52), Ferdinand (14), (Collymore 3), Wright I (28), Scholes (4)
Oct 11	Rome	ITALY	D 0-0		81,200	Seaman (38), Beckham (11), Le Saux (21), Southgate (21), **Adams** (48), Campbell (11), Gascoigne (53), (Butt 4), Batty (27), Wright I (29), Sheringham (29), Ince (34)

Friendly

DATE	VENUE	OPPONENTS	SCORE	GOALSCORERS	ATTENDANCE	TEAM
Nov 15	Wembley, London	CAMEROON	W 2-0	Fowler, Scholes	46,176	Martyn (5), Beckham (12), Hinchcliffe (4), Neville P (8), Southgate (22), (Ferdinand R 1), Campbell (12), McManaman (19), Gascoigne (54), (Lee 14), Fowler (7), Scholes (5), (Sutton 1), **Ince** (35)

1998

Friendlies

DATE	VENUE	OPPONENTS	SCORE	GOALSCORERS	ATTENDANCE	TEAM
Feb 11	Wembley, London	CHILE	L 0-2		65,228	Martyn (6), Lee (15), Neville P (9), (Le Saux 22), Neville G (24), **Adams** (49), Campbell (13), Butt (5), Batty (28), (Ince 36), Dublin (1), Sheringham (30), (Shearer 36), Owen (1)
Mar 25	Berne	SWITZERLAND	D 1-1	Merson	17,100	Flowers (10), Lee (16), Hinchcliffe (5), Southgate (23), Keown (16), Ferdinand R (2), McManaman (20), Ince (37), **Shearer** (37), Merson (16), (Batty 29), Owen (2), (Sheringham 31)
Apr 22	Wembley, London	PORTUGAL	W 3-0	Shearer 2, Sheringham	63,463	Seaman (39), Beckham (13), (Merson 17), Le Saux (23), Neville G (25), (Neville P 10), Adams (50), Campbell (14), Batty (30), Ince (38), **Shearer** (38), Sheringham (32), (Owen 3), Scholes (6)
May 23	Wembley, London	SAUDI ARABIA	D 0-0		63,733	Seaman (40), Anderton (17), Hinchcliffe (6), (Neville P 11), Neville G (26), Adams (51), Southgate (24), Beckham (14), (Gascoigne 55), Batty (31), **Shearer** (39), (Ferdinand 15), Sheringham (33), (Wright I 30), Scholes (7)

King Hassan II Cup

DATE	VENUE	OPPONENTS	SCORE	GOALSCORERS	ATTENDANCE	TEAM
May 27	Casablanca	MOROCCO	W 1-0	Owen	80,000	Flowers (11), Anderton (18), Le Saux (24), Southgate (25), Keown (17), Campbell (15), McManaman (21), Gascoigne (56), Dublin (2), (Ferdinand 16), Wright I (31), (Owen 4), **Ince** (39)
May 29	Casablanca	BELGIUM	D 0-0	(England lost 4-3 on penalties)	25,000	Martyn (7), Neville G (27), (Owen 5), Neville P (12), (Ferdinand R 3), Gascoigne (57), (Beckham 15), Keown (18), **Campbell** (16), (Dublin 3), Lee (17), Butt (6), Ferdinand (17), Merson (18), Le Saux (25)

THE WORLD CUP FINALS 1998 (FRANCE)

Group Stage – Group G

DATE	VENUE	OPPONENTS	SCORE	GOALSCORERS	ATTENDANCE	TEAM
Jun 15	Marseille	TUNISIA	W 2-0	Shearer, Scholes	54,587	Seaman (41), Anderton (19), Le Saux (26), Southgate (26), Adams (52), Campbell (17), Scholes (8), Batty (32), **Shearer** (40), Sheringham (34), (Owen 6), Ince (40)
Jun 22	Toulouse	ROMANIA	L 1-2	Owen	37,500	Seaman (42), Neville G (28), Le Saux (27), Batty (33), Adams (53), Campbell (18), Anderton (20), Ince (41), (Beckham 16), **Shearer** (41), Sheringham (35), (Owen 7), Scholes (9)
Jun 26	Lens	COLOMBIA	W 2-0	Anderton, Beckham	41,275	Seaman (43), Neville G (29), Le Saux (28), Beckham (17), Adams (54), Campbell (19), Anderton (21), (Lee 18), Ince (42), (Batty 34), **Shearer** (42), Scholes (10), (McManaman 22), Owen (8)

Second Round

DATE	VENUE	OPPONENTS	SCORE	GOALSCORERS	ATTENDANCE	TEAM
Jun 30	St Etienne	ARGENTINA	D 2-2	Shearer (pen), Owen (England lost 4-3 on penalties)	30,600	Seaman (44), Neville G (30), Le Saux (29), (Southgate 27), *Beckham* (18), Adams (55), Campbell (20), Anderton (22), (Batty 35), Ince (43), **Shearer** (43), Scholes (11), (Merson 19), Owen (9)

Group G

	P	W	D	L	F	A	Pts
ROMANIA	3	2	1	0	4	2	7
ENGLAND	3	2	0	1	5	2	6
COLOMBIA	3	1	0	2	1	3	3
TUNISIA	3	0	1	2	1	4	1

1998 (continued)

European Championship Qualifiers

DATE	VENUE	OPPONENTS	SCORE	GOALSCORERS	ATTENDANCE	TEAM
Sep 5	Stockholm	SWEDEN	L 1-2	Shearer	35,394	Seaman (45), Campbell (21), (Merson 20), Le Saux (30), *Ince* (44), Adams (56), Southgate (28), Anderton (23), (Lee 19), Redknapp (9), **Shearer** (44), Owen (10), Scholes (12), (Sheringham 36)
Oct 10	Wembley, London	BULGARIA	D 0-0		72,974	Seaman (46), Neville G (31), Hinchcliffe (7), (Le Saux 31), Lee (20), Campbell (22), Southgate (29), Anderton (24), (Batty 36), Redknapp (10), **Shearer** (45), Owen (11), Scholes (13), (Sheringham 37)
Oct 14	Luxembourg	LUXEMBOURG	W 3-0	Southgate, Shearer, Owen	8,000	Seaman (47), Ferdinand R (4), Neville P (13), Batty (37), Campbell (23), Southgate (30), Beckham (19), Anderton (25), (Lee 21), **Shearer** (46), Owen (12), Scholes (14), (Wright I 32)

Friendly

DATE	VENUE	OPPONENTS	SCORE	GOALSCORERS	ATTENDANCE	TEAM
Nov 18	Wembley, London	CZECH REPUBLIC	W 2-0	Anderton, Merson	38,535	Martyn (8), Ferdinand R (5), Le Saux (32), Butt (7), **Campbell** (24), Keown (19), Beckham (20), Anderton (26), Dublin (4), Wright I (33), (Fowler 8), Merson (21), (Hendrie 1)

1999

(CARETAKER-MANAGER: HOWARD WILKINSON)

Friendly

DATE	VENUE	OPPONENTS	SCORE	GOALSCORERS	ATTENDANCE	TEAM
Feb 10	Wembley, London	FRANCE	L 0-2		74,111	Seaman (48), (Martyn 9), Dixon (22), (Ferdinand R 6), Le Saux (33), Ince (45), Keown (20), (Wilcox 2), Adams (57), Beckham (21), Redknapp (11), (Scholes 15), **Shearer** (47), Owen (13), (Cole 3), Anderton (27)

MANAGER CHANGED TO: KEVIN KEEGAN

European Championship Qualifier

DATE	VENUE	OPPONENTS	SCORE	GOALSCORERS	ATTENDANCE	TEAM
Mar 27	Wembley, London	POLAND	W 3-1	Scholes 3	73,836	Seaman (49), Neville G (32), Le Saux (34), Sherwood (1), Campbell (25), Keown (21), Beckham (22), (Neville P 14), Scholes (16), (Redknapp 12), **Shearer** (48), Cole (4), McManaman (23), (Parlour 1)

1999 (continued)

Friendly

DATE	VENUE	OPPONENTS	SCORE	GOALSCORERS	ATTENDANCE	TEAM
Apr 28	Budapest	HUNGARY	D 1-1	Shearer (pen)	20,000	Seaman (50), Brown W (1), (Gray 1), Neville P (15), Batty (38), Ferdinand R (7), (Carragher 1), Keown (22), Butt (8), Sherwood (2), **Shearer** (49), Phillips (1), (Heskey 1), McManaman (24), (Redknapp 13)

European Championship Qualifiers

DATE	VENUE	OPPONENTS	SCORE	GOALSCORERS	ATTENDANCE	TEAM
Jun 5	Wembley, London	SWEDEN	D 0-0		75,824	Seaman (51), Neville P (16), Le Saux (35), (Gray 2), Sherwood (3), Campbell (26), Keown (23), (Ferdinand R 8), Beckham (23), (Parlour 2), Batty (39), **Shearer** (50), Cole (5), *Scholes* (17)
Jun 9	Sofia	BULGARIA	D 1-1	Shearer	22,000	Seaman (52), Neville P (17), Gray (3), Southgate (31), Campbell (27), Woodgate (1), (Parlour 3), Redknapp (14), Batty (40), **Shearer** (51), Sheringham (38), Fowler (9), (Heskey 2)
Sep 4	Wembley, London	LUXEMBOURG	W 6-0	Shearer 3, McManaman 2, Owen	68,772	Martyn (10), Dyer (1), (Neville G 33), Pearce (77), Batty (41), Keown (24), Adams (58), (Neville P 18), Beckham (24), (Owen 14), Parlour (4), **Shearer** (52), Fowler (10), McManaman (25)
Sep 8	Warsaw	POLAND	D 0-0		17,000	Martyn (11), Neville G (34), (Neville P 19), Pearce (78), *Batty* (42), Keown (25), Adams (59), Beckham (25), Scholes (18), **Shearer** (53), Fowler (11), (Owen 15), McManaman (26), (Dyer 2)

Friendly

DATE	VENUE	OPPONENTS	SCORE	GOALSCORERS	ATTENDANCE	TEAM
Oct 10	Sunderland	BELGIUM	W 2-1	Shearer, Redknapp	40,897	Seaman (53), (Martyn 12), Dyer (3), (Neville P 20), Guppy (1), Southgate (32), Keown (26), Adams (60), Lampard (1), (Wise 13), Redknapp (15), **Shearer** (54), (Heskey 3), Phillips (2), (Owen 16), Ince (46)

European Championship Qualifiers

DATE	VENUE	OPPONENTS	SCORE	GOALSCORERS	ATTENDANCE	TEAM
Nov 13	Hampden Park, Glasgow	SCOTLAND	W 2-0	Scholes 2	50,132	Seaman (54), Campbell (28), Neville P (21), Ince (47), Keown (27), Adams (61), Beckham (26), Scholes (19), **Shearer** (55), Owen (17), (Cole 6), Redknapp (16)
Nov 17	Wembley, London	SCOTLAND	L 0-1		75,848	Seaman (55), Campbell (29), Neville P (22), Ince (48), Southgate (33), Adams (62), Beckham (27), Scholes (20), (Parlour 5), **Shearer** (56), Owen (18), (Heskey 4), Redknapp (17)

2000

Friendlies

DATE	VENUE	OPPONENTS	SCORE	GOALSCORERS	ATTENDANCE	TEAM
Feb 23	Wembley, London	ARGENTINA	D 0-0		74,008	Seaman (56), Dyer (4), (Neville P 23), Campbell (30), Wise (14), Keown (28), (Ferdinand R 9), Southgate (24), Beckham (28), (Parlour 6), Scholes (21), **Shearer** (57), (Phillips 3), Heskey (5), (Cole 7), Wilcox (3)
May 27	Wembley, London	BRAZIL	D 1-1	Owen	73,956	Seaman (57), Neville G (35), Neville P (24), Ince (49), (Parlour 7), (Barmby 11), Keown (29), Campbell (31), Beckham (29), Scholes (22), **Shearer** (58), (Fowler 12), Owen (19), (Phillips 4), Wise (15)
May 31	Wembley, London	UKRAINE	W 2-0	Adams, Fowler	55,975	Martyn (13), Gerrard (1), (Dyer 5), Neville P (25), (Barry 1), Southgate (25), Campbell (32), Adams (63), Beckham (30), Scholes (23), (Barmby 12), **Shearer** (59), Fowler (13), (Heskey 6), McManaman (27)
Jun 3	Valletta	MALTA	W 2-1	Keown, Heskey	10,023	Wright R (1), Neville G (36), Neville P (26), Wise (16), (Ince 50), Keown (30), (Southgate 26), Campbell (33), Beckham (31), (Barry 2), Scholes (24), (McManaman 28), **Shearer** (60), (Heskey 7), Phillips (5), (Fowler 14), Barmby (13)

EUROPEAN CHAMPIONSHIP FINALS 2000

Group Stage – Group A

DATE	VENUE	OPPONENTS	SCORE	GOALSCORERS	ATTENDANCE	TEAM
Jun 12	Eindhoven	PORTUGAL	L 2-3	Scholes, McManaman	33,000	Seaman (58), Neville G (37), Neville P (27), Ince (51), Campbell (34), Adams (64), (Keown 31), Beckham (32), Scholes (25), **Shearer** (61), Owen (20), (Heskey 8), McManaman (29), (Wise 17)
Jun 17	Charleroi	GERMANY	W 1-0	Shearer	30,000	Seaman (59), Neville G (38), Neville P (28), Ince (52), Keown (32), Campbell (35), Beckham (33), Scholes (26), (Barmby 13), **Shearer** (62), Owen (21), (Gerrard 2), Wise (18)
Jun 20	Charleroi	ROMANIA	L 2-3	Shearer (pen), Owen	30,000	Martyn (14), Neville G (39), Neville P (29), Ince (53), Keown (33), Campbell (36), Beckham (34), Scholes (27), (Southgate 27), **Shearer** (63), Owen (22), (Heskey 9), Wise (19), (Barmby 14)

Group A

	P	W	D	L	F	A	Pts
PORTUGAL	3	3	0	0	7	2	9
ROMANIA	3	1	1	1	4	4	4
ENGLAND	3	1	0	2	5	6	3
GERMANY	3	0	1	2	1	5	1

2000 (continued)

Friendly

DATE	VENUE	OPPONENTS	SCORE	GOALSCORERS	ATTENDANCE	TEAM
Sep 2	Paris	FRANCE	D 1-1	Owen	70,000	Seaman (60), Campbell (37), Barry (3), Wise (20), Keown (34), **Adams** (65), (Southgate 28), Beckham (35), Scholes (28), (Owen 23), Cole (8), Barmby (15), (McManaman 30), Anderton (28), (Dyer 6)

World Cup Qualifiers

DATE	VENUE	OPPONENTS	SCORE	GOALSCORERS	ATTENDANCE	TEAM
Oct 7	Wembley, London	GERMANY	L 0-1		76,377	Seaman (61), Neville G (40), (Dyer 7), Le Saux (36), (Barry 4), Southgate (29), Keown (35), **Adams** (66), Beckham (36), (Parlour 8), Scholes (29), Cole (9), Owen (24), Barmby (16)

(CARETAKER-MANAGER: HOWARD WILKINSON)

| Oct 11 | Helsinki | FINLAND | D 0-0 | | 36,210 | Seaman (62), Neville P (30), Barry (5), (Brown W 2), Wise (21), **Keown** (36), Southgate (30), Parlour (9), Scholes (30), Cole (10), Sheringham (39), (McManaman 31), Heskey (10) |

(CARETAKER-MANAGER: PETER TAYLOR)
Friendly

| Nov 15 | Turin | ITALY | L 0-1 | | 22,000 | James (2), Neville G (41), Barry (6), (Johnson 1), Butt (9), (Carragher 2), Ferdinand R (10), Southgate (31), **Beckham** (37), Parlour (10), (Anderton 29), Heskey (11), (Phillips 6), Barmby (17), Dyer (8), (Fowler 15) |

2001

MANAGER CHANGED TO: SVEN-GORAN ERIKSSON
Friendly

DATE	VENUE	OPPONENTS	SCORE	GOALSCORERS	ATTENDANCE	TEAM
Feb 28	Villa Park, Birmingham	SPAIN	W 3-0	Barmby, Ehiogu, Heskey	42,129	James (3), (Martyn 15), Neville P (31), (Neville G 42), Powell (1), (Ball 1), Butt (10), (Lampard 2), Ferdinand R (11), (Ehiogu 2), Campbell (38), **Beckham** (38), (McCann 1), Scholes (31), (Heskey 12), Cole (11), Owen (25), Barmby (18)

World Cup Qualifiers

| Mar 24 | Anfield, Liverpool | FINLAND | W 2-1 | Beckham, Owen | 44,262 | Seaman (63), Neville G (43), Powell (2), Gerrard (3), Ferdinand R (12), Campbell (39), **Beckham** (39), Scholes (32), Cole (12), (Fowler 16), Owen (26), Butt (11), McManaman (32), (Heskey 13) |
| Mar 28 | Tirana | ALBANIA | W 3-1 | Scholes, Cole, Owen | 18,000 | Seaman (64), Neville G (44), Cole A (1), Butt (12), Ferdinand R (13), Campbell (40), (Brown W 3), **Beckham** (40), Scholes (33), Cole (13), Owen (27), (Sheringham 40), McManaman (33), (Heskey 14) |

2001 (continued)

Friendly

DATE	VENUE	OPPONENTS	SCORE	GOALSCORERS	ATTENDANCE	TEAM
May 25	Derby	MEXICO	W 4-0	Beckham, Scholes, Fowler, Sheringham	33,597	Martyn (16), (James 4), Neville P (32), Cole A (2), (Powell 3), Gerrard (4), (Butt 13), Ferdinand R (14), (Carragher 3), Keown (37), (Southgate 42), **Beckham** (41), (Cole J 1), Scholes (34), (Carrick 1), Fowler (17), (Sheringham 41), Owen (28), (Smith 1), Heskey (15), (Mills 1)

World Cup Qualifier

DATE	VENUE	OPPONENTS	SCORE	GOALSCORERS	ATTENDANCE	TEAM
Jun 6	Athens	GREECE	W 2-0	Beckham, Scholes,	46,000	Seaman (65), Neville P (33), Cole A (3), Gerrard (5), Ferdinand R (15), Keown (38), **Beckham** (42), Scholes (35), (Butt 14), Fowler (18), (Smith 2), Owen (29), Heskey (16), (McManaman 34)

Friendly

DATE	VENUE	OPPONENTS	SCORE	GOALSCORERS	ATTENDANCE	TEAM
Aug 15	White Hart Lane, London	HOLLAND	L 0-2		35,238	Martyn (17), (James 5), (Wright 2), Neville G (45), (Mills 2), Cole A (4), (Powell 4), Carragher (4), Keown (39), (Ehiogu 3), Brown (4), (Southgate 43) **Beckham** (43), (Lampard 3), Scholes (36), (Carrick 2), Cole (14), (Smith 3), Fowler (19), (Owen 30), Hargreaves (1), (Barmby 20)

World Cup Qualifiers

DATE	VENUE	OPPONENTS	SCORE	GOALSCORERS	ATTENDANCE	TEAM
Sep 1	Munich	GERMANY	W 5-1	Owen 3, Gerrard, Heskey	63,000	Seaman (66), Neville G (46), Cole A (5), Gerrard (6), (Hargreaves 2), Campbell (41), Ferdinand R (16), **Beckham** (44), Scholes (37), (Carragher 5), Heskey (17), Owen (31), Barmby (21), (McManaman 35)
Sep 5	St. James' Park Newcastle	ALBANIA	W 2-0	Fowler, Owen	51,046	Seaman (67), Neville G (47), Cole A (6), Gerrard (7), (Carragher 6), Campbell (42), Ferdinand R (17), **Beckham** (45), Scholes (38), Heskey (18), (Fowler 20), Owen (32), Barmby (22), (McManaman 36)
Oct 6	Old Trafford, Manchester	GREECE	D 2-2	Sheringham, Beckham	66,009	Martyn (18), Neville G (48), Cole A (7), (McManaman 37), Gerrard (8), Keown (40), Ferdinand R (18), **Beckham** (46), Scholes (39), Heskey (19), Fowler (21), (Sheringham 42), Barmby (23), (Cole 15)

Friendly

DATE	VENUE	OPPONENTS	SCORE	GOALSCORERS	ATTENDANCE	TEAM
Nov 10	Old Trafford Manchester	SWEDEN	D 1-1	Beckham (pen)	64,413	Martyn (19), Neville G (49), (Mills 3), Carragher (7), (Neville P 34), Southgate (44), Ferdinand R (19), **Beckham** (47), Butt (15), (Murphy 1), Heskey (20), (Sheringham 43), Phillips (7), (Fowler 22), Scholes (40), (Lampard 4), Sinclair (1), (Anderton 30)

2002

Friendlies

DATE	VENUE	OPPONENTS	SCORE	GOALSCORERS	ATTENDANCE	TEAM
Feb 13	Amsterdam	HOLLAND	D 1-1	Vassell	48,500	Martyn (20), (James 6), Neville G (50), (Neville P 35), Bridge (1), (Powell 5), Gerrard (9), (Lampard 5), Campbell (43), (Southgate 45), Ferdinand R (20), **Beckham** (48), Ricketts (1), (Phillips 8), Heskey (21), Vassell (1), (Cole J 2), Scholes (41), (Butt 16)
Mar 27	Elland Road, Leeds	ITALY	L 1-2	Fowler	36,635	Martyn (21), (James 7), Mills (4), (Neville P 36), Bridge (2), (Neville G 51), Butt (17), (Hargreaves 3), Campbell (44), (King 1), Southgate (46), (Ehiogu 4), **Beckham** (49), (Murphy 2), Lampard (6), (Cole J 3), Heskey (22), (Fowler 23), Owen (33), (Vassell 2), Sinclair (2), (Sheringham 44)
Apr 17	Anfield, Liverpool	PARAGUAY	W 4-0	Owen, Murphy, Vassell, own goal	42,713	Seaman (68), Neville G (52), (Lampard 7), Bridge (3), (Neville P 37), Butt (18), (Hargreaves 4), Keown (41), (Mills 5), Southgate (47), (Carragher 8), Gerrard (10), (Sinclair 3), Scholes (42), (Murphy 3), Vassell (3), (Sheringham 45), **Owen** (34), (Fowler 24), Dyer 9, (Cole J 4)
May 21	Seoguipo	SOUTH KOREA	D 1-1	Owen	39,876	Martyn (22), (James 8), Mills (6), (Brown 5), Cole A (8), (Bridge 4), Scholes (43), (Cole J 5), Campbell (45), (Keown 42), Ferdinand R (21), (Southgate 48), Murphy (4), (Sinclair 4), Vassell (4), Heskey (23), **Owen** (35), (Sheringham 46), Hargreaves (5)
May 26	Kobe	CAMEROON	D 2-2	Fowler, Vassell	42,000	Martyn (23), (James 9), Brown (6), Bridge (5), Scholes (44), (Mills 7), Campbell (46), (Keown 43), Ferdinand R (22), (Southgate 49), Cole J (6), Vassell (5), (Fowler 25), Heskey (24), (Sinclair 5), **Owen** (36), (Sheringham 47), Hargreaves (6)

THE WORLD CUP FINALS 2002 (JAPAN/KOREA)

Group Stage – Group F

DATE	VENUE	OPPONENTS	SCORE	GOALSCORERS	ATTENDANCE	TEAM
Jun 2	Saitama	SWEDEN	D 1-1	Campbell	52,271	Seaman (69), Mills (8), Cole A (9), Scholes (45), Campbell (47), Ferdinand R (23), **Beckham** (50), (Dyer 10), Vassell (6), (Cole J 7), Heskey (25), Owen (37), Hargreaves (7)
Jun 7	Sapporo	ARGENTINA	W 1-0	Beckham (pen)	35,927	Seaman (70), Mills (9), Cole A (10), Butt (19), Campbell (48), Ferdinand R (24), **Beckham** (51), Scholes (46), Heskey (26), (Sheringham 48), Owen (38), (Bridge 6), Hargreaves (8), (Sinclair 6)
Jun 12	Osaka	NIGERIA	D 0-0		44,864	Seaman (71), Mills (10), Cole A (11), (Bridge 7), Butt (20), Campbell (49), Ferdinand R (25), **Beckham** (52), Scholes (47), Heskey (27), (Sheringham 49), Owen (39), (Vassell 7), Sinclair (7)

Second Round

DATE	VENUE	OPPONENTS	SCORE	GOALSCORERS	ATTENDANCE	TEAM
Jun 15	Niigata	DENMARK	W 3-0	Owen, Ferdinand, Heskey	40,582	Seaman (72), Mills (11), Cole A (12), Butt (21), Campbell (50), Ferdinand R (26), **Beckham** (53), Scholes (48), (Dyer 11), Heskey (28), (Sheringham 50), Owen (40), (Fowler 26), Sinclair (8)

Quarter-final

DATE	VENUE	OPPONENTS	SCORE	GOALSCORERS	ATTENDANCE	TEAM
Jun 21	Shizuoka	BRAZIL	L 1-2	Owen	47,436	Seaman (73), Mills (12), Cole A (13), (Sheringham 51), Butt (22), Campbell (51), Ferdinand R (27), **Beckham** (54), Scholes (49), Heskey (29), Owen (41), (Vassell 8), Sinclair (9), (Dyer 12)

Group F

	P	W	D	L	F	A	Pts
SWEDEN	3	1	2	0	4	3	5
ENGLAND	3	1	2	0	2	1	5
ARGENTINA	3	1	1	1	2	2	4
NIGERIA	3	0	1	2	1	3	1

2002 (continued)

Friendly

DATE	VENUE	OPPONENTS	SCORE	GOALSCORERS	ATTENDANCE	TEAM
Sept 7	Villa Park, Birmingham	PORTUGAL	D 1-1	Smith	40,058	James (10), Mills (13), (Bridge 8), Cole A (14), (Hargreaves 9), Gerrard (11), (Dunn 1), Ferdinand (28), (Woodgate 2), Southgate (50), Bowyer (1), (Sinclair 10), Butt (23), (Murphy 5), Smith (4), **Owen** (42), (Cole J 8), Heskey (30)

European Championship Qualifiers

DATE	VENUE	OPPONENTS	SCORE	GOALSCORERS	ATTENDANCE	TEAM
Oct 12	Bratislava	SLOVAKIA	W 2-1	Beckham, Owen	30,000	Seaman (74), Neville G (53), Cole A (15), Gerrard (12), (Dyer 13), Woodgate (3), Southgate (51), **Beckham** (55), Scholes (50), Heskey (31), (Smith 5), Owen (43), (Hargreaves 10), Butt (24)
Oct 16	St Mary's, Southampton	MACEDONIA	D 2-2	Beckham, Gerrard	32,095	Seaman (75), Neville G (54), Cole A (16), Gerrard (13), (Butt 25), Woodgate (4), Campbell (52), **Beckham** (56), Scholes (51), *Smith* (6), Owen (44), Bridge (9), (Vassell 9)

2003

Friendly

DATE	VENUE	OPPONENTS	SCORE	GOALSCORERS	ATTENDANCE	TEAM
Feb 12	Upton Park, West Ham	AUSTRALIA	L 1-3	Jeffers	34,590	James (11), (Robinson 1), Neville G (55), (Mills 14), Cole A (17), (Konchesky 1), Lampard (8), (Hargreaves 11), Ferdinand (29), (Brown 7), Campbell (53), (King 2), **Beckham** (57), (Murphy 6), Scholes (52), (Jenas 1), Beattie (1), (Vassell 10), Owen (45), (Jeffers 1), Dyer (14), (Rooney 1)

European Championship Qualifiers

DATE	VENUE	OPPONENTS	SCORE	GOALSCORERS	ATTENDANCE	TEAM
Mar 29	Vaduz	LIECHTENSTEIN	W 2-0	Owen, Beckham	3,548	James (12), Neville G (56), Bridge (10), Gerrard (14), (Butt 26), Ferdinand (30), Southgate (52), **Beckham** (58), (Murphy 7), Scholes (53), Heskey (32), (Rooney 2), Owen (46), Dyer (15)
Apr 2	Stadium of Light, Sunderland	TURKEY	W 2-0	Vassell, Beckham (pen)	47,667	James (13), Neville G (57), Bridge (11), Gerrard (15), Ferdinand (31), Campbell (54), **Beckham** (59), Scholes (54), Rooney (3), (Dyer 16), Owen (47), (Vassell 11), Butt (27)

2003 (continued)

Friendlies

DATE	VENUE	OPPONENTS	SCORE	GOALSCORERS	ATTENDANCE	TEAM
May 22	Durban	SOUTH AFRICA	W 2-1	Southgate, Heskey	48,000	James (14), (Robinson 2), Mills (15), Neville P (38), Gerrard (16), (Barry 7), Ferdinand (32), Upson (1), Southgate (53), **Beckham** (60), (Jenas 2), Scholes (55), (Cole J 9), Heskey (33), (Vassell 12), Owen (48), Sinclair (11), (Lampard 9)
Jun 3	Walkers Stadium, Leicester	SERBIA & MONTENEGRO	W 2-1	Gerrard, Cole J	30,900	James (15), Mills (16), (Carragher 9), Cole A (18), (Bridge 12), Gerrard (17), (Hargreaves 12), Upson (2), (Barry 8), Southgate (54), (Terry 1), Lampard (10), (Cole J 10), Scholes (56), (Jenas 3), Heskey (34) (Vassell 13), **Owen** (49), (Rooney 4), Neville P (39), (Beattie 2)

European Championship Qualifier

DATE	VENUE	OPPONENTS	SCORE	GOALSCORERS	ATTENDANCE	TEAM
Jun 11	Riverside Stadium, Middlesbrough	SLOVAKIA	W 2-1	Owen 2 (1 pen)	35,000	James (16), Mills (17), (Hargreaves 13), Cole A (19), Gerrard (18), Upson (3), Southgate (55), Lampard (11), Scholes (57), Rooney (5), (Vassell 14), **Owen** (50), Neville P (40)

Friendly

DATE	VENUE	OPPONENTS	SCORE	GOALSCORERS	ATTENDANCE	TEAM
Aug 20	Ipswich	CROATIA	W 3-1	Beckham (pen) Owen, Lampard	28,700	James (17), (Robinson 3), Neville P (41), (Mills 18), Cole A (20), (Bridge 13), Butt (28), (Lampard 12), Terry (2), Ferdinand (33), (Upson 4), **Beckham** (61), (Sinclair 12), Scholes (58), (Cole J 11), Heskey (35), (Beattie 3), Owen (51), (Dyer 17), Gerrard (19), (Murphy 8)

European Championship Qualifiers

DATE	VENUE	OPPONENTS	SCORE	GOALSCORERS	ATTENDANCE	TEAM
Sept 6	Skopje	MACEDONIA	W 2-1	Rooney, Beckham (pen)	20,500	James (18), Neville G (58), Cole A (21), Butt (29), Terry (3), Campbell (55), **Beckham** (62), Lampard (13), (Heskey 36), Rooney (6), (Neville P 42), Owen (52), (Dyer 18), Hargreaves (14)
Sept 10	Old Trafford, Manchester	LIECHTENSTEIN	W 2-0	Owen, Rooney	64,931	James (19), Neville G (59), Bridge (14), Gerrard (20), (Neville P 43), Terry (4), Upson (5), **Beckham** (63), (Hargreaves 15), Rooney (7), (Cole J 12), Owen (53), Beattie (4), Lampard (14)
Oct 11	Istanbul	TURKEY	D 0-0		42,000	James (20), Neville G (60), Cole A (22), Butt (30), Terry (5), Campbell (56), **Beckham** (64), Gerrard (21), Heskey (37), (Vassell 15), Rooney (8), (Dyer 19), Scholes (59), (Lampard 15)

Friendly

DATE	VENUE	OPPONENTS	SCORE	GOALSCORERS	ATTENDANCE	TEAM
Nov 15	Old Trafford, Manchester	DENMARK	L 2-3	Rooney, Cole J	64,159	James (21), (Robinson 4), Neville G (61), (Johnson 1), Cole A (23), (Bridge 15), Butt (31), (Neville P 44), Terry (6), Upson (6), **Beckham** (65), (Jenas 4), Lampard (16), Heskey (38), (Beattie 5), Rooney (9), (Parker 1), Cole J (13), (Murphy 9)

2004

Friendlies

DATE	VENUE	OPPONENTS	SCORE	GOALSCORERS	ATTENDANCE	TEAM
Feb 18	Faro-Loule	PORTUGAL	D 1-1	King	27,000	James (22), Neville P (45), (Mills 19), Cole A (24), (Bridge 16), (Carragher 10), Butt (32), (Jenas 5), Southgate (56), King (3), **Beckham** (66), (Hargreaves 16), Rooney (10), (Heskey 39), Owen (54), (Smith 7), Scholes (60), (Dyer 20), Lampard (17), (Cole J 14)
Mar 31	Gothenburg	SWEDEN	L 0-1		40,464	James (23), Neville P (46), Carragher (11), Butt (33), (Parker 2), Terry (7), (Gardner 1), Woodgate (5), (Southgate 57), Hargreaves (17), (Jenas 6), **Gerrard** (22), (Cole J 15), Rooney (11), (Smith 8), Vassell (16), Defoe (1), Thompson (1), (Heskey 40)
Jun 1	City of Manchester Stadium	JAPAN	D 1-1	Owen	38,581	James (24), Neville G (62), (Neville P 47), Cole A (25), Gerrard (23), (Hargreaves 18), Terry (8), (King 4), Campbell (57), **Beckham** (67), (Cole J 16), Lampard (18), (Butt 34), Rooney (12), (Heskey 41), Owen (55), (Vassell 17), Scholes (61), (Dyer 21)
Jun 5	City of Manchester Stadium	ICELAND	W 6-1	Lampard, Rooney 2 Vassell 2, Bridge	43,500	Robinson (5), (Walker 4), Neville G (63), (Neville P 48), Cole A (26), (Bridge 17), Gerrard 24 (Hargreaves 19), Carragher (12), (Defoe 2), Campbell (58), (King 5), **Beckham** (68), (Dyer 22), Lampard (19), (Butt 35), Rooney (13), (Vassell 18), Owen (56), (Heskey 42), Scholes (62), (Cole J 17)

EUROPEAN CHAMPIONSHIP FINALS 2004

Group Stage – Group B

DATE	VENUE	OPPONENTS	SCORE	GOALSCORERS	ATTENDANCE	TEAM
Jun 13	Estadio Da Luz, Lisbon	FRANCE	L 1-2	Lampard	62,487	James (25), Neville G (64), Cole A (27), Gerrard (25), Campbell (59), King (6), **Beckham** (69), Lampard (20), Rooney (14), (Heskey 43) Owen (57), (Vassell 19), Scholes (63), (Hargreaves 20)
Jun 17	Coimbra	SWITZERLAND	W 3-0	Rooney 2, Gerrard	30,616	James (26), Neville G (65), Cole A (28), Gerrard (26), Terry (9), Campbell (60), **Beckham** (70), Lampard (21), Rooney (15), (Dyer 23), Owen (58), (Vassell 20), Scholes (64), (Hargreaves 21)
Jun 21	Estadio Da Luz, Lisbon	CROATIA	W 4-2	Scholes, Rooney 2 Lampard	63,000	James (27), Neville G (66), Cole A (29), Gerrard (27), Terry (10), Campbell (61), **Beckham** (71), Lampard (22), (Neville P 49), Rooney (16), (Vassell 21), Owen (59), Scholes (65), (King 7)

Group B

	P	W	D	L	F	A	Pts
FRANCE	3	2	1	0	7	4	7
ENGLAND	3	2	0	1	8	4	6
CROATIA	3	0	2	1	4	6	2
SWITZERLAND	3	0	1	2	1	6	1

Quarter-final

Jun 24	Estadio Da Luz, Lisbon	PORTUGAL	D 2-2	Owen, Lampard England lost 6-5 on penalties	62,564	James (28), Neville G (67), Cole A (30), Gerrard (28), (Hargreaves 22), Terry (11), Campbell (62), **Beckham** (72), Lampard (23), Rooney (17), (Vassell 22), Owen (60), Scholes (66), (Neville P 50)

2004 (continued)

Friendly

DATE	VENUE	OPPONENTS	SCORE	GOALSCORERS	ATTENDANCE	TEAM
Aug 18	St James' Park, Newcastle	UKRAINE	W 3-0	Beckham, Owen, Wright-Phillips	35,387	James (29), Neville G (68), (Johnson G 2), Cole A (37), (Carragher 13), Butt (37), (Wright-Phillips 1), Terry (12), King (8), **Beckham** (73), Lampard (24), (Jenas 7), Owen (61), Smith (9), (Defoe 3), Gerrard (29), (Dyer 24)

World Cup Qualifiers

DATE	VENUE	OPPONENTS	SCORE	GOALSCORERS	ATTENDANCE	TEAM
Sep 4	Vienna	AUSTRIA	D 2-2	Lampard, Gerrard	48,500	James (30), Neville G (69), Cole A (38), Gerrard (30), (Carragher 14), Terry (13), King (9), **Beckham** (74), Lampard (25), Owen (62), Smith (10), (Defoe 4), Bridge (18), (Cole J 18)
Sep 8	Katowice	POLAND	W 2-1	Defoe, own goal	38,000	Robinson (6), Neville G (70), (Carragher 15), Cole A (39), Gerrard (31), Terry (14), King (10), **Beckham** (75), (Hargreaves 23), Lampard (26), Owen (63), Defoe (5), (Dyer 25), Bridge (19)
Oct 9	Old Trafford, Manchester	WALES	W 2-0	Lampard, Beckham	65,224	Robinson (7), Neville G (71), Cole A (40), Butt (38), Campbell (63), Ferdinand (34), **Beckham** (76), (Hargreaves 24), Lampard (27), Owen (64), Defoe (6), (Smith 11), Rooney (18), (King 11)
Oct 13	Baku	AZERBAIJAN	W 1-0	Owen	20,000	Robinson (8), Neville G (72), Cole A (41), Butt (39), Campbell (64), Ferdinand (35), Jenas (8), (Wright-Phillips 2), Lampard (28), **Owen** (65), Defoe (7), (Smith 12), Rooney (19), (Cole J 19)

Friendly

Nov 17	Madrid	SPAIN	L 0-1		48,000	Robinson (9), Neville G (73), Cole A (31), (Defoe 8), Butt (36), Terry (15), (Upson 7), Ferdinand (36), (Carragher 16), **Beckham** (77), (Wright-Phillips 3), Lampard (29), (Jenas 9), Owen (66), Rooney (20), (Smith 13), Bridge (20)

2005

Friendly

DATE	VENUE	OPPONENTS	SCORE	GOALSCORERS	ATTENDANCE	TEAM
Feb 9	Villa Park, Birmingham	HOLLAND	D 0-0		40,705	Robinson (10), Neville G (74), Cole A (32), Gerrard (32), (Dyer 26), Brown (8), Carragher (17), **Beckham** (78), (Jenas 10), Lampard (30), (Hargreaves 25), Wright-Phillips (4), (Johnson A 1), Owen (67), Rooney (21), (Downing 1)

World Cup Qualifiers

DATE	VENUE	OPPONENTS	SCORE	GOALSCORERS	ATTENDANCE	TEAM
Mar 26	Old Trafford, Manchester	NORTHERN IRELAND	W 4-0	Cole J, Owen, own goal, Lampard	65,239	Robinson (11), Neville G (75), Cole A (33), Gerrard (33), (Hargreaves 26), Terry (16), Ferdinand (37), **Beckham** (79), (Dyer 27), Lampard (31), Owen (68), Rooney (22), (Defoe 9), Cole J (20)
Mar 30	St James' Park Newcastle	AZERBAIJAN	W 2-0	Gerrard, Beckham	49,046	Robinson (12), Neville G (76), Cole A (34), Gerrard (34), Terry (17), Ferdinand (38), King (12), **Beckham** (80), (Dyer 28), Lampard (32), Owen (69), Rooney (23), (Defoe 10), Cole J (21)

Friendlies

DATE	VENUE	OPPONENTS	SCORE	GOALSCORERS	ATTENDANCE	TEAM
May 28	Chicago	USA	W 2-1	Richardson 2	45,000	James (31), Johnson G (3), Cole A (35), (Defoe 11), Carrick (3), **Campbell** (65), (Knight 1), Brown (9), Jenas (11), Smith (14), Johnson A (2), (Young 1), Cole J (22), Richardson (1), (Neville P 51)
May 31	New Jersey	COLOMBIA	W 3-2	Owen 3	58,000	James (32), (Green 1), Neville P (52), Cole A (36), Carrick (4), Knight (2), Johnson G (4), **Beckham** (81), (Defoe 12), Owen (70), (Richardson 2), Crouch (1), (Smith 15), Cole J (23), (Young 2), Jenas (12)
Aug 17	Copenhagen	DENMARK	L 1-4	Rooney	41,438	Robinson (13), (James 33), Neville P (77), (Johnson G 5), Cole A (42), Gerrard (35), (Jenas 13), Terry (18), (Owen 71), Ferdinand (39), **Beckham** (82), Lampard (33), (Hargreaves 27), Defoe (13), (Carragher 18), Cole J (24), Rooney (24)

World Cup Qualifiers

DATE	VENUE	OPPONENTS	SCORE	GOALSCORERS	ATTENDANCE	TEAM
Sep 3	Millennium Stadium, Cardiff	WALES	W 1-0	Cole J	70,715	Robinson (14), Young (3), Cole A (43), Gerrard (36), (Richardson 3), Carragher (19), Ferdinand (40), **Beckham** (83), Lampard (34), Rooney (25), Cole J (25), (Hargreaves 28), Wright-Phillips (5), (Defoe 14)
Sep 7	Windsor Park, Belfast	NORTHERN IRELAND	L 0-1		14,000	Robinson (15), Young (4), Cole A (44), Gerrard (37), (Defoe 15), Carragher (20), Ferdinand (41), **Beckham** (84), Lampard (35), (Hargreaves 29), Owen (72), Rooney (26), Wright-Phillips (6), (Cole J 26)
Oct 8	Old Trafford, Manchester	AUSTRIA	W 1-0	Lampard (pen)	64,822	Robinson (16), Young (5), Carragher (21), Gerrard (38), Terry (19), Campbell (66), (Ferdinand 42), *Beckham* (85), Lampard (36), Crouch (2), Owen (73), (Richardson 4), Cole J (27), (King 13)
Oct 12	Old Trafford, Manchester	POLAND	W 2-1	Owen, Lampard	65,467	Robinson (17), Young (6), Carragher (22), King (14), Terry (20), Ferdinand (43), Wright-Phillips (7), (Crouch 3), Lampard (37), **Owen** (74), (Jenas 14), Rooney (27), Cole J (28), (Smith 16)

Friendly

DATE	VENUE	OPPONENTS	SCORE	GOALSCORERS	ATTENDANCE	TEAM
Nov 12	Geneva	ARGENTINA	W 3-2	Rooney, Owen 2	29,000	Robinson (18), Young (7), (Crouch 4), Bridge (21), (Konchesky 2), King (15), (Cole J 29), Terry (21), Ferdinand (44), **Beckham** (86), Lampard (38), Owen (75), Rooney (28), Gerrard (39)

2006

Friendlies

DATE	VENUE	OPPONENTS	SCORE	GOALSCORERS	ATTENDANCE	TEAM
Mar 1	Anfield, Liverpool	URUGUAY	W 2-1	Crouch, Cole J	40,013	Robinson (19), Neville G (78), Bridge (22), (Carragher 23), Gerrard (40), (Jenas 15), Terry (22), (King 16), Ferdinand (45), **Beckham** (87), (Wright-Phillips 8), Carrick (5), Bent D (1), (Defoe 16), Rooney (29), (Crouch 5), Cole J (30)
May 30	Old Trafford, Manchester	HUNGARY	W 3-1	Gerrard, Terry, Crouch	56,323	Robinson (20), Neville G (79), (Hargreaves 30), Cole A (45), Carragher (24), Terry (23), Campbell (67), Ferdinand (46), **Beckham** (88), Lampard (39), Owen (70), (Crouch 6), Cole J (31), Gerrard (41), (Walcott 1)
Jun 3	Old Trafford, Manchester	JAMAICA	W 6-0	Lampard, own goal, Crouch 3, Owen	70,373	Robinson (21), (James 34), Carragher (25), Cole A (46), (Bridge 23), Gerrard (42), (Downing 2), Terry (24), Campbell 68), Ferdinand (47), **Beckham** (89), (Lennon 1), Lampard (40), (Carrick 6), Crouch (7), Owen (77), Cole J (32)

THE WORLD CUP FINALS 2006 (GERMANY)

Group Stage – Group B

DATE	VENUE	OPPONENTS	SCORE	GOALSCORERS	ATTENDANCE	TEAM
Jun 10	Frankfurt	PARAGUAY	W 1-0	own goal	43,324	Robinson (22), Neville G (80), Cole A (47), Gerrard (43), Terry (25), Ferdinand (48), Beckham (90), Lampard (41), Crouch (8), Owen (78), (Downing 3), Cole J (33), (Hargreaves 31)
Jun 15	Nuremberg	TRINIDAD & TOBAGO	W 2-0	Crouch, Gerrard	41,000	Robinson (23), Carragher (26), (Lennon 2), Cole A (48), Gerrard (44), Terry (26), Ferdinand (49), Beckham (91), Lampard (42), Crouch (9), Owen (79), (Rooney 30), Cole J (34), (Downing 4)
Jun 20	Cologne	SWEDEN	D 2-2	Cole J, Gerrard	45,000	Robinson (24), Carragher (27), Cole A (49), Hargreaves (32), Terry (27), Ferdinand (50), (Campbell 69), Beckham (92), Lampard (43), Owen (80), (Crouch 10), Rooney (31), (Gerrard 45), Cole J 35

Second Round

DATE	VENUE	OPPONENTS	SCORE	GOALSCORERS	ATTENDANCE	TEAM
Jun 25	Stuttgart	ECUADOR	W 1-0	Beckham	52,000	Robinson (25), Terry (28), Ferdinand (51), Cole A (50), Hargreaves (33), Carrick (7), Beckham (93), (Lennon 3), Lampard (44), Rooney (32), Cole J (36), (Carragher 28), Gerrard (46), (Downing 5)

Quarter-final

DATE	VENUE	OPPONENTS	SCORE	GOALSCORERS	ATTENDANCE	TEAM
Jul 1	Gelsenkirchen	PORTUGAL	D 0-0	England lost 3-1 on penalties	52,000	Robinson (26), Neville G (81), Cole A (51), Gerrard (47), Terry (29), Ferdinand (52), Beckham (94), (Lennon 4), (Carragher 29), Rooney (33), Cole J (37), (Crouch 11), Hargreaves (34)

2006 (continued)

MANAGER CHANGED TO: STEVE McCLAREN

Friendly

DATE	VENUE	OPPONENTS	SCORE	GOALSCORERS	ATTENDANCE	TEAM
Aug 16	Old Trafford, Manchester	GREECE	W 4-0	Terry, Lampard, Crouch 2	45,864	Robinson (27), (Kirkland 1), Neville G (82), (Carragher 30), Cole A (52), (Bridge 11), Gerrard (48), (Bent D 2), Terry (30), Ferdinand (53), Hargreaves (35), Lampard (46), Crouch (12), Defoe (17), (Lennon 5), Downing (6), (Richardson 5)

European Championship Qualifiers

DATE	VENUE	OPPONENTS	SCORE	GOALSCORERS	ATTENDANCE	TEAM
Sep 2	Old Trafford, Manchester	ANDORRA	W 5-0	Gerrard, Defoe 2, Crouch 2	56,290	Robinson (28), Neville P (53), (Richardson 6), Cole A (53), Gerrard (49), Terry (31), Brown (10), Hargreaves (36), Lampard (47), Crouch (13), Defoe (18), Johnson A 3), Downing (7), (Lennon 6)
Sep 6	Skopje	MACEDONIA	W 1-0	Crouch	16,500	Robinson (29), Neville P (54), Cole A (54), Gerrard (50), Terry (32), Ferdinand (54), Hargreaves (37), Lampard (48), (Carrick 8), Crouch (14), (Johnson A 4), Defoe (19), (Lennon 7), Downing (8)
Oct 7	Old Trafford, Manchester	MACEDONIA	D 0-0		72,062	Robinson (30), Neville G (83), Cole A (55), Gerrard (51), Terry (33), King (17), Carrick (9), Lampard (49), Crouch (15), Rooney (34), (Defoe 20), Downing (9), (Wright-Phillips 9)
Oct 11	Zagreb	CROATIA	L 0-2		38,000	Robinson (31), Neville G (84), Cole A (56), Carragher (31), (Richardson 7), Terry (34), Ferdinand (55), Carrick (10), Lampard (50), Crouch (16), (Defoe 21), Rooney (35), Parker (3), (Wright-Phillips 10)

Friendly

DATE	VENUE	OPPONENTS	SCORE	GOALSCORERS	ATTENDANCE	TEAM
Nov 15	Amsterdam	HOLLAND	D 1-1	Rooney	44,000	Robinson (32), Richards (1), Cole A (57), Gerrard (52), Terry (35), Ferdinand (56), Carrick (11), Lampard (51), Johnson A (5), (Wright-Phillips 11), Rooney (36), Cole J (38), (Richardson 8)

2007

Friendly

DATE	VENUE	OPPONENTS	SCORE	GOALSCORERS	ATTENDANCE	TEAM
Feb 7	Old Trafford, Manchester	SPAIN	L 0-1		58,247	Foster (1), Neville G (85), (Richards 2), Neville P (55), (Downing 10), Gerrard (53), (Barry 1), Woodgate (6), (Carragher 32), Ferdinand (57), Carrick (12), Lampard (52), (Barton 1), Crouch (17), Dyer (29), Wright-Phillips (12), (Defoe 22)

2007 (continued)

European Championship Qualifiers

DATE	VENUE	OPPONENTS	SCORE	GOALSCORERS	ATTENDANCE	TEAM
Mar 24	Tel Aviv	ISRAEL	D 0-0		35,000	Robinson (33), Neville P (56) (Richards 3), Carragher (33), Gerrard (54), Ferdinand (58), **Terry** (36), Lennon (8) (Downing 11), Lampard (53), Johnson A (6) (Defoe 23), Rooney (37), Hargreaves (38)
Mar 28	Barcelona	ANDORRA	W 3-0	Gerrard 2, Nugent	12,800	Robinson (34), Richards (4) (Dyer 30), Cole A (58), Gerrard (55), Ferdinand (59), **Terry** (37), Lennon (9), Hargreaves (39), Johnson A (7), (Nugent 1), Rooney (38) (Defoe 24), Downing (12)